THE GENERAL LINEAR MODEL

**McGRAW-HILL
INTERNATIONAL
BOOK COMPANY**

New York
St. Louis
San Francisco
Auckland
Beirut
Bogotá
Düsseldorf
Johannesburg
Lisbon
London
Lucerne
Madrid
Mexico
Montreal
New Delhi
Panama
Paris
San Juan
São Paulo
Singapore
Sydney
Tokyo
Toronto

RAYMOND L. HORTON
Lehigh University

The General Linear Model

DATA ANALYSIS IN THE SOCIAL
AND BEHAVIORAL SCIENCES

This book was set in Times Roman, Series 327

British Library Cataloging in Publication Data

Horton, Raymond L.
   The general linear model.
   1. Statistics
   I. Title
   519.5′02′43   HA29   77-30078
ISBN 0-07-030418-1

THE GENERAL LINEAR MODEL

Copyright © 1978 by McGraw-Hill, Inc. All rights reserved.
Printed in the United States of America. No part of this publication may be reproduced, stored in a retrival system, or transmitted, in any form or by any means, electronic, mechanical, photocopying, recording or otherwise, without the prior permission of the publisher.

1 2 3 4 5 MPMP 80 7 9 8

Printed and Bound in the United States of America

To my mother and the memory of my father
Lucile and Harry Horton

CONTENTS

Preface		ix
1	**The General Linear Model**	**1**
	1-I Importance and Generality of the General Linear Model in the Social and Behavioral Sciences	2
	1-II Orientation of Book	3
	1-III General Linear Model	4
	1-IV A Note on Scales of Measurement	17
	1-V A Numerical Example	19
	1-VI Summary	24
2	**Additional Assumptions Necessary for Valid Statistical Tests of Hypotheses Concerning the Parameters of the General Linear Model**	**25**
	2-I A Review of Some Important Statistical Concepts	26
	2-II Three Assumptions Underlying the F Test	37
	2-III Summary	58
3	**Factorial Analysis of Variance Designs**	**59**
	3-I Research Uses of Factorial Designs	61
	3-II The Basic Model	63
	3-III Graphical Interpretation of Main Effects and Interaction Effects	79
	3-IV A Note on the Scale of Measurement and "Artificial" Interactions	80
	3-V Hypotheses Concerning Linear Combinations of the Coefficients of the General Linear Model	82
	3-VI Analysis of $2 \times 3 \times 3$ Factorial Design Using Packaged (Canned) Computer Programs	90
	3-VII Variations on the Factorial Design	111
	3-VIII Summary	114

4 Latin Square Designs — 115

- 4-I   Research Uses of Latin Square Designs — 117
- 4-II   The Basic Model — 118
- 4-III   The Absence of Interactions Assumption — 123
- 4-IV   Advanced Latin Square Designs — 134
- 4-V   Summary — 138

5 Repeated Measures Designs — 139

- 5-I   Research Uses of Repeated Measures Designs — 140
- 5-II   The Basic Model — 142
- 5-III   The Covariance Assumption — 148
- 5-IV   More Complex Repeated Measures Designs — 151
- 5-V   Rules for Constructing Expected Mean Squares — 161
- 5-VI   The Variance Components Model — 162
- 5-VII   Summary — 167

6 Analysis of Covariance — 168

- 6-I   Research Uses of Covariance Designs — 171
- 6-II   The Basic Model — 174
- 6-III   Assumptions Underlying the Analysis of Covariance — 186
- 6-IV   A Comparison of Covariance Analysis and Randomized Blocks — 198
- 6-V   Advanced Covariance Designs — 199
- 6-VI   Summary — 204

7 General Regression Analysis — 205

- 7-I   Research Uses of General Regression Analysis — 207
- 7-II   The Basic Model — 208
- 7-III   Some Procedures for Interpreting the Regression Equation — 211
- 7-IV   Problems Associated with Multicollinearity — 224
- 7-IV   Some Comments on Stepwise Regression Techniques — 230
- 7-VI   Summary — 231

Postscript — 233

Appendix A—Review of Some Basic Matrix Algebra — 235

Appendix B—Statistical Tables — 238

References — 267

Author Index — 270

Subject Index — 272

PREFACE

During the past five years I have taught a graduate course on advanced data analysis with primary emphasis on analysis of variance and regression analysis, which are the major variants of the General Linear Model. Students in this course have come primarily from the social and behavioral sciences, have generally had two semesters of statistics, and have been motivated by a desire for training in the use of sophisticated, computer-based, data analysis procedures, usually as an aid in conducting research for a master's thesis or a doctoral dissertation. In teaching this course, and in searching for suitable texts I came to several conclusions which provided the motivation for the writing of this book.

Much to my surprise and dismay most of my students have been under the misimpression that analysis of variance and regression analysis are distinct, even unrelated, analytical tools. Even within analysis of variance many have not grasped the essential commonality which underlies the many variants, e.g., Latin squares and repeated measures, of analysis of variance. Much of this confusion seems attributable to the focus of traditional statistics courses and texts on sampling theory and the detailed computational methods appropriate to each specific formulation of the General Linear Model. It is especially this emphasis on computational methods—which are somewhat redundant in this day of computerized data analysis—which has deflected attention from the essential commonality which underlies all General Linear Model procedures, and from the all-important relationships between the researcher's substantive questions and the precise structure of the specific, special formulation of the General Linear Model chosen by the researcher to guide his data analysis.

This book has been written with a view to overcoming these perceived problems. The product, hopefully, is a text which will prove especially useful to students studying for careers in applied research in the various social and behavioral sciences and as a reference source for individuals actively engaged in such research.

In broad outline the text is structured as follows. In Chapter 1 the General Linear Model is developed in matrix form,[1] the minimal assumptions of the model are stated, and the squared error function is constructed as the criterion to be minimized in deriving the parameters of the postulated General Linear Model. The concluding section of this chapter carefully states what is and what is not required for various uses of the General Linear Model. The advantage of this approach is that once the matrix of independent variables X and the associated vector of dependent variables y have been formed *every* specialized regression analysis and analysis of variance formulation of the General Linear Model reduces to solving the matrix equation:

$$\theta = (X'X)^{-1}X'y$$

for the coefficient vector θ of the parameters of the General Linear Model. This makes detailed computational formulas and examples unnecessary and frees space for a detailed, but concise, discussion of the various models from the perspective of research questions and the assumption structures underlying each model.

In Chapter 2 the additional assumptions necessary for valid statistical tests of hypotheses are discussed. This chapter also discusses methods of testing these assumptions, the consequences of violation of the various assumptions, and corrective procedures when the assumptions are not met. A particularly unique section of this chapter reviews studies which allow the researcher to specify the direction, and often the rough magnitude, of distortions of significance tests and power caused by specific assumption violations. This procedure is a decided improvement over transformations of the dependent variable, which almost invariably violate additional assumptions in the process of correcting any specific assumption violation. Placing this material in a separate chapter is meant to emphasize the fact that the assumptions of normality, independence, and homogeneity are *not* necessary if the General Linear Model is used only as a descriptive, rather than as an inferential, model. The concluding section of Chapter 2 emphasizes this point by carefully distinguishing between the significance and magnitude of the treatment effects vis-à-vis the dependent variable.

The five remaining chapters examine the most frequently encountered special forms of the General Linear Model: factorial, Latin square, repeated measures, covariance, and regression analysis designs. The orientation of these chapters is to the applied researcher. Each chapter begins with a discussion of the research applications of the basic design, and then specifies the assumed underlying structural model which presumably generated the observed data. The next section examines the necessary assumptions, in addition to those specified in Chapters 1 and 2, to use validly the particular form of the General Linear Model under study. Other sections discuss statistical tests of the assumptions, the consequences

---

[1] Appendix A provides the necessary matrix algebra. Only the simplest matrix procedures are required.

of violations of the assumptions and the corrective procedures which are used when the assumptions are violated. Where appropriate, detailed procedures for interpreting the output of the analyses are discussed, e.g., interpreting interaction effects.

Each chapter also includes numerical examples to illustrate specific uses of each design in behavioral and social research and/or analytical problems associated with each design. Many of these examples are in the form of computer printouts from the widely distributed BioMedical (BMD) and Statistical Package for the Social Sciences (SPSS) computer program packages, with discussion in the text of the procedures necessary for using the power of the computer in data analysis.

As always many individuals have provided both valuable criticisms and suggestions and encouragement which have immeasurably improved the quality of this book. In particular, I would like to acknowledge the contributions of my former colleagues at the University of North Carolina at Greensboro, Professors John Hoftyzer and Terry Seaks, and my present colleagues at Lehigh University, Professors John Bonge, Ed Kay, Art King, Gary Lutz, and Robert Thornton. My greatest debt is to my wife Pat, who is currently a graduate student in psychology studying for a research career in behavioral science, for her constant encouragement and student perspective on the readability of the manuscript, which has greatly improved the clarity and understandability of the resulting text. Finally, I must express my gratitude to Ms. Sharon Ruhf for her skillful typing of the manuscript.

Raymond L. Horton
Bath, Pa.
April 6, 1977

CHAPTER
ONE
THE GENERAL LINEAR MODEL

1-I Importance and Generality of the General Linear Model in the Social and Behavioral Sciences

1-II Orientation of Book

1-III General Linear Model

1-III-1 Terminology and Notation
1-III-2 An Introduction to the General Linear Model
    1-III-2-1 Some simple linear models
    1-III-2-2 Basic form of the GLM
1-III-3 Minimal Assumptions Underlying the GLM
1-III-4 The General Linear Model Cast in Matrix Form
    1-III-4-1 Matrix notation for GLM
    1-III-4-2 Least-squared-errors criterion
    1-III-4-3 Least-squares estimate of $\hat{\theta}$
1-III-5 Interpretation of Normal Equation
    1-III-5-1 $\hat{\theta}$
    1-III-5-2 Covariance of $\hat{\theta}$
    1-III-5-3 Geometric representation of dependent and independent variables
    1-III-5-4 Partitioning the total sum of squares

1-IV A Note on Scales of Measurement

1-IV-1 Nominal Scales
1-IV-2 Ordinal Scales
1-IV-3 Interval Scales
1-IV-4 Ratio Scales

1-V A Numerical Example

1-V-1 Construction of Artificial Data
1-V-2 Independent Variable Coding Procedures
1-V-3 Data Analysis
1-V-4 Reader Test Problem

1-VI Summary

This chapter sets the stage for the chapters to follow by casting the General Linear Model (GLM) in its most minimal form. Our goal is to show the essential commonality underlying all regression analysis and analysis of variance techniques. This commonality is shown by fully developing the General Linear Model and showing that regression analysis and the many variants of analysis of variance are all special cases of the GLM.

With the assumptions specified in this chapter the GLM may be used as a *descriptive* model of any phenomenon which satisfies the assumptions. As a descriptive model, each component of the GLM may be given a specific interpretation and a number of quantities may be derived which are useful in interpreting the GLM for any specific set of empirical data. These aspects of the GLM are described fully, first in general terms and then in terms of a numerical example which is small enough to be worked easily by hand. Carefully note that we shall need the additional assumptions specified in Chap. 2 to make valid statistical tests of hypotheses.

1-I IMPORTANCE AND GENERALITY OF THE GENERAL LINEAR MODEL IN THE SOCIAL AND BEHAVIORAL SCIENCES

Underlying the vast majority of all data analysis in the social and behavioral sciences is a model known to mathematicians as the General Linear Model. Different research traditions have historically made almost exclusive use of one of two familiar variants of the GLM:

1. Analysis of variance.
2. Regression analysis.

Psychology, for example, with a strong experimental tradition, relies primarily on techniques associated with analysis of variance. In contrast, sociology, with a strong field research tradition, has relied more heavily on techniques associated with regression analysis.

The emphasis of disciplines which primarily use one or the other of the two versions of the GLM is quite distinct. Data analyzed by analysis of variance techniques is typically presented in terms of experimental factors, sums of squares attributable to each factor, mean squares, and tests of significance. Data analyzed by regression techniques is typically presented in terms of independent variables, regression coefficients, prediction equations, and the multiple correlation between the independent and dependent variables.

In the context of the GLM it will become apparent that in their essentials analysis of variance and regression analysis are identical. What information is available in one is available in the other. It is only by tradition that certain disciplines have focused on various subsets of this information. In the demonstration of these facts lies the basis for more powerful and more relevant data analysis in the social and behavioral sciences.

1-II ORIENTATION OF BOOK

This book is written for applied researchers in the social and behavioral sciences and for students studying for such a career. Some familiarity on the part of the reader with regression analysis and analysis of variance is presumed. We also presume that the actual analysis will be done on a computer—in fact, many of our examples will be computer printouts. Thus, we will not present detailed computational formulas.[1] Indeed, it is the author's belief that the focus on computational methods of traditional books on experimental design is the single greatest cause for the confusion regarding the relationships among various analysis of variance and regression techniques, especially the common belief that these two techniques are quite distinct.

While much of the material in this book is necessarily technical, no proofs of well-known conclusions will be offered. For example, no attempt will be made to prove that the ratio of two independent chi-squares follows an F distribution. What we will show is that underlying each special formulation (e.g. Latin squares) of the GLM is a very specific set of assumptions. The focus of the discussion will be on the types of research problems for which each GLM design is best suited; the nature of the assumptions underlying each design; the consequences of violating these assumptions; potential corrective actions which the researcher may take when he determines the assumptions have been violated; and the interpretation of the numerical output of the analysis under the assumptions posited.

The formulas, and especially the derivations of these formulas, are presented for two essential reasons. First, these formulas concisely display the structure of any GLM design and the relationships among the many components which are needed to completely describe empirical data analyzed via GLM techniques. Second, most computer programs have been written for a specific purpose and, therefore, information which is relevant to the research may not be supplied in the

---

[1] Excellent texts which discuss computational methods suitable for hand or electronic calculator computations are available. Two of the better ones are Winer (1971) and Hays (1963).

printout. Often, however, this information may easily be derived with a few simple hand calculations from the printed output by using the formulas which relate the various components of any GLM design to one another.

1-III GENERAL LINEAR MODEL

1-III-1 Terminology and Notation

Figure 1-1 defines frequently encountered symbols. More detailed definitions will be given for each symbol when it is introduced. Population parameters will be indicated by Greek letters (e.g., α). The independent variables corresponding to these parameters will be designated with a corresponding Latin letter (e.g., A). Parameter estimates will carry a caret (e.g., $\hat{\alpha}$). Means will be indicated by a bar (e.g., $\bar{A}_j$), it being understood that the mean is taken over all subscripts not appearing.

N	Total number of observations
n	Number of observations per cell
m	Number in parameters model
y	N-element vector of observations of dependent variable
X	N by m matrix of independent variables, called the design matrix
θ	General notation for m-element vector of parameters
ε	N-element vector of residual error terms
σ_ε^2	Variance of population errors
SS	Sum of squares; will carry a subscript to indicate which parameters of GLM are being referenced.
MS	Mean squares; will carry a subscript to indicate which parameters of GLM are being referenced.
df	Degrees of freedom
r	Vector of correlation coefficients
R	Correlation Matrix
$N(\mu, \sigma^2 I)$	Indicates variable is normally distributed with mean μ, and variance $\sigma^2 I$, I being an identity matrix with 1's on the diagonal and 0's elsewhere
p_I	Type I error; significance level of statistical test
p_II	Type II error; $1 - p_\mathrm{II}$ equals the power of the statistical test
$E(z)$	Expected value of a random variable z.
λ	Noncentrality parameter
ϕ	$(\lambda/m)^{\frac{1}{2}}$, standardized λ used to table noncentral F distribution
l	Linear contrast among coefficients in θ.
ln	Natural logarithm

Figure 1-1 Frequently used symbols.

Vectors will be represented by boldface lower case letters.[2] A vector of the form $_N\mathbf{y}_1$ defines a column vector with N rows. Generally we shall use the row and column subscripts only when initially defining a variable, the subscripts being implied thereafter. The jth element of $\mathbf{y}$ is referenced by y_j, where j is a subscript running from 1 to N. Matrices will be represented by upper case letters. A matrix of the form $_N\mathbf{X}_m$ indicates a matrix with N rows and m columns. The ith row and jth column of $\mathbf{X}$ is referenced by x_{ij}, where i runs from 1 to N and j from 1 to m. A single row or column of $\mathbf{X}$ will be designated $\mathbf{x}_i$. The transpose of a vector or matrix, i.e., the operation of interchanging rows and columns, will be designated by a prime (e.g., $\mathbf{X}'$). An exponent of minus one indicates the inverse of a matrix (e.g., $\mathbf{X}^{-1}$).

1-III-2 An Introduction to the General Linear Model

1-III-2-1 Some simple linear models The linear models considered in this book all have the following general form. The dependent variable y is hypothesized to be a weighted linear combination of one or more independent variables x. The weights are often called regression or beta coefficients in regression analysis and treatment effects in analysis of variance.

A few examples may clarify what is meant by a linear model. For example, the equation

$$y_i = \alpha + \beta x_i \tag{1-1}$$

is one of the simplest linear models. Equation (1-1) states that the observed dependent variable for each subject y_i is hypothesized to be a function of a term common to all subjects α and an independent variable for the ith subject x_i which is related to the dependent variable by a weighting (i.e., regression) coefficient β. Or consider the model

$$y_i = \alpha + \beta x_i^2 \tag{1-2}$$

Equation (1-2) is still a linear model. To see why, let $z_i = x_i^2$, then

$$y_i = \alpha + \beta z_i \tag{1-3}$$

which is clearly linear. z_i is simply measured on a scale which equals the square of the scale on which x_i is measured.

Equations (1-1)–(1-3) all follow a form recognizable to readers familiar with regression analysis. For those familiar with analysis of variance, consider a two-factor design with two levels per factor. The structural model would be

$$y_{ijk} = \mu + \alpha_i + \beta_j + \alpha\beta_{ij}, \tag{1-4}$$

Equation (1-4) appears rather different from Eqs. (1-1)–(1-3).

We may put Eq. (1-4) in a form which is similar to Eqs. (1-1)–(1-3) by writing

---

[2] Readers unfamiliar with vector and matrix notation and manipulations should carefully read App. A.

6 THE GENERAL LINEAR MODEL

$$y_{ijk} = \mu x_0 + \alpha_1 x_1 + \alpha_2 x_2 + \beta_1 x_3 + \beta_2 x_4 + \alpha\beta_{11} x_5 + \alpha\beta_{12} x_6 + \alpha\beta_{21} x_7 + \alpha\beta_{22} x_8$$
(1-5)

Each x in Eq. (1-5) will be either 0 or 1 depending on which treatment combination the subject received. For example, for a subject in level 1 of both factors x_0 would be 1 because the grand mean μ is attributed to all subjects: x_1, x_3, and x_5 would also be 1 because these are the terms corresponding to the main effects α_1 and β_1 and the interaction effect $\alpha\beta_{11}$. All other x's would be 0 because this subject was not observed under the relevant treatment conditions. Symbolically,

$$y_{11k} = \mu(1) + \alpha_1(1) + \beta_1(1) + \alpha\beta_{11}(1)$$
$$= \mu + \alpha_1 + \beta_1 + \alpha\beta_{11}$$

Standard texts on analysis of variance typically write the structural model in the form of Eq. (1-4) with the values of the x's, i.e., the independent variables, being implied. Two things about Eq. (1-5) are noteworthy. First, the general form is the same as Eqs. (1-1)–(1-3). Each dependent variable is a weighted combination of the independent variables, the weights being called treatment effects in the language of analysis of variance. Second, the interaction terms are represented by single variables in the same manner as x_i^2 was recoded as $z_i = x_i^2$ in Eq. (1-3).

1-III-2-2 Basic form of the GLM With this background we may state that the linear models we shall discuss are *linear in their parameters*. Each independent variable is related to the dependent variable by a weighting factor called a regression coefficient or treatment effect and the dependent variable is hypothesized to be the additive (i.e., linear) sum of all weighted independent variables. In discussions of analysis of variance this linearity is often called additivity.

Consolidating these results we may write the GLM in the following completely general form

$$y_i = \theta_1 x_{i1} + \theta_2 x_{i2} + \cdots + \theta_m x_{im} + \varepsilon_i \qquad (i = 1, 2, \ldots, N) \qquad (1-6)$$

where y_i is an observation of an intervally-scaled, dependent variable which is by hypothesis a linear function of m unknown constants (i.e., parameters) $\theta_1 \ldots \theta_m$, where $x_{i1} \ldots x_{im}$ are m observed independent variables for the ith observation, and ε_i is the residual error for the ith observation.[3] The independent variables $x_{i1} \ldots x_{im}$ are restricted only in that they may *not* be ordinally scaled.[4]

We should note that Eq. (1-6) is called the basic structural (or response generating) model because it represents the researcher's hypothesis of the underlying forces which generated the observed response. It is important to recognize that underlying all data analysis is a specific model. The challenges to the researcher are to postulate the research model correctly, be certain that the postulated model

---

[3] Strictly speaking, an error term should be added to each of the structural equations, (1-1)–(1-5). This in no way affects the discussion concerning these equations.

[4] The characteristics of nominal, ordinal, and interval scales of measurement are reviewed in Sec. 1-IV of this chapter.

and the model underlying the data analysis technique are the same, and extract all information from the empirical data (via his chosen basic analytical technique) which is relevant to the postulated research model. These are not easy tasks, particularly in this day of packaged computer programs, which encourage the use of analytical tools without adequate grounding in their conceptual basis and research uses, and without proper interpretation of the often voluminous numerical output of many computer programs.

We might also add that the form of the output of many computer programs is virtually uninterpretable to the uninitiated. It is our hope to provide a small part of that initiation.

1-III-3 Minimal Assumptions Underlying the GLM

The general linear model consists of Eq. (1-6) along with the following three assumptions, which are partially reflected in this equation:

1. The functional form relating dependent and independent variables is linear.
2. Equation (1-6) is completely specified, i.e., all relevant independent variables are represented.
3. $E(\varepsilon_i) = 0$, for all i, i.e., the expected value of the residual error for each observation is zero.

These three assumptions are necessary to use the GLM as a *descriptive* model or representation of the data.

Figure 1-2 illustrates the consequences if the true functional form is not linear.

$$y = \theta_1 e^{\theta_2 x_1} \quad (1)$$

$$y = \theta_1 + \theta_2 x_1 \quad (2)$$

True functional form specified in Eq. (1)

Assumed functional form specified in Eq. (2)

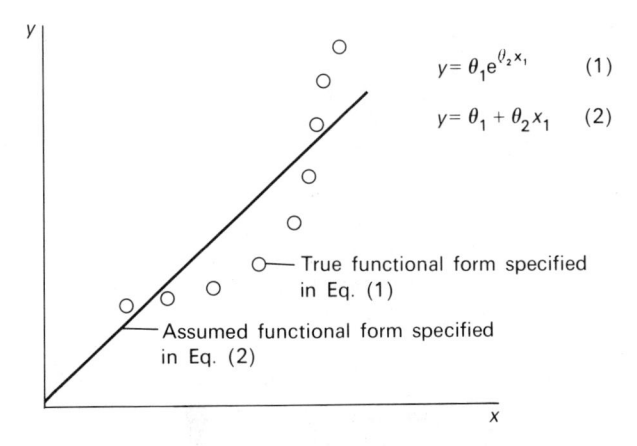

Figure 1-2 Illustration of effects of violation of the linearity assumption.
Note that linearity may be restored by taking logarithms on both sides of Eq. (1) so that

$$\ln y = \ln \theta_1 + \theta_2 x_1 \ln e$$
$$= \ln \theta_1 + \theta_2 x_1$$

where e, which equals 2.71828..., is the base of the Naperian system of logarithms. ln e is equal to 1.

First, the fit of the data to the model will not be as good as if the proper model had been specified. Second, the parameter estimates, i.e., estimates of the regression coefficients or treatment effects, will be biased. As noted in Figure 1-2, however, it will often be possible to find a transformation which will restore linearity. The topic of finding such transformations is further pursued in Chaps. 2 and 3.

The effects of violating assumption (2) given above are dependent on whether or not the independent variables are correlated. If an omitted variable is uncorrelated or orthogonal[5] with all other independent variables the variance attributable to the omitted variable will lodge entirely in the error term. If the omitted variable is correlated with one or more of the independent variables the parameter estimates for these variables will generally be distorted, sometimes greatly distorted. The error variance will also be increased, making it more difficult to pass a specific test of statistical significance.

Violation of assumption (3) will result in biased parameter estimates. The causes and remedies, however, are quite different from those discussed under assumptions (1) and (2). The causes are numerous: "yea-saying" tendencies; interviewer or response bias; experimenter effects; halo effects—ad infinitum. Remedies are to be found primarily in the procedures used to elicit and record responses and will be heavily dependent on the substantive area being researched. More will be said about biased errors in Chap. 3.

1-III-4 The General Linear Model Cast in Matrix Form

In this section and the next subsection the GLM is developed formally. In Sec. 1-V a numerical example which is small enough to be worked by hand is presented. Readers unfamiliar with the GLM, especially its development in matrix terms, may find it desirable to read these sections twice, working the numerical example as they reread the material.

The matrix algebra used in this book is probably new to many readers. And, until one acquires a basic familiarity with matrix notation and manipulations, it may seem more cumbersome than the simple algebraic expressions it replaces. Therefore, we should briefly consider the rationale for the matrix methods adopted here.

The primary reason for use of matrix algebra is that it allows us to show that all techniques of analysis of variance and regression analysis are based on the solution of a single matrix equation. This equation is called the normal equation. The substantive information contained in this equation and the interpretation of this information will be conditional on a set of assumptions about the dependent and independent variables on which this normal equation is based. The most important advantage of matrix algebraic methods is that they free us from the need to present detailed computational formulas, which tend to be somewhat unique for each specific formulation of the GLM.

---

[5] Orthogonal is a term often used synonymously with uncorrelated in more mathematical discussions of methods of analysis of variance.

1-III-4-1 Matrix notation for GLM[6] In order to put Eq. (1-6) in matrix form let us adopt the following notation:

$$y = {}_N y_1 = \begin{bmatrix} y_1 \\ y_2 \\ \vdots \\ y_N \end{bmatrix} \qquad \hat{y} = {}_N \hat{y}_1 = \begin{bmatrix} \hat{y}_1 \\ \hat{y}_2 \\ \vdots \\ \hat{y}_N \end{bmatrix}$$

$$X = {}_N X_m = \begin{bmatrix} x_{11} & x_{12} & \cdots & x_{1m} \\ x_{21} & & & \\ \vdots & & & \vdots \\ x_{N1} & x_{N2} & \cdots & x_{Nm} \end{bmatrix}$$

$$\theta = {}_m \theta_1 = \begin{bmatrix} \theta_1 \\ \theta_2 \\ \vdots \\ \theta_m \end{bmatrix} \qquad \hat{\theta} = {}_m \hat{\theta}_1 = \begin{bmatrix} \hat{\theta}_1 \\ \hat{\theta}_2 \\ \vdots \\ \hat{\theta}_m \end{bmatrix}$$

$$\varepsilon = {}_N \varepsilon_1 = \begin{bmatrix} \varepsilon_1 \\ \varepsilon_2 \\ \vdots \\ \varepsilon_N \end{bmatrix} \qquad \hat{\varepsilon} = {}_N \hat{\varepsilon}_1 = \begin{bmatrix} \hat{\varepsilon}_1 \\ \hat{\varepsilon}_2 \\ \vdots \\ \hat{\varepsilon}_N \end{bmatrix}$$

y is a column vector of *observed* dependent variables on N subjects. $\hat{y}$ is a column vector of *predicted* dependent variables on the same N subjects. X is an N-row, m-column matrix of m observed independent variables on the N subjects. θ is a m-element column vector of unknown parameters and $\hat{\theta}$ is the sample estimate of θ. Finally, ε is a column vector of N residual error terms and $\hat{\varepsilon}$ is the sample estimate of ε.

In matrix terms the observed data may be represented as

$$\begin{bmatrix} y_1 \\ \vdots \\ y_N \end{bmatrix} = \begin{bmatrix} x_{11} & \cdots & x_{1m} \\ \vdots & & \vdots \\ x_{N1} & \cdots & x_{Nm} \end{bmatrix} \begin{bmatrix} \theta_1 \\ \vdots \\ \theta_m \end{bmatrix} + \begin{bmatrix} \varepsilon_1 \\ \vdots \\ \varepsilon_N \end{bmatrix}$$

or

$$y = X\theta + \varepsilon.$$

Similarly, the *predicted* dependent vector may be represented as

$$\begin{bmatrix} \hat{y}_1 \\ \vdots \\ \hat{y}_N \end{bmatrix} = \begin{bmatrix} x_{11} & \cdots & x_{1m} \\ \vdots & & \vdots \\ x_{N1} & \cdots & x_{Nm} \end{bmatrix} \begin{bmatrix} \hat{\theta}_1 \\ \vdots \\ \hat{\theta}_m \end{bmatrix}$$

or

$$\hat{y} = X\hat{\theta}$$

---

[6] Readers unfamiliar with basic matrix notation and manipulations should read App. A carefully before proceeding.

1-III-4-2 Least-squared-errors criterion One of the researcher's most important objectives is to minimize the error of his research predictions. Using the notation developed above this error is

$$\hat{\varepsilon}_i = y_i - \hat{y}_i$$

i.e., the discrepancy between the observed and predicted values of the dependent variable for each subject. The sum of these errors is, by definition, zero. The error criterion we shall use is the sum of the squared errors.[7] In matrix notation this may be written as

$$\hat{\varepsilon}'\hat{\varepsilon} = \hat{\varepsilon}_1^2 + \hat{\varepsilon}_2^2 + \cdots + \hat{\varepsilon}_N^2 \qquad (1\text{-}7)$$

which many readers will recognize as the quantity to be minimized in the least squares estimates of the parameters of the GLM.

1-III-4-3 Least squares estimate of $\hat{\theta}$[8] Having defined the sum of squared errors as the quantity to be minimized, we may now proceed to select a set of parameter estimates $\hat{\theta}$ which will in fact minimize this criterion. To do this we must differentiate $\hat{\varepsilon}'\hat{\varepsilon}$ with respect to the estimated parameters $\hat{\theta}$, set the derivative equal to zero, and solve the derivative for a set of numbers $\hat{\theta}$ which will minimize the squared-errors criterion. This we now do.

First $\hat{\varepsilon}'\hat{\varepsilon}$ may be expanded to as follows:

$$\begin{aligned}\hat{\varepsilon}'\hat{\varepsilon} &= (y - \hat{y})'(y - \hat{y}) \\ &= (y - X\hat{\theta})'(y - X\hat{\theta}) \\ &= y'y + \hat{\theta}'X'X\hat{\theta} - 2\hat{\theta}'X'y\end{aligned} \qquad (1\text{-}8)$$

since $\hat{\varepsilon} = y - \hat{y}$ and $\hat{y} = X\hat{\theta}$.

The first step required to minimize the squared errors in Eq. (1-8) requires taking the partial derivative of $\hat{\varepsilon}'\hat{\varepsilon}$ with respect to the parameter estimates $\hat{\theta}$. This derivative is[9]

$$\frac{\partial \hat{\varepsilon}'\hat{\varepsilon}}{\partial \hat{\theta}} = 2X'X\hat{\theta} - 2X'y \qquad (1\text{-}9)$$

Equation (1-9) gives the rate of change of the sum of squared errors with respect to any parameter estimates. For Eq. (1-8) to be at a minimum Eq. (1-9) must equal

---

[7] Other error criterions are possible. One that may have come to the reader's mind is the sum of the absolute value of the errors. Some use has been made of this criterion. Mathematically, however, it is much more difficult to manipulate than the squared-errors criterion.

[8] This is the only time we shall use the differential calculus. Readers without a working knowledge of basic calculus are urged to follow the logic of this section, realizing that the objective of the calculus is to determine a set of parameter estimates $\hat{\theta}$ which will minimize the sum of squared errors.

[9] The differentiation of Eq. (1-8) is not as difficult as it may look. First, $y'y$ is a constant and thus does not enter the derivative. Second, $-2\hat{\theta}X'y$ is the matrix equivalent of $k\hat{\theta}$, where $k = -2X'y$ and the derivative is simply k or $-2X'y$. Third, $\hat{\theta}X'X\hat{\theta}$ is the matrix equivalent of $k\hat{\theta}^2$, where $k = X'X$ and the derivative is $2k\hat{\theta}$ or $2X'X\hat{\theta}$.

zero, i.e., the rate of change of the total squared errors with respect to changes in $\hat{\theta}$ must be zero. Therefore, Eq. (1-9) is set equal to zero and solved for $\hat{\theta}$, the least squares estimates of the parameters of the GLM, as follows

$$2X'X\hat{\theta} - 2X'y = 0$$

$$X'X\hat{\theta} = X'y$$

$$(X'X)^{-1}X'X\hat{\theta} = (X'X)^{-1}X'y$$

and since

$$(X'X)^{-1}X'X\hat{\theta} = I\hat{\theta} = \hat{\theta}$$

we have

$$\hat{\theta} = (X'X)^{-1}X'y \tag{1-10}$$

which is the matrix equivalent of the well-known normal equations of regression and analysis of variance that minimize the sum of squared errors.

Equation (1-10) is a most important result. It requires only that y be intervally scaled, X *not* be ordinally scaled, and that the inverse of $X'X$ exist. Using this single equation we may formulate all the familiar designs: e.g., factorial, Latin square, repeated measures. There is no requirement that the independent variables in X be uncorrelated and no restriction on how nominal and interval scales are mixed in X. All of these factors, however, shall affect the relevance of each design for specific research problems and questions. And these factors shall affect the interpretation of such outputs as the estimated coefficients $\hat{\theta}$. But none of the factors concerning such things as the scale of measurement or the correlations among the independent variables affects the validity of Eq. (1-10).

1-III-5 Interpretation of Normal Equation

Each of the terms X, $X'X$, $(X'X)^{-1}$, $X'y$, and $\hat{\theta}$ may be given a specific interpretation and shown to have some useful properties. It is also possible to derive a number of additional quantities which are useful in interpreting the GLM.

1-III-5-1 $\hat{\theta}$ The interpretation of $\hat{\theta}$, the estimated vector of regression weights, depends on the manner in which the columns (independent variables) of X have been coded. The problem of coding the independent variables is best discussed with an example and is therefore postponed until the next section.

It is easy to show, however, that $\hat{\theta}$ is unbiased since

$$\hat{\theta} = (X'X)^{-1}X'y$$

Replacing y with its expected value $E(y) = X\theta$ gives

$$E(\hat{\theta}) = (X'X)^{-1}X'E(y)$$
$$= (X'X)^{-1}X'X\theta$$
$$= \theta$$

which shows that $\hat{\theta}$ is unbiased, i.e., that taken over many samples the expected value of the parameter estimates $\hat{\theta}$ will equal the actual parameters θ in the underlying population.

1-III-5-2 Covariance of $\hat{\theta}$ We may easily find the covariance of the estimated parameters as

$$\operatorname{cov} \hat{\theta} = \hat{\theta}\hat{\theta}'$$

and since $\hat{\theta} = (X'X)^{-1}X'y$

$$\operatorname{cov} \hat{\theta} = (X'X)^{-1}X'yy'X(X'X)^{-1} \quad (1\text{-}11)$$

In repeated sampling, yy' will vary only as a function of the error variance in the data, σ_ε^2. In fact, it is relatively easy to show that in repeated sampling the expected value of yy' is

$$E(yy') = E[\operatorname{cov} y] = \sigma_\varepsilon^2 I$$

Setting $yy' = \sigma_\varepsilon^2 I$ in Eq. (1-11) yields

$$\operatorname{cov} \hat{\theta} = (X'X)^{-1}X'\sigma_\varepsilon^2 IX(X'X)^{-1}$$
$$= (X'X)^{-1}X'X(X'X)^{-1}\sigma_\varepsilon^2$$
$$= (X'X)^{-1}\sigma_\varepsilon^2$$

In practice, σ_ε^2 must be estimated from sample data. Procedures for estimating σ_ε^2 are given below.

There are two basic uses of the information contained in $\operatorname{cov} \hat{\theta}$. First, and here we shall need the additional assumptions of Chap. 2, $\operatorname{cov} \hat{\theta}$ is needed for statistical tests of hypotheses concerning $\hat{\theta}$. Second, the diagonal elements of $\operatorname{cov} \hat{\theta}$ provide information on the variance of the individual parameter estimates in $\hat{\theta}$. The larger these elements are the more we can expect $\hat{\theta}$ to vary from sample to sample. Another way of putting this is to say the larger the diagonal of $\operatorname{cov} \hat{\theta}$ the less faith we can put in the estimated value of $\hat{\theta}$.

1-III-5-3 Geometric representation of dependent and independent variables X, y, $X'X$, and $X'y$ may be given geometric representations which will prove very useful in determining the structure of any specific GLM and in interpreting empirical data in the context of a specific GLM design. To aid this discussion, Fig. 1-3a presents a simple data matrix X defining three observations (rows) with two variables per observation and the cross-products XX' and $X'X$. Geometrically, the observations may be represented as three points in a variable space of two dimensions. Figure 1-3b presents such a geometric representation where each point represents a row of X and the projections of each point onto each axis gives the independent variables for each observation. Each point is joined to the origin by a line known as a vector. We may also invert the graph in Fig. 1-3b (as is done in Fig. 1-3c) to picture the variables in a subject space. Although we shall eventually be more interested in the second graph, we postpone discussion

THE GENERAL LINEAR MODEL 13

Figure 1-3 Geometric portrayal of a data matrix $_3X_2$ defining 3 empirical observations and 2 independent variables per observation:

(a) data matrix and cross products matrices;

$$X = \begin{bmatrix} x_{11} & x_{12} \\ x_{21} & x_{22} \\ x_{31} & x_{32} \end{bmatrix} = \begin{bmatrix} v_1 & v_2 \\ 2 & 4 \\ 2 & 2 \\ 6 & 3 \end{bmatrix}$$

$$XX' = \begin{bmatrix} 20 & 12 & 24 \\ 12 & 8 & 18 \\ 24 & 18 & 45 \end{bmatrix} \qquad X'X = \begin{bmatrix} 44 & 30 \\ 30 & 29 \end{bmatrix}$$

(a)

(b) subjects in a variable space;

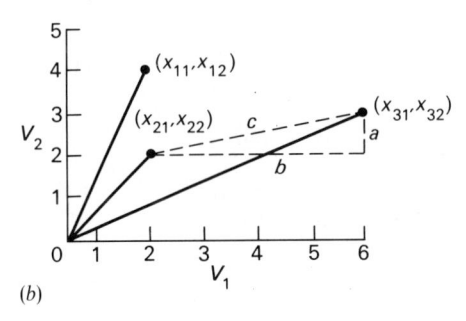

(b)

(c) variables in a subject space.

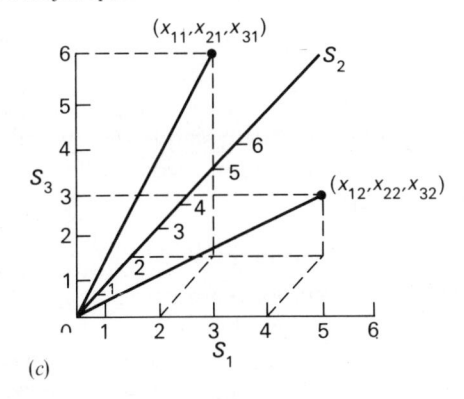

(c)

of it for the moment because we presume most readers are not familiar with such a graph.

Now, we might ask what the distance to the origin of any point is in Fig. 1-3b. The answer is to be found in XX' which is N times the *subject* covariance matrix.[10]

---

[10] For sample data an unbiased estimate of the subject covariance matrix would be obtained by dividing XX' by $N - 1$.

14 THE GENERAL LINEAR MODEL

The distance of any point i to the origin equals the square root of the ith diagonal element in XX'. For the third point (X_{31}, X_{32}) this is $\sqrt{45} = 6.71$. The ith diagonal of XX' is also equal to N times the variance of the ith subject over all variables.[11] If y were added as an additional column in X the above interpretation would hold exactly; y would simply appear as an added dimension in the graph in Fig. 1-3b.

We may also use information contained in XX' to determine how far it is between any two points (rows) in Fig. 1-3b. This is done by use of the Pythagorean theorem, which states that the distance between two points equals the square root of the sum of squared lengths of the sides of a right-angled triangle formed between the two points. If, as is done in Fig. 1-3b, the two sides of the triangle are labeled a and b and the hypotenuse (the straight line between the two points) is labeled c then the distance d_{ij} between the two points is

$$c = (a^2 + b^2)^{\frac{1}{2}}$$

For points (x_{21}, x_{22}) and (x_{31}, x_{32}), the two points forming the triangle in Fig. 1-3b, this distance is

$$d_{23} = c = (1^2 + 4^2)^{\frac{1}{2}} = 4.12$$

The Pythagorean theorem generalizes directly to any number of dimensions. In matrix notation the squared distance between any two points is

$$d_{ij}^2 = (x_{i1} - x_{j1})^2 + (x_{i2} - x_{j2})^2 + \cdots + (x_{im} - x_{jm})^2 \quad (1\text{-}12)$$

which is simply the sum of the squared differences on each of the m axes. Equation (1-12) may be written more compactly as

$$\begin{aligned} d_{ij}^2 &= (x_i - x_j)'(x_i - x_j) \\ &= x_i'x_i + x_j'x_j - 2x_i'x_j \end{aligned} \quad (1\text{-}13)$$

But note that the first two terms in Eq. (1-13) are simply the ith and jth diagonal elements of XX'. To get the last expression in a more useful form we may show, by the cosine rule of trigonometry, that

$$x_i'x_j = (x_i'x_i)^{\frac{1}{2}}(x_j'x_j)^{\frac{1}{2}} \cos(i, j)$$

The cosine of the angle between the vectors representing points i and j is, by definition, equal to the correlation r_{ij} between these two points.

It is easy to transform XX' into a matrix of correlation coefficients by recalling that a correlation is simply a covariance standardized to remove the effects of the variances of the two variables. The correlation between any two points r_{ij} may be found from XX' by the relationship

$$r_{ij} = \frac{x_i'x_j}{(x_i'x_i)^{\frac{1}{2}}(x_j'x_j)^{\frac{1}{2}}}$$

---

[11] Again, the proper divisor for sample data is $N - 1$.

For the second and third points the correlation is

$$r_{ij} = \frac{18}{(8)^{\frac{1}{2}}(45)^{\frac{1}{2}}} = 0.948$$

Combining these results we may write the following general formula for the distance between any two points

$$d_{ij}^2 = x_i'x_i + x_j'x_j - 2(x_i'x_i)^{\frac{1}{2}}(x_j'x_j)^{\frac{1}{2}}r_{ij}$$

For points 2 and 3 this would be

$$d_{23}^2 = 8 + 45 - 2(8)^{\frac{1}{2}}(45)^{\frac{1}{2}}(0.948)$$
$$= 8 + 45 - 2(2.828)(6.708)(0.948)$$
$$= 17$$

Thus $\qquad d_{23} = (17)^{\frac{1}{2}} = 4.12$

which is the same distance obtained from the more direct application of the Pythagorean theorem.

The above relationships were all developed in the context of the matrix XX', which summarizes the interrelationships among all subjects over the independent variables. The normal equation requires the term $X'X$ which summarizes the relationships among the independent variables over subjects. Figure 1-3c gives a geometrical representation of X which emphasizes the relationships among the independent variables. In Fig. 1-3c we have simply reversed the figure in Fig. 1-3b, letting the axes represent subjects and picturing the two variables as vectors in a subject space of three dimensions. With more than three subjects, of course, we cannot draw such a figure. Mathematically, however, the relationships pictured in Fig. 1-3c hold for any number of subjects. Note carefully that all information concerning X is available in both graphs. The first simply emphasizes the information in XX', i.e., the relationships among subjects over variables, while the second emphasizes the information in $X'X$, i.e., the relationships among variables over subjects.

$X'y$ is N times the covariance between the independent and dependent variables.[12] $X'y$ may easily be transformed into a vector of correlation coefficients by the relationship

$$r_{iy} = \frac{x_i'y}{(x_i'x_i)^{\frac{1}{2}}(y'y)^{\frac{1}{2}}}$$

As we shall subsequently explore more fully, the correlation of each independent variable with the dependent variable is one of the most useful tools we have for interpreting the results of any GLM analysis.

The role of $X'X$ and $X'y$ in the normal equation should now be clear. $X'X$ contains all the information concerning the interrelationships among the in-

---

[12] Again, the proper divisor for sample data is $N - 1$.

dependent variables. $X'y$ contains all the information concerning the relationship between each independent variable and the dependent variable.

1-III-5-4 Partitioning the total sum of squares The last thing we shall do in this section is show how the total sum of squares of the dependent variable may be partitioned. First define the total sum of squares SS_y as

$$SS_y = y'y = y_1^2 + y_2^2 + \cdots + y_N^2$$

We may find the portion of $y'y$ which is accounted for by the GLM as follows. First recall that the *predicted* dependent vector is

$$\hat{y} = X\hat{\theta}$$

The sum of squares accounted for by the GLM, SS_R, is therefore $\hat{y}'\hat{y}$. Substituting $X\hat{\theta}$ for $\hat{y}$ yields

$$SS_R = \hat{y}'\hat{y} = \hat{\theta}'X'X\hat{\theta} \tag{1-14}$$

Since $\hat{\theta} = (X'X)^{-1}X'y$, we may substitute this for the far right $\hat{\theta}$ in Eq. (1-14)

$$SS_R = \hat{\theta}'X'X(X'X)^{-1}X'y$$
$$= \hat{\theta}'X'y$$

The residual error sum of squares, SS_E, is simply

$$SS_E = SS_y - SS_R$$

Since the first element of $\hat{\theta}$ will often be the mean[13] of y we can separate the sum of squares due the mean, SS_M, from the sum of squares due the GLM as follows

$$SS_M = (\mathbf{1}'y)^2/N$$
$$= (y_1^2 + y_2^2 + \cdots + y_n^2)/N$$

where $\mathbf{1}$ is a column vector of N 1's. SS_M is the matrix equivalent of the correction for the mean.

The proportion of variance "explained" by the GLM, R^2, is

$$R^2 = \frac{SS_R}{SS_y}$$

If the m independent variables are uncorrelated it is possible to partition SS_R into m independent components, giving a unique interpretation to each of the independent variables. When the independent variables are correlated this unique partition will not be possible, and although it is still possible to interpret each independent variable this interpretation becomes more difficult and less certain as the intercorrelations among the independent variables increase.

---

[13] In textbooks the mean is usually represented as a in regression analysis and μ in analysis of variance. GLM discussions often subscript this element β_0.

Table 1-1 Partition of total sum of squares

Source of variation	Sum of squares	Degrees of freedom
General Linear Model†	$\hat{\theta}'X'y$	m
Mean	$(1'y)^2/N$	1
GLM, excluding mean	$\hat{\theta}'X'y - (1'y)^2/N$	$m - 1$
Residual	$y'y - \hat{\theta}'X'y$	$N - m$
Total	$y'y$	N

† This is often denoted as the sum of squares due to regression or the sum of squares due to treatment.

Finally, with N observations there are N degrees of freedom which may be partitioned and attributed, sometimes uniquely, to each sum of squares. We shall have more to say about the concept of degrees of freedom in Chap. 3. Table 1-1 summarizes the partition of the sum of squares and the corresponding degrees of freedom in the usual analysis of variance table format.

1-IV A NOTE ON SCALES OF MEASUREMENT

Before proceeding to the numerical example presented in the next section it will be useful to digress for a moment to consider the four different types of measurement scales on which the dependent and independent variables may be measured. Of the four scales one is specifically excluded from GLM analytical techniques, one contains properties which are stronger than those required by the GLM, and of the remaining two types of scale one is most frequently encountered in regression designs while the other is most frequently found in analysis of variance designs.

1-IV-1 Nominal Scales

Nominal scales indicate group membership. An observation is either in a group or it is not. No ordering among the groups is possible. Mathematically, the only operation allowed is equivalence, i.e., determining whether the observation is a member of a specific group or not. Familiar examples of nominal scales are the numbering of football players, telephone numbers, and social security numbers. Nominal scales are invariant over (i.e., the information contained in the measurement scale is not changed by) any assignment of numbers which preserves group membership. As we shall demonstrate shortly, analysis of variance designs use a special form of nominally-scaled, independent variables.

1-IV-2 Ordinal Scales

In addition to equivalence, ordinal scales allow tests of whether one observation is greater or less than another. Social class is a good example of an ordinal scale. While we can rank the various classes in terms of social status we generally cannot say anything about the relative differences in status between different pairs of social classes, i.e., if lower class = 1, middle class = 2, and upper-middle class = 3, we cannot say the status *difference* between lower and middle class individuals equals the status *difference* between the middle and upper-middle class individuals. Any positive monotone transformation[14] of the measurement scale is allowable for an ordinal scale since it preserves ordering among the observations. Ordinal scales may not be used in GLM designs although any ordinal scale may be downgraded to a nominal scale by disregarding the ordering among groups. For a readable discussion of procedures for analyzing ordinal data see Seigel (1956).

1-IV-3 Interval Scales

Interval scales allow tests of equivalence and order, and comparisons of inter-point distances. If in the previous example social class had been measured on an interval scale it would have been legitimate to compare the difference in status between lower and middle class individuals with the difference in status between middle and upper-middle class individuals. Examples of interval scales are certain attitude and intelligence scales. It is worth noting that many of the scales traditionally regarded as having interval properties have been severely criticized by some researchers who believe that these scales can only legitimately be regarded as ordinal. A good example of such a situation is provided by the attitude scales developed by Thurstone's method of equal appearing intervals.

Any transformation of the form

$$y^* = a + by \quad (b > 0)$$

is legitimate for an interval scale. In such a transformation a locates the center of the scale and b sets the unit of measurement. For example, in the Stanford–Binet intelligence test, a is set so that the average intelligence is 100 and b is set so that the standard deviation (the unit of measurement) is 15. An important point is that the mean of an interval scale is arbitrary and therefore conveys no information by itself.

Independent variables encountered in regression discussions are almost always intervally scaled. In fact, the use of intervally-scaled independent variables in regression analysis and nominally-scaled independent variables in analysis of variance is the principal distinction between the two major variants of the GLM. As we shall demonstrate, a moment's reflection indicates that the covariance analysis encountered as one of the last topics in most analysis of variance texts is simply a mixture of nominal and interval independent variables in a single GLM design. In all GLM designs, however, the *dependent* variable at least must be intervally scaled.

---

[14] A positive monotone transformation is one where if one observation had a score higher than another observation on the original scale this relationship is preserved on the transformed scale.

1-IV-4 Ratio Scales

Ratio scales represent the élite of measurement scales. These scales have a natural origin, i.e., a non-arbitrary zero point. Reinforcement schedules are one example of a ratio scale. Ratio scales allow not only comparisons of interpoint distances but also comparisons of the ratio of the absolute values of two observations. For example, if one rat is given 2 grams of food for each correct response and another rat only 1 gram we can say the first rat is receiving twice as much food per correct response as the second rat. Ratio scales are invariant over transformations of the form

$$y^* = by \quad (b > 0)$$

The mean of such a scale conveys meaning by itself and it is permissible to test hypotheses concerning the value of the mean of a ratio scaled variable. In general, however, we shall not need the additional property of a fixed natural origin to use the GLM legitimately.

With this background on measurement scales we can now construct a very simple set of data which contains both nominally-scaled and intervally-scaled dependent variables.

1-V A NUMERICAL EXAMPLE

Sections 1-III and 1-IV covered a great deal of material very quickly and rather abstractly. In this section we shall work through an artificially constructed set of data to illustrate the principles discussed above. Artificial data has been used for two primary reasons. First, the amount of data is small enough that the reader can work through all calculations by hand. Second, the analysis of artificial data, whose characteristics are known by definition, is an excellent device for learning the characteristics of an analytical technique for it allows us to compare what is revealed by the analysis with what we know to be true a priori.

1-V-1 Construction of Artificial Data

To construct artificial data it is necessary to assume a basic structural model. This model is sometimes called the response-generating model because it is our hypothesis of the forces which caused the observed response. With artificial data, of course, we may insure the congruence of our data and the response-generating model.[15] Section (*a*) of Table 1-2 presents the structural model used to construct the data. Readers familiar with analysis of variance will recognize this as a single factor covariance design where the factor has two treatment levels.

In Table 1-2*b* the data is constructed by giving numerical values to each component of the structural model. The term μ represents the grand mean, an

---

[15] We may also purposefully construct data which violates one or more assumptions of our model to determine the effects of the assumption violations.

20 THE GENERAL LINEAR MODEL

Table 1-2 Construction and analysis of artificial data

(a) Structural model

$$y_{ji} = \mu + \alpha_i + \beta x_j \quad (j = 1, 8)$$
$$\Sigma \alpha_i = 0 \quad (i = 1, 2)$$

(b) Construction of artificial data

Treatment level	Subject	Dependent variable y_{ji}	μ	Independent variables α_1	α_2	$x_j^\dagger$
1	1	44.5	40	10		5.5
1	2	46.5	40	10		3.5
1	3	53.5	40	10		-3.5
1	4	55.5	40	10		-5.5
2	5	24.5	40		-10	5.5
2	6	26.5	40		-10	3.5
2	7	33.5	40		-10	-3.5
2	8	35.5	40		-10	-5.5

(c) Analysis

(i) Matrix formulation of data

$$\mathbf{y} = \mathbf{X}\boldsymbol{\theta} \qquad \boldsymbol{\theta} = \begin{bmatrix} \mu \\ \alpha_1 \\ \beta \end{bmatrix}$$

$$\begin{bmatrix} 44.5 \\ 46.5 \\ 53.5 \\ 55.5 \\ 24.5 \\ 26.5 \\ 33.5 \\ 35.5 \end{bmatrix} = \begin{bmatrix} 1 & 1 & 5.5 \\ 1 & 1 & 3.5 \\ 1 & 1 & -3.5 \\ 1 & 1 & -5.5 \\ 1 & -1 & 5.5 \\ 1 & -1 & 3.5 \\ 1 & -1 & -3.5 \\ 1 & -1 & -5.5 \end{bmatrix} \begin{bmatrix} 40 \\ 10 \\ -1 \end{bmatrix}$$

(ii) Cross products

$$\mathbf{X}'\mathbf{X} = \begin{bmatrix} 8 & 0 & 0 \\ 0 & 8 & 0 \\ 0 & 0 & 170 \end{bmatrix} \qquad \mathbf{X}'\mathbf{y} = \begin{bmatrix} 320 \\ 80 \\ -170 \end{bmatrix}$$

(iii) Inverse of $\mathbf{X}'\mathbf{X}^\ddagger$

$$(\mathbf{X}'\mathbf{X})^{-1} = \begin{bmatrix} 1/8 & 0 & 0 \\ 0 & 1/8 & 0 \\ 0 & 0 & 1/170 \end{bmatrix}$$

Table 1-2 Continued

(iv) Estimated regression coefficients of GLM

$$\hat{\theta} = (X'X)^{-1}X'y$$

$$= \begin{bmatrix} 1/8 & 0 & 0 \\ 0 & 1/8 & 0 \\ 0 & 0 & 1/170 \end{bmatrix} \begin{bmatrix} 320 \\ 80 \\ -170 \end{bmatrix} = \begin{bmatrix} 40 \\ 10 \\ -1 \end{bmatrix}$$

(v) Sum of squares attributable to GLM§

$$SS_R = \hat{\theta}'X'y$$

$$= \begin{bmatrix} 40 & 10 & -1 \end{bmatrix} \begin{bmatrix} 320 \\ 80 \\ -170 \end{bmatrix}$$

$$= 12{,}800 + 800 + 170$$

$$= 13{,}770$$

(vi) Correlation matrix

$$R_{xx} = \begin{bmatrix} 1 & 0 & 0 \\ 0 & 1 & 0 \\ 0 & 0 & 1 \end{bmatrix}$$

$$r_{xy} = \begin{bmatrix} 320/(\sqrt{8} \cdot \sqrt{13770}) \\ 80/(\sqrt{8} \cdot \sqrt{13770}) \\ -170/(\sqrt{170} \cdot \sqrt{13770}) \end{bmatrix} = \begin{bmatrix} 0.9642 \\ 0.2410 \\ -0.1109 \end{bmatrix}$$

---

† $\beta = -1$, therefore the constructed observation for the first subject is $y_{11} = 40 + 10 - 5.5 = 44.5$.
‡ When the columns of X are orthogonal (uncorrelated) the inverse of $X'X$ is simply the reciprocal of the diagonal elements of $X'X$. It is easily verified that $(X'X)^{-1}$ is the inverse of $X'X$ by computing $(X'X)^{-1}X'X$, which is indeed an identity matrix.
§ Since there is no error in our data and the structural is correct

$$SS_R = \hat{\theta}'X'y = y'y$$

i.e., the explained sum of squares is equal to the total sum of squares.
¶ Note that because R_{xx} is an identity matrix, i.e., all independent variables are uncorrelated, $r'_{xy}r_{xy} = SS_R/SS_y$. This means that a unique portion of the total variance in y can be attributed to each of the three independent variables. This will be the case *only* if $X'X$ is a diagonal matrix.

effect common to all subjects, and is set equal to 40. The treatment effects for subjects in the first treatment condition α_1 is 10. By the usual analysis of variance restriction that the sum of the effects for each factor is equal to zero, α_2 must equal $-\alpha_1$ or -10. βx_j is the standard linear regression term where x_j is an intervally-scaled independent variable and β is the slope coefficient relating x_j to y_{ji}. In analysis of variance terminology x_j is a covariate. β is equal to -1. Note that no error term is specified. This has been done to allow perfect recovery of the underlying model. At the end of this section an error term is added to the data and the reader is encouraged to work this problem to be sure he understands the basics of the GLM. The structural model, of course, is linear and each y_{ji} is simply the sum of the terms to the right of it.

1-V-2 Independent Variable Coding Procedures

In section (c) of Table 1-2 we begin the analysis. First, the data must be properly coded. The vector of dependent variables y is reproduced from Table 1-2b without alteration, and is, of course, intervally scaled. In coding the independent variables it will simplify our discussion to consider the three variables in reverse order.

The third independent variable is an intervally-scaled variable. In analysis of variance terminology this variable is called a covariate. In a learning study involving rats, for example, the covariate might be the initial weight of each rat. In an attitude change study it might be each subject's pretreatment attitude. For coding purposes the data in Table 1-2b under x_j is simply recorded as the third column of the matrix of independent variables X. By hypothesis, y will change by β units for every unit change in x_3.

The second independent variable codes the two treatments A_1 and A_2 as a single nominal variable. In the literature this type of variable is usually called a dummy or indicator variable. If an observation was observed under the first treatment of the factor A_1, a 1 is recorded in the second column of X for that observation. Since the treatment effects (α's) are defined as deviations from the grand mean μ it follows that the sum of the α's is zero and that therefore α_2 equals $-\alpha_1$, i.e.,

$$\alpha_1 + \alpha_2 = 0$$

$$\alpha_2 = -\alpha_1$$

Thus if an observation is not observed under A_1 it must, by definition, have been observed under A_2 and since $\alpha_2 = -\alpha_1$ a -1 is recorded under x_2 if the observation was made under A_2.

In general, if there are k treatment groups it requires $k - 1$ dummy variables to completely code them. Table 1-3 shows the coding for an example with three groups.

Finally, the first column in X has all 1's because our structural model hypothesizes a term μ, the grand mean, which is common to all observations.

The complete matrix X is called the design matrix because it contains all the information available concerning the independent variables. There is no restriction in the GLM which requires or prohibits any particular combination of dummy independent variables and intervally-scaled independent variables.

Table 1-3 Dummy variable coding for three groups

Observation in group	Dummy variable code x_1	x_2
1	1	0
2	0	1
3	-1	-1

Indeed, the example we have constructed is an analysis of covariance design which is the meeting place of traditional regression analysis and traditional analysis of variance.

We should note, before proceeding to the data analysis, that the dummy variable coding procedure presented in this chapter is only one of a great many ways in which the treatment effects can be coded. Considerably more will be said about different coding procedures in Chap. 3.

1-V-3 Data Analysis

In Table 1-2 (c-ii) the necessary cross products are computed. Notice that $X'X$ is a diagonal matrix. This means that the independent variables are uncorrelated. When this is the case the inverse of $X'X$ is obtained by simply replacing the diagonal elements with their reciprocals as is done in Table 1-2 (c-iii). In section (c-iv) of this table the vector of regression coefficients $\hat{\theta}$ is computed. Note that these are exactly the coefficients used to construct the data. Of course, in the presence of error and/or an inappropriate model this will normally not be true.

In Table 1-2 (c-v) the explained sum of squares is derived. Since there is no error in the data and the structural model is correct the explained sum of squares equals the total sum of squares. Finally, the correlation matrix is presented in Table 1-2 (c-vi). The independent variables are, as previously noted, uncorrelated. When this is true r_{xy}, the correlation between each independent variable and dependent variable, has a very useful interpretation. The squared elements of r_{xy} give the proportion of the total explained variance which is uniquely attributable to each variable in X. When R_{xx} is not an identity matrix this is not true and the interpretation of the GLM becomes more difficult.

Table 1-4 Artificial data with small random error, estimated $\hat{\theta}$, and r_{xy}[†]

$$y = \begin{bmatrix} 43.5 \\ 43.5 \\ 55.5 \\ 56.5 \\ 25.5 \\ 24.5 \\ 36.5 \\ 38.5 \end{bmatrix} \quad \hat{\theta} = \begin{bmatrix} 40.5 \\ 9.25 \\ -1.34 \end{bmatrix} \quad r_{xy} = \begin{bmatrix} 0.9640 \\ 0.2202 \\ -0.1466 \end{bmatrix}$$

[†] The reader is urged to work this problem entirely to insure his basic understanding of the GLM. This table presents only changes in the data in Table 1-2, which the reader will need to refer to for the remainder of the data necessary to work this problem.

24 THE GENERAL LINEAR MODEL

1-V-4 Reader Test Problem

To check your understanding of the GLM try analyzing the data in Table 1-4. This is the same data as in Table 1-2 with a random error added to each observation. The structural model is the same and enough information is given to check your work. Notice that $\hat{\theta} \neq \theta$. This is because although the *expected* value of $\hat{\varepsilon}$ is zero, in any one sample the actual value of $\hat{\varepsilon}$ will not normally be zero. To see what would happen if the structural model were not correctly specified drop one of the variables (columns) from X and reanalyze the data.

1-VI SUMMARY

In this chapter we have shown that all analysis of variance and regression analysis designs involve solving the same general normal equation:

$$\hat{\theta} = (X'X)^{-1}X'y$$

To solve this equation it need only be assumed that $(X'X)^{-1}$ exists, which will generally be true. Also discussed were the assumptions necessary to use the GLM as a descriptive model and the concept of scales of measurement. The role of each component of the normal equation and a number of derived quantities in interpreting empirical data within the context of a GLM design was discussed in detail. Table 1-5 summarizes the major equations developed in this chapter.

Table 1-5 Summary of most important equations in Chap. 1

Observed data

$$y = X\theta + \varepsilon$$

Predicted data

$$\hat{y} = X\hat{\theta}$$

Normal equation

$$\hat{\theta} = (X'X)^{-1}X'y$$

Covariance of estimated parameters

$$\text{cov } \hat{\theta} = (X'X)^{-1}\sigma_\varepsilon^2$$

Correlations

$$r_{ij} = \frac{x_i' x_j}{(x_i' x_i)^{\frac{1}{2}} (x_j' x_j)^{\frac{1}{2}}} \qquad r_{iy} = \frac{x_i' y}{(x_i' x_i)^{\frac{1}{2}} (y' y)^{\frac{1}{2}}}$$

Sum of squares predicted by GLM

$$SS_R = \hat{\theta}' X' y$$

CHAPTER
TWO

ADDITIONAL ASSUMPTIONS NECESSARY FOR VALID STATISTICAL TESTS OF HYPOTHESES CONCERNING THE PARAMETERS OF THE GENERAL LINEAR MODEL

2-I A Review of Some Important Statistical Concepts

2-I-1 Statistical Hypotheses
2-I-2 Construction of a Test of the "Null" Hypothesis
    2-I-2-1 Discrepancy between estimated parameters and parameters specified by the null hypothesis
    2-I-2-2 Expected value of a random variable
    2-I-2-3 Test statistic and sampling distribution of a test statistic
    2-I-2-4 Critical value of test statistic
2-I-3 Significance and Power of the F Test
    2-I-3-1 Significance and power defined
    2-I-3-2 Calculating the power of a test
    2-I-3-3 Planning sample size to insure power and significance
2-I-4 Magnitude of Coefficients of the GLM
2-I-5 A Note on the Interrelationships Among the Z, χ^2, F and t Tests

2-II Three Assumptions Underlying the F Test

2-II-1 Actual Significance and Power of the F Test
2-II-2 Characteristics of the Actual Distribution of the F Test Statistic
2-II-3 The Independence of Errors Assumption
    2-II-3-1 Rationale for assumption
    2-II-3-2 Consequences of assumption violation
    2-II-3-3 Preventive procedures
    2-II-3-4 Corrective procedures

2-II-4 The Homogeneity of Error Variance Assumption
    2-II-4-1 Rationale for assumption
    2-II-4-2 Procedures for detecting violation of homogeneity assumption
    2-II-4-3 Consequences of violating homogeneity assumption
    2-II-4-4 Corrective procedures
2-II-5 The Normality of Errors Assumption
    2-II-5-1 Rationale for assumption
    2-II-5-2 Procedures for detecting violation of normality assumption
    2-II-5-3 Theoretical reasons for unimportance of normality assumption
    2-II-5-4 Consequences of violating normality assumption
    2-II-5-5 Corrective procedures
2-II-6 Heterogeneous Variances and Non-Normality
2-II-7 Reader Test Problem

2-III Summary

This chapter has two primary purposes. First, we shall briefly review some important statistical concepts. Second, we shall investigate three assumptions which are necessary if the standard t and F tests of statistical hypotheses are to be correct. Specifically, it is necessary to assume that the residual errors are (1) normally distributed with (2) constant variance, and (3) that the errors are independent. We shall also inquire into the consequences of violating these assumptions and suggest corrective procedures when the assumptions are severely violated.

2-I A REVIEW OF SOME IMPORTANT STATISTICAL CONCEPTS[1]

This section is presented only as a refresher. Readers needing a more thorough review are referred to one of the following sources: Ferguson (1959), Hays and Winkler (1971), or Winer (1971), Chap. 1.

2-I-1 Statistical Hypotheses

A statistical hypothesis is an assertion about the state of some defined population whose truth is to be tested. It was Sir Ronald Fisher (1925) who first presented this definition of a "null" hypothesis and stated the criterion that this null

---

[1] For convenience in this chapter we shall use N to designate the total number of observations and n to designate various subsets of N. Subscripts will be carried by n to indicate the appropriate observations. The number of levels of an experimental factor will be indicated by k.

hypothesis should be rejected when the probability of the observed sample data occurring, *given* that the null hypothesis is true, becomes unacceptably small. This probability is the traditional significance level of a statistical hypothesis test.

Three years later Neyman and Pearson (1928) observed that rejection of the null hypothesis implies the existence of an alternative hypothesis. In subsequent sections the null hypothesis is labeled H_0 and the alternative hypothesis H_1.

2-I-2 Construction of a Test of the "Null" Hypothesis

To test a null hypothesis we must (1) define a statistic, such as t or F, which measures the departure of the population parameters estimated from sample data $\hat{\theta}$ from the assumed population parameters specified by the null hypothesis θ_H, (2) determine the sampling (i.e., probability) distribution of the test statistic, and (3) set a critical value of the test statistic which will cause rejection of the null hypothesis.

Table 2-1 presents data which will help illustrate these ideas. The data is for a three-level, single factor design with three observations per cell. The data have been centered to zero mean; the marginal means are therefore equivalently the treatment effects or the coefficients $\hat{\theta}$ of the GLM.[2]

2-I-2-1 Discrepancy between estimated parameters and parameters specified by the null hypothesis
As a first step in constructing a statistic which measures the departure of the estimated parameters from the parameters specified by the null hypothesis, recall that in Chap. 1 we defined the sum of squares explained by $\hat{\theta}$ as $\hat{\theta}'X'y$. If we replace $\hat{\theta}$ with θ_H, the sum of squares explained by the null hypothesis is $\theta'_H X'y$. Our measure of the departure of the estimated parameters from those specified by the null hypothesis is simply the difference between these two sums of squares. Usually θ_H will be a vector of zeros and hence the sum of squares explained by the null hypothesis will be zero in these cases. From sections b(i) to b(iii) in Table 2-1 we see that the sum of squares due to departure of the sample data from the null hypothesis is 6. Section (b-iv) in the table gives the residual sum of squares which is needed to estimate the error variance of the data $\hat{\sigma}_\varepsilon^2$.

Of course, these sums of squares are based on different numbers of observations. Each sum of squares is also defined about different means, requiring different adjustments of the number of observations to obtain the proper degrees of freedom. For example, the three treatment effects are defined as deviations from the grand mean, allowing only two effects to vary independently. Hence there are only two degrees of freedom available to estimate the treatment effects.[3]

---

[2] The third coefficient, of course, is not given directly in the GLM.

[3] Strictly speaking the degrees of freedom due a source of variation equals the number of observations minus the number of linear constraints on which the variance is defined. For our purposes the number of linear constraints is the same as the number of means estimated from the data on which the variance is defined.

28 THE GENERAL LINEAR MODEL

Table 2-1 Construction of F test statistic for statistical test of the null hypothesis that $\hat{\theta} = \theta_H$

(a) Data

Subject	Factor A		
	A_1	A_2	A_3
1	−6	−3	0
2	0	0	−3
3	3	3	6
Mean	−1	0	1

(b) Sums of squares (i) Due to A

$$SS_A = \hat{\theta}'X'y = \begin{bmatrix} -1 & 0 \end{bmatrix} \begin{bmatrix} 111 & 000 & -1 & -1 & -1 \\ 000 & 111 & -1 & -1 & -1 \end{bmatrix} \begin{bmatrix} -6 \\ 0 \\ 3 \\ -3 \\ 0 \\ 3 \\ 0 \\ -3 \\ 6 \end{bmatrix}$$

$$= 6$$

(ii) Due to null hypothesis

$$SS_H = \theta'_H X'y = \begin{bmatrix} 0 & 0 \end{bmatrix} \begin{bmatrix} 111 & 000 & -1 & -1 & -1 \\ 000 & 111 & -1 & -1 & -1 \end{bmatrix} \begin{bmatrix} -6 \\ 0 \\ 3 \\ -3 \\ 0 \\ 3 \\ 0 \\ -3 \\ 6 \end{bmatrix}$$

$$= 0$$

(iii) Due to difference between sample parameter estimates and null hypothesis

$$SS_D = \hat{\theta}'X'y - \theta'_H X'y = 6 - 0 = 6$$

(iv) Sum of squares error

$$SS_E = y'y - \hat{\theta}'X'y = 108 - 6 = 102$$

(v) Mean squares

$$MS_D = SS_D/(k-1) = 6/2 = 3$$

$$MS_E = SS_E/(N-k) = 102/6 = 17$$

(vi) Test statistic

$$\Delta_{(k-1, N-k)} = \frac{SS_D/(k-1)}{SS_E/(N-1)} = \frac{MS_D}{MS_E} = \frac{n\sigma_\alpha^2 + \sigma_\varepsilon^2}{\sigma_\varepsilon^2} = \frac{3}{17} < 1$$

In order to make sums of squares with different degrees of freedom comparable we divide each sum of squares by its degrees of freedom. This quantity is called a mean square. Section $b(v)$ of Table 2-1 gives the mean square difference (which is identical here to the treatment mean square) and the mean square error.

2-I-2-2 Expected value of a random variable[4] As a second step in our efforts to construct a test of the null hypothesis we shall need to know the expected values of various mean squares. More generally we shall need the concept of the expected value of a random variable. By a random variable we mean, somewhat loosely, that the variable may take on different values. For example y, the dependent variable in the GLM, is a random variable. If $\text{pr}(y)$ is the probability that the random variable takes a given value of y then the expected value of y is

$$E(y) = \Sigma \, \text{pr}(y) \cdot y$$

where the summation is taken over all values of y. The expected value of y, of course, is the grand mean of the population from which y was sampled.

To determine the expected mean squares of the sources of variance underlying the data in Table 2-1 we shall need the structural model for the data which is

$$y_{ij} = \mu + \alpha_i + \varepsilon_{ij}$$

Within any treatment level i the mean ($\bar{y}_i$) is

$$\bar{y}_i = \mu + \alpha_i + \bar{\varepsilon}_i$$

since μ and α_i are constants. Thus the difference between any observation and its within level mean is

$$\hat{\varepsilon}_{ij} = y_{ij} - \bar{y}_i$$
$$= \mu + \alpha_i + \varepsilon_{ij} - \mu - \alpha_i - \bar{\varepsilon}_j$$
$$= \varepsilon_{ij} - \bar{\varepsilon}_j$$
$$= \varepsilon_{ij}$$

under the assumption that the errors are unbiased. The expected value of the mean square error then is

$$E(\text{MS}_E) = E(\varepsilon_{ij}^2)$$
$$= \frac{\Sigma(y_{ij} - \bar{y}_i)^2}{(N - k)}$$
$$= \sigma_\varepsilon^2$$

where N is the number of observations, k is the number of levels of the factor, and $(N - k)$ is the number of degrees of freedom available to estimate the error variance.

Similarly let us define $\hat{\tau}_i$ as the difference between the mean of treatment

---

[4] For a detailed discussion of the algebra of expectations, see Hays and Winkler (1971), pp. 139–43.

level i, $\bar{y}_i$, and the grand mean $\bar{y}$ as follows

$$\hat{\tau}_i = \bar{y}_i - \bar{y}$$
$$= \mu + \alpha_i + \bar{\varepsilon}_i - \mu$$
$$= \alpha_i + \bar{\varepsilon}_i$$

If there are n observations per treatment the expected value of the mean square treatment is

$$E(MS_T) = \frac{n\Sigma(\bar{y}_i - \bar{y})^2}{(k-1)}$$

$$= \frac{n\Sigma\tau_i^2}{(k-1)}$$

which under the assumption that α_i and ε_{ij} are independent yields

$$E(MS_T) = \frac{n\Sigma\alpha_i^2}{(k-1)} + \frac{n\Sigma\bar{\varepsilon}_i^2}{(k-1)}$$

$$= n\sigma_\alpha^2 + n\sigma_{\bar{\varepsilon}}^2$$

and since the variance of the mean of n observations equals $1/n$ times the variance of the individual observations

$$E(MS_T) = n\sigma_\alpha^2 + \sigma_\varepsilon^2$$

2-I-2-3 Test statistic and sampling distribution of a test statistic Now let us define the test statistic

$$\Delta_{(k-1,N-k)} = \frac{SS_D/(k-1)}{SS_E/(N-k)} = \frac{MS_D}{MS_E}$$

where Δ is based on $(k-1)$ degrees of freedom in the numerator and $(N-k)$ degrees of freedom in the denominator. Replacing the mean squares with their expectations yields

$$\frac{E(MS_D)}{E(MS_E)} = \frac{n\sigma_\alpha^2 + \sigma_\varepsilon^2}{\sigma_\varepsilon^2} \tag{2-1}$$

Under the null hypothesis $n\sigma_\alpha^2 = 0$. To the extent that the treatment effects are different from one another, σ_α^2 will be larger. Also, for positive σ_α^2, $E(MS_D)$ will be larger the greater the number of observations per cell.

Next we must determine the sampling distribution of Δ. Now the reader may think the choice of symbols peculiar since Δ is easily recognized as the F test statistic familiar from analysis of variance and regression. We have done this to make an important point. Δ will follow an F probability distribution *only* if a specific set of assumptions are met. These assumptions are discussed in Sec. 2-II. For the remainder of this section we shall assume these assumptions have been met.

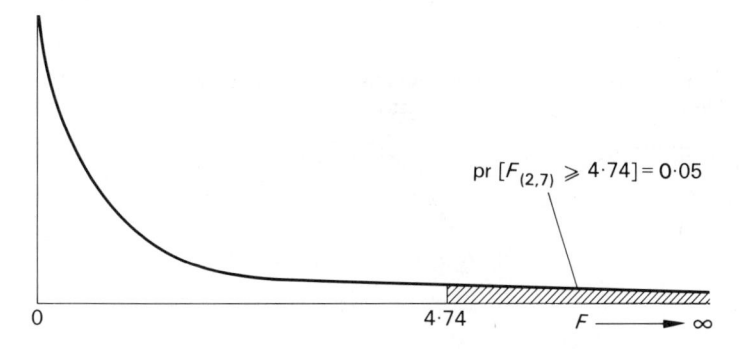

ADDITIONAL ASSUMPTIONS NECESSARY FOR TESTS OF HYPOTHESES 31

pr $[F_{(2,7)} \geq 4.74] = 0.05$

Figure 2-1 F distribution with 2 degrees of freedom in numerator and 6 degrees of freedom in denominator.

2-I-2-4 Critical value of test statistic *If* the assumptions underlying the F distribution are met and, *if* the null hypothesis is true then we can set a critical value for F which will give a specific probability of rejecting the null hypothesis given that it is true. For the data in Table 2-1 the obtained F must exceed 4.74 for us to have no more than a 5 percent chance of rejecting the null hypothesis given that it is true. Figure 2-1 presents a graph of the relevant F distribution. Note that the precise shape of the F distribution depends on the degrees of freedom in both the numerator and denominator. An extensive set of F values is presented in App. B, Table B-2.

2-I-3 Significance and Power of the F Test

2-I-3-1 Significance and power defined We have previously defined the significance level of a test as the probability of rejecting the null hypothesis given that it is true. Symbolically,

$$\text{pr}\left[F > F_{(m, N-m, p_\text{I})} \,|\, \text{H}_0\right] = p_\text{I} \qquad (2\text{-}2)$$

which is read the probability, pr, that the value of F calculated from the sample data, with N observations and m parameters in the model, exceeds the critical value of $F[F_{(m, N-m, p_\text{I})}]$ given the truth of the null hypothesis H_0 equals p_I. The probability of not rejecting H_0, given that H_0 is true, then must be

$$\text{pr}\left[F \leq F_{(m, N-m, p_\text{I})} \,|\, \text{H}_0\right] = 1 - p_\text{I} \qquad (2\text{-}3)$$

since, given H_0, the two alternatives are both mutually exclusive and exhaustive. This probability is often referred to as the confidence level of the test.

The rejection of H_0 implies the existence of an alternative hypothesis H_1. We may then define

$$\text{pr}\left[F \leq F_{(m, N-m, p_\text{I})} \,|\, \text{H}_1\right] = p_\text{II} \qquad (2\text{-}4)$$

where p_II is the probability of failing to reject H_0 given that it is false. The power

32 THE GENERAL LINEAR MODEL

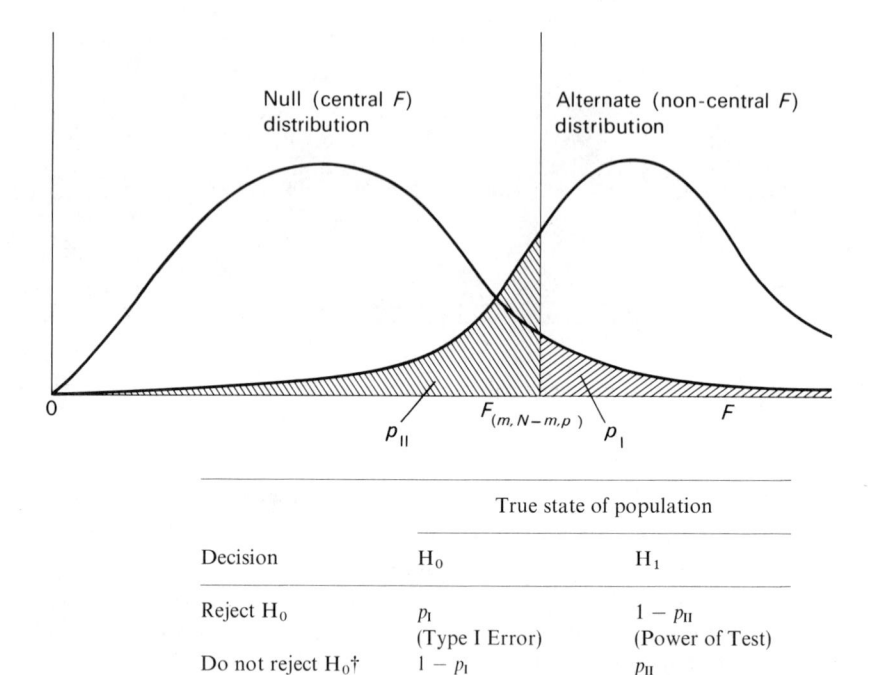

Figure 2-2 Significance and power of F test.

	True state of population	
Decision	H₀	H₁
Reject H₀	p_I (Type I Error)	$1 - p_{II}$ (Power of Test)
Do not reject H₀†	$1 - p_I$ (Confidence Level)	p_{II} (Type II Error)

    † Note that we "fail to reject" the null hypothesis rather than accept it. This is because our sample data may be consistent with *both* the null hypothesis and some other unspecified hypothesis.

of a test to reject H_0 given that it is false is

$$\text{pr}\left[F > F_{(m, N-m, p_I)} \big| H_1\right] = 1 - p_{II} \tag{2-5}$$

In the statistical literature p_I and p_{II} are often referred to as Type I and Type II errors, respectively. The above relationships are summarized in Figure 2-2.

2-I-3-2 Calculating the power of a test The distribution of $F_{(m, N-m)}$ is called the central F distribution and is based on the assumption that H_0 is true. If H_1 is true then the expected value of the computed F will be greater than the expected value of F assuming H_0. The effect will be to shift the F distribution to the right. How far the distribution will be shifted is a function of the magnitude of the coefficients in $\hat{\theta}$. This new distribution is called the non-central F distribution and is a function of the three parameters m, $N - m$, and λ. The "shape" of the non-central F distribution will be affected by λ as well as the degrees of freedom.

    The variable λ, which measures the degree of shift of the non-central F distribution, is defined as

$$\frac{\hat{\theta}'X'X\hat{\theta}}{\hat{\sigma}_\varepsilon^2} = \frac{\hat{\theta}'X'y}{\hat{\sigma}_\varepsilon^2} \qquad (2\text{-}6)$$

i.e., λ is simply the explained sum of squares divided by the mean square error.

Tables of the non-central F distribution are usually tabulated in terms of the parameter

$$\phi = \left(\frac{\lambda}{k}\right)^{\frac{1}{2}}$$

where k is the number of levels of the factor. A table of the non-central F distribution appears in App. B, Table B-4.

We may illustrate the idea of power with the data in Table 2-1. ϕ may be calculated as follows

$$\lambda = \frac{[-1 \ 0]\begin{bmatrix} 6 & 3 \\ 3 & 6 \end{bmatrix}\begin{bmatrix} -1 \\ 0 \end{bmatrix}}{17} = 0.35$$

$$\phi = \left(\frac{0.35}{3}\right)^{\frac{1}{2}} = 0.34$$

Referring to App. B, Table B-4, indicates that the power of the test, assuming a significance level of 0.05, is only approximately 0.07.

Patnaik (1949) gives a useful procedure for approximating the non-central F distribution from the central F distribution, which is very useful since extensive tables of the former are not readily available. First, calculate

$$g = \frac{[(k-1)+\lambda]^2}{[(k-1)+2\lambda]}$$

$$k^* = \frac{(k-1)+\lambda}{(k-1)}$$

$$F^* = \frac{F_{(k-1,N-k,p_1)}}{k^*}$$

Then the non-central $F[F_{(k-1,N-k,\lambda)}]$ will be approximately distributed as the central $F[F^*_{(g,N-k)}]$. Using the data in Table 2-1,

$$g = \frac{(2+0.34)^2}{2+2(0.34)} = 2.01$$

$$k^* = \frac{2+0.34}{2} = 1.17$$

$$F^* = \frac{5.14}{1.17} = 4.39$$

and

$$\text{pr}\,[F^* > 4.39\,|\,H_1] = 0.07$$

When the statistical test is very powerful, F^* will tend to be very small. In such a case we may use a standard central F table by making use of the following identity:

$$\text{pr}\left[F^* > F_{(m,N-m)}\right] = \text{pr}\left[1/F^* < F_{(N-m,m)}\right]$$

i.e., by taking the reciprocal of F^* and interchanging the degrees of freedom.

2-I-3-3 Planning sample size to insure power and significance

For designs involving equal cell size the following formula is very useful for planning a sample size which will guarantee a minimum power for a given decision rule, i.e., for a given significance level:

$$\phi = \sqrt{n}\left(\frac{\Sigma\tau_j^2}{k\sigma_\varepsilon^2}\right)^{\frac{1}{2}} \tag{2-7}$$

where n is the number of observations used to estimate each of the k treatment effects τ_j. To use this formula we must have an estimate of σ_ε^2 and we must specify $\Sigma\tau_j^2$, i.e., we must say how large the treatment effects must be before we consider it worthwhile to detect them.

To see how Eq. (2-7) is used, suppose we considered it important to detect the alternative hypothesis suggested by the treatment effects in Table 2-1. Then $\Sigma\tau_j^2 = 2$, the best estimate of σ_ε^2 is 17, and $k = 3$. Substituting these values into Eq. (2-7), we obtain

$$\phi = \sqrt{n}\left(\frac{2}{3 \times 17}\right)^{\frac{1}{2}}$$
$$= \sqrt{n}(0.1980) \tag{2-8}$$

To find the power of the planned test we need to substitute different values of n into Eq. (2-8), calculate ϕ, and read the power from App. B, Table B-4. Several calculations yield the following results:

n	5	10	15	20
ϕ	0.44	0.63	0.77	0.89
Power for $p_1 = 0.05$	0.07	0.16	0.23	0.30
Power for $p_1 = 0.01$	0.01	0.06	0.09	0.12

These figures show very low power even for relatively large sample sizes. In fact for $p_1 = 0.05$ it will take approximately $n = 60$ to guarantee a power of 0.7.

Fortunately, so-called constant power curves (a number of which are reproduced in App. B, Table B-6) eliminate the need to calculate ϕ for each sample size. Figure 2-3 presents such a graph for planning tests on a factor with three levels. The horizontal axis is calibrated in terms of ϕ' which is defined as

$$\left(\frac{\Sigma\tau_j^2}{k\sigma_\varepsilon^2}\right)^{\frac{1}{2}}$$

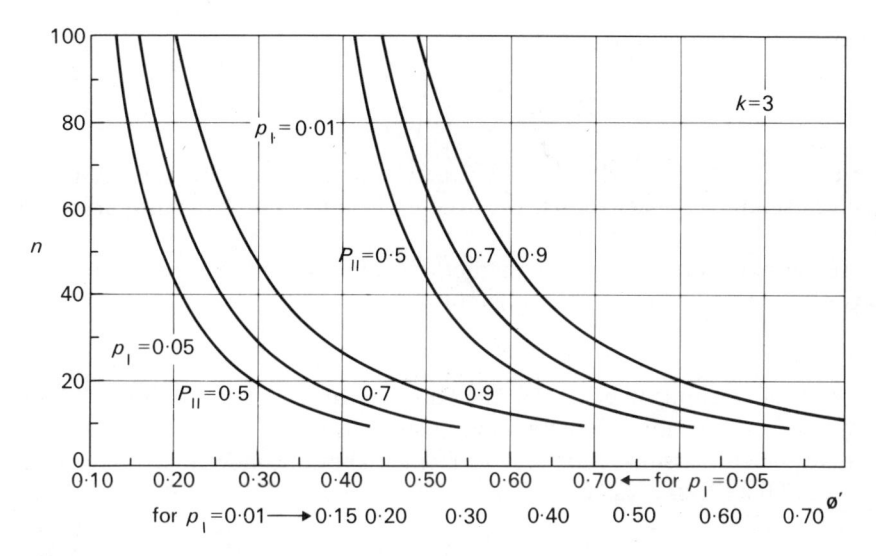

ADDITIONAL ASSUMPTIONS NECESSARY FOR TESTS OF HYPOTHESES

Figure 2-3 Constant power curve for main effect of factor with three levels. *(Reproduced from L. S. Feldt and M. W. Mahmoud (1958), with the kind permission of the authors and the editor of Psychometrika.)*

which equals $(\phi/\sqrt{n})$. For the alternative hypothesis suggested by the data in Table 2-1, ϕ' has already been calculated at 0.1980. Finding this value on the horizontal axis for $p_I = 0.05$ and reading up to the $p_{II} = 0.7$ power curve indicates approximately 60 observations per treatment are needed to ensure a 70 percent chance of detecting the alternative hypothesis, given that it is true, when a $p_I = 0.05$ significance test is used to test the null hypothesis.

2-I-4 Magnitude of Coefficients of the GLM

The previous section emphasized the interrelationships and the trade-offs among the significance, power, and sample size of a statistical test. The point we wish to emphasize here, however, is that no matter how small the coefficients of the GLM, and hence the relative sum of squares explained by the GLM, *it is always possible to achieve a significant result by having a sufficiently large sample size.* Therefore we must make a sharp distinction between the significance of a result and its magnitude or relative importance in explaining the behavior under investigation.

Perhaps the simplest index of the magnitude of the treatment effects is

$$R^2 = \frac{\hat{\theta}'X'y}{y'y} \tag{2-9}$$

the explained sum of squares relative to the total sum of squares. Generally, the grand mean is considered arbitrary and therefore both the numerator and denominator of R^2 are adjusted to

$$R^2 = \frac{\theta'X'y - (1'y)^2/N}{y'y - (1'y)^2/N}$$

In the case of orthogonal designs $\theta'X'y$ may be partitioned into components uniquely attributable to each term in the structural model underlying the particular GLM.

A somewhat more satisfactory method is as follows. First define π_α^2 as the average squared treatment effect for a factor A

$$\pi_\alpha^2 = \Sigma \hat{\alpha}_i^2 / k$$

where $\hat{\alpha}_i$ is the treatment effect for the ith level of a factor A with k levels. Similarly define $a\pi^2$ for all other components in the structural model. For illustrative purposes assume there are two factors. Then one index of the estimated magnitude of the effects of factor A is

$$\hat{\omega}_A^2 = \frac{\pi_\alpha^2}{\pi_\alpha^2 + \pi_\beta^2 + \pi_{\alpha\beta}^2 + \hat{\sigma}_\varepsilon^2} \qquad (2\text{-}10)$$

The magnitude of the effects of factor B and the interaction effect are similarly defined by placing the proper π^2 in the numerator.

An especially convenient feature of Eq. (2-10) is that it may be rewritten in terms of the F ratio and degrees of freedom for each source of variation and the total number of observations as follows

$$\hat{\omega}_A^2 = \frac{(p-1)(F_a-1)}{(p-1)(F_a-1) + (q-1)(F_b-1) + (p-1)(q-1)(F_{ab}-1) + N} \qquad (2\text{-}11)$$

where factors A and B have p and q levels, respectively. Again the effects for factor B and the A–B interaction may be obtained by substituting the proper term in the numerator.

The index presented in Eqs. (2-10) and (2-11) is originally due to Hays (1963). For further details and a comparison with other possible indices of the magnitude of the treatment effects the reader is referred to Fleiss (1969).

2-1-5 A Note on the Interrelationships Among the Z, χ^2, F, and t Tests

At numerous points in this text we refer to the χ^2, F, and t tests of statistical hypotheses. Here we shall indicate the general relationships among these tests. For a more detailed argument the reader is referred to Hays and Winkler (1971), pp. 364–67.[5]

First, consider the chi-square test statistic. Of its many uses one of the most important is in the study of sample variances. The chi-square statistic is defined

---

[5] For a more sophisticated discussion of the interrelationships among a number of statistical tests, including many not discussed here, see Rulon and Brooks (1968).

as

$$\chi^2 = \frac{\Sigma(y_i - \mu)^2}{\sigma^2}$$

i.e., as the sum of squared standardized deviates. Now—and this is the important point—for the χ^2 test statistic to follow a chi-square distribution it is necessary that the population from which the standardized deviates are drawn be normally distributed. In a sense, then, the normal distribution is the "parent" distribution of the chi-square distribution. Also as the number of observations on which the chi-square is based increases without limit the chi-square distribution approaches the normal distribution.

The F distribution is defined as the ratio of two chi-squares each divided by its degrees of freedom, i.e., the ratio of two mean squares. As the chi-square distribution rests on the assumption of normality so does the F distribution.

Finally, the t distribution is a special case of the F distribution. Specifically, for a t distribution with v degrees of freedom,

$$t_{(v)} = [F_{(1,v)}]^{\frac{1}{2}}$$

In certain situations we shall find the t test more convenient than the corresponding F test.

2-II THREE ASSUMPTIONS UNDERLYING THE F TEST

This section investigates three assumptions underlying the F test. In decreasing order of importance they are:

1. Errors are independent.
2. Errors have constant variance.
3. Errors are normally distributed.

The first assumption is crucial. The second is primarily important in the case of unequal sample sizes. The third is not generally of major importance.

In addition to specifying the consequences of assumption violations we shall suggest corrective procedures. Our suggestions here, however, are different from those typically recommended. Most texts suggest transformations of the data to restore normality or equality of variances. Unfortunately a transform which changes the variance of a distribution or restores normality also changes the distribution's shape (e.g., if normal to begin with the distribution will not be normal after the transformation) and changes the appropriateness of the linearity assumption, assuming it was correct in the first instance. Fortunately, enough is known concerning the behavior of significance levels in the face of assumption violations to be able to recommend approximate direct adjustments of the nominal significance level in the face of specific types of violation. To a lesser extent we may also make adjustments to the nominal power of statistical tests of significance.

38 THE GENERAL LINEAR MODEL

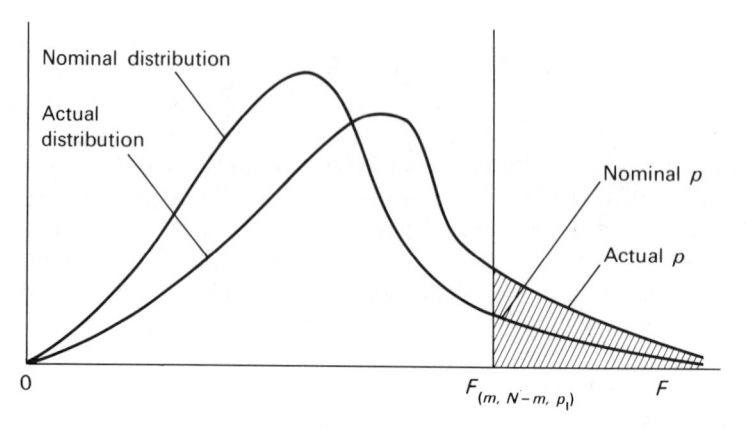

Figure 2-4 Nominal versus actual distribution of obtained F test statistic.

2-II-1 Actual Significance and Power of the F Test

If the assumptions underlying the F test are not met then the distribution of the calculated F will not be an F distribution and the significance of the test will not be p_1. Figure 2-4 illustrates these points graphically. The vertical line at $F_{(m,N-m,p_1)}$ defines the critical value which will cause us to reject the null hypothesis. If the assumptions underlying the F distribution are met the calculated F will follow an F distribution (called the nominal distribution in Fig. 2-4) and the actual p_1 and the nominal p_1 will be the same. Failure to meet one or more of the assumptions will cause the calculated F to follow some other distribution (called the actual distribution in Fig. 2-4). In this case the nominal p_1 will not equal the actual p_1, as is evident from Fig. 2-4. Usually, although not necessarily, the actual p_1 will exceed the nominal p_1, resulting in a higher probability of rejecting the null hypothesis, given that it is true, than the researcher expects. A similar argument holds with respect to the power of a test.

2-II-2 Characteristics of the Actual Distribution of the F Test Statistic

When we inquire about the consequences of the failure of the computed F test statistic to follow an F distribution we enter an intellectual quagmire. This is because there are an infinite number of ways in which the assumptions on which the F distribution is based may be violated. In the next few paragraphs we show how any distribution may be characterized in terms of its first four moments. While the first four moments do not adequately describe all distributions they do provide a great deal of information regarding the shape of a distribution. In addition most studies of the effects of assumption violations report the extent of the violations in terms of the second, third, and fourth moments.

The mean of a distribution is defined as

$$E(y) = \mu$$

i.e., as the expected deviation of the dependent variable from zero. This is the first moment of a distribution about the origin. We could similarly define second and higher moments about the origin. For most purposes, however, it is desirable to remove the effects of central location and define higher order moments about the mean of a distribution. The variance of a distribution is defined as

$$E(y - \mu)^2 = \sigma^2$$

which is the second moment about the mean.

Similarly, we may define the third and fourth moments as

$$E(y - \mu)^3$$

and

$$E(y - \mu)^4$$

An important characteristic of a distribution is whether or not it is symmetric about its mean. A nonsymmetric distribution is said to be skewed. A common measure of the skewness γ_1 of a distribution is defined in terms of the third moment,

$$\gamma_1 = \frac{E(y - \mu)^3}{(\sigma^2)^{3/2}} = \frac{E(y - \mu)^3}{\sigma^3}$$

The denominator is necessary to standardize γ_1, i.e., to remove the effects of σ^2. If the distribution is skewed right γ_1 will be positive and if skewed left it will be negative. Figure 2-5 illustrates both skew right and skew left distributions with respect to a normal distribution. The normal distribution is symmetrical, i.e., $\gamma_1 = 0$.

Another important characteristic is the peakedness of the distribution. A

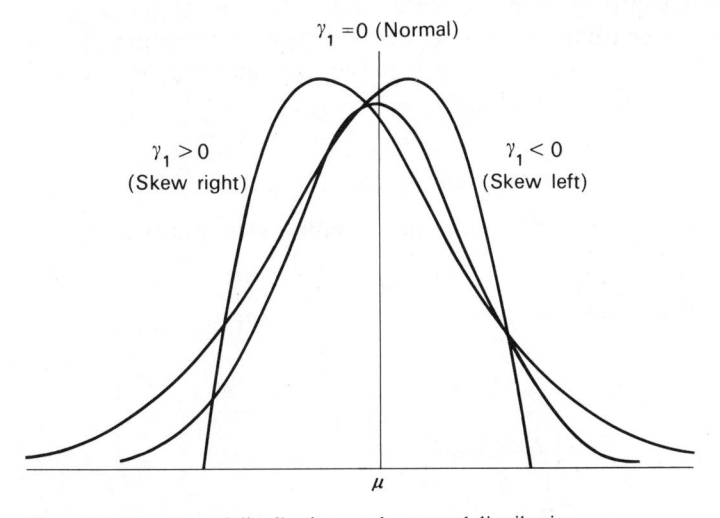

Figure 2-5 Two skewed distributions and a normal distribution.

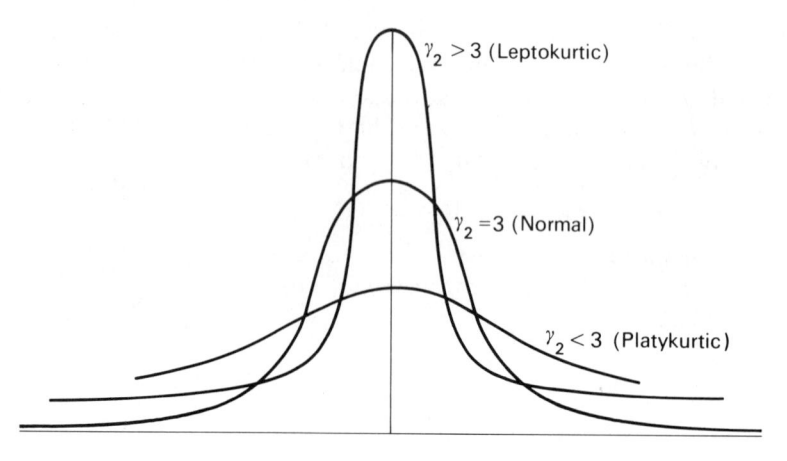

Figure 2-6 Leptokurtic, platikurtic, and normal distribution.

common measure of peakedness, called kurtosis, is defined as

$$\gamma_2 = \frac{E(y-\mu)^4}{(\sigma^2)^2} = \frac{E(y-\mu)^4}{\sigma^4}$$

where again the denominator is used to standardize γ_2. For a normal distribution γ_2 is 3. If the distribution is more peaked than the normal distribution γ_2 will be greater than 3, and if less peaked it will be smaller than 3. A peaked distribution is said to be leptokurtic. A flat distribution is platykurtic. The normal distribution is mesokurtic. Figure 2-6 presents three such distributions. The reader should note that the kurtosis of a distribution is sometimes reported as $\gamma_2 - 3$.

We should note before leaving this section that most computer installations have one or more packaged programs which provide much valuable descriptive information about the distribution of a set of data. The computation of such descriptive statistics should be one of the first steps in the data analysis. We shall illustrate such a program in the next chapter.

2-II-3 The Independence of Errors Assumption[6]

2-II-3-1 Rationale for assumption
Formally, this assumption may be written

$$E(\varepsilon\varepsilon') = \begin{bmatrix} E(\varepsilon_1^2) & E(\varepsilon_1\varepsilon_2) & \cdots & E(\varepsilon_1\varepsilon_N) \\ E(\varepsilon_2\varepsilon_1) & E(\varepsilon_2^2) & & \\ \vdots & & \ddots & \vdots \\ E(\varepsilon_N\varepsilon_1) & & \cdots & E(\varepsilon_N^2) \end{bmatrix} = \begin{bmatrix} \sigma_\varepsilon^2 & 0 & \cdots & 0 \\ 0 & \sigma_\varepsilon^2 & & \\ \vdots & & \ddots & \vdots \\ 0 & & \cdots & \sigma_\varepsilon^2 \end{bmatrix} \quad (2\text{-}12)$$

---
[6] For a much more thorough theoretical discussion of this assumption see Johnston (1972), Chap. 8.

The diagonal of Eq. (2-12) states the homogeneity assumption which is considered next. The off-diagonal entries state the independence assumption. Note carefully that the independence assumption requires the expected value of the covariances among the errors to be zero. Of course, in any sample of data the errors will not be completely uncorrelated.

It is usually stated that the assumption of independence is required for the F statistic to follow an F distribution. As we shall see in Chap. 5, however, a somewhat weaker assumption than complete independence will suffice.

2-II-3-2 Consequences of assumption violation In terms of its effect on the discrepancy between the actual and nominal significance of a statistical test, violation of the independence assumption can be little short of devastating. For example, it is not unlikely that when the researcher is testing at the nominal significance level of 0.05 the actual significance level is closer to 0.25. To take a very simple example, assume the errors are "serially" correlated with the correlation being ρ.[7] Then for a test conducted at $p_1 = 0.05$ the actual significance for various ρ values is[8]

ρ	−.4	−.3	−.2	−.1	0	.1	.2	.3	.4
Actual significance	1.10^{-5}	.002	.011	.028	.05	.074	.098	.12	.14

The test will be either conservative or liberal, depending on whether ρ is negative or positive, respectively. More complex patterns of intercorrelated errors may produce even more severe consequences.

We can specify certain additional consequences of violating the independence assumption. First, the parameter estimates $\hat{\theta}$ will be unbiased. Second, we will normally underestimate the variances of the parameter estimates, i.e., normally ρ will be positive. And, third, the predicted values of the dependent variable will have larger sampling variances than if the errors were uncorrelated.

2-II-3-3 Preventive procedures With the exception of designs we shall consider in Chap. 5, good research design procedures will generally prevent the errors from being correlated. Specifically, treatments should be randomly assigned to subjects and observations should be taken in such a way that one subject's response does not influence other subject's responses.

2-II-3-4 Corrective procedures Since the only designs where correlated errors can be expected are discussed in Chap. 5, we postpone further discussion of this rather serious problem.

---

[7] By serially correlated we mean that the expected value of an error δ_t is dependent on the error of the previously drawn observation δ_{t-1}. Mathematically, if ρ is the first order serial correlation

$$\delta_t = \rho\, \delta_{t-1} + \varepsilon_t$$

where δ_t equals the total error of observation t and ε_t equals that part of δ_t which satisfies the independence assumption as well as the normality and homogeneity assumptions.

[8] Data taken from Scheffé (1959), p. 339, with the kind permission of the publisher.

2-II-4 The Homogeneity of Error Variance Assumption

2-II-4-1 Rationale for assumption
Formally, this assumption may be written

$$\text{diag } E(\varepsilon\varepsilon') = \sigma_\varepsilon^2 I \tag{2-13}$$

i.e., the expected error variance of each observation is a constant. In general terms the rationale for this assumption is as follows. σ_ε^2 may be thought of as inversely related to the amount of information we possess about an observation, i.e., the smaller σ_ε^2 the better is the quality of our information. Now our empirical estimate of σ_ε^2 is the denominator of the F statistic. But $\hat{\sigma}_\varepsilon^2$ is a pooled estimate, i.e., it is averaged over all observations. Hence if the errors are not homogeneous the pooled estimate of σ_ε^2 will not adequately reflect the variance of the errors over the entire distribution.

2-II-4-2 Procedures for detecting violation of homogeneity assumption
A widely used test for homogeneity is Bartlett's chi-square test (Bartlett 1937), where

$$\chi^2_{(k-1)} = \frac{2.303}{C}(f \log \hat{\sigma}_\varepsilon^2 - \Sigma f_i \hat{\sigma}_{\varepsilon_i}^2) \tag{2-14}$$

where

$$f_i = n_i - 1 = \text{degrees of freedom for } \hat{\sigma}_{\varepsilon_i}^2$$

$$f = \Sigma f_i = \text{degrees of freedom for } \hat{\sigma}_\varepsilon^2$$

$$C = 1 + \frac{1}{3(k-1)}\left[\Sigma\left(\frac{1}{f_i}\right) - \frac{1}{f}\right]$$

This chi-square is distributed with $(k-1)$ degrees of freedom, where k equals the number of cells in the research design, i.e., the number of values of $\sigma_{\varepsilon_i}^2$.[9]

We have included the Bartlett test for two reasons. First, it is widely used. Second, it is so sensitive to departures from the underlying assumption of normality as to be extremely misleading in practical applications. How misleading can be seen from Table 2-2. This table gives the true percentage chance of rejecting the null hypothesis at $p_1 = 0.05$ for various values of γ_2 and k. It is readily apparent that the distortions are quite substantial. For example, with 10 groups and $\gamma_2 = 5$ there is almost a 50 percent chance of rejecting the null hypothesis when the nominal $p_1 = 0.05$.

Fortunately, the F test is not sufficiently sensitive to the homogeneity assumption to justify a particularly sensitive test. A very simple test proposed by Hartley (1950) is sufficient. Hartley's test statistic is

$$F_{\max(k, n-1)} = \frac{\text{largest of } k \text{ variances}}{\text{smallest of } k \text{ variances}} \tag{2-15}$$

---

[9] In regression analysis, where the independent variables are continuous the homogeneity assumption applies at each point on the regression line or plane. In practice the homogeneity assumption may be tested by arbitrarily dividing the regression plane into k subsamples and computing separate variances within each of the subsamples.

Table 2-2 True percentage chance of rejecting null hypothesis for Bartlett's homogeneity of variance test for various values of kurtosis γ_2 and number of groups k†

γ_2	\multicolumn{6}{c}{k}
	2	3	5	10	20	30
5	16.6	22.4	31.5	48.9	71.8	84.9
4	11.0	13.6	17.6	25.7	38.9	49.8
3	5.0	5.0	5.0	5.0	5.0	5.0
2	0.56	0.25	0.08	0.01	0.0004	0.00001

† Data due to Box (1953), p. 320, reproduced with the kind permission of the trustees of *Biometrika*.

where each of the k variances is based on n observations. In the case of unequal cell sizes where the cell sizes are not greatly unequal the largest cell size may be used to approximate the number of degrees of freedom. A table of the F_{max} statistic is presented in App. B, Table B-5.

2-II-4-3 Consequences of violating homogeneity assumption In the case of two samples van der Vaart (1961, cited in Glass et al. 1972, p. 245) has shown that for large sample sizes the t test statistic is distributed as zd where z is the unit normal deviate and

$$d = \left[\frac{\left(\frac{n_1}{n_1 + n_2}\right) + \left(1 - \frac{n_1}{n_1 + n_2}\right)\frac{\sigma_{\varepsilon_2}^2}{\sigma_{\varepsilon_1}^2}}{1 - \left(\frac{n_1}{n_1 + n_2}\right) + \left(\frac{n_1}{n_1 + n_2}\right)\frac{\sigma_{\varepsilon_2}^2}{\sigma_{\varepsilon_1}^2}} \right]^{\frac{1}{2}} \quad (2\text{-}16)$$

Table 2-3 True percentage chance of rejecting the null hypothesis of equal means for two groups for various group sizes and variances for large sample sizes†

Ratio of sample sizes and variances in group 1 to group 2

Ratio of sample sizes	\multicolumn{7}{c}{Ratio of variances}
	0‡	0.2	0.5	1	2	5	∞‡
1	5.0	5.0	5.0	5.0	5.0	5.0	5.0
2	17.0	12.0	8.0	5.0	2.9	1.4	0.6
5	38.0	22.0	12.0	5.0	1.4	0.2	0.001
∞	100.0	38.0	17.0	5.0	0.6	0.001	0

† Data due to Scheffé (1959), p. 340. Reproduced with the kind permission of the publisher.

‡ Unattainable limiting cases to show bounds.

Table 2-4 Norton data on heterogeneous variances[†]

Nominal p_t error		0.50	0.25	0.20	0.10	0.05	0.25	0.01	0.005	0.001
Number of cases	Number of groups[‡]	Observations per group				Actual p_t probability (empirically estimated)				
3333	3	3	0.5012	0.2748	0.2301	0.1347	0.0726	0.0429	0.0213	0.0213	0.0036
3000	3	10	0.4946	0.2683	0.2156	0.1173	0.0656	0.0383	0.0200	0.0120	0.0037

[†] Data due to Norton (cited in Lindquist 1953, p. 82). Reproduced with the kind permission of the publisher.
[‡] The variances of the three groups are $\sigma_{\varepsilon_1}^2 = 25$, $\sigma_{\varepsilon_2}^2 = 100$, $\sigma_{\varepsilon_3}^2 = 225$.

Table 2-5 Percentage chances of rejecting null hypothesis of equal group means with heterogeneous variances and unequal group sizes for $p_\text{I} = 0.05$†

No. of groups (k)	Ratio of $\sigma_{\varepsilon_i}^2$'s	Sample sizes (n)	Actual chances of Type error
3	1:2:3	5, 5, 5	05.6
	(For example, $\sigma_{\varepsilon_1}^2 = 10$,	3, 9, 3	05.6
	$\sigma_{\varepsilon_2}^2 = 20$, $\sigma_{\varepsilon_3}^2 = 30$.)	7, 5, 3	09.3
		3, 5, 7	04.0
3	1:1:3	5, 5, 5	05.9
	(For example, $\sigma_{\varepsilon_1}^2 = \sigma_{\varepsilon_2}^2 = 10$,	7, 5, 3	10.7
	$\sigma_{\varepsilon_3}^2 = 30$.)	9, 5, 1	17.4
		1, 5, 9	01.3
5	1:1:1:1:3	5, 5, 5, 5, 5	07.4
	(For example, $\sigma_{\varepsilon_1}^2 = \sigma_{\varepsilon_2}^2 =$	9, 5, 5, 5, 1	14.6
	$\sigma_{\varepsilon_3}^2 = \sigma_{\varepsilon_4}^2 = 10$, $\sigma_{\varepsilon_5}^2 = 30$.)	1, 5, 5, 5, 9	02.5
7	1:1:...:1:7	3, 3, ..., 3	12.0

† Data due to Box (1954), pp. 229 and 301. Reproduced with the kind permission of the publisher.

given that the null hypothesis is true. Note carefully that whenever $n_1 = n_2$, i.e., whenever the sample sizes are equal, $d = 1$. Thus in the case of two groups, a condition of unequal error variances does not affect the distribution of the statistic if the cell sizes are equal.[10] Table 2-3 gives selected values of the actual p_I error for a nominal $p_\text{I} = 0.05$ for various combinations of unequal variances and sample sizes for two groups.[11]

The finding that, for large sample sizes, the condition of equal cell sizes eliminates the need for the homogeneity assumption does not extend to the general case with more than two groups. Simulation studies, however, suggest that discrepancies between actual and nominal significance when there are equal numbers of observations per cell will be relatively small except in the extreme tails of the distribution, i.e., for very small p_I significance levels. Table 2-4 presents relevant data.

Table 2-5 presents data for the cases with equal and unequal cell size. Note that for equal cell sizes the data confirm the findings in Table 2-4; even substantial differences among the variances produce only a modest discrepancy between the nominal and actual significance levels.

In the case of unequal cell sizes the discrepancy can be substantial. For example, Table 2-5 shows (line 7) an actual p_I of 0.174 for a nominal value of 0.05. Note carefully the pattern in this table. When the *smaller* variances come from cells with *larger* sample sizes the actual p_I may greatly *exceed* the nominal p_I.

---

[10] Recall that the t distribution is a special case of the F distribution.
[11] This table is taken from Scheffé (1959, p. 340) who gives a superficially different formula which yields the same results as van der Vaart's formula.

46 THE GENERAL LINEAR MODEL

When the *smaller* variances come from cells with *smaller* sample sizes the actual p_1 may be greatly *exceeded by* the nominal p_1.

We can also make several observations concerning the power of the F test under heterogeneous variances. First, we may find the actual power of a test under heterogeneous variances just as we found the actual significance level. Second, and this is a crucial point, the nominal *theoretical* power of a test conducted under heterogeneous variances is not defined. This is because the non-central F distribution is partially defined by the parameter λ, which is defined only on the assumption that σ_ε^2 is equal for all cells in the design.

Several simulation studies, however, have investigated the actual power of the F test under heterogeneous variances. As a point of reference these studies have defined what is sometimes mislabeled as a "theoretical" power based on the

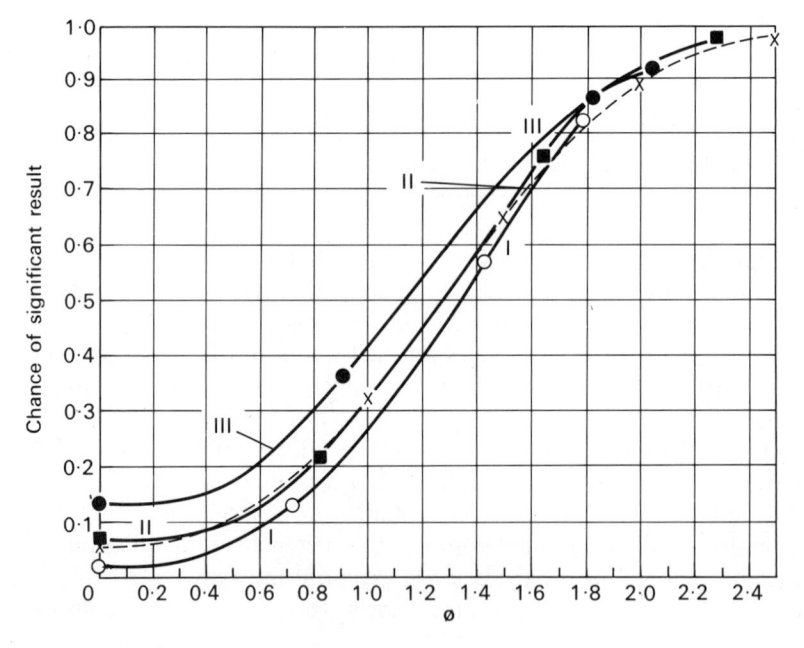

Divergent mean is in a group with low variance.
Note:

		$\sigma_{\varepsilon_1}^2$	$\sigma_{\varepsilon_2}^2$	$\sigma_{\varepsilon_3}^2$	$\sigma_{\varepsilon_4}^2 = 1:1:1:3$
Ratio of variance					
Sample sizes		n_1	n_2	n_3	n_4
Group	I	7	7	7	19
	II	10	10	10	10
	III	12	12	12	4

(- - -) = equal variances.

(Data due to Horsnell (1953), p. 134. Reproduced with the kind permission of the trustees of Biometrika.)

Figure 2-7 Probability of significant result for different alternative hypotheses measured by ϕ and different patterns of heterogeneous variances and group means.

average of the within cell variances. The actual question addressed by "these studies is whether standard power charts can be adapted to approximate the actual power of the F test when the group variances are heterogeneous" (Glass, et al. 1972, p. 268).

Figures 2-7 and 2-8 summarize the relationship between the actual power of the F test and the power approximated from standard power charts under various conditions. Both figures are based on four groups of observations. In Fig. 2-7 the divergent mean comes from the group with low variance and in Fig. 2-8 the divergent mean comes from the group with high variance. For equal sample sizes the power approximation tends to be quite good up to about a power of 0.6. Above 0.6 the estimated power tends to be a bit low when the divergent mean comes from the low variance group and a bit high in the reverse case. Note

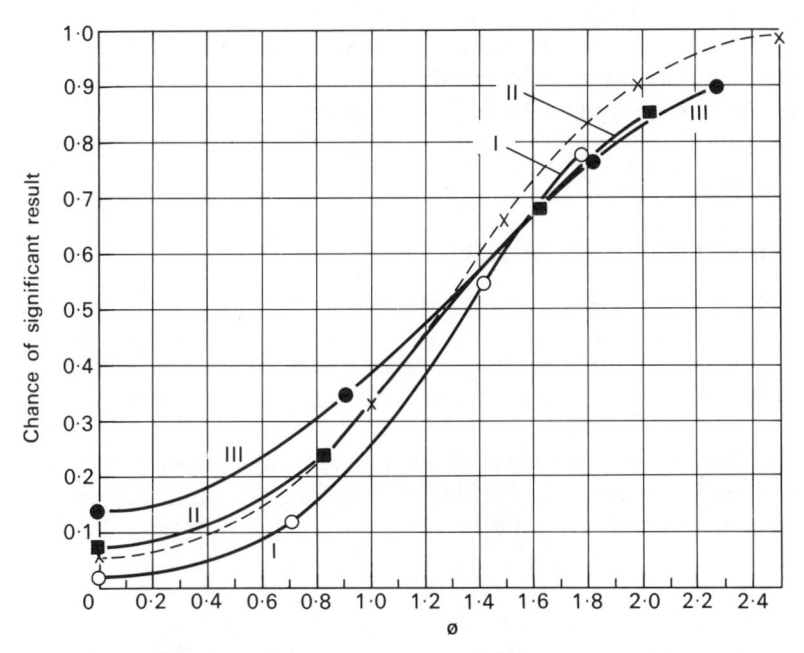

Divergent mean is in the group with high variance.
Note:

Ratio of variance		$\sigma^2_{\varepsilon_1}$	$\sigma^2_{\varepsilon_2}$	$\sigma^2_{\varepsilon_3}$	$\sigma^2_{\varepsilon_4} = 1:1:1:3$
Sample sizes		n_1	n_2	n_3	n_4
Group	I	7	7	7	19
	II	10	10	10	10
	III	12	12	12	4

(- - -) = equal variances.
(Data due to Horsnell (1953), p. 134. Reproduced with the kind permission of the trustees of Biometrika.)

Figure 2-8 Probability of significant result for different alternative hypotheses measured by ϕ and different patterns of heterogeneous variances and group means.

carefully that in the case of unequal cell sizes the actual and estimated power may be quite different. When the large variance comes from the large sample group the actual power will tend to be less than the estimated power for powers of approximately 0.6 to 0.7 or less. When the large variance comes from the small sample group the actual power will tend to be greater than the estimated power.

2-II-4-4 Corrective procedures There are several transformations which are useful for restoring homogeneous variances. If the cell variances tend to be proportional to the cell means, taking the square root of each observation tends to restore homogeneity. When dealing with proportions a transformation of the form

$$y_t = 2 \arcsin \sqrt{y}$$

is often recommended.

For the reasons cited above, i.e., a transformation which changes within groups variances also alters such things as the shape of the distribution and the appropriateness of an additive model, we do not recommend transforming the data to achieve homogeneity of variance. Rather we suggest the use of the tables and figures presented in Section 2-II to make rough direct adjustments to the nominal significance level.

2-II-5 The Normality of Errors Assumption

2-II-5-1 Rationale for assumption This assumption is necessary if the distributions of the mean squares are to have chi-square distributions. And since the F distribution is the distribution of the ratio of two independent chi-squares the normality assumption is required for the F test statistic to follow an F distribution.

2-II-5-2 Procedures for detecting violation of normality assumption There are numerous methods for testing the normality assumption. The most complete is the chi-square goodness of fit test of the actual errors to the hypothesis[12]

$$\varepsilon \quad \text{is} \quad N(0, \sigma_\varepsilon^2 I)$$

Only rarely, however, will the researcher have sufficient data for such a test; and fortunately the effects of non-normality are not sufficiently severe to justify it.

As a rough check on normality the researcher can plot the residual errors against the independent variables and determine the percent of errors which are within $\pm 1\hat{\sigma}_\varepsilon^2$, $\pm 2\hat{\sigma}_\varepsilon^2$, and $\pm 3\hat{\sigma}_\varepsilon^2$.[13] For a normal distribution these percentages are 68.2, 95.4, and 99.7, respectively.

The researcher may also calculate various descriptive measures including the skewness and kurtosis of the errors which can be compared to the normal

---

[12] Ferguson (1959), pp. 162–165, gives a detailed discussion of how to make such a test.

[13] Such a residual plot will also reveal substantial heterogeneity of error variance. For a good discussion of procedures for examining residuals see Draper and Smith (1966), Chap. 3, and Anscombe and Tukey (1963).

distribution values of 0 and 3, respectively. Most of the simulation studies reviewed below have measured the departure from normality in terms of the skewness and kurtosis of the actual distribution.

2-II-5-3 Theoretical reasons for unimportance of normality assumption[14]
It has been widely reported that the F test is not very sensitive to departure from normally distributed errors. As it happens there is a good theoretical explanation for this finding. The argument is based on approximating the variances and covariances of the treatment mean square and the error mean square and approximating the ratio of these mean squares (i.e., the F test statistic) in the general case where normality is not assumed.

First, Pearson (1931) showed that

$$\sigma^2_{MS_T} \doteq 2\sigma^4 \left[1 + \frac{\frac{1}{2}(\gamma_2 - 3)(k - 1)}{nk} \right] \Big/ (k - 1)$$

$$\sigma^2_{MS_E} \doteq 2\sigma^4 \left[1 + \frac{\frac{1}{2}(\gamma_2 - 3)(n - 1)}{n} \right] \Big/ [k(n - 1)]$$

$$\sigma_{MS_T, MS_E} \doteq \sigma^2 \frac{(\gamma_2 - 3)}{kn}$$

where $\doteq$ is read "is approximately equal to," k equals the number of levels of the treatment factor, and n equals the number of observations per cell. Note carefully that the kurtosis γ_2, but not the skewness, of the distribution enters into the approximations of the variances and covariances of the mean squares.

Earlier, Pearson (1897) had shown that the variance of a ratio of two variables can be approximated by

$$\sigma^2_{x/y} \doteq \frac{\mu^2_x}{\mu^2_y} \left[\frac{\sigma^2_x}{\mu^2_x} + \frac{\sigma^2_y}{\mu^2_y} - \frac{2\sigma_{xy}}{\mu_x \mu_y} \right]$$

Letting $x = MS_T$ and $y = MS_E$ and simplifying yields

$$\sigma^2_{MS_T, MS_E} \doteq \frac{2}{(k - 1)} + \frac{2}{k(n - 1)}$$

given that the null hypothesis is true.

Kendall and Stuart (1963, p. 378) show that

$$\sigma^2_{MS_T/MS_E} = \frac{2[k(n - 1)]^2[(k - 1) + k(n - 1) - 2]}{(k - 1)[k(n - 1) - 2]^2[k(n - 1) - 4]} \quad (2\text{-}17)$$

given that the null hypothesis is true and that the errors are normally distributed. For large n, however, Eq. (2-17) simplifies to

$$\sigma^2_{MS_T, MS_E} \doteq \frac{2}{(k - 1)} + \frac{2}{k(n - 1)}$$

[14] This section closely follows the discussion by Glass et al. (1972), pp. 253–254.

Table 2-6 Actual probabilities (theoretically approximated) of rejecting the null hypothesis at $p_1 = 0.05$ for various non-normal distributions and values of ϕ†

	Skewness	Kurtosis	\multicolumn{10}{c}{Values of ϕ‡}
			\multicolumn{2}{c}{0}	\multicolumn{2}{c}{1.0}	\multicolumn{2}{c}{1.5}	\multicolumn{2}{c}{2.0}	\multicolumn{2}{c}{2.5}
1.	0	2.0	0.054	0.052	0.249	0.308	0.531	0.649	0.819	0.908	0.967	0.993
2.¶	0	3.0	0.050	0.050	0.262	0.319	0.551	0.659	0.821	0.907	0.957	0.988
3.	0	3.5	0.048	0.049	0.268	0.325	0.561	0.664	0.822	0.907	0.952	0.986
4.	0	4.0	0.046	0.048	0.275	0.330	0.571	0.669	0.823	0.906	0.947	0.983
5.	0	5.0	0.042	0.045	0.288	0.342	0.590	0.679	0.824	0.906	0.937	0.978
6.	0	5.4	0.041	0.044	0.290	0.346	0.598	0.683	0.825	0.905	0.933	0.976
7.	0.25	2.0	0.055	0.053	0.248	0.307	0.532	0.649	0.820	0.908	0.967	0.993
8.	0.25	3.0	0.051	0.050	0.261	0.318	0.552	0.659	0.822	0.907	0.957	0.988
9.	0.25	3.5	0.049	0.049	0.267	0.324	0.562	0.664	0.823	0.907	0.953	0.985
10.	0.25	5.0	0.044	0.045	0.287	0.341	0.501	0.679	0.825	0.906	0.938	0.978
11.	0.49	5.4	0.043	0.045	0.291	0.345	0.600	0.683	0.827	0.906	0.934	0.976

† Data due to Srivastava (1959). Reproduced with the kind permission of the trustees of *Biometrika*. In each of the five pairs of columns, the left entry is for $k = 5$, $n = 3$ and the right entry is for $k = 5$, $n = 5$.
‡ For $\phi = 0$ power and significance are identical.
¶ The normal distribution.

Table 2-7 Actual (empirical) probabilities of rejecting the null hypothesis at $p_1 = 0.05$ for various non-normal distributions and values of ϕ†

Nature of distribution	Skewness	Kurtosis	\multicolumn{10}{c}{Values of ϕ‡}
			\multicolumn{2}{c}{0}	\multicolumn{2}{c}{0.5}	\multicolumn{2}{c}{1.0}	\multicolumn{2}{c}{1.5}	\multicolumn{2}{c}{2.5}
Normal	0	2.90	0.046	0.059	0.098	0.091	0.200	0.275	0.430	0.519	0.851	0.945
Slightly skewed	0.45	3.53	0.052	0.052	0.077	0.096	0.193	0.266	0.410	0.556	0.848	0.947
Square root transformation	0	2.91	0.054	0.046	0.086	0.098	0.201	0.286	0.518	0.575	0.834	0.946
Moderately skewed	0.64	3.53	0.058	0.054	0.080	0.100	0.188	0.273	0.446	0.563	0.858	0.943
Logarithm transformation	0	2.82	0.058	0.057	0.094	0.097	0.213	0.268	0.445	0.594	0.828	0.941
Extremely skewed	2.04	9.54	0.048	0.037	0.108	0.078	0.264	0.326	0.541	0.559	0.854	0.910
Reciprocal transformation	0.03	2.88	0.059	0.057	0.134	0.120	0.325	0.485	0.536	0.657	0.792	0.964
Leptokurtic	0	9.16	0.049	0.036	0.101	0.109	0.269	0.338	0.522	0.584	0.874	0.924
Rectangular	0	1.80	0.070	0.058	0.106	0.094	0.209	0.258	0.400	0.538	0.856	0.954
Theoretical (nominal) power			0.050	0.050	0.087	0.097	0.206	0.261	0.417	0.540	0.851	0.954

† Data due to Games and Lucas (1966). Reproduced with the kind permission of the editor. In each of the five pairs of columns, the left entry is based on $k = 3$, $n = 3$ and the right entry is based on $k = 3$, $n = 6$.
‡ For $\phi = 0$ power and significance are identical.

Table 2-8 Power for three distributions†

k	n_j	$\Delta\mu$‡	ϕ§	Normal 0.10	Normal 0.05	Normal 0.01	Exponential 0.10	Exponential 0.05	Exponential 0.01	Lognormal 0.10	Lognormal 0.05	Lognormal 0.01
2	4		0.00	0.101	0.018	0.009	0.087	0.042	0.007	0.074	0.031	0.005
		5.000	0.50	0.163	0.089	0.020	0.199	0.109	0.025	0.259	0.152	0.037
		10.000	1.00	0.349	0.224	0.065	0.446	0.310	0.108	0.552	0.419	0.189
		15.000	1.50	0.586	0.425	0.162	0.672	0.539	0.266	0.749	0.648	0.396
		20.000	2.00	0.802	0.654	0.312	0.825	0.723	0.447	0.869	0.788	0.575
		25.000	2.50	0.925	0.835	0.502	0.908	0.844	0.615	0.917	0.873	0.704
		30.000	3.00	0.978	0.938	0.685	0.954	0.913	0.753	0.949	0.918	0.799
2	8		0.00	0.098	0.049	0.009	0.098	0.044	0.007	0.085	0.035	0.005
		3.536	0.50	0.170	0.098	0.025	0.195	0.115	0.030	0.238	0.145	0.060
		7.072	1.00	0.380	0.260	0.092	0.445	0.325	0.128	0.537	0.417	0.201
		10.608	1.50	0.647	0.505	0.244	0.687	0.573	0.328	0.751	0.663	0.449
		14.144	2.00	0.852	0.749	0.465	0.849	0.773	0.553	0.874	0.815	0.653
		17.680	2.50	0.960	0.909	0.709	0.937	0.887	0.735	0.934	0.899	0.789
		21.216	3.00	0.993	0.978	0.875	0.975	0.951	0.856	0.966	0.949	0.877
2	16		0.00	0.100	0.050	0.009	0.099	0.046	0.007	0.094	0.038	0.004
		2.500	0.50	0.174	0.102	0.028	0.199	0.117	0.030	0.217	0.132	0.037
		5.000	1.00	0.399	0.276	0.105	0.443	0.325	0.140	0.504	0.391	0.181
		7.500	1.50	0.669	0.544	0.276	0.704	0.586	0.349	0.750	0.656	0.438
		10.000	2.00	0.869	0.787	0.548	0.871	0.797	0.595	0.882	0.824	0.667
		12.500	2.50	0.967	0.932	0.782	0.952	0.917	0.791	0.931	0.917	0.818
		15.000	3.00	0.995	0.987	0.927	0.986	0.970	0.906	0.977	0.971	0.904
2	32		0.00	0.098	0.049	0.010	0.099	0.049	0.009	0.096	0.046	0.007
		1.768	0.50	0.186	0.108	0.030	0.188	0.113	0.029	0.212	0.130	0.036
		3.536	1.00	0.408	0.289	0.114	0.426	0.307	0.129	0.479	0.361	0.112
		5.304	1.50	0.681	0.556	0.307	0.685	0.575	0.336	0.729	0.627	0.409
		7.072	2.00	0.876	0.795	0.573	0.877	0.798	0.595	0.877	0.818	0.655
		8.840	2.50	0.967	0.934	0.803	0.964	0.933	0.807	0.952	0.918	0.820
		10.608	3.00	0.995	0.987	0.937	0.991	0.980	0.929	0.979	0.967	0.913
4	4		0.00	0.097	0.048	0.010	0.083	0.041	0.010	0.076	0.035	0.008
		2.500	0.56	0.190	0.110	0.028	0.204	0.117	0.032	0.265	0.158	0.049
		5.000	1.12	0.468	0.324	0.120	0.544	0.400	0.172	0.631	0.513	0.266
		7.500	1.68	0.793	0.666	0.348	0.811	0.711	0.453	0.840	0.770	0.574
		10.000	2.24	0.958	0.902	0.669	0.936	0.885	0.714	0.931	0.887	0.769
		12.500	2.80	0.997	0.985	0.892	0.980	0.960	0.867	0.967	0.949	0.876
4	8		0.00	0.096	0.047	0.009	0.086	0.040	0.007	0.076	0.034	0.006
		1.768	0.56	0.206	0.119	0.034	0.224	0.129	0.034	0.251	0.153	0.047
		3.536	1.12	0.528	0.386	0.165	0.574	0.441	0.216	0.640	0.519	0.296
		5.304	1.68	0.851	0.753	0.496	0.854	0.770	0.555	0.868	0.808	0.637
		7.072	2.24	0.977	0.952	0.828	0.965	0.935	0.822	0.945	0.913	0.821

Table 2-8 Continued

Parameters			Power							
			Normal (α)¶			Exponential (α)¶			Lognormal (α)¶		
k	n_j	$\Delta\mu$‡	ϕ§	0.10	0.05	0.01	0.10	0.05	0.01	0.10	0.05	0.01
4	16	0.00	0.00	0.095	0.048	0.011	0.099	0.047	0.009	0.085	0.037	0.006
		1.250	0.56	0.212	0.129	0.036	0.224	0.136	0.039	0.248	0.152	0.047
		2.500	1.12	0.550	0.416	0.194	0.574	0.449	0.224	0.626	0.510	0.288
		3.750	1.68	0.870	0.786	0.559	0.869	0.764	0.590	0.879	0.817	0.647
		5.000	2.24	0.985	0.966	0.879	0.977	0.956	0.867	0.964	0.941	0.871
4	32	0.00	0.00	0.102	0.051	0.010	0.092	0.045	0.007	0.092	0.044	0.008
		0.884	0.56	0.221	0.131	0.041	0.217	0.131	0.036	0.244	0.145	0.040
		1.768	1.12	0.561	0.434	0.211	0.580	0.454	0.218	0.613	0.491	0.271
		2.652	1.68	0.882	0.804	0.584	0.878	0.804	0.607	0.882	0.816	0.645
		3.536	2.24	0.988	0.970	0.901	0.984	0.967	0.888	0.970	0.952	0.884
8	4	0.00	0.00	0.100	0.053	0.013	0.086	0.044	0.009	0.079	0.040	0.009
		1.222	0.56	0.221	0.135	0.040	0.240	0.141	0.041	0.282	0.175	0.059
		2.444	1.12	0.621	0.475	0.217	0.927	0.538	0.283	0.726	0.613	0.384
		3.660	1.68	0.941	0.878	0.647	0.988	0.868	0.687	0.920	0.876	0.741
		4.888	2.24	0.998	0.993	0.946	0.999	0.976	0.915	0.977	0.980	0.904

† Data due to Donaldson (1968), pp. 665 and 666. Reproduced with the kind permission of the editor of the *Journal of the American Statistical Association*.
‡ Difference between successive means.
§ For $\phi = 0$ power and significance are identical.
¶
	Normal	Exponential	Lognormal
Skewness (γ_1)	0	2	4
Kurtosis (γ_2)	3	9	41

which shows that for large n the variance of the F test statistic calculated under non-normal errors is approximately equal to the variance of the central F distribution. This result accounts for the widely reported insensitivity of the F test to violation of the normality assumption for a true null hypothesis.

In true experimental designs, where subjects are randomly assigned to treatment conditions, the randomization procedure itself provides a basis for drawing accurate statistical inferences. More specifically, for a particular randomization procedure a null distribution of the test statistic may be calculated. Fortunately, in such situations statistical tests based on normal theory assumptions are usually good approximations to the precise distribution.[15]

2-II-5-4 Consequences of violating normal assumption
Tables 2-6, 2-7, and 2-8 present data from three different simulation studies which show the departure of

---
[15] Scheffé (1959, Chap. 9) presents a thorough but somewhat technical discussion of so-called randomization models.

both the significance and power of different distributions from the corresponding values estimated under the assumption of normally distributed errors. Figure 2-9 graphically presents the data in Table 2-8. Each of these distributions has been characterized by its skewness γ_1 and kurtosis γ_2. In reading these tables remember that when $\phi = 0$ the null distribution is also the true distribution of the F statistic and $p_\text{I} = 1 - p_\text{II}$, i.e., the power and significance level of a test are identical.

Examination of these tables reveals several significant results. First, and this

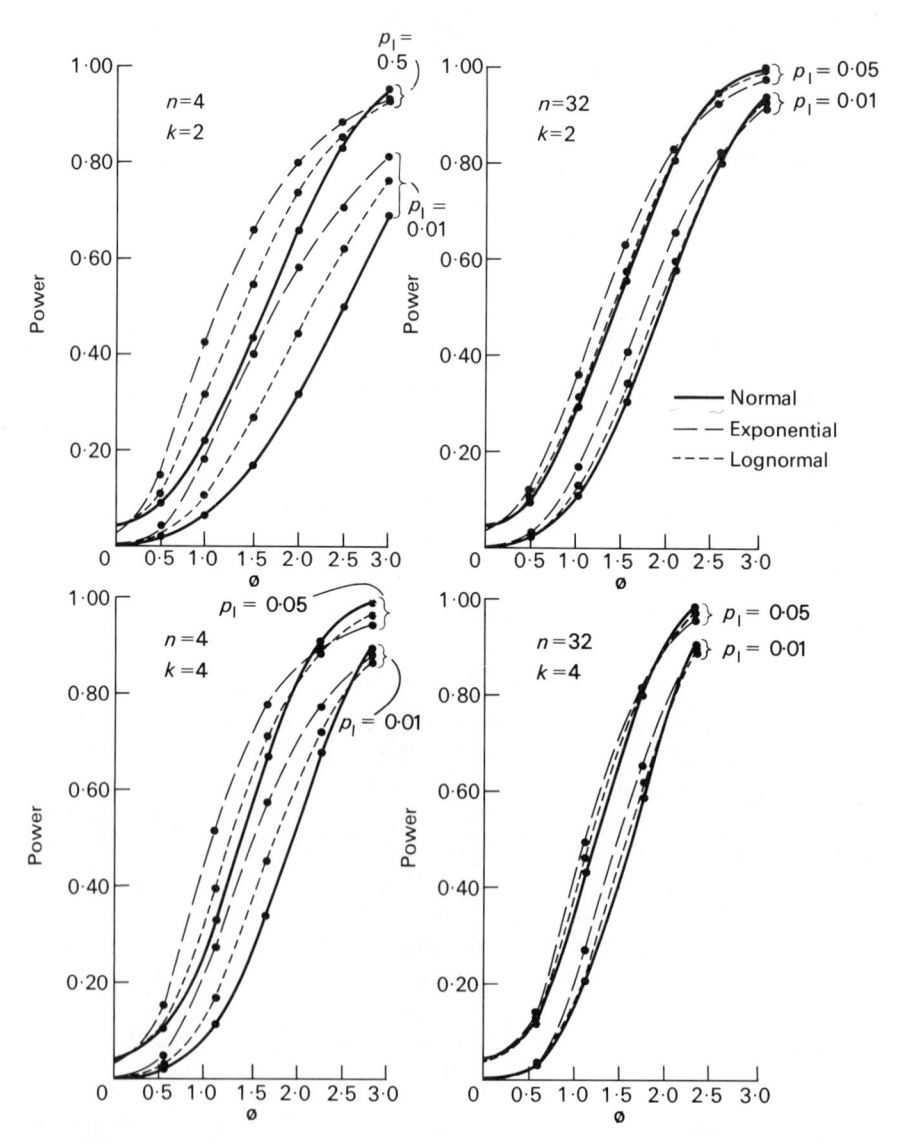

Figure 2-9 Graphical presentation of power calculations for three distributions presented in Table 2-8. (*Data due Donaldson (1968), p. 667. Reproduced with the kind permission of the editor.*)

was to be expected on the basis of the theoretical observations in the above section, skewness has virtually no effect on the nominal significance level of the F test. Skewness also has little effect on the power of the F test when the null hypothesis is false. Carefully note, however, that these results apply only to two-tailed tests. For one-tailed tests of significance skewness can have substantial effects. The F test, however, is by definition a non-directional or two-tailed test.

Second, and this was also to be partially expected, the kurtosis of the distribution may have a moderate effect on the significance level of a test, especially for small sample sizes and distributions with extreme kurtosis. For situations likely to occur frequently the distortions are rarely likely to be more than one or two hundredths off. For platykurtic distributions ($\gamma_2 < 3$) the actual p_1 value will exceed the nominal p_1 value. The reverse is true for leptokurtic distributions.

To get some idea of the magnitude of the effect when the null hypothesis is true, note in Table 2-8 that the most extreme deviation at $p_1 = 0.05$ is -0.019, i.e., for a lognormal distribution with $\gamma_2 = 41$ the actual p_1 is 0.031. While this is a large relative deviation, absolutely it is small. Note also that the distortions are greater for small significance values and less for larger sample sizes and larger numbers of treatment levels.

The kurtosis of a distribution, however, may substantially affect the power of the F test when the null hypothesis is not true. Note, especially from Table 2-8 and Figure 2-9, that the largest discrepancies are produced for moderate power values, e.g., 0.25 to 0.60. For platykurtic distributions the actual power is less than the nominal power. The reverse is true for leptokurtic distributions. For example, for $k = 2$, $n_j = 4$ and $\phi = 1$ the power calculated under normal assumptions is 0.224 at $p_1 = 0.05$ but is actually 0.419 for a lognormal distribution, a 47 percent discrepancy. When ϕ rises to 2.5 the discrepancy falls to a mere 4.3 percent.

Glass, et al. (1972) indicate that the results for unequal sample size cases are similar.

Table 2-9 Reader test problem for calculating F test, F_{max} test, checking skewness and kurtosis, and estimating power

(a) Data

Subject	A_1	A_2	A_3	A_4
1	6	8	12	21
2	9	7	15	30
3	4	9	10	18
4	3	8	15	28
5	8	8	13	28

(b) Answers

$F_{mean} = 350.99$ $\gamma_1 = -0.50$
$F_A = 37.75$ $\gamma_2 = 2.53$
$F_{max} = 54$ Power $= 0.97$

Table 2-10 Summary of consequences of violation of assumptions underlying the general linear model†

Type of violation	Equal n's — Effect on p_t	Equal n's — Effect on power	Unequal n's — Effect on p_t	Unequal n's — Effect on power
Non-independece of errors	Non-independence of errors seriously affects both the level of significance and power of the F test regardless of whether the n's are equal or unequal.			
Non-normality — Skewness	Skewed populations have very little effect on either the level of significance or the power of the fixed-effects model F test; distortions of nominal significance levels of power values are rarely greater than a few hundredths. (However, skewed populations can seriously affect the level of significance and power of *directional* — or "one-tailed" — tests.)			
Kurtosis	Actual p_t is less than nominal p_t when populations are leptokurtic (i.e., $\gamma_2 > 3$). Actual p_t exceeds nominal p_t for platykurtic populations.	Actual power is less than nominal power when populations are platykurtic. Actual power exceeds nominal power when populations are leptokurtic. Effects can be substantial for small n.	Actual p_t is less than nominal p_t when populations are leptokurtic (i.e., $\gamma_2 > 3$). Actual p_t exceeds nominal p_t for platykurtic populations.	Actual power is less than nominal power when populations are platykurtic. Actual power exceeds nominal power when populations are leptokurtic. Effects can be substantial for small n's.
Heterogeneous variances	Very slight effect on p_t, which is seldom distorted by more than a few hundredths. Actual p_t seems always to be slightly increased over the nominal p_t.	(No theoretical power value exists when variances are heterogeneous.)	p_t may be seriously affected. Actual p_t exceeds nominal p_t when smaller samples are drawn from more variable populations; actual p_t is less than nominal p_t when smaller samples are drawn from less variable populations.	(No theoretical power value exists when variances are heterogeneous.)
Combined non-normality and heterogeneous variances	Non-normality and heterogeneous variances appear to combine additively ("non-interactively") to affect either level of significance or power. (For example, the depressing effect on p_t of leptokurtosis could be expected to be counteracted by the elevating effect on p_t of having drawn smaller samples from the more variable, leptokurtic populations.)			

† Taken from Glass et al. (1972, p. 273). Reproduced with the kind permission of the editor.

2-II-5-5 Corrective procedures

Often it will be possible to find a transformation which will restore normality. For example, if the distribution has an extreme positive skew one might take the logarithm of the observations. Rarely, if ever, however, will such an adjustment be worthwhile. Rather, if substantial kurtosis is found, rough adjustments on the reported p_I and $1 - p_{II}$ values should be made on the basis of data presented in Tables 2-6 to 2-8.

2-II-6 Heterogeneous Variances and Non-Normality

Finally, we note the conclusion of Glass et al. (1972) that the effects of simultaneous violations of the homogeneity and normality assumptions are additive. For example, if it is determined that we should add 0.08 to p_I to adjust for heterogeneous variances and -0.03 to adjust for non-normality the net adjustment would be 0.05.

Table 2-11 Summary of most important equations in Chap. 2

Power of test

$$\lambda = \frac{\hat{\theta}'X'y}{\sigma_\varepsilon^2}$$

$$\phi = \left(\frac{\lambda}{k}\right)^{\frac{1}{2}}$$

$$g = \frac{[(k-1)+\lambda]^2}{(k-1)+2\lambda}$$

$$k^* = \frac{(k-1)+\lambda}{k-1}$$

$$F^* = \frac{F_{(k-1,N-k,p_I)}}{k^*}$$

Magnitude of effects coefficient

$$\omega_i^2 = \frac{\pi_i^2}{\sum_{j=1}^{m} \pi_j}$$

where m = number of terms in structural model.

Skewness

$$\gamma_1 = \frac{E(y-\mu)^3}{\sigma^3}$$

Kurtosis

$$\gamma_2 = \frac{E(y-\mu)^4}{\sigma^4}$$

F_{max}

$$F_{max(k,n-1)} = \frac{\text{largest of } k \text{ variances}}{\text{smallest of } k \text{ variances}}$$

2-II-7 Reader Test Problem

Table 2-9 presents data which the reader may use to test his understanding of the concepts discussed in this chapter.

2-III SUMMARY

The first section of this chapter reviewed basic statistical concepts. The second section investigated three assumptions underlying the F test of statistical significance. Table 2-10 summarizes the consequences of violating these assumptions. Table 2-11 summarizes the most important equations presented in this chapter.

CHAPTER
THREE
FACTORIAL ANALYSIS OF VARIANCE DESIGNS

3-I Research Uses of Factorial Designs
3-I-1 Importance of Interaction Effects
3-I-2 Two General Uses for Factorial Designs

3-II The Basic Model
3-II-1 Assumed Underlying (Response-Generating) Structural Model
3-II-2 Assumptions Underlying Factorial Designs
      3-II-2-1 Assumption 1—additivity of effects
      3-II-2-2 Assumption 2—complete model specification
      3-II-2-3 Assumption 3—unbiased errors
      3-II-2-4 Assumptions 4, 5, and 6—ε is $N(0, \sigma_\varepsilon^2 I)$
      3-II-2-5 Assumption 7—freedom from other treatment effects
      3-II-2-6 Assumption 8—fixed effects model
      3-II-2-7 Assumption 9—equal cell sizes
3-II-3 Estimating Coefficients of the GLM and Partitioning the Total Sum of Squares—a Numerical Example
      3-II-3-1 Dummy variable coding procedures
      3-II-3-2 Coefficient estimation and partition of sum of squares
3-II-4 A Comparison of GLM Procedures with Standard Procedures for Partitioning the Total Sum of Squares
3-II-5 Tests of Significance
      3-II-5-1 Aggregate tests of significance of main effects and interaction effects

        3-II-5-2 Test of significance of grand mean
        3-II-5-3 General test of significance for any single coefficient in $\hat{\theta}$
3-II-6 Power of Tests of Significance

3-III Graphical Interpretation of Main Effects and Interaction Effects

3-IV A Note on the Scale of Measurement and "Artificial" Interactions

3-V Hypotheses Concerning Linear Combinations of the Coefficients of the General Linear Model

3-V-1 General Linear Contrasts
3-V-2 Orthogonal Contrasts, Degrees of Freedom, and Independent Questions
3-V-3 Orthogonal Polynomials
        3-V-3-1 General logic of orthogonal polynomials
        3-V-3-2 Coding procedures for orthogonal polynomials
        3-V-3-3 Aggregating polynomial trend components
        3-V-3-4 A comparison of the two dummy variable coding procedures
3-V-4 A Note on a priori and post hoc Tests of Significance

3-VI Analysis of 2 × 3 × 3 Factorial Design Using Packaged (Canned) Computer Programs

3-VI-1 Preliminary Analysis
        3-VI-1-1 General reasons for preliminary analysis
        3-VI-1-2 Preliminary analysis of data in Table 3-7
3-VI-2 Analysis of Variance
        3-VI-2-1 General information
        3-VI-2-2 Sum of squares and tests of significance
        3-VI-2-3 Analysis of errors
        3-VI-2-4 Regression coefficients
        3-VI-2-5 Predicted dependent variable
3-VI-3 Orthogonal Polynomial Analysis
        3-VI-3-1 General comments
        3-VI-3-2 Orthogonal polynomial analysis for main effects
        3-VI-3-3 Orthogonal polynomial analysis for two-way effects
        3-VI-3-4 Orthogonal polynomial analysis for three-way and higher interaction effects
        3-VI-3-5 Reduced form structural model
3-VI-4 Reader Test Problem

3-VII Variations on the Factorial Design

3-VII-1 Single Factor Designs
3-VII-2 Randomized Blocks—the Logic of Causal and Associative Models
3-VII-3 Advanced Designs

3-VIII Summary

This chapter investigates the properties of a class of General Linear Models (GLM) known as factorial designs. The distinguishing feature of factorial designs is that they allow the researcher to assess the extent to which interactions among two or more independent variables account for the variation in the dependent variable. In texts on analysis of variance the independent variables are typically referred to as experimental factors.

Most of the formulas presented in this chapter are appropriate for any GLM design. Where a formula would not be correct for certain designs this fact is explicitly noted. Most of these cases involve simplified formulas appropriate only for equal cell sizes. As will become evident in later chapters, however, some of these formulas have no meaning in certain other designs and the interpretation of the numerical output will often be different in designs other than factorial designs.

We should also note that while the independent variables are typically experimental factors, i.e., the levels of each factor are randomly assigned to subjects, this is not required for any of the computations presented in this chapter. The interpretation of the numerical output, of course, is heavily dependent on whether the independent variables were randomly assigned to subjects. This distinction is considered in some detail in the last section of this chapter.

This chapter is divided into six major sections. The first discusses the research uses of factorial designs. The second develops the basic factorial analysis of variance model in detail. This section is especially important because we shall treat all other GLM designs discussed in this book from the perspective of modifications of the basic factorial design. Sections 3-III and 3-IV are devoted to a discussion of interaction effects. Section 3-V discusses the general linear contrast procedure for making statistical tests of hypotheses on the model. Finally, Sec. 3-VI shows how a three-factor factorial design can be analyzed using standard, and readily available, computer programs.

3-I RESEARCH USES OF FACTORIAL DESIGNS

Factorial designs are said to be fully crossed. By fully crossed we mean that every level of each factor is observed at least once under every level of every other factor. As we have already stated, the importance of this feature is that it allows the researcher to assess the extent of interaction effects among the independent variables.

3-I-1 Importance of Interaction Effects

It is difficult to overemphasize the importance of interaction effects in the social and behavioral sciences. Many, perhaps most, important research findings in these sciences are proving to be a function of complex contingent relationships among a number of variables. Familiar examples are the sociological concepts of family life cycle and social class, both of which are defined on the basis of complex interactions among more basic independent variables.

3-I-2 Two General Uses for Factorial Designs

Factorial designs are especially useful in two types of research situation. In the first set of situations can be included preliminary, pilot, and exploratory studies. Such studies are characterized by a general lack of detailed substantive knowledge, and they have many different objectives. Some of the more important are (1) to make a preliminary determination of which of a set of potential explanatory factors do in fact explain the dependent variable; (2) to make a preliminary determination of which interactions may be safely ignored; and (3) to investigate different research methodologies, i.e., the levels of one or more of the factors represent different methodologies which might be used in the full experiment. An example of this last situation might be the use of two or more different experimental cover stories in an experiment which requires the deception of subjects.

In the second set of situations are included research questions where prior knowledge suggests the existence of interaction effects. The general objective in these studies is to explore the precise nature of the interactions. Depending on whether the factors are nominally or intervally scaled and, if intervally scaled, on whether a relatively simple continuous relationship between dependent and independent variables can be found, two rather different uses of interaction effects can be distinguished.

First, consider situations where the levels of each factor represent points along an underlying interval scale. Here the objective is often to find a simple continuous relationship between independent and dependent variables which will specify the dependent variable for all values of the independent variables. Further discussion of this use of interaction effects is postponed until we have considered, in detail, the geometrical interpretation of interaction effects.

Second, consider situations where the factors are nominally scaled or where no simple continuous relationship seems to exist between the dependent and independent variables. In these situations each cell in the factorial design is a potential member of a taxonomic structure. Such a taxonomy is typically built by grouping together cells which exhibit essentially similar responses on the dependent variable and then, hopefully, interpreting the differences among the groups in terms of the independent variables.[1]

An example of how such taxonomic classification structures are developed may help. In a study of the relationship between social class, income, and automobile purchasing behavior Coleman (1961) found that to successfully predict whether a consumer would purchase a luxury, standard, or economy car one needed to know *both* the social class and the income of the consumer. Within each social class individuals who had higher incomes than the average member of their social class tended to purchase luxury cars and those with relatively lower incomes tended to purchase economy cars. Coleman interpreted his findings to mean that a consumer judges his economic position *relative* to the average economic position of other individuals in his class and, to the extent that his economic position differs from this social class average, the consumer views himself

---

[1] For a review of methods for developing taxonomies, generally called cluster analysis, see Sokal and Sneath (1963), and Frar and Green (1968).

Table 3-1 Numerical example of a 3 × 4 factorial design

Factor A level	Factor B level				Mean
	B_1	B_2	B_3	B_4	
A_1	40 53 31 28 18	45 66 38 46 34	40 69 32 50 20	48 51 26 53 25	40.65
A_2	67 62 37 57 62	65 77 50 54 69	65 56 36 27 52	62 50 34 39 56	53.85
A_3	27 44 49 68 29	39 49 33 43 35	35 41 35 48 23	45 43 51 52 28	40.85
Mean	44.80	49.53	41.93	44.20	45.12

as relatively under- or over-privileged. For our purposes the important point is that this taxonomy of over-, average-, and under-privileged consumers is defined by the interaction pattern between social class and relative income.

3-II THE BASIC MODEL

A numerical example will be used to facilitate the discussion in this and the next two sections. Table 3-1 presents artificially contrived data for a so-called 3 × 4 design, i.e., the first factor (labeled A) has $p = 3$ levels, the second factor B has $q = 4$ levels, and since the design is fully crossed, there are $pq = 12$ cells in the design. Further, there are $n = 5$ observations in each cell and the total number of observations N is

$$N = pqn = 3 \times 4 \times 5 = 60 \qquad (3\text{-}1)$$

As Eq. (3-1) generalizes to any number of factors it is immediately apparent that the number of required observations increases very rapidly as the number of factors and the number of levels per factor increase. If needlessly large numbers of observations are to be avoided,[2] this requires the researcher to give very careful consideration to each factor included in the research design and the number of levels per factor.

---

[2] On this point see Cox (1958), Chap. 9.

3-II-1 Assumed Underlying (Response-Generating) Structural Model

The complete structural model underlying any two factor design, such as the one for the data in Table 3-1, is

$$y_{ijk} = \mu + \alpha_i + \beta_j + \alpha\beta_{ij} + \varepsilon_{ijk} \tag{3-2}$$

$$\sum_i \alpha_i = \sum_j \beta_j = \sum_i \alpha\beta_{ij} = \sum_j \alpha\beta_{ij} = 0 \quad (i = 1, p; j = 1, q; k = 1, n) \tag{3-3}$$

Equation (3-2) states that the magnitude of an observation y_{ijk} under level i of factor A and level j of factor B is a function of five additive effects. μ is the mean response for the population from which the observations were drawn, and α_i is the added effect of being influenced by level i of factor A. β_j is similarly defined. α_i and β_j are called main effects because each is defined over all levels of the other factors. $\alpha\beta_{ij}$ is the interaction effect of being *jointly* influenced by level i of factor A and level j of factor B. Note that the term is written $\alpha\beta_{ij}$ and *not* $\alpha_i\beta_j$. This means that $\alpha\beta_{ij}$ is a single term and not the product of α_i and β_j. Finally, ε_{ijk} is the residual error. As we shall see it contains *all* effects not explicitly included in Eq. (3-2), including incorrect model specification and omission of relevant variables.

Equation (3-3) states the usual analysis of variance restriction that the treatment effects are defined as deviations from the mean with the consequence that the sum of the effects for each factor equals zero. Note that the interaction effects sum to zero across levels of both factors A and B.

With three factors the structural model is

$$y_{ijkh} = \mu + \alpha_i + \beta_j + \gamma_k + \alpha\beta_{ij} + \alpha\gamma_{ik} + \beta\gamma_{jk} + \alpha\beta\gamma_{ijk} + \varepsilon_{ijkh} \tag{3-4}$$

$$\sum_i \alpha_i = \sum_j \beta_j = \sum_k \gamma_k = \sum_i \alpha\beta_{ij} = \sum_j \alpha\beta_{ij} = \sum_i \alpha\gamma_{ik} = \sum_k \alpha\gamma_{ik}$$

$$= \sum_j \beta\gamma_{jk} = \sum_k \beta\gamma_{jk} = \sum_i \alpha\beta\gamma_{ijk} = \sum_j \alpha\beta\gamma_{ijk} = \sum_k \alpha\beta\gamma_{ijk} = 0 \tag{3-5}$$

In general, the number of terms in the structural model can be found from the combinatorial formula[3]

$$\sum_{r=0}^{n} \binom{n}{r} + 1 = \sum \frac{n!}{(n-r)!r!} + 1 \tag{3-6}$$

where n equals the number of factors and the 1 represents the residual error. The number of terms of order r is easily found from Eq. (3-6). For example, with $n = 3$ factors $r = 2$ there are

$$\frac{3 \times 2 \times 1}{1 \times 2 \times 1} = 3$$

---

[3] Thus: $n! = n(n-1)(n-2)\ldots 1$
$r! = r(r-1)(r-2)\ldots 1$
$(n-r)! = (n-r)(n-r-1)\ldots 1$
By convention $0! = 1$.

Third degree polynomial
    True form $y = 10 + 1x - 2x^2 + 3x^3$
    Approximation $y = 10 + 1x - 2x^2 + 3x^3$

Natural logarithmic
    True form $y = \ln x$
    Approximation $y = -1.15 + 1.44x - 0.31x^2 + 0.03x^3$

Square root
    True form $y = x^{\frac{1}{2}}$
    Approximation $y = 0.44 + 0.64x - 0.09x^2 + 0.01x^3$

Square
    True form $y = x^2$
    Approximation $y = x^2$

Figure 3-1 Approximation of four different functions by third degree polynomial equation.†

    † x takes on the values 1, 2, 3, and 4.

two-way interaction terms. With three factors there are 9 terms in the complete structural model, with four factors 17, and with five factors 33. The number of required terms increases rapidly as we get much beyond five factors.

3-II-2 Assumptions Underlying Factorial Designs

In this section we examine the assumptions underlying the factorial design. We also indicate the conditions under which each assumption may be omitted.

3-II-2-1 Assumption 1—Additivity of effects

We have already encountered this assumption in Chap. 1 where it was noted that if the true model underlying the data is not additive the fit of the data to the hypothesized model will be poorer than if the proper model had been specified. Parameter estimates, of course, will be biased.

Coding the p levels of a factor into $(p - 1)$ dummy or indicator variables, however, has the effect of substantially reducing the importance of the linearity assumption.[4] Specifically, dummy variable coding allows $(p - 1)$ of the treatment effects to move independently of one another. The pth treatment effect is, by definition, equal to the negative of the sum of the first $(p - 1)$ treatment effects. The mathematical consequence of this is that the p treatment means may *always* be represented by a polynomial equation of degree $(p - 1)$. Of more practical importance is the fact that a great many functions may be approximated quite closely by a polynomial of sufficient degree.

Figure 3-1 illustrates the above principles by using a third degree polynomial of the form

$$y = b_0 + b_1 x + b_2 x^2 + b_3 x^3$$

to approximate four different functional forms. The independent variable was represented by the integers 1, 2, 3, and 4, i.e., four equally spaced treatment

---

[4] Recall from our discussion in Chap. 1 that the linearity assumption means the model is linear in its parameters, *not* that all points fall along a straight line on any given measurement scale.

levels. Dependent observations were generated for each independent variable using the true functional form and then this data was fitted to a third degree polynomial equation.

Several things are noteworthy about Fig. 3-1. First, by definition, the polynomial approximation accounts for all variation in the dependent variables. Second, polynomial approximations tend to be very accurate within the range of the independent variables. For example, the natural logarithm of 1.5 is 0.40546 while the polynomial approximation of the dependent variable corresponding to 1.5 is 0.39921. Polynomial approximations, however, are notoriously untrustworthy when extrapolated beyond the range of the independent variables used to construct the equation. For example, the natural logarithm of 10 is 2.30259 while the polynomial approximation is 10.16640. And, third, the polynomial approximation will often require more parameters than the true functional form. For example, both the natural logarithm and square root functions require only one parameter while their polynomial approximations require four, i.e., the grand mean plus the three degrees of the polynomial.

Later in this chapter we shall explore procedures for fitting treatment means to a polynomial equation. In Chap. 7, more general curve-fitting procedures are discussed. For present purposes, however, we wish to emphasize the flexibility created when an independent variable is coded as a series of dummy variables.

The relationship among two or more factors and the dependent variable may, of course, not be additive. In such situations it may be possible to find a transformation of the dependent variable which will restore additivity. In the social and behavioral sciences the most frequent choice is between an additive or multiplicative model. The logic of the additive model is that each factor contributes an effect to the dependent variable which is independent of the level of all other factors. A multiplicative model, on the other hand, weights each factor by the product of the other factors. Examples of multiplicative models abound in the social and behavioral sciences. Hull's learning theory is one well-known example where

$$_sE_R = VDK\,_sH_R \qquad (3\text{-}7)$$

Equation (3-7) states that the response potential $_sE_R$ is a multiplicative function of the intensity of the stimulus V, motive strength D, incentive value of the stimulus K, and habit strength $_sH_R$. Another example is the definition of decision risk as a multiplicative function of the negative consequences of a bad decision and the probability that these negative consequences will occur.

When we suspect that a multiplicative model is appropriate, additivity can often be restored by taking the logarithm of the dependent variable. Hull's learning theory model, for example, would then take the form[5]

---

[5] Logarithms are defined only for positive numbers. While an interval scale is invariant over any transformation of the form

$$y^* = a + by \qquad (b > 0)$$

the product of two or more interval scales is not invariant when the underlying scales are subject to such a transformation. For the composite scale to be invariant, the underlying scales must be ratio-scaled variables.

$$\ln {}_sE_R = \ln V + \ln D + \ln K + \ln {}_sH_R \tag{3-8}$$

When we consider that many of the measurement scales used in research in the social and behavioral sciences are rather arbitrary, the argument for finding the most parsimonious representation of the data becomes even more compelling.

3-II-2-2 Assumption 2—Complete model specification In the context of factorial designs *with* an equal number of observations per cell the violation of this assumption will cause whatever variance is accounted for by the omitted variables to be lodged in the residual error term. Parameter estimates will not be affected. When there are an unequal number of observations per cell the factors will not necessarily, and usually will not, be uncorrelated. In this case the variance attributable to the omitted variables will be partially confounded with the included variables, and parameter estimates will be affected.

3-II-2-3 Assumption 3—Unbiased errors If this assumption is not met our parameter estimates will be biased. The violation of this assumption is perhaps one of the most troublesome problems in research in the social and behavioral sciences. Survey research methods are plagued by problems of response refusals, inadequate sample frames, interviewer and response bias, and a host of other problems too numerous to mention.[6] Even true experimental research is not free from bias as Rosenthal (1966) has so well documented.[7]

Often, however, the researcher is more interested in the differences between treatment means than in the actual estimates of the treatment means themselves. In this case it need only be assumed that the bias is constant across treatments. For example, in contrasting the treatment means for A_1 and A_2 we have

$$\overline{A}_1 - \overline{A}_2 = (\mu + \alpha_1 + \bar{\varepsilon}_1) - (\mu + \alpha_2 + \bar{\varepsilon}_2)$$
$$= \alpha_1 - \alpha_2 + \bar{\varepsilon}_1 - \bar{\varepsilon}_2$$

and if the error bias is constant

$$= \alpha_1 - \alpha_2$$

because, by the restrictions that the sum of the treatment effects equal zero, all other effects cancel out. While constant bias is a weaker assumption than unbiased errors there is no guarantee it will hold in any actual investigation. Nevertheless, even if the assumption is not completely valid the bias across the different treatment groups will normally be in the same direction.

3-II-2-4 Assumptions 4, 5, and 6—ε is $N(0, \sigma_\varepsilon^2 I)$ The assumptions that the errors are normally and independently distributed with constant variance were investi-

---

[6] Kish (1967, Chap. 13) gives an excellent general discussion of so-called non-sampling errors. For recent attempts to assess non-sampling errors see Brown (1969), Neter (1970), and Mayer (1970).

[7] Anyone planning to conduct an experiment should read the discussion by Aronson and Carlsmith (1968) of experimentation in social psychology, particularly with respect to minimizing response bias.

gated in detail in Chap. 2. Here we shall merely note that these assumptions are needed only if statistical tests of significance are to be made. Even then the strict validity of the first and third assumptions will not be crucial. If substantial violations are detected, rough adjustments of the nominal significance level may be made on the basis of the tables reported in the previous chapter.

3-II-2-5 Assumption 7—Freedom from other treatment effects This assumption states that the observed response of each observation should not be influenced by the assignment of subjects to other treatment conditions. To take a very simple example, consider an experiment where a chain of stores in a metropolitan area randomly assigns a high, medium, and low price to a new product in different stores to determine the price which results in the greatest profit. The problem with this procedure is that a substantial number of consumers may be aware of this differential price. Presumably, many of these consumers will patronize the store with the lowest price. On the basis of the experiment, however, a single price will be set for all stores.

To put assumption 7 more generally we must make a sharp distinction between internal validity and external validity. An experiment is internally valid to the extent that the treatments, and not some extraneous variable, produced the observed response. An experiment is externally valid to the extent the observed response may be generalized to a larger population in a nonexperimental setting. In the pricing experiment, even if the experiment were internally valid, the adoption of the experimentally optimum price might not produce the predicted effects because the interference among the different price conditions would no longer be present.

Interference effects are especially prominent in research in the social and behavioral sciences. The researcher should carefully consider this problem; especially important is whether the interference is an experimental artifact or a reflection of behavior in the population about which generalizations are to be made. If the latter is the case it is generally wise to try to isolate the effect of the interference in terms of an interaction effect.

3-II-2-6 Assumption 8—Fixed effects model There are really two quite distinct analysis of variance models. The first model is called the fixed effects model or model I. In this class of models the object of investigation is the difference among two or more treatment means. The estimated variance of the treatment effects in these models $\hat{\sigma}_\tau^2$ is used as a descriptive measure of the distances among the means rather than as a parameter describing the variance of the treatment effects in some larger population. Another way of putting this is to say that in the fixed effects model either all treatments have been included or the treatments which are included were selected in a non-probabilistic manner and the findings can be generalized only to these particular treatments in the larger population.

In the second model, called the random effects model or model II, the treatment levels of each factor are considered to be randomly selected from a larger set of treatment levels. The primary object of investigation is the variance of the treatment effects σ_τ^2 rather than the means. In the random effects model

σ_τ^2 is a distribution parameter describing the variance of the treatment effects in some larger population, and is usually assumed to be distributed $N(0, \sigma_\tau^2)$.

Parameter estimates, sum of squares, mean squares, and degrees of freedom due to each component of the structural model are identical in the two models. The mathematical theory underlying the two models, however, is quite different, often leading to different expected mean squares and, consequently, requiring different procedures for the tests of significance. We might also note that model II is rather sensitive to violation of the assumptions of normality and equal variance of errors.[8]

Except in Chap. 5, where we consider a model with both fixed and random factors and briefly review an aspect of model II called variance components analysis, we assume all factors or independent variables to be fixed. This assumption reflects the fact that the random effects model is only rarely encountered in research in the social and behavioral sciences. And even when it is used, close inspection will usually show it to have been misused since the treatment levels are almost invariably selected in a non-probabilistic manner.[9]

3-II-2-7 Assumption 9—Equal cell sizes This assumption is made so that the total sum of squares may be uniquely partitioned and attributed to each factor in the model. With unequal cell sizes the factors will typically be correlated and the sum of squares cannot be uniquely attributed to each factor. This, of course, makes interpretation of the data much more difficult since we must somehow account for these intercorrelations among the factors. In Chap. 7 we shall remove this assumption and consider various interpretation procedures for correlated factors.

While the advantages of uncorrelated factors are often loudly proclaimed we should add a methodological caution. Often the goal of social and behavioral research is to generalize the experimental findings to a larger population. The experimental factors often, indeed usually, are correlated in this larger population. Strictly speaking, projections of the experimental findings are legitimate only to a hypothetical population where all factors are uncorrelated. To make accurate predictions in the actual population we need to know the correlations among the factors.

Finally, we note that while the interpretation of the data will be affected, most of the formulae presented in this chapter apply to both equal and unequal cell sizes. Unless otherwise specified the reader may assume the formulae presented apply to both the equal and unequal cell size cases.

3-II-3 Estimating Coefficients of the GLM and Partitioning the Total Sum of Squares—a Numerical Example

3-II-3-1 Dummy variable coding procedures Table 3-2 presents information necessary to code the data in Table 3-1 in a form suitable for analysis via the

---

[8] For details on this point see Scheffé (1959), Chap. 9.

[9] For further discussion of the random effects model see Winer (1970), pp. 167–168, 244–245, 321–332, and 425–428 and Scheffé (1959), Chaps. 7 and 10.

Table 3-2 Coding of data in Table 3-1

(a) Structural model

$$y_{ijk} = \mu + \alpha_i + \beta_j + \alpha\beta_{ij} + \varepsilon_{ijk}$$
$$(i = 1, p; j = 1, q; k = 1, n)$$
$$\sum_i \alpha_i = \sum_j \beta_j = \sum_i \alpha\beta_{ij} = \sum_j \alpha\beta_{ij} = 0$$

(b) Matrix representation of structural model

$$_N y_1 = {_N}X_{m\ m}\theta_1 + {_N}\varepsilon_1$$

(c) Coding, procedures, for experimental factors

Level of factor								Treatment effects coded as dummy variables					
A	B	μ	α_1	α_2	β_1	β_2	β_3	$\alpha\beta_{11}$	$\alpha\beta_{12}$	$\alpha\beta_{13}$	$\alpha\beta_{21}$	$\alpha\beta_{22}$	$\alpha\beta_{23}$
1	1	1	1	0	1	0	0	1	0	0	0	0	0
1	2	1	1	0	0	1	0	0	1	0	0	0	0
1	3	1	1	0	0	0	1	0	0	1	0	0	0
1	4	1	1	0	−1	−1	−1	−1	−1	−1	0	0	0
2	1	1	0	1	1	0	0	0	0	0	1	0	0
2	2	1	0	1	0	1	0	0	0	0	0	1	0
2	3	1	0	1	0	0	1	0	0	0	0	0	1
2	4	1	0	1	−1	−1	−1	0	0	0	−1	−1	−1
3	1	1	−1	−1	1	0	0	−1	0	0	−1	0	0
3	2	1	−1	−1	0	1	0	0	−1	0	0	−1	0
3	3	1	−1	−1	0	0	1	0	0	−1	0	0	−1
3	4	1	−1	−1	−1	−1	−1	1	1	1	1	1	1

GLM. Section (a) in Table 3-2 merely repeats the assumed structural model with Sec. (b) giving the general matrix representation. The most important part of Table 3-2 is Sec. (c) which gives the dummy variable codes for observations in each of the 12 cells of the 3 × 4 factorial design. This, of course, is the design matrix X of independent variables.

Consider the coding for observations under level 1 of both factors A and B. The grand mean μ is attributed to these observations, along with all other observations, and a 1 is recorded under μ. In the next two columns a 1 is recorded under α_1 and a 0 is recorded under α_2 because these subjects were observed under A_1 and not A_2. A similar logic holds for the remaining columns and the next two rows.

Coding procedures for subjects observed under $A_1 B_4$ need to reflect the fact that B_4 is not defined directly. By the restriction that the sum of the treatment effects for each factor sum to zero we have

$$\beta_1 + \beta_2 + \beta_3 + \beta_4 = 0$$
$$\beta_4 = -\beta_1 - \beta_2 - \beta_3$$

and a minus one is recorded under each β column. The interaction term $\alpha\beta_{14}$ is similarly defined since

$$\alpha\beta_{14} = -\alpha\beta_{11} - \alpha\beta_{12} - \alpha\beta_{13}$$

The logic for observations in A_3B_4 is similar although a bit more complicated. First,

$$\alpha\beta_{34} = -\alpha\beta_{14} - \alpha\beta_{24}$$

Although neither $\alpha\beta_{14}$ or $\alpha\beta_{24}$ is directly defined the restrictions that the sum of the interaction effects across both rows and columns equal zero implies that

$$\alpha\beta_{14} = -\alpha\beta_{11} - \alpha\beta_{12} - \alpha\beta_{13}$$

and

$$\alpha\beta_{24} = -\alpha\beta_{21} - \alpha\beta_{22} - \alpha\beta_{23}$$

Hence,

$$\alpha\beta_{34} = \alpha\beta_{11} + \alpha\beta_{12} + \alpha\beta_{13} + \alpha\beta_{21} + \alpha\beta_{22} + \alpha\beta_{23}$$

and a 1 is recorded under each of the interaction columns.

The above coding procedure for interaction terms appears rather cumbersome. Note, however, that the terms under each interaction effect are simply the product of the terms under the corresponding main effects. This result generalizes to any number of factors and interactions of any order.

3-II-3-2 Coefficient estimation and partition of sum of squares With this much background we may proceed to the analysis which is presented in Table 3-3. The raw data is not presented. It would consist of a column vector y of dependent variables and a design matrix X of independent variables, each row of which would be determined by the cell of the design from which the observed dependent variable was obtained (see Table 3-2c).

Table 3-3a presents the cross products matrix $X'X$. Note carefully the pattern of zeros. For example, the first row gives the cross products of μ with all other variables. The first entry is 60 which is the number of subjects involved in estimating the grand mean. This is followed by zeros which indicate the mean is not correlated with any of the remaining variables.

Next, look at the second row of $X'X$. This corresponds to α_1. The second column is 40. This is because, as can be seen from the column labeled α_1 in Table 3-2c, α_1 has been coded as a contrast between $\bar{A}_1$ and $\bar{A}_3$. This contrast involves the 20 observations in A_1 and the 20 observations in A_3. The third column of row two of $X'X$ tells us that 20 subjects—those in A_2—were not involved in this contrast. The fact that all other entries in the second row are zero tells us that factor A is uncorrelated with all other factors. Each row then sums to 60 and each component (α, β, $\alpha\beta$) of the structural model is uncorrelated with every other component. Note, however, that the levels of each component are correlated among themselves. This is an artifact of our coding procedure. Other coding

72 THE GENERAL LINEAR MODEL

Table 3-3 Analysis of 3 × 4 factorial data†

(a) Cross products

$$X'X = \begin{bmatrix} 60 & 0 & 0 & 0 & 0 & 0 & 0 & 0 & 0 & 0 & 0 & 0 \\ 0 & 40 & 20 & 0 & 0 & 0 & 0 & 0 & 0 & 0 & 0 & 0 \\ 0 & 20 & 40 & 0 & 0 & 0 & 0 & 0 & 0 & 0 & 0 & 0 \\ 0 & 0 & 0 & 30 & 15 & 15 & 0 & 0 & 0 & 0 & 0 & 0 \\ 0 & 0 & 0 & 15 & 30 & 15 & 0 & 0 & 0 & 0 & 0 & 0 \\ 0 & 0 & 0 & 15 & 15 & 30 & 0 & 0 & 0 & 0 & 0 & 0 \\ 0 & 0 & 0 & 0 & 0 & 0 & 20 & 10 & 10 & 0 & 0 & 0 \\ 0 & 0 & 0 & 0 & 0 & 0 & 10 & 20 & 10 & 0 & 0 & 0 \\ 0 & 0 & 0 & 0 & 0 & 0 & 10 & 10 & 20 & 0 & 0 & 0 \\ 0 & 0 & 0 & 0 & 0 & 0 & 0 & 0 & 0 & 10 & 5 & 5 \\ 0 & 0 & 0 & 0 & 0 & 0 & 0 & 0 & 0 & 5 & 10 & 5 \\ 0 & 0 & 0 & 0 & 0 & 0 & 0 & 0 & 0 & 5 & 5 & 10 \\ 0 & 0 & 0 & 0 & 0 & 0 & 0 & 0 & 0 & 10 & 10 & 20 \end{bmatrix} \qquad X'y = \begin{bmatrix} 2707 \\ -4 \\ 260 \\ 9 \\ 80 \\ -34 \\ -31 \\ 46 \\ 45 \\ 46 \\ 94 \\ 32 \end{bmatrix}$$

(b) Inverse of $X'X$

$$\begin{bmatrix} 0.0167 & 0 & 0 & 0 & 0 & 0 & 0 & 0 & 0 & 0 & 0 & 0 \\ 0 & 0.0333 & -0.0167 & 0 & 0 & 0 & 0 & 0 & 0 & 0 & 0 & 0 \\ 0 & -0.0167 & 0.0333 & 0 & 0 & 0 & 0 & 0 & 0 & 0 & 0 & 0 \\ 0 & 0 & 0 & 0.0500 & -0.0167 & -0.0167 & 0 & 0 & 0 & 0 & 0 & 0 \\ 0 & 0 & 0 & -0.0167 & 0.0500 & -0.0167 & 0 & 0 & 0 & 0 & 0 & 0 \\ 0 & 0 & 0 & -0.0167 & -0.0167 & 0.0500 & 0 & 0 & 0 & 0 & 0 & 0 \\ 0 & 0 & 0 & 0 & 0 & 0 & 0.1000 & -0.0333 & -0.0333 & 0.0167 & 0.0167 & 0.0167 \\ 0 & 0 & 0 & 0 & 0 & 0 & -0.0333 & 0.1000 & -0.0333 & -0.0333 & -0.0333 & -0.0500 \\ 0 & 0 & 0 & 0 & 0 & 0 & -0.0333 & -0.0333 & 0.1000 & 0.0167 & 0.0167 & -0.0500 \\ 0 & 0 & 0 & 0 & 0 & 0 & -0.0500 & 0.0167 & 0.0167 & 0.1000 & -0.0333 & -0.0333 \\ 0 & 0 & 0 & 0 & 0 & 0 & 0.0167 & -0.0500 & 0.0167 & -0.0333 & 0.1000 & -0.0333 \\ 0 & 0 & 0 & 0 & 0 & 0 & 0.0167 & 0.0167 & -0.0500 & -0.0333 & -0.0333 & 0.1000 \end{bmatrix}$$

(c) Estimated regression coefficients

$$\hat{\boldsymbol{\theta}} = \begin{bmatrix} \hat{\mu} \\ \hat{\alpha}_1 \\ \hat{\alpha}_2 \\ \hat{\beta}_1 \\ \hat{\beta}_2 \\ \hat{\beta}_3 \\ \widehat{\alpha\beta}_{11} \\ \widehat{\alpha\beta}_{12} \\ \widehat{\alpha\beta}_{13} \\ \widehat{\alpha\beta}_{21} \\ \widehat{\alpha\beta}_{22} \\ \widehat{\alpha\beta}_{23} \end{bmatrix} = (\mathbf{X}'\mathbf{X})^{-1}\mathbf{X}'\mathbf{y} = \begin{bmatrix} 45.12 \\ -4.47 \\ 8.73 \\ -0.32 \\ 4.42 \\ -3.18 \\ -6.33 \\ 0.73 \\ 4.73 \\ 3.47 \\ 4.73 \\ -3.47 \end{bmatrix}$$

(d) Explained variance

$$\begin{aligned}
\text{SS}_R = \hat{\boldsymbol{\theta}}'\mathbf{X}'\mathbf{y} = \quad & (45.12)(2707) = 122{,}139.84 \\
& +(-4.47)(-4) +17.88 \\
& +(8.73)(260) +2269.80 \\
& +(-0.32)(9) +(-2.88) \\
& +(4.42)(80) +353.60 \\
& +(-3.18)(-34) +108.12 \\
& +(-6.33)(-31) +196.23 \\
& +(0.73)(46) +33.58 \\
& +(4.73)(45) +212.85 \\
& +(3.47)(46) +159.62 \\
& +(4.73)(94) +444.62 \\
& +(-3.47)(32) +(-111.04) \\
& \overline{125{,}822.22}
\end{aligned}$$

† Raw data is located in Table 3-1. Procedures for coding the factors as dummy variables are given in Table 3-2.

procedures, discussed below, which will remove the correlations among the levels of each factor are available. The interpretation of the coefficients $\hat{\theta}$ of the GLM as deviations from various means will, however, no longer be correct.

Table 3-3a also gives $X'y$. The first row is simply the sum of the dependent variable over the 60 observations. As we remarked in the above paragraph, α_1 was coded as a contrast between $\overline{A}_1$ and $\overline{A}_3$. The second row of $X'y$ then is simply the difference between the sum of the y's observed under A_1 and the sum of the y's observed under A_3. The fact that this number (-4) is very small tells us that the estimated values of α_1 and α_3 will be very close. A similar interpretation holds for the remaining rows of $X'y$.

The inverse of $X'X$ is given in Table 3-3b. The reader may easily verify that $(X'X)^{-1}X'X$ is an identity matrix. Except for obtaining $\hat{\theta}$ this matrix will be of little interest until we consider tests of significance. The reader is reminded that $\hat{\sigma}_\varepsilon^2(X'X)^{-1}$ is the estimated covariance matrix of the parameter coefficient vector $\hat{\theta}$.

Table 3-3c presents the estimated parameters of the hypothesized structural model. By comparing these results with the treatment means in Table 3-1 the reader may easily verify that the coefficients of $\hat{\theta}$ may be interpreted as means or deviations from means. For example, $\hat{\mu}$ is estimated at 45.12. Adding $-4.47(\hat{\alpha}_1)$ one obtains 40.65 which is equal to the mean of the observations under A_1. The value of $\hat{\alpha}_3$ is not obtained directly but is given by

$$\hat{\alpha}_3 = -\hat{\alpha}_1 - \hat{\alpha}_2$$
$$= -(-4.47) - (8.73)$$
$$= -4.26$$

A similar interpretation holds for $\hat{\beta}_j$.

The interaction effects may be interpreted as deviations from the main effect means of the corresponding cells. For example, the mean of AB_{11} is 34. Now, if $\overline{AB}_{11}$ were estimated using only the main effects we would have

$$\overline{AB}_{11} = \hat{\mu} + \hat{\alpha}_1 + \hat{\beta}_1$$
$$= 45.12 + (-4.47) + (-0.32)$$
$$= 40.33$$

The difference between the actual mean of AB_{11} and the corresponding mean estimated using only the main effects is -6.33. This, of course, equals $\hat{\alpha\beta}_{11}$. Thus, we may subtract 6.33 from an observation's estimated response and attribute this to the fact that the subject was simultaneously influenced by treatments A_1 and B_1.

Finally, Table 3-3d presents the sum of squares due to regression—the explained sum of squares—broken down by independent variables. Because each factor is independent of all other factors the sum of squares attributable to each factor is simply the sum of the relevant terms in Table 3-3d. For example, the sum of squares attributable to factor A is the sum of the second and third entries in Table 3-3d. Table 3-4 presents a standard analysis of variance table computed from Table 3-3d.

FACTORIAL ANALYSIS OF VARIANCE DESIGNS 75

Table 3-4 Analysis of variance table for 3 × 4 factorial example†

Source of variation	Sum of squares	Degrees of freedom	Mean square	Expected mean square
Mean	122,130.82	1	122,130.82	$\sigma_\varepsilon^2 + npq\sigma_\mu^2$
A	2,288.53	2	1,144.27	$\sigma_\varepsilon^2 + nq\sigma_\alpha^2$
B	458.72	3	152.91	$\sigma_\varepsilon^2 + np\sigma_\beta^2$
AB	936.53	6	156.09	$\sigma_\varepsilon^2 + n\sigma_{\alpha\beta}^2$
Error	7,976.40	48	166.17	σ_ε^2
Total	133,791.00	60		

† The numbers in this table were calculated by computer which accounts for the slight discrepancies with Table 3-3.

3-II-4 A Comparison of GLM Procedures with Standard Procedures for Partitioning the Total Sum of Squares

We pause briefly here to compare the results obtained by the matrix methods presented above with a more familiar method of partitioning the total sum of squares. An observation may be broken into a series of components each of which represents a deviation from a mean. For example, any observation in the 3 × 4 factorial data may be represented as

$$y_{ijk} = \bar{G} + (\bar{A}_i - \bar{G}) + (\bar{B}_j - \bar{G}) + (\overline{AB}_{ij} - \bar{A}_i - \bar{B}_j + \bar{G}) + (y_{ijk} - \overline{AB}_{ij}) \quad (3\text{-}9)$$

Reading the terms to the right of the equals sign in Eq. (3-9) we have that y_{ijk} is attributed to a grand mean $\bar{G}$; a deviation of the treatment mean $\bar{A}_i$ from the grand mean; a similar deviation corresponding to the relevant level of factor B; a deviation attributable to the interaction effect; and a residual term reflecting the deviation of observation k from its cell mean. Note that all terms on the righthand side of Eq. (3-9) except y_{ijk} cancel out and we are left with the identity $y_{ijk} = y_{ijk}$.

Now if we subtract $\bar{G}$ from both sides of Eq. (3-9), square, and sum over all observations we have

$$\sum_i \sum_j \sum_k (y_{ijk} - \bar{G})^2 = nq \sum_i (\bar{A}_i - \bar{G})^2 + np \sum_j (\bar{B}_j - \bar{G})^2$$
$$+ n \sum_i \sum_j (\overline{AB}_{ij} - \bar{A}_i - \bar{B}_j + \bar{G})^2 + \sum_i \sum_j \sum_k (y_{ijk} - \overline{AB}_{ij})^2 \quad (3\text{-}10)$$

Six cross-product terms of the form

$$n \sum_i \sum_j (\bar{A}_i - \bar{G})(\bar{B}_j - \bar{G}) = 0$$

drop out because each involves the sum of deviations about its own mean which is by definition equal to zero. Equation (3-10) states that for any two-factor design with equal cell sizes we may partition the total sum of squares into four components which are exhaustive and mutually exclusive (i.e., independent).

Under this scheme the sum of squares attributable to factor A is

$$20(-4.47)^2 + 20(8.73)^2 + 20(-4.27)^2 = 2284.40 \tag{3-11}$$

which is, within rounding error, equal to the figure in Table 3-4. Note that three terms (as opposed to the two in the GLM) are involved in Eq. (3-11). The third component of the sum of squares due to A is completely specified by the first two because of the restriction that the sums of the treatment effects equal zero.

3-II-5 Tests of Significance

The tests of significance presented in this section require the assumptions

$$\varepsilon \text{ is } N(0, \sigma_\varepsilon^2 I)$$

These assumptions, including the consequences of violations, were reviewed in detail in Chap. 2. In addition, we must assume that all factors are fixed. If they are not, the form of the expected mean squares will be different from those presented here, and our F ratios may not have the proper denominators.

3-II-5-1 Aggregate tests of significance of main effects and interaction effects
Referring back to Table 3-4, the expected mean squares indicate that the appropriate F ratios may be obtained by dividing the mean square for each factor by the mean square error. For the data in Table 3-4 these F ratios are

$$\text{Mean} \quad F_{(1,48)} = 734.95$$
$$A \quad F_{(2,48)} = 6.89$$
$$B \quad F_{(3,48)} = 0.92$$
$$AB \quad F_{(6,48)} = 0.94$$

Ignoring the mean, only the main effect for factor A is significant at anything even close to an acceptable significance level (e.g., $p_1 = 0.10$).[10] With 2 and 48 degrees of freedom the main effect for A is significant beyond the 0.005 level.

3-II-5-2 Test of significance of grand mean
The F test for the mean requires some explanation. The reader is probably familiar with a statement to the effect that with N observations there are only $(N - 1)$ degrees of freedom since the total sum of squares is defined in terms of deviations from the grand mean and the grand mean is estimated from the sample data. What is often not pointed out is that the lost degree of freedom may be used to test a hypothesis concerning the value of the mean. The hypothesis above is that the true mean equals zero. Obviously, with $F = 735$ this hypothesis is not tenable.

More often than not in social and behavioral research the means of our scales are arbitrary. Hence a hypothesis that the mean equals zero is usually meaningless. We might, however, wish to test the hypothesis that our mean equals

---

[10] We speak of an acceptable significance level because *every* F test is significant at some level.

some specific value other than zero. For example, assume the artificial data used for illustration is a measure of reading ability and that we know from past experience that the mean in the general population from which our subjects were randomly selected is 50. We might then wish to test the hypothesis that the obtained mean is not significantly (at say $p_1 = 0.05$) different from 50. It can be shown that an appropriate test of the hypothesis that the estimated mean $\hat{\mu}$ is not significantly different from a hypothesized value μ_h is the t test

$$t_{(N-m)} = \frac{\hat{\mu} - \mu_h}{\hat{\sigma}_\varepsilon (C_{ii})^{\frac{1}{2}}}$$

where C_{ii} is the diagonal element of $(X'X)^{-1}$ which corresponds to μ. The term $\hat{\sigma}_\varepsilon$ is the square root of the MS_E and, as we remarked in Chap. 1, $\hat{\sigma}_\varepsilon(C_{ii})^{\frac{1}{2}}$ is the square root (standard error) of the variance of the ith element in $\hat{\theta}$, which in this case is $\hat{\mu}$. With N observations and m estimated parameters there are $(N - m)$ degrees of freedom left to estimate the error variance.

For example, to test the hypothesis

$$H_0: \mu = 50$$

we have

$$t_{(48)} = \frac{45.12 - 50}{(166.17)^{\frac{1}{2}}(0.0167)^{\frac{1}{2}}} = \frac{-4.88}{1.67}$$

$$= -2.92$$

which is significant well beyond the $p_1 = 0.01$ level. Therefore, we do not accept the null hypothesis.

3-II-5-3 General test of significance for any single coefficient in $\hat{\theta}$

The result obtained above is completely general. Any hypothesis of the form that one element of $\hat{\theta}(\hat{\theta}_i)$ equals a specific value (θ_{iH}) may be tested by[11]

$$t_{(N-m)} = \frac{\hat{\theta}_i - \theta_{iH}}{\hat{\sigma}_\varepsilon (C_{ii})^{\frac{1}{2}}} \tag{3-12}$$

A confidence interval for any significance level may also be placed around $\hat{\theta}_i$ by

$$\hat{\theta}_i \pm [t_{(N-m)p_1/2} \times \hat{\sigma}_\varepsilon (C_{ii})^{\frac{1}{2}}] \tag{3-13}$$

For the hypothesis tested above that the grand mean is not significantly different from 50 at $p_1 = 0.05$ the confidence interval would be

$$45.12 \pm 2.02(1.67) = 45.12 \pm 3.37$$

or

$$41.75 \leq \mu \leq 48.49$$

[11] We use the t test because it is more convenient than the F test. It is relatively easy to show that

$$t_{(N-m)} = [F_{(1, N-m)}]^{\frac{1}{2}}$$

In a sense Eqs. (3-12) and (3-13) are equivalent because if θ_{iH} is included in the confidence interval in (3-13) the hypothesis represented in (3-12) cannot be rejected. The two equations, however, put this information in a somewhat different form.

The test represented in Eq. (1-12) is an extremely versatile and useful one. For example, a theory may predict a specific value for one or more of the coefficients in $\hat{\theta}$. Or we might wish in a replication study to test the hypothesis that $\hat{\theta}_i$ is equal to a value estimated for this element in a previous study. Many other uses of this test might easily be envisaged.

3-II-6 Power of Tests of Significance

The power of a statistical test was defined in Chap. 2. Here we will illustrate power calculations for the illustrative data for factor A. First we must calculate the noncentrality parameter

$$\lambda = \frac{\hat{\theta}' X' X \hat{\theta}}{\sigma_\varepsilon^2}$$

it being understood that $\hat{\theta}$ and $X'X$ contain only elements corresponding to the coefficients being tested.

For factor A, λ would be

$$\frac{(-4.47, 8.73) \begin{bmatrix} 40 & 20 \\ 20 & 40 \end{bmatrix} \begin{bmatrix} -4.47 \\ 8.73 \end{bmatrix}}{(166.17)} = 13.76$$

Dividing λ by the number of levels of factor A and taking the square root yields

$$\phi = \left(\frac{13.76}{3}\right)^{\frac{1}{2}} = 2.14$$

Referring to the non-central F table we find

$$\text{Power} = \text{pr}\left[F_{(p-1, N-m, \phi)} > F_{(p-1, N-m)}\right]$$
$$= \text{pr}\left[F_{(2, 48, 2.14)} > F_{(2, 48)}\right]$$
$$= 0.87$$

for the 0.05 significance level. This means that using a decision rule of the form "reject the null hypothesis if the probability of its truth given the sample data is less than 0.05" we will reject the null hypothesis approximately 87 percent of the time if the distribution defined by the non-centrality parameter λ is the true distribution. If we set the significance at 0.01 the power falls by almost a third. Thus we clearly see the tradeoff between type I and type II errors.

It is important for the purposes of planning an experiment to note that the power formula may be solved for n, i.e., for a given decision rule we may vary n to achieve any power we desire. This, of course, requires an estimate of σ_ε^2 and a prior decision about how large the coefficients in θ must be before we consider it "worthwhile" to detect them. For further details refer to Sec. 2-I-3-3.

3-III GRAPHICAL INTERPRETATION OF MAIN EFFECTS AND INTERACTION EFFECTS

In Sec. 3-V we will consider mathematical and statistical procedures for examining the pattern of the treatment effects of each factor. In this section we present a simple graphical heuristic which will reveal much about the structure of our data. Figure 3-2 presents a number of graphs for different two-factor experiments. In

(a) No interaction: linear main effects in A and B.

(b) Interaction: no main effects in A or B.

(c) No interaction: quadratic trend in A, linear trend in B.

(d) Graph (c) drawn to show simple effects for factor B.

(e) No interaction: main effects in B, no main effects in A.

(f) Interaction and main effects in both factors.

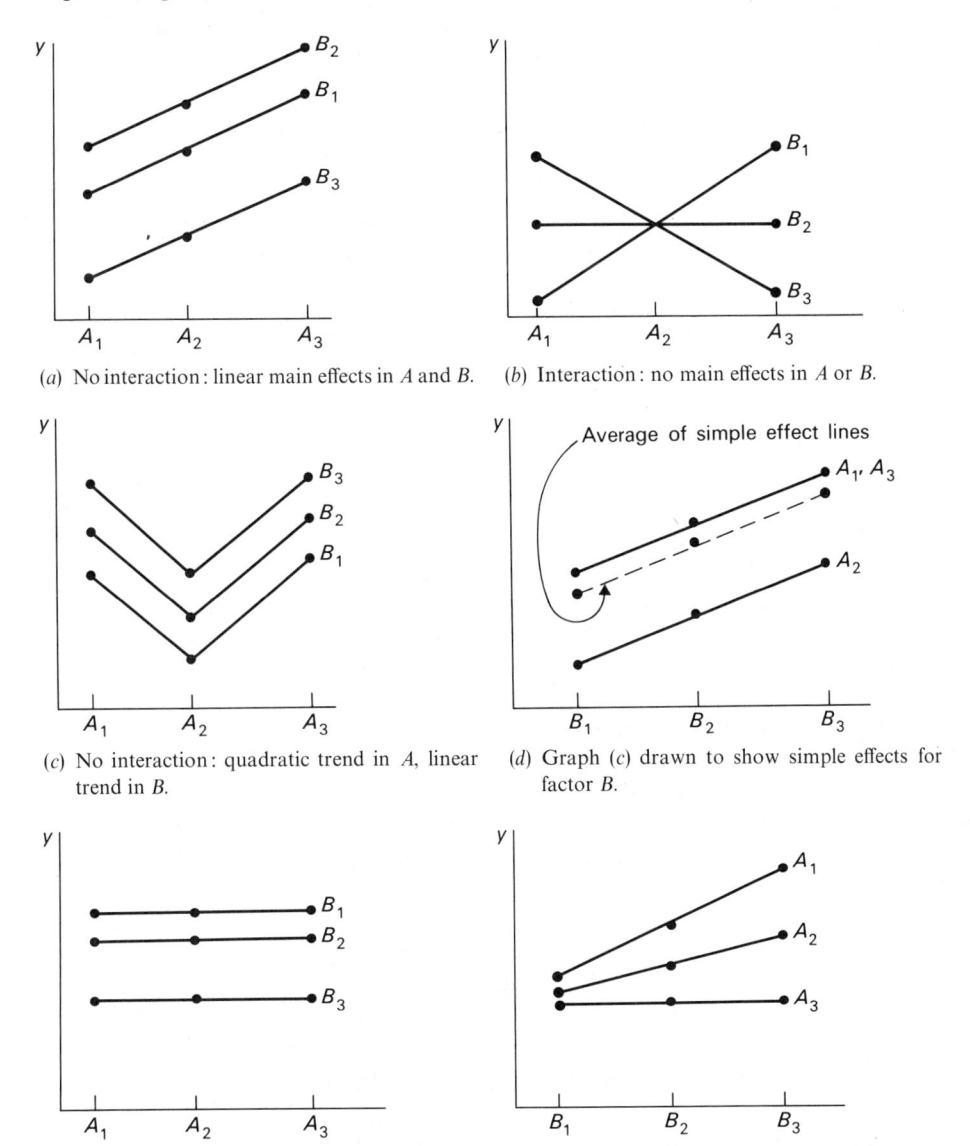

Figure 3-2 Illustrative patterns of main effects and interaction effects.

each graph the dependent variable is plotted on the vertical axis and it is assumed that the levels of factor A are equally spaced on an underlying interval scale. The treatment means for each level of factor A are plotted separately for each level of factor B. Each such line represents the so-called simple effects of factor A, i.e., the main effects of a factor at a specific level of each other factor. Simple effects may be defined similarly for each factor in the experiment.

The graphs a, c, d, and e in Figure 3-2 contain no interaction effects. Note that all simple effect lines are parallel in these graphs. This is a graphical representation of no interaction effects. Note also that although there is an obvious quadratic trend in factor A, at each level of factor B in the third graph there is no interaction since the simple effect lines are equidistant at each level of A.

Figure 3-2d is the same as 3-2c except that the former displays the simple effects of factor B. The dashed line is the average of the simple effects for factor B. The average of the simple effects of a factor is, of course, the main effects for that factor. Between Figs. 3-2c and d then it is clear that the data represented in the two graphs can be accounted for by a grand mean, a quadratic trend in A, and a linear trend in B. This requires a model with only three terms rather than the nine terms which are present in the full structural model for a 3×3 factorial design. We shall have considerably more to say about the construction of these so-called reduced form models in Sec. 3-V.

Figure 3-2b displays data where there is only an interaction effect. The average of the simple effects for factor A is a horizontal line, indicating no main effect for factor A. Similarly the average of the simple effects for factor B is a vertical line. Finally, Fig. 3-2f presents a situation with main effects for both factors and an interaction effect. The interaction is indicated by the fact that the simple effects for factor A are not parallel. The main effects for A and B are indicated by the slope of the average of the simple effects for each factor.

Of course this simple graphical procedure cannot tell us if an apparent effect is statistically significant or how much of the total variance an effect accounts for. We shall consider these questions in Sec. 3-V after a brief digression.

3-IV A NOTE ON THE SCALE OF MEASUREMENT AND "ARTIFICIAL" INTERACTIONS

We have already remarked on the arbitrariness of the measurement scales on which many social and behavioral phenomena are measured. We pause here to show how, under certain conditions, interaction effects may be removed by an appropriate change in the scale of measurement. The goals of such a change in the measurement scale are generally to describe the data with as few and as simple parameters as possible in order that the model used to represent the data be as parsimonious and comprehensible as possible.

Table 3-5 presents illustrative data. In Section (a) of the table simple effect profiles for factor A are plotted at each level of factor B. The fact that these profiles are not parallel indicates the presence of an interaction effect between

Table 3-5 An example of a monotone transformation of dependent variable to restore additivity

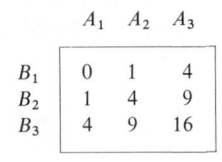

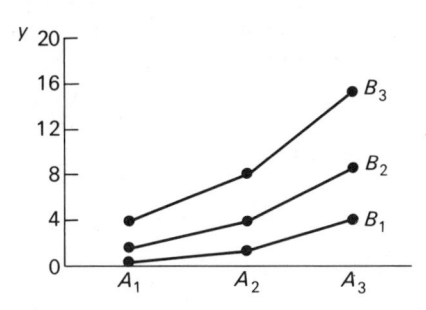

(a) Original data

	A_1	A_2	A_3
B_1	0	1	4
B_2	1	4	9
B_3	4	9	16

(b) Data after square root transformation

	A_1	A_2	A_3
B_1	0	1	2
B_2	1	2	3
B_3	2	3	4

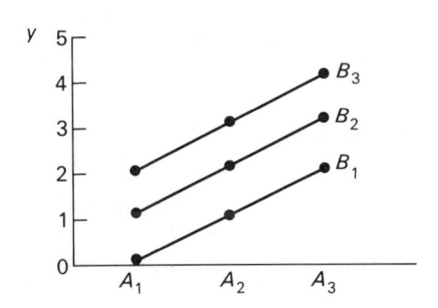

factors A and B. Section (b) of the table presents the same data after a square root transformation. The simple effect profiles are now parallel indicating that the interaction between factors A and B has been removed by taking the square root of each observation. In a sense, the apparent interaction effect in the original data was simply an artifact of the scale of measurement.

The practical problem, of course, is to determine the form of the required transformation. Often a visual inspection of various data plots will reveal the proper transformation. It is also relatively easy to try several different standard transformations (e.g., square, square root, or logarithmic) and observe the relative change in the sum of squares attributable to interaction effects.[12] In recent years Anscombe and Tukey (1963) have developed a procedure for estimating a power transform y_t of the form

$$y_t = y^p$$

which will remove what they term removable nonadditivity. The exponent p may take on values which allow most of the transformations frequently encountered in analysis of variance discussions. As the logic of their procedures is somewhat complicated the reader is referred to the original paper for details.

---

[12] It is the relative sum of squares which is relevant because a transformation will usually change the total sum of squares substantially.

As a general guide for deciding when it is appropriate to seek a transformation which will remove interaction effects we offer the following heuristics. First, the interaction effects, before any transformation, should be statistically significant and of sufficient magnitude that they cannot be ignored without substantially impairing the predictive or explanatory power of the model. Second, the simple effect profiles should not cross at any point. If the simple effect profiles cross, the required transformation will be non-monotonic, i.e., the rank order of the observations will not be preserved. In such a case it seems best to regard any interaction as fundamental and not as a measurement artifact. And, third, the simple effect profiles should be relatively smooth so that a relatively simple transformation will suffice.

3-V HYPOTHESES CONCERNING LINEAR COMBINATIONS OF THE COEFFICIENTS OF THE GENERAL LINEAR MODEL

In this section we will discuss mathematical and statistical procedures for testing hypotheses concerning the specific form of the estimated coefficients in $\hat{\theta}$. As we shall see these procedures take many different specific forms, e.g., comparison among treatment means, trend analysis, Newman–Keuls, Scheffé test—ad infinitum. All of these procedures, however, are based on a linear contrast among the coefficients in $\hat{\theta}$.

3-V-1 General Linear Contrasts

A contrast l among the regression coefficients may be defined as

$$l = C_1\hat{\theta}_1 + C_2\hat{\theta}_2 + \cdots + C_m\hat{\theta}_m$$
$$= C'\hat{\theta} \quad (\Sigma C_j = 0) \tag{3-14}$$

where the contrast coefficients C sum to zero. Some elements of C may, of course, be zero. A typical example of a linear contrast would be

$$l = (1)\hat{\alpha}_1 + (-2)\hat{\alpha}_2 + (1)\hat{\alpha}_3 \tag{3-15}$$

Equation (3-15) defines a contrast between $\hat{\alpha}_2$ and the average effect of $\hat{\alpha}_1$ and $\hat{\alpha}_3$. A test of the hypothesis that this contrast is within sampling error of zero is equivalent to testing the hypothesis that $\hat{\alpha}_2$ equals the average of $\hat{\alpha}_1$ and $\hat{\alpha}_3$.

If we let l represent the value of the contrast and l_H represent the hypothesized value of the contrast (which will usually be zero) we need only find the variance of the linear contrast l to construct a significance test. From elementary algebra and basic statistics we know that if every element of a variable is multiplied by a constant the variance of that variable is increased by the square of the constant. Generalizing this principle it is easy to show that the variance of a contrast l is

$$\text{Var}(l) = [C'(X'X)^{-1}C]\hat{\sigma}_\varepsilon^2$$

Combining these results we have the familiar t test with $(N - m)$ degrees of freedom

$$t_{(N-m)} = \frac{l - l_H}{\hat{\sigma}_\varepsilon [C'(X'X)^{-1}C]^{\frac{1}{2}}} \tag{3-16}$$

where $\hat{\sigma}_\varepsilon$ is the square root of the mean square error, i.e., the sample estimate of σ_ε.

We might also note that we can place a confidence interval around l in the same manner as we did with the individual elements in $\hat{\theta}$. In general terms the interval is

$$l \pm \{t_{(N-m)p_l/2} \times \hat{\sigma}_\varepsilon [C'(X'X)^{-1}C]^{\frac{1}{2}}\}$$

To take a simple example, consider the hypothesis that for the data in Table 3-3 $\hat{\alpha}_1 = \hat{\alpha}_2$. Then

$$l = (1)(-4.47) + (-1)(8.73) = -13.20$$
$$l_H = 0 \tag{3-17}$$

$$\text{Var}(l) = (1 \; -1) \begin{bmatrix} 0.0333 & -0.0167 \\ -0.0167 & 0.0333 \end{bmatrix} \begin{pmatrix} 1 \\ -1 \end{pmatrix} = 0.10 \tag{3-18}$$

and

$$t_{(48)} = \frac{-13.20}{(166.17)^{\frac{1}{2}}(0.10)^{\frac{1}{2}}} = -3.24$$

which is significant well beyond the 0.005 level. Note that in Eqs. (3-17) and (3-18) we have omitted zero entries to conserve space.

To take another example, assume that factor A in the illustrative data represents race, where A_2 designates white subjects and A_1 and A_3 designate subjects from two different minority races. The treatment effects clearly suggest the hypothesis that most of the racial effects are accounted for by the difference between the mean effect for minority subjects and the mean effect for white subjects. To test this hypothesis we first define the contrast between the effects for minority and white subjects as

$$l = (1)\hat{\alpha}_1 + (-2)\hat{\alpha}_2 + (1)\hat{\alpha}_3$$
$$= (1)(-4.47) + (-2)(8.73) + (1)(-4.27) = -26.19 \tag{3-19}$$

To use the t test defined in Eq. (3-16) we must modify Eq. (3-19) to reflect the fact that $\hat{\alpha}_3$ is not defined directly but is equal to the negative of $\hat{\alpha}_1 + \hat{\alpha}_2$. Making this substitution into Eq. (3-19) yields

$$l = (1)\hat{\alpha}_1 + (-2)\hat{\alpha}_2 + (1)(-\hat{\alpha}_1 - \hat{\alpha}_2)$$
$$= -3\hat{\alpha}_2$$
$$= -3(8.73) = -26.19$$

which is identical to the value of l derived in Eq. (3-19).

Finding the variance of l is quite easy since it simply equals 9, i.e., the square of the contrast coefficient, times the variance of $\hat{\alpha}_2$. In matrix notation this is

$$\text{Var}(l) = -3[(166.17)(0.0333)] - 3 \tag{3-20}$$
$$= 50.10$$

The number 0.0333 in Eq. (3-20) is the diagonal element of $(X'X)^{-1}$ corresponding to $\hat{\alpha}_2$. Combining Eqs. (3-19) and (3-20) gives a t test of the hypothesis that $\hat{\alpha}_1 + \hat{\alpha}_3$ is not significantly different from $\hat{\alpha}_2$

$$t_{(48)} = \frac{-26.19}{(50.10)^{\frac{1}{2}}} = -3.70$$

which is highly significant.[13]

3-V-2 Orthogonal Contrasts, Degrees of Freedom, and Independent Questions

Many other hypotheses could be suggested, especially if l_H is given values other than zero. The reader, for example, might try to test the hypothesis that $\hat{\alpha}_2 = \hat{\alpha}_3$. The t value for this hypothesis is 3.19.

A very important set of contrasts are known as orthogonal contrasts. The word orthogonal is equivalent to independent and means that each of the contrasts accounts for a different part of the variation in the dependent variable. A complete set of orthogonal contrasts accounts for all variations in the dependent variable. Formally, any two contrasts, C_1 and C_2, are orthogonal if, and only if,

$$\frac{C_{11}C_{21}}{n_1} + \frac{C_{12}C_{22}}{n_2} + \cdots + \frac{C_{1k}C_{2k}}{n_k} = 0 \tag{3-21}$$

where

$$C_1 = C_{11} + C_{12} + \cdots + C_{1k}$$
$$C_2 = C_{21} + C_{22} + \cdots + C_{2k}$$

For equal cell sizes the n's in Eq. (3-21) may be omitted.

To take an example, consider the following four contrasts for the main effects of factor A in our illustrative data

---

[13] Since the inverse of $X'X$ will often not be readily available we note that an equivalent test of a linear contrast is

$$F_{(1, N-m)} = \frac{[n(C_1\hat{\theta}_1 + \cdots C_m\hat{\theta}_m)]^2}{n(C_1^2 + \cdots C_m^2)}$$

The reader may easily verify the equality of this test and the t test in Eq. (3-16) by recalling that

$$t_{(N-m)} = [F_{(1, N-m)}]^{\frac{1}{2}}$$

The formula in this note, however, requires equal cell sizes.

Contrast	$\hat{\alpha}_1$	$\hat{\alpha}_2$	$\hat{\alpha}_3$
1	1	−1	0
2	1	1	−2
3	0	1	−1
4	1	0	−1

Since each α is estimated on the basis of 20 observations we may test each pair of contrasts for orthogonality via Eq. (3-21) with the n's omitted. For l_1 and l_3 this is

$$(1)(0) + (-1)(1) + (0)(-1) = -1$$

which indicates l_1 and l_3 are not orthogonal. The reader may easily verify that only l_1 and l_2 are orthogonal.

That there are only two independent contrasts among the three coefficients for the main effects of factor A is no accident. The number of orthogonal contrasts for a set of coefficients is identically equal to the number of degrees of freedom for the set of coefficients. In effect we may ask one entirely separate and independent question of our data for each degree of freedom. We may ask other questions, but these questions will be, at least partially, merely our old questions rephrased.

3-V-3 Orthogonal Polynomials

When one or more of the experimental factors is an intervally-scaled variable, such as electric shock, advertising expenditure, or person density, it will often be desirable to determine the form of the function linking independent and dependent variables. These techniques fall under a variety of headings such as trend analysis and response surface fitting techniques. In general, all of these techniques represent special applications of the general linear regression techniques discussed fully in Chap. 7. Here we discuss a very special but extremely useful and flexible form of analysis known as orthogonal polynomial or trend analysis. More general methods of fitting response surfaces are described in Chap. 7.

Earlier in this chapter we noted that a factor with p levels could always be represented by a polynomial equation of degree $(p - 1)$, i.e., of degree equal to the number of degrees of freedom for the factor. We now proceed to show how the total sum of squares due a factor may be partitioned into a series of components which represent the *addition* to the explained sum of squares from adding to the model a term which is linear, quadratic, cubic, etc. Although not completely necessary we shall assume that the levels of the factor for which the orthogonal polynomials are being constructed are equally spaced along an intervally-scaled continuum.[14]

---

[14] For procedures when the levels are unequally spaced see Robson (1959). The reader should be careful when using computer programs which provide a polynomial breakdown of the total sum of squares, for these programs assume that the levels of each factor are equally spaced. If this is not true the results will not be meaningful.

3-V-3-1 General logic of orthogonal polynomials Each column of the design matrix X is coded as a contrast between certain parameters in the GLM. The essential logic of the orthogonal polynomial procedure is to find a set of transformations of X which will yield the desired polynomial equation. In the transformed design matrix the first column for the main effects of each factor will carry the contrast coefficients which represent the linear trend in the factor, the second column captures the quadratic trend, and so on. As the mathematics are somewhat complicated we proceed by example. The interested reader is referred to Anderson and Bancroft (1952) for further details.

3-V-3-2 Coding procedures for orthogonal polynomials An extensive table of orthogonal polynomial coefficients is presented in App. B, Table B-7. Table 3-6a excerpts the coefficients necessary to code the illustrative 3 × 4 factorial design

Table 3-6 Orthogonal polynomials for a 3 × 4 factorial design†

(a) Orthogonal polynomial coefficients

Treatment levels	Polynomial trend	Level 1	Level 2	Level 3	Level 4
3	Linear	−1	0	1	
	Quadratic	1	−2	1	
4	Linear	−3	−1	1	3
	Quadratic	1	−1	−1	1
	Cubic	−1	3	−3	1

(b) Orthogonal polynomial coding procedures for main effects

Level of factor A	B	$\hat{\alpha}_1$	$\hat{\alpha}_2$	$\hat{\beta}_1$	$\hat{\beta}_2$	$\hat{\beta}_3$
1	1	−1	1	−3	1	−1
1	2	−1	1	−1	−1	3
1	3	−1	1	1	−1	−3
1	4	−1	1	3	1	1
2	1	0	−2	−3	1	−1
2	2	0	−2	−1	−1	3
2	3	0	−2	1	−1	−3
2	4	0	−2	3	1	1
3	1	1	1	−3	1	−1
3	2	1	1	−1	−1	3
3	3	1	1	1	−1	−3
3	4	1	1	3	1	1

Table 3-6 Continued

(c) Orthogonal coding procedures for interaction effects

Level of factor		Interaction effects coded as orthogonal polynomials					
A	B	$\hat{\alpha\beta}_{11}$	$\hat{\alpha\beta}_{12}$	$\hat{\alpha\beta}_{13}$	$\hat{\alpha\beta}_{21}$	$\hat{\alpha\beta}_{22}$	$\hat{\alpha\beta}_{23}$
1	1	3	−1	1	−3	1	−1
1	2	1	1	−3	−1	−1	3
1	3	−1	1	3	1	−1	−3
1	4	−3	−1	−1	3	1	1
2	1	0	0	0	6	−2	2
2	2	0	0	0	2	2	−6
2	3	0	0	0	−2	2	6
2	4	0	0	0	−6	−2	−2
3	1	−3	1	−1	−3	1	−1
3	2	−1	−1	3	−1	−1	3
3	3	1	−1	−3	1	−1	−3
3	4	3	1	1	3	1	1

† An extensive table of orthogonal polynomials is presented in App. B, Table B-7

used throughout this chapter. Several things about these coefficients are noteworthy. First, the coefficients for a specific trend will be different, depending on the number of levels of each factor. Second, there will be $(k-1)$ trends for a factor with k levels. Third, the number of times the sign of the coefficients change equals the order of the trend, e.g., reading from left to right the sign of the contrast coefficients for the cubic trend changes three times.

Table 3-6b presents the contrast codes for the trends in the main effects for each of the 12 cells in the 3 × 4 factorial design. The column labeled $\hat{\alpha}_1$ carries the linear contrast for factor A. Note that this column is simply the first row in Table 3-6a expanded to reflect the fact that A_1 is observed under each level of factor B. The column $\hat{\alpha}_2$ carries the quadratic contrast for factor A. Note that $\hat{\alpha}_2$ is orthogonal to $\hat{\alpha}_1$. This means that $\hat{\alpha}_2$ captures the increase in explained variation from adding a quadratic term to the assumed structural model.

Somewhat earlier we noted that the graphical equivalent of an interaction effect is the departure of the simple effect lines from being parallel.[15] Here we shall present precise methods for determining exactly how the simple effect lines depart from parallelism. In the simplest case we might ask to what extent the simple effect profiles would be non-parallel if each factor had only a linear trend. Then, just as was done for the main effects, we could add a quadratic trend to one factor and determine the increase in the explained sum of squares due to the interaction effects between the quadratic trends in one factor and the linear trend in another factor. Continuing this logic it may be shown that for our illustrative

---
[15] For a graphical presentation of simple effects see Fig. 3-2 in Sec. 3-III.

3 × 4 design the interaction term has six degrees of freedom which may be decomposed as follows

Interaction between trend in factor		Product of main effects in Table 3-6b		
A	B			
Linear by	linear	$\hat{\alpha}_1$	$\hat{\beta}_1$	(3-22a)
Linear by	quadratic	$\hat{\alpha}_1$	$\hat{\beta}_2$	(3-22b)
Linear by	cubic	$\hat{\alpha}_1$	$\hat{\beta}_3$	(3-22c)
Quadratic by linear		$\hat{\alpha}_2$	$\hat{\beta}_1$	(3-22d)
Quadratic by quadratic		$\hat{\alpha}_2$	$\hat{\beta}_2$	(3-22e)
Quadratic by cubic		$\hat{\alpha}_2$	$\hat{\beta}_3$	(3-22f)

The coefficients necessary to code those six interaction effects are given in Table 3-6c. Note carefully that the linear by linear contrast is simply the product of the coefficients for the main linear effects of A and the main linear effects of B given in Table 3-6b. Each of the other contrasts is similarly defined. This procedure may be directly generalized to interactions of any order.

Each component of the polynomial may be tested for significance by dividing the sum of squares by the mean square error. Since each component has one degree of freedom the result will be distributed as $F_{(1, N-m)}$.

3-V-3-3 Aggregating polynomial trend components Certain aggregations of the decomposed sum of squares represented by Eqs. (3-22) are especially interesting. For example, the sum of (3-22a), (3-22b), and (3-22c) gives the total sum of squares attributable to the fact that the linear trends in the simple effect profiles of factor A at each level of factor B are not parallel. Similarly, the nonparallelism of the quadratic trends in the simple effects of factor A is captured by the remaining three terms. Factor B may be similarly analyzed. Each of these aggregated terms may be tested for significance by dividing the appropriate sum of squares by its degrees of freedom, i.e., the number of terms aggregated, dividing this by the mean square error and determining the significance level for the quantity $F_{(k, N-m)}$, where k is the number of terms in the aggregation.

We have said that trend analysis is meaningful only if the levels of a factor have been drawn from an intervally-scaled variable. The orthogonal contrast coefficients, however, are legitimate even when this is not true. The resulting partition of the sum of squares for the interaction effect will have no intrinsic meeting. The aggregations we spoke of in the above paragraph will have the meanings attributed to them for any factor which is intervally scaled.

3-V-3-4 A comparison of the two dummy variable coding procedures Finally, we should consider the relationship between coding systems presented in Table 3-6a and b, and Table 3-2c. First, $X'X$ will be a diagonal matrix for the orthogonal polynomial coding and hence $(X'X)^{-1}$ will simply be the reciprocal of the elements in $X'X$. For the illustrative data $X'X$ will simply be the sum of squares in each column of Table 3-6b and c multiplied by 5, the number of observations per cell. As an example the second and third diagonal elements of $X'X$, corresponding to $\hat{\alpha}_1$ and $\hat{\alpha}_2$, would be 40 and 120, respectively. Note carefully from Table 3-6b that $\hat{\alpha}_1$ has been coded as a contrast between $\overline{A}_1$ and $\overline{A}_3$. Thus the $X'y$ element corresponding to $\hat{\alpha}_1$ is equal to the sum of the observations in A_3 minus the sum of the observations in A_1. This figure is 4 which when divided by 40 yields $\hat{\alpha}_1 = 0.1$. By a similarly logic $\hat{\alpha}_2 = -4.36$.

Now, if we denote the $\hat{\alpha}$'s as coded in Table 3-2c as $\hat{\alpha}^*$ to distinguish them from the $\hat{\alpha}$'s estimated under the orthogonal polynomial coding system the two sets of coefficients are related as follows

$$\hat{\alpha}_1^* = \hat{\alpha}_1 x_{11} + \hat{\alpha}_2 x_{12} = (0.1)(-1) + (-4.36)(1) = -4.46$$
$$\hat{\alpha}_2^* = \hat{\alpha}_1 x_{21} + \hat{\alpha}_2 x_{22} = (0.1)(0) + (4.36)(-2) = 8.72$$
$$\hat{\alpha}_3^* = \hat{\alpha}_1 x_{31} + \hat{\alpha}_2 x_{32} = (0.1)(1) + (-4.36)(1) = -4.26$$

where x_{ij} references a row corresponding to the ith level of factor A and jth column of the orthogonal polynomial design matrix X. The importance of this relationship between the two coding systems is that it clearly demonstrates that the two systems are displaying the *same* data from two *different* perspectives.

We shall pursue polynomial trend analysis further in Sec. 3-VI which analyzes a somewhat more complex factorial design via packaged computer programs.

3-V-4 A Note on a priori and post hoc Tests of Significance

Implicit in the discussion in Sec. 3-V of this chapter is the assumption that all contrasts were planned before the data was analyzed, i.e., all tests were a priori tests. It should be kept clearly in mind that tests of significance on main effects and interaction effects are also contrasts. To take an extreme example, assume a researcher was interested in the effects of five factors on some behavior but that he had no explicit hypotheses. Now as we said early in this chapter with five factors there are 32 main effects and interaction effects in the structural model[16] to be tested for significance in addition to any other contrasts or polynomial analysis. It may be shown that, under the present conditions, the probability of at least one significant result at the p_1 significance level is given by the formula

$$1 - (1 - p_1)^k$$

where k is the number of significance tests to be made. If $k = 32$ and $p_1 = 0.05$ there is slightly more than a 0.48 probability that at least one test will be significant given the null hypothesis is true for each test. More detailed tests would compound the problem.

---

[16] If the grand mean is included there would be 33 terms.

One implication of the above paragraph is that it is not necessary, and indeed may be undesirable, to test every possible main effect and every possible interaction effect. This is especially true for high order interaction effects which often prove virtually uninterpretable. What is required is very careful consideration of the questions which the research is designed to answer. The resulting a priori questions may then be tested without undue inflation of the significance level from random searching of the data.

With regard to post hoc tests, i.e., those suggested by the data, we may offer a certain heuristic rule. It is often said that post hoc tests should be made on a factor only if the aggregate significance test on that factor is significant. This rule seems much too harsh and even counter-productive. A better rule would be to simply report the observed regularity in the data as a potential hypothesis rather than as a conclusion. Of course, it may also be possible to calculate approximately the actual as opposed to the nominal probability of the result given the null hypothesis. In general, however, we should not ignore results which in hindsight seem plausible simply because we failed to postulate a relevant hypothesis. But we should be certain that we understand that the methodological ground we stand upon may not be terribly firm.

Finally, we note that a great many procedures for testing post hoc hypotheses have been developed in recent years. Some of the more familiar of these are Newman–Kuels, Scheffé, and Duncan tests. Each of these testing procedures is concerned with testing the significance of differences among two or more treatment means. They differ primarily in how each adjusts the significance level to reflect the fact that the tests are post hoc. The reader is cautioned that the adjusting procedures are such that different tests may lead to different results even if the same nominal significance level is used in each test. For further discussion the reader is referred to Winer (1971, pp. 196–201).

3-VI ANALYSIS OF 2 × 3 × 3 FACTORIAL DESIGN USING PACKAGED (CANNED) COMPUTER PROGRAMS

In this section we completely analyze a somewhat more complex factorial design than we have dealt with to this point. No new principles are needed to handle this added complexity. We shall proceed by analyzing the data much as any researcher might; selecting the best computer program for each aspect of the analysis and deriving some useful interpretative data from the computer printouts by hand where this is more convenient than setting up the necessary programs. As we shall see in the following discussion most canned programs have one or more peculiarities which tend to render them uninterpretable to the unitiated. The raw data is presented in Table 3-7.

3-VI-1 Preliminary Analysis

3-VI-1-1 General reasons for preliminary analysis A preliminary data analysis is particularly important when the data is analyzed via computer. First, simple

Table 3-7 Data for $2 \times 3 \times 3$ factorial analysis of variance design

	\multicolumn{3}{c}{A_1}	\multicolumn{3}{c}{A_2}
	B_1	B_2	B_3	B_1	B_2	B_3
C_1	51, 42, 51, 50, 46	86, 81, 80, 79, 90	94, 93, 92, 80, 82	93, 89, 94, 95, 88	57, 51, 63, 53, 60	55, 57, 63, 58, 60
C_2	37, 43, 24, 28, 38	36, 43, 35, 40, 51	47, 57, 52, 51, 52	51, 53, 46, 49, 48	36, 42, 37, 43, 36	38, 34, 30, 23, 32
C_3	17, 15, 13, 15, 25	28, 15, 22, 32, 28	79, 65, 73, 75, 70	63, 71, 67, 66, 68	50, 45, 38, 54, 53	8, 1, 0, 10, 10

coding errors which would be obvious in hand calculations may not be detected in programs which report aggregated results. Coding errors, however, are often highly visible in such simple things as data printouts and such statistics as the minimum and maximum.

Second, it is quite easy to make an error in inputing data into computer programs. Analysis of variance programs, which require each observation to be placed in the proper design cell, are especially prone to this problem. A preliminary calculation of within-cell means, for example, is a good device for preventing such errors since these means may be checked against those printed out by other programs. It is especially important to remember that the more complex the calculations performed by the computer and the less obvious the printed results the greater is the need for such checks to ensure the absence of errors.

Third, and perhaps most importantly, computerized data analysis has tended to place a barrier between the researcher and his data. When calculations are made by hand the researcher is forced to know each individual observation. And in the process of numerous "passes" over the data the researcher may often recognize some peculiar, and often important, pattern in the data which would not be obvious or even present in the results of the analysis for which the computations were being performed. A computer, of course, cannot recognize such patterns unless it is specifically instructed to search for them.

The specific preliminary analyses will depend on the exact nature of the data. Generally, however, we can say that in addition to procedural checks the primary purpose of preliminary data analysis is to give the researcher a "feel" for the data. Thus, in addition to looking for specific patterns, the researcher should attempt to retain a mental openness and flexibility which will help him to recognize the unexpected. A cognitive psychologist would call this the "ah ha!" phenomena, the sudden and somewhat unexplainable recognition of a pattern which in the context of the researcher's accumulated experience "makes sense."

3-VI-1-2 Preliminary analysis of data in Table 3-7 For the present data the preliminary analysis consisted of calculating within-cell means and variances,

Table 3-8 SPSS BREAKDOWN analysis of raw data in Table 3-7

```
VOGELBACK COMPUTING CENTER
NORTHWESTERN UNIVERSITY
S P S S  - -  STATISTICAL PACKAGE FOR THE SOCIAL SCIENCES
VERSION 6.50 -- APRIL 1, 1976


RUN NAME         PRELIMINARY ANALYSIS OF 2 X 3 X 3 FACTORIAL DESIGN
VARIABLE LIST    A,B,C,DEPEN
INPUT MEDIUM     CARD
INPUT FORMAT     FIXED(3F1.0,F3.0/)

ACCORDING TO YOUR INPUT FORMAT, VARIABLES ARE TO BE READ AS FOLLOWS

VARIABLE   FORMAT   RECORD   COLUMNS

 A          F 1.0      1         1
 B          F 1.0      1         2
 C          F 1.0      1         3
 DEPEN      F 3.0      1       4-  6

THE INPUT FORMAT PROVIDES FOR  4 VARIABLES.   4 WILL BE READ
IT PROVIDES FOR  2 RECORDS (*CARDS*) PER CASE.  A MAXIMUM OF   6 *COLUMNS* ARE USED ON A RECORD.

N OF CASES       90
BREAKDOWN        TABLES = DEPEN BY A BY B BY C
STATISTICS       ALL
READ INPUT DATA

GIVEN 3 DIMENSIONS, INITIAL CM ALLOWS FOR  1047 CELLS, MAXIMUM CM ALLOWS FOR  4151 CELLS.
```

PRELIMINARY ANALYSIS OF 2 X 3 X 3 FACTORIAL DESIGN

FILE   NONAME   (CREATION DATE = 02/05/77)   02/05/77   PAGE   2

- - - CRITERION VARIABLE DEPEN - - - D E S C R I P T I O N   O F   S U B P O P U L A T I O N S - - -
BROKEN DOWN BY A
             BY B
             BY C

VARIABLE	CODE	VALUE LABEL	SUM	MEAN	STD DEV	VARIANCE	N
FOR ENTIRE POPULATION			4531.0000	50.3444	23.8069	566.7677	90
A B C	1 1 1		2293.0000	50.9556	24.6825	609.2253	45
C	1		495.0000	33.0000	14.1472	200.1429	15
C	2		248.0000	48.0000	13.9370	15.5000	5
C	3		170.0000	34.0000	7.7782	60.5000	5
B C	1		18.0000	17.0000	4.6904	22.0000	5
B C	2		746.0000	49.7333	26.0068	676.3524	15
C	1		416.0000	83.2000	4.5830	21.0000	5
C	2		205.0000	41.0000	6.4420	41.5000	5
C	3		125.0000	25.0000	6.6332	44.0000	5
B	3		1052.0000	70.1333	17.2373	297.1238	15
C	1		441.0000	88.2000	6.5581	244.2000	5
C	2		249.0000	49.8000	6.0554	36.7000	5
C	3		362.0000	72.4000	5.2726	27.8000	5
A B C	2 1 1		2238.0000	49.7333	23.1609	536.4273	45
C	1		1049.0000	69.9333	18.2044	331.4000	15
C	2		459.0000	91.8000	4.1145	7.7000	5
C	3		245.0000	49.0000	2.9155	8.5000	5
B	2		718.0000	47.8667	8.9751	80.5524	15
C	1		284.0000	56.8000	4.9193	24.2000	5
C	2		194.0000	38.8000	3.4205	11.7000	5
C	3		240.0000	48.0000	6.5955	43.5000	5
B	3		479.0000	31.9333	22.7236	516.3524	15
C	1		293.0000	58.6000	5.0496	19.3000	5
C	2		157.0000	31.4000	5.4498	30.8000	5
C	3		129.0000	25.8000	4.9193	24.2000	5

TOTAL CASES = 90
PRELIMINARY ANALYSIS OF 2 X 3 X 3 FACTORIAL DESIGN

Table 3-9 Descriptive analysis of data in Table 3-7

(a) Within-cell means and variances

	A_1			A_2		
	B_1	B_2	B_3	B_1	B_2	B_3
C_1	48.0† 15.5‡	83.2 21.7	88.2 44.2	91.8 9.7	56.8 24.2	58.6 9.3
C_2	34.0 60.5	41.0 41.5	49.8 36.7	51.4 7.3	38.8 11.7	31.4 30.8
C_3	17.0 22.0	25.0 44.0	72.4 27.8	67.0 8.5	48.0 43.5	5.8 24.2

† Mean. ‡ Variance.

(b) Marginal means

	A_1	A_2
B_1	33.00	69.40
B_2	49.73	47.87
B_3	70.13	31.93
	50.96	49.73

	B_1	B_2	B_3
C_1	69.90	70.00	73.40
C_2	41.70	39.90	40.60
C_3	42.00	36.50	39.10
	51.20	48.80	51.03

	C_1	C_2	C_3
A_1	73.13	41.60	38.13
A_2	69.07	39.87	40.27
	71.10	40.73	39.20

(c) Statistics describing total distribution

Mean	50.34	Range	95.00
Mode	51.00	Variance	566.77
Median	50.50	Standard deviation	23.807

marginal means, and several other simple descriptive statistics. Two programs from the widely distributed Statistical Package for the Social Sciences (SPSS) were used to make these calculations. The SPSS program BREAKDOWN was used to calculate within-cell means and variances. For the present data four variables were input into the BREAKDOWN program. The first three variables give the level of each factor under which the observation was made. The fourth was the dependent variable. BREAKDOWN was instructed to completely cross the data on the first three variables and calculate means, variances, standard deviations, and cell sizes for each cell in the design. A sample of the computer printout is given in Table 3-8.[17] Table 3-9a summarizes the BREAKDOWN analysis. Note that the F_{max} statistic

$$F_{max} = 60.5/7.3 = 8.29$$

[17] It is worth noting that most analysis of variance programs, even those that handle unequal cell sizes, do not calculate within-cell variances. Indeed very few of these programs calculate any quantities which can be used to test the assumptions upon which the analysis is based.

does not even begin to approach significance at $p_1 = 0.05$, indicating the assumption of homogeneity of variance is tenable. Table 3-9b presents marginal means. These means were actually calculated by the analysis of variance programs we shall present shortly. Finally, Table 3-9c presents some general descriptive measures calculated by an SPSS program called CODEBOOK. We shall present a CODEBOOK printout shortly.

3-VI-2 Analysis of Variance

For the analysis of variance and certain related analyses we have used two programs from the widely distributed UCLA BioMedical (BMD) programs. Their characteristics are fairly representative of most analysis of variance programs available at medium to large computer installations.

The first program used in the analysis of variance is the BMD program 10V.[18] This program, which is also called the General Linear Hypothesis, can be used to handle any design we shall consider in this book, including unequal cell size designs and general regression designs. Table 3-10 presents the 10V output.

3-VI-2-1 General information Table 3-10a lists information which partially describes the analysis. The problem code is simply a label. When a large number of computer runs are to be made it is important that the output of each run be carefully labeled. No covariates were used in this run. Skipping the dummy variable cards the next two lines indicate there were 90 observations and three factors (indices) in this problem.

As given in Table 3-10a, to analyze this particular problem required eight so-called dummy variable cards. Each of these cards describes one source of variation of the data. Each source of variation is described by the degrees of freedom it receives from each factor as follows

Source of variation	Degrees of freedom attributable to factor		
	A	B	C
Mean			
A	1		
B		2	
C			2
AB	1	2	
AC	1		2
BC		2	2
ABC	1	2	2

Note that the product of the entries in each row gives the degrees of freedom for each source of variation, i.e., for each component in the structural model

---

[18] In earlier releases of the BMD programs 10V was labeled X64.

Table 3-10 BMD10V analysis of $2 \times 3 \times 3$ factorial design data in Table 3-7

(c)

ANALYSIS OF VARIANCE TABLE

SOURCE	SUM OF SQUARES	D.F.	MEAN SQUARE	F
MEAN	228110.67778	1	228110.67778	8499.25937†
A	33.61111	1	33.61111	1.25233
B	107.75556	2	53.87778	2.00745
AB	1342.02222	2	971.01111	36.80625†
C	20874.02222	2	10437.01111	388.87642†
AC	147.08889	2	73.54444	2.74022
BC	139.51111	4	34.87778	1.29952
ABC	7786.97778	4	1946.74444	72.53446†
ERROR	1932.40000	72	26.83889	

(d)

CELL INDICES	CELL SIZE	PREDICTED VALUE	GENERATED VARIABLES

† $p_i < 0.001$.

except the error variance which is calculated as a residual. This procedure is particularly useful because it allows us easily to construct any reduced form model we might be interested in. By reduced form we mean a model with fewer than all components in the full structural model.

Finally note the variable format card. The entry 3F1.0 tells us the first three columns of each data card contain three variables each of which is allocated one column with zero points to the right of the decimal point. These variables are the treatment levels of the factors *A*, *B*, and *C*, respectively, which informs the program of the cell into which the observation should be placed. The major advantage of this input procedure is that it eliminates the need to have the data in a precise order. 1X instructs the computer to skip the next spaces and F2.0 describes the location of the dependent variable which is located in columns 6 and 7 of each data card. For more detailed descriptions of (data) input format statements the reader is referred to any good manual on the FORTRAN computer language.

3-VI-2-2 Sum of squares and tests of significance Table 3-10c presents the sum of squares, degrees of freedom, mean square, and *F* ratio for each component of the structural model. Significance values are given by an appended table note. The *F* ratios for the Mean, *C*, *AB*, and *ABC* are highly significant. No other *F* ratios reached the $p_I = 0.05$ significance level.

3-VI-2-3 Analysis of errors Table 3-11 presents a CODEBOOK analysis of the residual error term. By definition, the mean of the errors is zero. The mode, median, and skewness information describe central location and skewness of the errors. From Chap. 2, however, we know that the skewness has little effect on the actual significance level. The kurtosis value[19] of -0.604 indicates the error distribution is somewhat flat. Reference to Tables 2-2–2-8 and Figs. 2-7–2-9 indicates this should have the effect of raising the actual significance level very slightly, e.g., 0.055 to 0.06 for a nominal p_I value of 0.05.

3-VI-2-4 Regression coefficients Table 3-10b gives the regression coefficients for a series of hypotheses that a particular component of the structural model is zero. This is the same as dropping that component from the model. The last column, labeled NONE, gives the regression coefficients when all components specified by the dummy variable cards are included in the model.

The first entry under the column NONE is the grand mean μ. The second is $\hat{\alpha}_1$. The term $\hat{\alpha}_2$ is not given directly but is easily found since $\hat{\alpha}_2 = -\hat{\alpha}_1 = -0.61111$. The effects for *B* and *C* are similarly defined. The terms for the *AB*

---

[19] The kurtosis value of the normal distribution as calculated by CODEBOOK is 0. The reader is reminded that the two definitions of kurtosis differ by 3. Care should be taken to determine which definition is being used.

Table 3-11 CODEBOOK analysis of the residual error term

```
RUN NAME         ANALYSIS OF RESIDUAL ERROR FOR 2 X 3 X 3 FACTORIAL DESIGN
VARIABLE LIST    RESID
INPUT MEDIUM     CARD
INPUT FORMAT     FIXED(/7X,F5.0)

ACCORDING TO YOUR INPUT FORMAT, VARIABLES ARE TO BE READ AS FOLLOWS

VARIABLE   FORMAT   RECORD   COLUMNS

RESID      F  5. 0     2      8-  12

THE INPUT FORMAT PROVIDES FOR   1 VARIABLES.   1 WILL BE READ
IT PROVIDES FOR  2 RECORDS (*CARDS*) PER CASE.  A MAXIMUM OF  12 *COLUMNS* ARE USED ON A RECORD.

         N OF CASES       90
         FREQUENCIES      GENERAL = RESID
         STATISTICS       ALL
         READ INPUT DATA

FREQUENCIES - INITIAL CM ALLOWS FOR  2745 VALUES, MAXIMUM CM ALLOWS FOR 11022 VALUES.

    MEAN          .000          STD ERR        .491        MEDIAN         .300
    MODE         3.000          STD DEV       4.660        VARIANCE     21.712
    KURTOSIS     -.604          SKEWNESS      -.195        RANGE        20.000
    MINIMUM    -10.000          MAXIMUM      10.000        SUM            .000
    C.V. PCT  .6148E+17         .95 C.I.      -.976   TO    .976

    VALID CASES     90          MISSING CASES     0
```

interaction may be found as follows

	B_1	B_2	B_3
A_1	−18.81	0.32	18.49
A_2	18.81	−0.32	−18.49

where $\widehat{\alpha\beta}_{11}$ and $\widehat{\alpha\beta}_{12}$ are given by the seventh and eighth columns under NONE and the remaining coefficients follow from the restriction that the coefficients in each row and column sum to zero.

The terms for the ABC interaction may be found as follows

| | A_1 ||| A_2 |||
	B_1	B_2	B_3	B_1	B_2	B_3
C_1	−5.12	10.84	−5.72	5.12	−10.84	5.72
C_2	10.24	−0.09	−10.15	−10.24	0.09	10.15
C_3	−5.12	−10.75	15.87	5.12	10.75	−15.87

where the four terms bracketed by the heavy lines are given directly and the remaining 14 terms follow from the restrictions that the effects sum to zero across each factor. Note carefully the order of the last four terms under the column NONE. They are $\widehat{\alpha\beta\gamma}_{111}$, $\widehat{\alpha\beta\gamma}_{121}$, $\widehat{\alpha\beta\gamma}_{112}$, and $\widehat{\alpha\beta\gamma}_{122}$, which is probably not the order the reader would have guessed since the middle subscript is changing fastest. We shall comment further on this shortly; the immediate point is to alert the reader to the fact that the output may often not be in the format expected.

3-VI-2-5 Predicted dependent variable Table 3-10d gives the predicted value of the dependent variable for each of the 18 design cells. Note that the predicted value is simply the cell mean. The independent variables are presented under the heading GENERATED VARIABLES. By generated it is meant that the computer generates these dummy variables on the basis of instructions given via the dummy variable cards. The generated variables, of course, are simply the design matrix X for a $2 \times 3 \times 3$ factorial design.

3-VI-3 Orthogonal Polynomial Analysis

3-VI-3-1 General comments In this section we use trend analysis to investigate the pattern of the coefficients for each effect found significant. The particular procedures we shall use require (1) that the levels of each factor be drawn from an underlying intervally-scaled variable, and (2) that the levels be equally spaced.

The first program we shall use is the BMD program 02V. The output of this program is somewhat more readable than 10V but the program does have a number of peculiarities. The most notable of these is the requirement that each replication of the design be read in sequentially. Typically our data will not be arranged this way.

The 02V program has one particular feature, however, which makes it ideally suited to the present purposes. This program will automatically perform an orthogonal polynomial analysis for up to four factors and all two-way interactions between the designated factors. Table 3-12 presents the 02V output with only a few labels added (see pages 102 and 103).

Section (a) presents identifying information; section (b) presents the standard analysis of variance table. For some unknown reason the programmers chose not to compute the relevant F ratios.

3-VI-3-2 Orthogonal polynomial analysis for main effects Table 3-12c presents the polynomial partition of the sum of squares attributed to each of the three main effects. With two levels all the variance accounted for by factor A is attributable to the linear trend since a straight line will always fit two points. Skipping to factor C we see that almost 79 percent of the sum of squares due to C is attributable to the linear trend in C. This strong linear trend is clearly evident in Fig. 3-3 which plots the means for each level of C. Note that $\bar{C}_2$ and $\bar{C}_3$ are virtually indistinguishable. If C were a nominal variable this might suggest a taxonomic dichotomy between C_1 versus C_2 and C_3.

3-VI-3-3 Orthogonal polynomial analysis for two-way effects Table 3-12, sections (d) through (f), present the orthogonal polynomial analysis for each of the three two-way interaction effects. Each of these sections is identical and each consists of three separate parts. We shall discuss only the AB interaction here as it was the only significant two-way interaction.

The first of the three sub-tables in Table 3-12d gives the total sum of squares

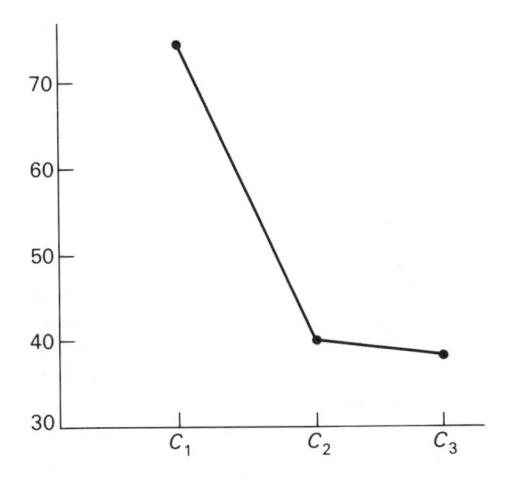

Figure 3-3 Main effects of factor C.

Table 3-12 Polynomial trend analysis of main effects and two-way interaction effects of data in Table 3-7

```
BMD02V - ANALYSIS OF VARIANCE FOR FACTORIAL DESIGN - REVISED FEBRUARY 3, 1972
HEALTH SCIENCES COMPUTING FACILITY, UCLA
```

(a) PROBLEM NO. 1

```
NUMBER OF VARIABLES      3
NUMBER OF REPLICATES     5
VARIABLE   NO. OF LEVELS
   1(A)           2
   2(B)           3
   3(C)           3
VARIABLE FORMAT CARD(S)
(3X,F3.0/)
```

GRAND MEAN   50.34444

(b)
SOURCE OF VARIATION	DEGREES OF FREEDOM	SUMS OF SQUARES	MEAN SQUARES
1(A)	1	33.61111	33.61111
2(B)	2	107.75556	53.87778
3(C)	2	19420.95556	9710.47778
12(AB)	2	20874.02222	10437.01111
13(AC)	2	147.08889	73.54444
23(BC)	4	139.51111	34.87778
123(ABC)	4	7786.97778	1946.74444
WITHIN REPLICATES	72	1932.40000	25.83889
TOTAL	89	50442.32222	

(c) ORDERED VARIABLES...   1   2   3

```
1  LINEAR       33.61111
1  TOTAL        33.61111

2  LINEAR       107.41667
2  QUADRATIC       .33889
2  TOTAL        107.75556

3  LINEAR     15264.15000
3  QUADRATIC   4156.80556
3  TOTAL      19420.95556
```

(d)
VARIABLE 1 ORDERED	LINEAR	QUADRATIC	VARIABLE 2 ORDERED CUBIC	REMAINDER	TOTAL
LINEAR	20869.35000	4.67222	.00000	-.00000	20874.02222
QUADRATIC	.00000	.00000	.00000	.00000	.00000
CUBIC	.00000	.00000	.00000	.00000	.00000
REMAINDER	.00000	.00000	.00000	-.00000	.00000
TOTAL	20869.35000	4.67222	.00000	-.00000	20874.02222

TABLE OF INTERACTIONS FOR
VARIABLE 1 (ROW)
VARIABLE 2 (COLUMN)

FACTORIAL ANALYSIS OF VARIANCE DESIGNS 103

```
           -18.81111     -.32222   18.48889
           -18.81111     -.32222  -18.48889
          TABLE OF MEANS
             .85556    -1.54444      .68889

           33.00000    49.73333   70.13333        .61111                                           VARIABLE 3 ORDERED
           69.40000    47.86667   31.93333       -.61111                           QUADRATIC       CUBIC       REMAINDER      TOTAL

           51.20000    48.80000   51.03333      50.34444                             2.93889       .00000       .00000      147.08889
                                                                                      .00000       .00000       .00000          .00000
(e) VARIABLE 1 ORDERED           LINEAR                                               .00000       .00000       .00000          .00000
         LINEAR                144.15000       50.95556
         QUADRATIC                 .00000      49.73333                              2.93889       .00000       .00000      147.08889
         CUBIC                     .00000
         REMAINDER                 .00000      50.34444
         TOTAL                  144.15000
    TABLE OF INTERACTIONS FOR
         VARIABLE 1 (ROW)
         VARIABLE 3 (COLUMN)
            1.42222    -.25556   -1.67778        .61111
           -1.42222    -.25556    1.67778       -.61111

           20.75556    -9.61111  -11.14444      50.34444
    TABLE OF MEANS
           73.13333    41.60000   38.13333      50.95556
           63.06667    39.86667   40.26667      49.73333

           71.10000    40.73333   39.20000      50.34444

                                                                                                   VARIABLE 3 ORDERED
                                                 QUADRATIC                         QUADRATIC       CUBIC       REMAINDER      TOTAL

(f) VARIABLE 2 ORDERED           LINEAR           6.53333                             .00000       .00000       .00000      108.93333
         LINEAR                102.40000         11.37778                             .00000       .00000       .00000       30.57778
         QUADRATIC              19.20000           .00000                             .00000       .00000       .00000          .00000
         CUBIC                     .00000         17.91111                            .00000       .00000       .00000      139.51111
         REMAINDER                 .00000
         TOTAL                  121.60000
    TABLE OF INTERACTIONS FOR
         VARIABLE 2 (ROW)
         VARIABLE 3 (COLUMN)
           -2.05556      .11111    1.94444        .85556
             .44444      .71111   -1.15556      -1.54444
            1.61111     -.82222    -.78889        .68889

           20.75556    -9.61111  -11.14444      50.34444
    TABLE OF MEANS
           69.90000    41.70000   42.00000      51.20000
           70.00000    39.90000   36.50000      46.80000
           73.40000    40.60000   39.10000      51.03333

           71.10000    40.73333   39.20000      50.34444
```

104 THE GENERAL LINEAR MODEL

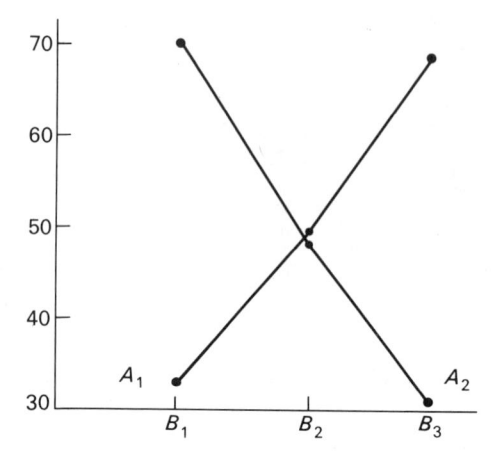

Figure 3-4 AB interaction effect.

due the AB interaction effect broken down by the interaction between the linear, quadratic, and cubic trends in factor A and the same trends in factor B. As A has two levels and B three levels the AB interaction is completely accounted for by a linear (A) by linear (B) interaction and a linear (A) by quadratic (B) interaction. Note that virtually all the AB effect is attributable to the relatively simple linear by linear effect.

Figure 3-4 graphs the AB cell means. These may be found in the third sub-table of Table 3-12d. Note that the simple effects for factor B at A_1 and A_2 form almost a perfect X. This is the geometric form of a two-way interaction where the interaction is accounted for primarily by linear trends in each of the two factors. Finally note that the second sub-table of Table 3-12d gives the treatment effects for the main effects of A, B, and the AB interaction. Carefully compare this sub-table with regression coefficients for the 10V program.

3-VI-3-4 Orthogonal polynomial analysis for three-way and higher interaction effects
The three-way interaction term may be partitioned into the following four trend components

A	B	C
Linear by	linear	by linear
Linear by	linear	by quadratic
Linear by	quadratic	by linear
Linear by	quadratic	by quadratic

Unfortunately the BMD program 02V does not provide such analysis of interaction terms involving more than two factors. The BMD program 10V or X64, however, allows for a general linear contrast of the form

$$C'\hat{\theta} = C_1\hat{\theta}_1 + \cdots + C_m\hat{\theta}_m = k$$

where C_i are the contrast coefficients and k is a constant which will usually be zero. In the present case we will need four sets of contrasts, one for each of the four trends specified in the above paragraph. To see how these orthogonal polynomial coefficients are obtained refer to Table 3-13. The first three columns give the levels for each of the 18 cells in the design. The next five columns give the orthogonal polynomial coefficients for the linear trend in A, the linear and quadratic trends in B, and the linear and quadratic trends in C, respectively. The coefficients for the linear by linear by linear trend are simply the product of the coefficients under α_1, β_1, and γ_1, i.e., the product of the linear trends for the main effects of each factor. The three other sets of coefficients are similarly defined. This procedure holds for any number of factors.

As we have already seen there are 18 three-way interaction terms of which only four are independent. To use X64 for the present analysis we must have a set of orthogonal polynomial coefficients defined in terms of the four independent three-way interaction effects. To see how this is done first write the following

Table 3-13 Orthogonal polynomial coefficients for three-way interaction

Levels of factor			Coefficients for main effects					Coefficients for interaction effects			
A	B	C	$\alpha_1{}^a$	$\beta_1{}^a$	$\beta_2{}^b$	$\gamma_1{}^a$	$\gamma_2{}^b$	$\alpha\beta\gamma_{111}{}^c$	$\alpha\beta\gamma_{112}{}^d$	$\alpha\beta\gamma_{121}{}^e$	$\alpha\beta\gamma_{122}{}^f$
1	1	1	−1	−1	1	−1	1	−1	1	1	−1
1	1	2	−1	−1	1	0	−2	0	−2	0	2
1	1	3	−1	−1	1	1	1	1	1	−1	−1
1	2	1	−1	0	−2	−1	1	0	0	−2	2
1	2	2	−1	0	−2	0	−2	0	0	0	−4
1	2	3	−1	0	−2	1	1	0	0	2	2
1	3	1	−1	1	1	−1	1	1	−1	1	−1
1	3	2	−1	1	1	0	−2	0	2	0	2
1	3	3	−1	1	1	1	1	−1	−1	−1	−1
2	1	1	1	−1	1	−1	1	1	−1	−1	1
2	1	2	1	−1	1	0	−2	0	2	0	−2
2	1	3	1	−1	1	1	1	−1	−1	1	1
2	2	1	1	0	−2	−1	1	0	0	2	−2
2	2	2	1	0	−2	0	−2	0	0	0	4
2	2	3	1	0	−2	1	1	0	0	−2	−2
2	3	1	1	1	1	−1	1	−1	1	−1	1
2	3	2	1	1	1	0	−2	0	−2	0	−2
2	3	3	1	1	1	1	1	1	1	1	1

Note: all interaction terms involve a linear trend in factor A. This has been omitted in the following labels since it is constant for each three-way interaction.

[a] Linear trend; [b] quadratic trend; [c] linear by linear; [d] linear (B) by quadratic (C); [e] quadratic (B) by linear (C); [f] quadratic by quadratic.

106 THE GENERAL LINEAR MODEL

equation for the linear by linear by linear contrast

$$
\begin{aligned}
&(-1)\alpha\beta\gamma_{111} + (0)\alpha\beta\gamma_{112} + (1)\alpha\beta\gamma_{113} \\
&+ (0)\alpha\beta\gamma_{121} + (0)\alpha\beta\gamma_{122} + (0)\alpha\beta\gamma_{123} \\
&+ (1)\alpha\beta\gamma_{131} + (0)\alpha\beta\gamma_{132} + (-1)\alpha\beta\gamma_{133} \\
&+ (1)\alpha\beta\gamma_{211} + (0)\alpha\beta\gamma_{212} + (-1)\alpha\beta\gamma_{213} \\
&+ (0)\alpha\beta\gamma_{221} + (0)\alpha\beta\gamma_{222} + (0)\alpha\beta\gamma_{223} \\
&+(-1)\alpha\beta\gamma_{231} + (0)\alpha\beta\gamma_{232} + (1)\alpha\beta\gamma_{233}
\end{aligned} \tag{3-23}
$$

The numbers in brackets are simply the polynomial coefficients for the linear by linear by linear contrast which were copied from the ninth column of Table 3-13. As the first simplification step note that since factor A has only two levels the last three lines in Eq. (3-23) are the same as the first three lines. This follows from the fact that the coefficients sum to zero across each factor, e.g., $\alpha\beta\gamma_{111} = -\alpha\beta\gamma_{211}$, and each pair of coefficients which have the same subscripts for all factors except A are modified by the same absolute coefficient with one positive and one negative, e.g.,

$$
\begin{aligned}
(-1)\alpha\beta\gamma_{111} &= (1)(\alpha\beta\gamma_{211}) \\
-\alpha\beta\gamma_{111} &= (1)(-\alpha\beta\gamma_{111}) \\
-\alpha\beta\gamma_{111} &= -\alpha\beta\gamma_{111}
\end{aligned}
$$

The next step is to find the definitional relation between each interaction effect and the four independent effects, i.e., 14 of the 18 effects may be defined as linear combinations of the four independent effects. These may then be substituted into the first three lines of Eq. (3-23) and the result multiplied by two to give the coefficients needed for the linear by linear by linear contrast as follows

$$
2 \begin{bmatrix}
(-1)\alpha\beta\gamma_{111} + (0)\alpha\beta\gamma_{112} + (1)(-\alpha\beta\gamma_{111} - \alpha\beta\gamma_{112}) \\
(0)\alpha\beta\gamma_{121} + (0)\alpha\beta\gamma_{122} + (0)(-\alpha\beta\gamma_{121} - \alpha\beta\gamma_{122}) \\
(1)(-\alpha\beta\gamma_{111} - \alpha\beta\gamma_{121}) + (0)(-\alpha\beta\gamma_{112} - \alpha\beta\gamma_{122}) \\
(-1)(\alpha\beta\gamma_{111} + \alpha\beta\gamma_{112} + \alpha\beta\gamma_{121} + \alpha\beta\gamma_{122})
\end{bmatrix} \tag{3-24}
$$

Consolidating terms yields

$$(-4)\alpha\beta\gamma_{111} + (-2)\alpha\beta\gamma_{112} + (-2)\alpha\beta\gamma_{121} + (-1)\alpha\beta\gamma_{122}$$

The remaining three sets of coefficients may be found by substituting the coefficients from each column of Table 3-13 into Eq. (3-24) and collecting terms. The reader may easily verify that these coefficients are[20]

---

[20] As it is only the relative magnitude of the coefficients which is important each row may be divided by a constant to yield smaller absolute contrast coefficients.

A	B	C	$\alpha\beta\gamma_{111}$	$\alpha\beta\gamma_{112}$	$\alpha\beta\gamma_{121}$	$\alpha\beta\gamma_{122}$
Linear	Linear	Linear	−4	−2	−2	−1
Linear	Linear	Quadratic	0	−12	0	−6
Linear	Quadratic	Linear	0	0	−12	−6
Linear	Quadratic	Quadratic	0	0	0	−18

Table 3-14 presents the analysis. Sections (a) and (d) of this table are exactly the same as in Table 3-10. Five extra rows appear in section (c). The first, (L–C), is the sum of squares accounted for by the linear trend in factor C. This contrast was included as a check. Note that it is, within rounding error, equal to the linear trend calculated in Table 3-12. The next four rows give the sum of squares attributable to the following trends

A	B	C	Coded as	Sum of Squares
Linear	Linear	Linear	L–L	1166.40
Linear	Linear	Quadratic	L–Q	3499.20
Linear	Quadratic	Linear	Q–L	3121.20
Linear	Quadratic	Quadratic	Q–Q	0.18

These four contrasts, of course, sum to the ABC sum of squares (7,786.98). With the exception of Q–Q all trends are highly significant.

Figure 3-5 summarizes these relationships graphically. First, note from the first three panels the strong linear trend for factor C with the means for C_2 and C_3 being very close. Notice also that there is relatively little variance within level C_2. Second, note the last panel which gives the AB means averaged over each level of factor C. Again we can clearly see the interaction between the linear trends in factors A and B. It is also evident from this panel that there are no main effects for either factors A or B.

A three-way interaction effect exists whenever the simple AB interaction effect lines for each level of factor C are not parallel to the AB interaction effect averaged over all levels of C.[21] We have already noted that factor C is characterized by a strong linear trend and somewhat weaker quadratic trend. From Fig. 3-5 we can see that factor B also has a strong linear trend and a somewhat weaker quadratic trend within each level of factor C. Note that the quadratic trend in B occurs primarily at level C_1. From Table 3-14 we can determine the extent to which this non-parallelism is attributable to interactions among different simple effect trends.

Finally, Fig. 3-6 presents the response surface for the data. Close inspection of this figure reveals all of the relationships described in the above two paragraphs.

---

[21] This statement will also hold for either the AC interaction at each level of B or the BC interaction at each level of A.

Table 3-14 BMDX64 analysis of 2 × 3 × 3 factorial design with polynomial breakdown of three-way interaction

FACTORIAL ANALYSIS OF VARIANCE DESIGNS 109

(c)

```
11   -2.05556  -2.05556  -2.05556  -2.05556  -2.05556
12      .44444     .44444     .44444     .44444     .44444
13      .11112     .11110     .11110     .11110     .11112
14      .17778     .02222     .17778     .11110     .22224
15     -5.04444  -10.04444   -5.04444   -5.04444   -5.04444
16     10.24444   10.04444   10.24444   10.24444   10.24444
17     -1.08889   -1.08889   -1.08889   -1.08889   -1.08889
18
TOLERANCE .56250    .56250     .56250     .56250     .56250
```

ANALYSIS OF VARIANCE TABLE

SOURCE	SUM OF SQUARES	D.F.	MEAN SQUARE	F
MEAN	228110.67778	1	228110.67778	8499.25937
A	333.77778	1	333.77778	12.09735
B	197.55556	2	97.75555...	...
AB	19420.22222	2	10437....	361.06242
C	2087.02222	2	104...	388.87640
AC	139.77778	4	34.9...	12.34952
BC	1786.97778	4	73.87...	...
ABC	15264.15000	4	1526...	568.73256
L1-C	114.99999	1	114.99999	4.37738
Q-C	3121.17778	1	3121.17778	130.13934
L-Q	1932.40000	1	...	1116....
ERROR	1932.40000	72	26.83883	.06662
```

(d)

CELL CELL PREDICTED GENERATED
SIZE INDICES VALUE VARIABLES

(A large block of generated predicted values and coded ±1/0 design variables follows.)
```

110 THE GENERAL LINEAR MODEL

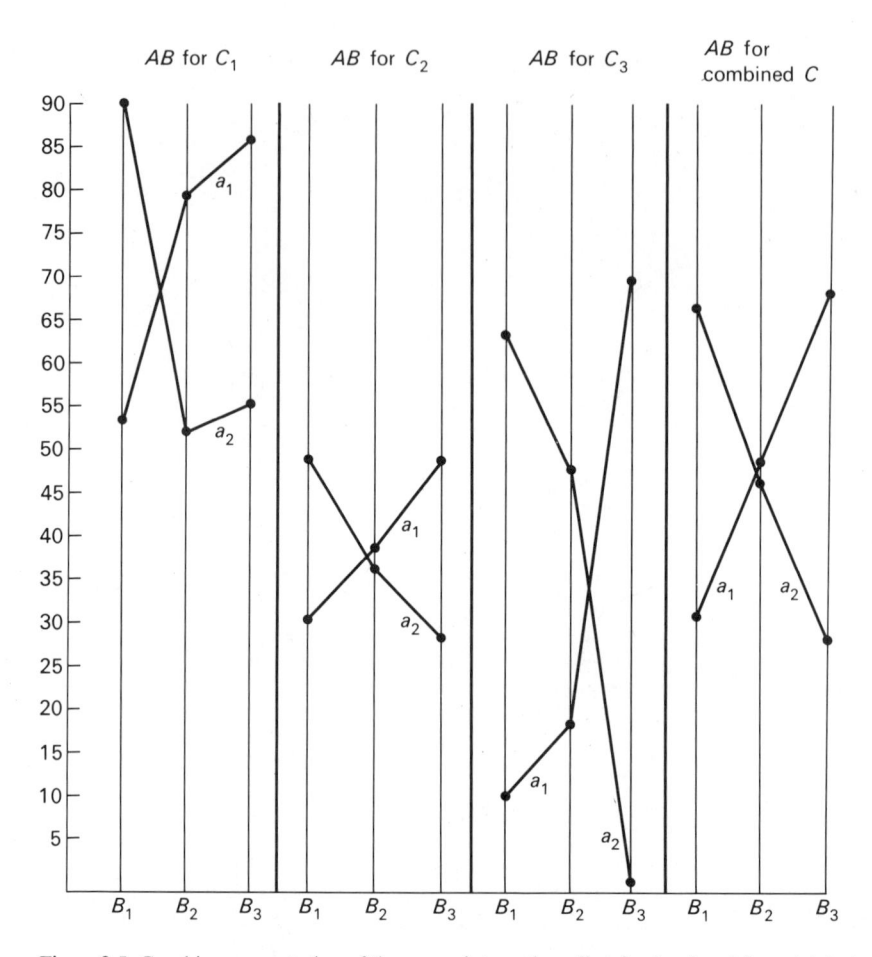

Figure 3-5 Graphic representation of three-way interaction effect for 2 × 3 × 3 factorial design.

Notice the roller coaster effect as one moves from the upper left-hand corner to the lower right-hand corner. The data can, of course, be pictured in many different ways. For the present data Fig. 3-5 is the most revealing.

3-VI-3-5 Reduced form structural model In concluding this section we should note that the complete structural model, ignoring the error term, for a 2 × 3 × 3 factorial design contains 18 terms. On the basis of our polynomial analysis we were able to reduce this to a much simpler and more interpretable seven terms: a grand mean; a linear and quadratic trend in C (which could be reduced to a single term if we could justify aggregating C_2 and C_3); a linear by linear interaction in the AB interaction terms; and a relatively complex ABC interaction effect requiring three terms. Further response surface analysis might reveal even more compact structural models which would adequately represent the data.

3-VI-4 Reader Test Problem

Table 3-15 presents data for a 3 × 3 factorial which the reader is encouraged to work through as a test problem. Sufficient data is provided for the reader to check his work.

3-VII VARIATIONS ON THE FACTORIAL DESIGN

3-VII-1 Single Factor Designs

We have not discussed single factor designs in this chapter because we presume some familiarity with analysis of variance techniques. Everything discussed in this chapter applies to single factor designs. Indeed, as we saw in the previous section,

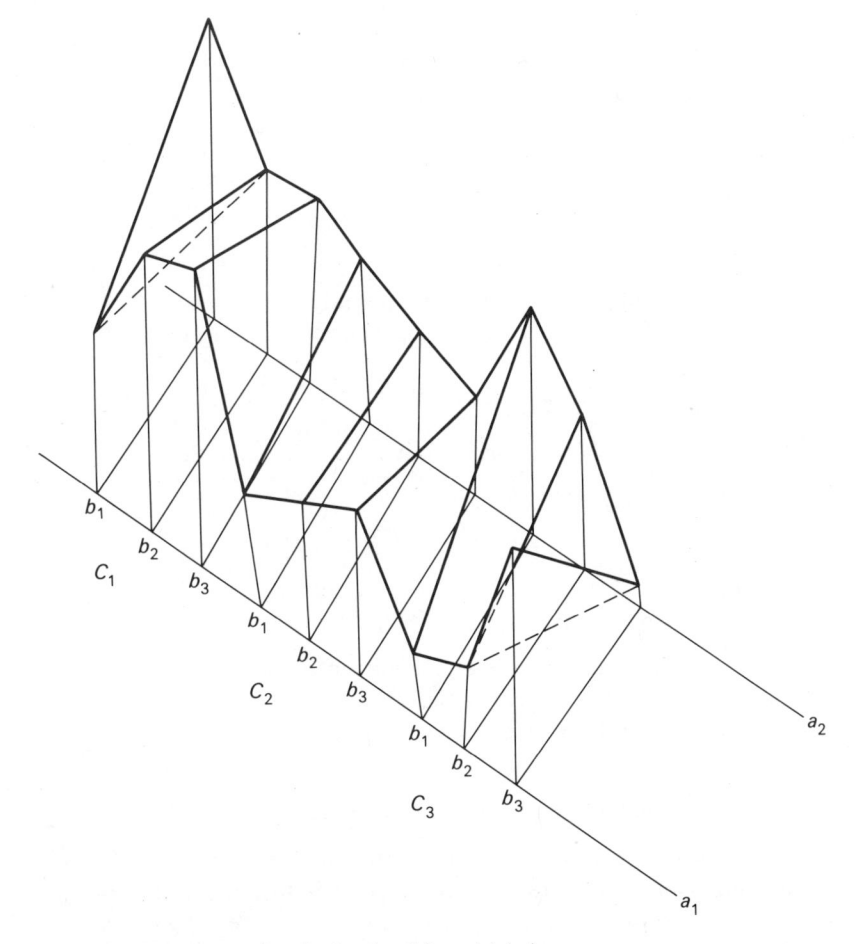

Figure 3-6 Response surface for 2 × 3 × 3 factorial design.

Table 3-15 Reader test problem

(a) Data

	B_1	B_2	B_3
A_1	95, 104, 82, 98, 76	52, 79, 78, 66, 62	98, 90, 101, 97, 84
A_2	84, 81, 83, 92, 106	54, 43, 59, 44, 68	84, 63, 82, 88, 86
A_3	62, 73, 76, 64, 59	46, 31, 46, 31, 29	78, 69, 81, 76, 58

(b) Answers

Anova table and power

Source of variation	Degrees of freedom	Mean square	Power†
A	2	2492.87	~1
B	2	4440.20	~1
AB	4	100.27	0.14
Error	36	93.49	

Polynomial trend analysis—sum of squares

A—Linear	4889.63	B—Linear	0.00
Quadratic	96.10	Quadratic	8880.40

AB—

	B Linear	B Quadratic
A Linear	8.45	104.02
A Quadratic	277.35	11.25

† Assuming $p_1 = 0.01$.

the *only* effect of omitting a factor is that the sum of squares and degrees of freedom for that factor will be lodged in the residual error term. Remember, however, that this will be true only when all factors are orthogonal.

3-VII-2 Randomized Blocks—the Logic of Causal and Associative Models

The so-called randomized blocks design is often presented in a separate chapter, sometimes following, but more often preceding, the first chapter on factorial designs. In these designs subjects are aggregated on some basis, e.g., age, race, sex, personality, etc., which is called the blocking factor. Within blocks the treatments are randomly assigned to subjects. Thus the design is fully crossed. The practical importance of this is that *computationally* the randomized blocks design is identical to the corresponding factorial design except that one factor is now called a block.

The logic underlying the two types of independent variables and the interpretation of the data analysis results, however, are quite different. In the case of a true experimental factor treatments are *randomly* assigned to subjects. It is the randomization procedure which allows us to interpret a significant result as indicating a causal relationship between the experimental factor and the dependent variable. Another way of putting this is to say that randomization allows us to probabilistically equate pre-experimental groups receiving different treatments. That is, we can say that the experimental groups differ systematically only in terms of the treatments they receive. Since the groups are equivalent, except for treatments, the treatment difference is the most probable cause of the observed differences in the dependent variable between subjects in different treatments.[22]

Such a causal interpretation is not possible for blocking variables. This is because we can never be sure that the blocking variable is not just a surrogate for a presumably more fundamental variable which is the true causal influence. To take a trivial example, there is a measurable relationship between the rate at which ice cream cones melt in New York City and the death rate in India. Both, of course, are related to a third variable—temperature.

To take a more important case, researchers often block subjects by sex. When they find, for example, that females are typically less aggressive than males to what can they attribute this behavior? Is it because typically females are not as strong physically as males? Is it due to some genetically based emotional influence, or perhaps to some complex social conditioning process? The fact of the matter is that *the procedure* for blocking does not allow the cause to be isolated.[23] All that can be said is that sex and aggression are empirically associated. What the blocking does do is remove from the error sum of squares the variance accounted for by the blocking factor. There is also a corresponding loss of degrees of freedom from the error term. This gives a more sensitive test on the treatment effects of the experimental factor by reducing the mean square error.

3-VII-3 Advanced Designs

Finally, as we shall see in the following chapters, more advanced designs may be basically regarded as modifications of the basic factorial design presented in this chapter.

---

[22] Randomization is the sine qua non of true experimentation. For a thorough discussion of randomization see Cox (1958), Chap. 5. Campbell and Stanley (1966) describe methods for dealing with situations where only partial randomization is possible. Finally, we should note that randomization provides a partial rationale for dispensing with the normal theory assumptions. For details on this latter point see Scheffé (1959), Chap. 9.

[23] The situation is not quite as bleak as this simple statement indicates. For procedures for making causal inferences from non-experimental data see Blalock (1961).

3-VIII SUMMARY

This chapter has investigated the properties of factorial analysis of variance designs. The chapter has been rather long because most of the relationships developed for factorial designs apply, usually with only minor modifications, to all analysis of variance designs. Indeed, as shall become evident in the next several chapters, the factorial design is really the parent of more advanced designs. Table 3-16 summarizes the major equations developed in this chapter.

Table 3-16 Summary of most important equations in Chap. 3

Hypothesis test of single GLM parameter

$$t_{(N-m)} = \frac{\hat{\theta}_i - \theta_{iH}}{\hat{\sigma}_\varepsilon (C_{ii})^{\frac{1}{2}}}$$

Confidence interval for single GLM parameter

$$\hat{\theta}_i \pm [t_{(N-m)p_l/2} \times \hat{\sigma}_\varepsilon (C_{ii})^{\frac{1}{2}}]$$

Linear contrast

$$l = C_1 \hat{\theta}_1 + C_2 \hat{\theta}_2 + \cdots + C_m \hat{\theta}_m = \mathbf{C}' \hat{\boldsymbol{\theta}}$$

Hypothesis test of linear contrast

$$t_{(N-m)} = \frac{l - l_H}{\hat{\sigma}_\varepsilon [\mathbf{C}'(\mathbf{X}'\mathbf{X})^{-1}\mathbf{C}]^{\frac{1}{2}}}$$

Confidence interval for linear contrast

$$l \pm \{t_{(N-m)p_l/2} \times \hat{\sigma}_\varepsilon [\mathbf{C}'(\mathbf{X}'\mathbf{X})^{-1}\mathbf{C}]^{\frac{1}{2}}\}$$

Orthogonal contrasts

$$\frac{C_{11}C_{21}}{n_1} + \frac{C_{12}C_{22}}{n_2} + \cdots + \frac{C_{1k}C_{2k}}{n_k} = 0$$

CHAPTER
FOUR
LATIN SQUARE DESIGNS

4-I Research Uses of Latin Square Designs
4-I-1 The Classic Agricultural Case
4-I-2 Double Blocking
4-I-3 Fractional Replication of a Factorial Design
4-I-4 Controlling Order Effects
4-I-5 Components in More Complex Experimental Designs

4-II The Basic Model
4-II-1 Assumed Underlying (Response-Generating) Structural Model
4-II-2 The Structure of Latin Squares
    4-II-2-1 Comparison with factorial designs
    4-II-2-2 Standard form
    4-II-2-3 Orthogonal squares
4-II-3 Assumptions Underlying Latin Square Designs
    4-II-3-1 Prior assumptions
    4-II-3-2 Absence of interaction effects
4-II-4 Partial Analysis of Example and Reader Test Problem
    4-II-4-1 Analysis of variance
    4-II-4-2 Additional analysis and test problem

4-III The Absence of Interactions Assumption
4-III-1 Consequences of Interactions
    4-III-1-1 Parameter estimates
    4-III-1-2 A residual interactions source of variation
    4-III-1-3 Expected mean squares
    4-III-1-4 A test of the no interactions assumption
    4-III-1-5 Statistical tests on main effects

4-III-2 Corrective Procedure when Interactions Exist
    4-III-2-1 Conservative F test
    4-III-2-2 Transformations
    4-III-2-3 Design change

4-IV Advanced Latin Square Designs

4-IV-1 Design 1
4-IV-2 Design 2

4-V Summary

This chapter investigates the properties of a class of General Linear Models (GLM) known as Latin squares. Latin squares provide an extremely efficient procedure for analyzing the main effects of a set of independent variables but assumes that the true response-generating process which produced the observed data contains no interaction terms.

By definition a Latin square design has three independent variables or factors, each with the same number of levels, arranged so that each level of every factor appears once and only once under every level of every other factor. Figure 4-1 shows one such arrangement for a 3×3 Latin square. It is because each level of a factor does *not* appear under *all combinations* of the levels of the other two factors, i.e., the design is *not* fully crossed, that we must assume the data contain no interactions.

A very important point which the reader should keep firmly in mind is that the Latin square design is simply a variation on the basic GLM discussed in the first three chapters of this book. If the assumption of no interactions in the data is correct everything written in the first three chapters applies directly to the analysis of data following the Latin square pattern.

This chapter is divided into four major sections. Section 4-I discusses some ways Latin square designs are used by researchers. Section 4-II develops the basic model, focusing on those aspects which are different from the full factorial design. Section 4-III is in many ways the most important as it discusses those special problems which arise when the crucial assumption of no interactions is violated. Finally, Sec. 4-IV briefly illustrates how more complex experimental designs may be built using Latin squares.

	B_1	B_2	B_3
A_1	C_1	C_2	C_3
A_2	C_2	C_3	C_1
A_3	C_3	C_1	C_2

Figure 4-1 Schematic of basic 3×3 Latin square design.

4-I RESEARCH USES OF LATIN SQUARE DESIGNS

4-I-1 The Classic Agricultural Case

The classic use of the Latin square design is in the assignment of experimental treatments to a plot of land divided into $p \times p$ units.

In Fig. 4-1, A and B might represent the rows and columns of a plot of ground and C some experimental treatment such as the level of nitrogen in the fertilizer. The purpose of this design is to control for the varying natural fertility of the land. In effect this is a single-factor design where the Latin square prescribes the randomization procedure necessary for the validity of the statistical tests.[1]

4-I-2 Double Blocking

An especially important use of Latin squares in social and behavioral research involves an extension of the randomized blocks design discussed in Sec. 3-VII-2. In this use A and B represent non-experimental blocking variables which represent characteristics of the subjects under study and C represents a true experimental factor which is randomly assigned to subjects.

The purpose of this design is to remove from the error term those sources of variation arising from variables A and B, thereby improving the power of the statistical tests. For example, in Fig. 4-1, C might represent three different persuasive communications aimed at junior high school students urging them not to smoke. The researcher might suspect, however, that the relative effectiveness of these communications might vary according to the size of city and the region of the country and therefore decide to block the data on both of these variables.

It is important to remember that, in addition to assuming that no interactions exist, the number of levels of all independent variables must be equal. Also, since A and B are not randomly assigned in this plan, the interpretations attached to variables A and B are those appropriate to an associative and not a causal model.[2]

4-I-3 Fractional Replication of a Factorial Design

A frequent use of the Latin square design in social and behavioral research is to select a partially balanced fractional replication from a full factorial design. Since a Latin square with p levels involves only $1/p$ as many cells as the corresponding factorial design the researcher gains great economy of observations by using this "fractional replication." The design, however, is only partially balanced, i.e., main effects, but not interaction effects, are controlled in the main effect parameter estimates and tests of significance. The relationship between a $p \times p$ Latin square and a $p \times p \times p$ factorial design is more fully pursued in Secs. 4-II-2-1 and 4-III.

---

[1] For a further description of this use of the Latin square design see Cochran and Cox (1957), pp. 117–127.

[2] For a discussion of the distinction between these two models see Sec. 3-VII-2.

118 THE GENERAL LINEAR MODEL

We might also note that computationally there is no difference between this use of Latin squares and the double blocking we discussed above. The distinction, of course, is that between associative and causal models discussed in Sec. 3-VII-2.

4-I-4 Controlling Order Effects

In social and behavioral research it is sometimes desirable to administer all treatments for one or more factors to every subject. These so-called repeated measures designs, which are the topic of the next chapter, are very powerful but present special problems. One of these problems is the effect that the order of presentation of the treatments may have on subjects. For example, in an experiment involving three depressant drugs of varying strengths the reaction of subjects may depend on the order in which the drugs are administered even if there is a time delay between administrations of the drugs. The Latin square design provides one procedure for partially controlling such order effects.

For example, in Fig. 4-1, A might represent three subjects receiving three drugs (factor C) in the order specified by factor B. Note, however, that while each drug is received once, second and third exactly once, all possible orders of presentation do not occur. Hence ordering effects are only partially controlled. We might also note that there may be more than three subjects in such a design, it is only required that the number of subjects be an even multiple of the number of treatments.

4-I-5 Components in More Complex Experimental Designs

In the previous section it was suggested how the Latin square might be used to provide partial control over order effects. There are also designs variously known as cross-over, change-over, or carry-over designs which allow explicit investigation of these order effects.[3]

More generally, the Latin square is often used as a basic component in more complex experimental designs. In all of these designs the basic tradeoff is between economy of observations versus the requirement that certain, but not necessarily all, interactions be assumed not to exist. Two good reference sources for some of these designs are Winer (1971) and especially Cochran and Cox (1957).

4-II THE BASIC MODEL

A numerical example will be used to facilitate the discussion in this section. Table 4-1 presents artificially contrived data for a 3×3 Latin square design with $n = 3$ observations per cell. While each of the three factors must have the same number of levels, n may be any integer greater than or equal to one. As we shall

---

[3] See, for example, Banks (1965), Chap. 6, Cochran and Cox (1957), pp. 127–131, and Cox (1958), Chap. 13.

Table 4-1 Numerical example basic Latin square design

(a) Arrangement of factor levels

	B_1	B_2	B_3
A_1	C_1	C_2	C_3
A_2	C_2	C_3	C_1
A_3	C_3	C_1	C_2

(b) Data—three observations per cell

30.22	24.14	15.48
20.91	20.69	−4.12
29.81	25.85	−0.64
47.27	28.27	26.21
41.48	31.08	21.30
38.78	41.25	20.00
20.22	22.49	16.31
31.56	13.96	2.40
16.78	18.61	−9.80

see in Sec. 4-III, however, if n is greater than one we can separate a pure error term from the residual variation which will prove useful in testing the assumption of no interaction effects in our data.

In the remainder of this chapter we shall, for convenience, refer to A, B, and C as factors. None of the computational or statistical procedures depend on whether any of the variables are randomly assigned or not. The propriety of causal interpretations of the data analysis, however, continues to rest largely on the random assignment of treatments to subjects.

4-II-1 Assumed Underlying (Response-Generating) Structural Model

The complete structural model assumed to be responsible for generating the data for any basic Latin square design, such as that in Table 4-1, is

$$y_{hijk} = \mu + \alpha_i + \beta_j + \gamma_k + \varepsilon_{hijk} \tag{4-1}$$

$$\sum_i \alpha_i = \sum_j \beta_j = \sum_k \gamma_k = 0 \tag{4-2}$$

$$(i = 1, p; j = 1, p; k = 1, p; h = 1, n) \tag{4-3}$$

where each factor has p levels and there are n observations per cell. Except for the omission of interaction terms, Eqs. (4-1)–(4-3) are precisely the same as those for a $p \times p \times p$ factorial design.

4-II-2 The Structure of Latin Squares

Since a $p \times p$ Latin square has only $1/p$ as many cells as the corresponding factorial an important question is exactly which cells should be selected. A useful way to approach this question is to consider the general structure of Latin squares.

4-II-2-1 Comparison with factorial designs Initially, any $p \times p \times p$ factorial may be partitioned into p Latin squares. Figure 4-2 illustrates this relationship for designs with three levels. Note that the cells have been partitioned in such a way that within a square under any level of a factor the levels of all other factors appear exactly once. It is this property of the Latin square, i.e., its balance for main effects, which allows us to estimate the main effects of any factor free from biases from the main effects of the other two factors. Under any level of a factor, however, only $1/p$ of the possible two- and three-way combinations of the levels of the other two factors occur. Thus the design is not balanced for interaction effects, i.e., to use a term common in the statistical literature, the main effects and interactions are "confounded."

4-II-2-2 Standard form A Latin square, such as that in Fig. 4-1, with its first row and first column in ascending order is said to be in standard form. Any other arrangement, e.g., Fig. 4-2b, is said to be non-standard. A 3×3 Latin square has one standard and 11 non-standard forms, i.e., $3!2! - 1 = 11$. A 4×4 Latin square has the following four standard forms

(1)	(2)	(3)	(4)
1 2 3 4	1 2 3 4	1 2 3 4	1 2 3 4
2 1 4 3	2 3 4 1	2 4 1 3	2 1 4 3
3 4 2 1	3 4 1 2	3 1 4 2	3 4 1 2
4 3 1 2	4 1 2 3	4 3 2 1	4 3 2 1

where the numbers represent the levels of factor C and factors A and B are implicit. For each standard form there are $4!3! - 1 = 143$ non-standard forms. An extensive set of standard forms for Latin squares of different sizes are given in Fisher and Yates (1955).

Choosing a specific Latin square for a research design requires a randomization procedure to ensure that all possible arrangements of cells have an equal probability of occurrence. A recommended procedure is:

1. For 3×3 squares randomize the rows and columns of the one standard square.
2. For 4×4 squares randomly select one of the four standard squares and then randomize the rows and columns.
3. For larger squares randomize the rows and columns of a standard form and then randomly assign specific treatments to the levels of factor C.

A suitable standard form for randomization of a 5×5 or larger Latin square may be obtained from a one-step cyclic permutation where the numbers $1 \ldots p$

(a) Factorial design

	C_1			C_2			C_3		
	B_1	B_2	B_3	B_1	B_2	B_3	B_1	B_2	B_3
A_1	L_1	L_2	L_3	L_3	L_1	L_2	L_2	L_3	L_1
A_2	L_3	L_1	L_2	L_2	L_3	L_1	L_1	L_2	L_3
A_3	L_2	L_3	L_1	L_1	L_2	L_3	L_3	L_1	L_2

(b) Latin square designs

Square L_1

	B_1	B_2	B_3
A_1	C_1	C_2	C_3
A_2	C_3	C_1	C_2
A_3	C_2	C_3	C_1

Square L_2

	B_1	B_2	B_3
A_1	C_3	C_1	C_2
A_2	C_2	C_3	C_1
A_3	C_1	C_2	C_3

Square L_3

	B_1	B_2	B_3
A_1	C_2	C_3	C_1
A_2	C_1	C_2	C_3
A_3	C_3	C_1	C_2

Figure 4-2 Relationship between 3×3 Latin square and $3 \times 3 \times 3$ factorial designs

are written in the first row and each succeeding row has the first number in the extreme left of the previous line moved to the extreme right, e.g., for a 5×5 Latin square, the standard square constructed by this procedure would be

$$\begin{array}{ccccc} 1 & 2 & 3 & 4 & 5 \\ 2 & 3 & 4 & 5 & 1 \\ 3 & 4 & 5 & 1 & 2 \\ 4 & 5 & 1 & 2 & 3 \\ 5 & 1 & 2 & 3 & 4 \end{array}$$

4-II-2-3 Orthogonal squares Two Latin squares are independent or orthogonal if, when combined, the same pair of symbols appear no more than once. The following squares, for example, are orthogonal:

$$\begin{array}{c}(1)\\ \begin{array}{cccc} 1 & 2 & 3 & 4 \\ 2 & 1 & 4 & 3 \\ 3 & 4 & 1 & 2 \\ 4 & 3 & 2 & 1 \end{array}\end{array} + \begin{array}{c}(2)\\ \begin{array}{cccc} 1 & 2 & 3 & 4 \\ 3 & 4 & 1 & 2 \\ 4 & 3 & 2 & 1 \\ 2 & 1 & 4 & 3 \end{array}\end{array} = \begin{array}{c}(3)\\ \begin{array}{cccc} 11 & 22 & 33 & 44 \\ 23 & 14 & 41 & 32 \\ 34 & 43 & 12 & 21 \\ 42 & 31 & 24 & 13 \end{array}\end{array}$$

The composite of two orthogonal Latin squares is called a Greco-Latin square and represents the addition of a fourth variable to the design, i.e., square one gives the assignment of the levels of C and square two the assignment of the levels of a new variable D. Greco-Latin squares, of course, contain no interaction terms. It is not always possible, however, to find orthogonal Latin squares; e.g., no orthogonal squares exist for 6×6 Latin squares.

4-II-3 Assumptions Underlying Latin Square Designs

4-II-3-1 Prior assumptions All of the assumptions discussed in Sec. 3-II-2 in the context of the full factorial design continue to hold. The consequences of violating these assumptions and the appropriate remedies also apply to the Latin square.

4-II-3-2 Absence of interaction effects As we have noted repeatedly in the special Latin square case of the GLM, we shall also need to assume that there are no interaction effects in the data. Because of its central importance we will devote Sec. 4-III to the examination of this assumption. Here we simply note that violation of this assumption tends to invalidate both our parameter estimates and tests of significance of the main effects of the data.

4-II-4 Partial Analysis of Example and Reader Test Problem

Although no new computational principles are involved it is convenient to analyze the data in Table 4-1 for a variety of reasons. First, it allows us to introduce the widely used Statistical Package for the Social Sciences[4] (SPSS) analysis of variance computer program ANOVA. Second, it provides a test problem for the reader to test his understanding of the principles discussed in the first three chapters as they apply to the special Latin square case of the GLM. And, third, this example will serve as a standard by which we can demonstrate the effects of violating the no interaction assumption in Sec. 4-III.

To tie the Latin squarely firmly to its GLM foundation we note that in matrix terms the model for the Latin square is

$$_N y_1 = {_N}X_{m\,m}\theta_1 + {_N}\varepsilon_1$$

where the terms are exactly the same as defined in the first three chapters.[4] The number of parameters in θ is

$$m = 3(p - 1) + 1$$

and parameter estimates may be found from

$$\hat{\theta} = (X'X)^{-1}X'y$$

as they are for any GLM model discussed in this book.

4-II-4-1 Analysis of variance[5] Table 4-2 is a printout of the analysis of the data in Table 4-1 using the SPSS program ANOVA. Section (a) of the table should give the reader sufficient information to easily reproduce the analysis. Several things in section (a) do merit specific mention. Note line 15 which begins with the procedure name ANOVA. The dependent variable, called DEPEND1, is listed before the SPSS keyword BY which separates dependent and independent variables. The factors are labeled A, B, and C, where the numbers in parentheses

---

[4] See especially Sec. 3-II-3 for a quick review.

[5] The general matrix procedures necessary to set up and solve this problem are discussed in Sec. 3-II-3. Those procedures relevant to interactions may simply be omitted.

indicate the range of the levels for each factor. The next line indicates that a second dependent variable, DEPEND2, was analyzed as part of this computer run. That analysis is presented in Table 4-5.

Table 4-2b presents the standard analysis of variance table which indicates factors A and B, but not C, are highly significant. Note that an AB interaction term with 2 degrees of freedom appears in the analysis of variance table. Since we know that it is not possible to isolate an AB interaction term, either a mistake has been made or this term has an interpretation which is different from the usual one. As we shall see in Sec. 4-III-1-4 the latter is the case and this AB term may be used as a test of the absence of interactions assumption. For the moment the AB term and its degrees of freedom should be pooled with the error variation. Table 4-2c presents the grand mean, main effects for each factor,[6] and magnitude of effects. The last, ETA, is the square root of each component sum of squares divided by the total sum of squares.

4-II-4-2 Additional analysis and test problem If interactions are not present in the data, the procedures for calculating power, making general linear contrasts, estimating polynomial trends, etc. apply directly to Latin squares.[7] The presence of interactions in the data will not effect any of the above computations. Interpretations or conclusions, however, may be incorrect when interactions are present.

To check your understanding of these procedures try analyzing the data in Tables 4-1 and 4-2 for power, polynomial trends, and linear contrasts. Table 4-3 presents sufficient data to check your work.

4-III THE ABSENCE OF INTERACTIONS ASSUMPTION

As we have noted repeatedly above the validity of the Latin square design rests upon the assumption that the true, as opposed to the assumed, response-generating model contains no interaction effects. In some cases the researcher will have theoretical and/or prior empirical justification for making this assumption. In other cases he may not. Always, however, there is the potential danger that the data contains interaction effects.

Tables 4-4, 4-5, and 4-6 will be used to facilitate this discussion. The first presents the same data as in Table 4-1 with an AB interaction term added to the data. The second table analyzes the data. This table is the second half of the SPSS computer run which analyzes the dependent variable DEPEND2 mentioned in Sec. 4-II-4-1. Table 4-6 shows the biasing effects of the AB interaction by comparing main effect parameter estimates and sums of squares for the data in Tables 4-1 and 4-4 with the known values used to construct these artificial data sets.

---

[6] UNADJUSTED DEV*N simply means that the deviations of the treatment means from the grand mean have not been adjusted for the correlation with other independent variables. Such adjustments are discussed in Chaps. 6 and 7.

[7] These topics are discussed in Secs. 3-II-6 and 3-V.

124 THE GENERAL LINEAR MODEL

Table 4-2 Analysis of data in Table 4-1 using the Statistical Package for the Social Sciences (SPSS) computer program ANOVA

(a)
```
     RUN NAME       LATIN SQUARE ANALYSIS
     VARIABLE LIST  A,B,C,DEPEND1,DEPEND2
     INPUT MEDIUM   CARD
     INPUT FORMAT   FIXED(3F1.0,2X,2F6.2)

 ACCORDING TO YOUR INPUT FORMAT, VARIABLES ARE TO BE READ AS FOLLOWS

     VARIABLE  FORMAT  RECORD  COLUMNS

     A         F1.0       1      1-  1
     B         F1.0       1      2-  2
     C         F1.0       1      3-  3
     DEPEND1   F6.2       1      6- 11
     DEPEND2   F6.2       1     12- 17

 THE INPUT FORMAT PROVIDES FOR  5 VARIABLES.  15 WILL BE READ
 IT PROVIDES FOR  1 RECORDS (*CARDS*) PER CASE.  A MAXIMUM OF  17 *COLUMNS* ARE USED ON A RECORD

     N OF CASES    27
     ANOVA         DEPEND1 BY A(1,3) B(1,3) C(1,3)/
                   DEPEND2 BY A(1,3) B(1,3) C(1,3)/
     STATISTICS    ALL
     READ INPUT DATA

 0045300 CM REQUIRED FOR ANOVA
```

(b) LATIN SQUARE ANALYSIS
```
* * * * * * * * * * * * * * * * * * * * * * * * * * * * * * * * * * * * * *
 FILE   NONAME   (CREATION DATE = 02/05/77 )
* * *   * * * A N A L Y S I S   O F   V A R I A N C E * * * * * * * * * *
*                         DEPEND1                                         *
*          BY            A                                                *
*                         B                                               *
*                         C                                               *
* * * * * * * * * * * * * * * * * * * * * * * * * * * * * * * * * * * * * *
*                         SUM OF           MEAN                  SIGNIF   *
* SOURCE OF VARIATION     SQUARES   DF    SQUARE      F          OF F     *
*   MAIN EFFECTS          3927.799   6   654.633    12.914       .001     *
*     A                   1779.741   2   889.870    17.555       .001     *
*     B                   2106.154   2  1053.077    20.775       .001     *
*     C                     41.903   2    20.952      .413       .668     *
*   2-WAY INTERACTIONS      25.913   2    12.956      .256       .777     *
*     A B                   25.913   2    12.956                          *
*                                                                         *
*   EXPLAINED             3953.711   8   494.214     9.750       .001     *
*   RESIDUAL               912.422  18    50.690                          *
*   TOTAL                 4866.133  26   187.159                          *
*                                                                         *
*  27 CASES WERE PROCESSED.                                               *
*   0 CASES (  0 PCT) WERE MISSING.                                       *
 LATIN SQUARE ANALYSIS
```

(c) FILE   NONAME   (CREATION DATE = 02/05/77)

* * * M U L T I P L E   C L A S S I F I C A T I O N   A N A L Y S I S * * *
        DEPEND1
    BY   A
         B
         C
* *

GRAND MEAN =   21.61

				ADJUSTED FOR[†] INDEPENDENTS		ADJUSTED FOR INDEPENDENTS +COVARIATES	
VARIABLE + CATEGORY	N	UNADJUSTED DEV≠N ETA		DEV≠N BETA		DEV≠N BETA	
A							
1	9	-3.57		-3.57			
2	9	11.24		11.24			
3	9	-7.66	.50	-7.66	.50		
B							
1	9	9.17		9.17			
2	9	2.76		2.76			
3	9	-11.93	.66	-11.93	.66		
C							
1	9	1.22		1.22			
2	9	-1.40		-1.40			
3	9	-1.63	.09	-1.63	.09		

MULTIPLE R SQUARED   .807
MULTIPLE R   .898
LATIN SQUARE ANALYSIS

---

† Same as previous two columns since all independent variables are orthogonal.

Table 4-3 Answers for reader test problem analyzing data in Tables 4-1 and 4-2

(a) Power of tests on main effects at $p_1 = 0.05$

$$\text{Power of } A = 0.99$$
$$\text{Power of } B = 0.99$$
$$\text{Power of } C = 0.12$$

(b) Sum of squares† for polynomial trends

Factors	Trends Linear	Quadratic
A	49.57	1627.68
B	2001.97	145.27
C	31.18	17.69

(c) Sum of squares† for selected post hoc linear contrasts

Contrast	Sum of squares
$\hat{\alpha}_1 - \hat{\alpha}_2 = 0$	987.16
$\hat{\beta}_1 + \hat{\beta}_2 - 2\hat{\beta}_3 = 0$	2004.83

† Remember that each polynomial trend and each contrast requires only one degree of freedom. Therefore each sum of squares is also a mean square.

4-III-1 Consequences of Interactions

4-III-1-1 Parameter estimates To illustrate the problem let us determine which terms of a full factorial model are present in our estimate of the parameter γ_2 for the data in Table 4-4. This calculation requires us to first average the means of all cells in which C_2 appears, i.e.,

$$ABC_{122} = \mu + \alpha_1 + \beta_2 + \gamma_2 + \alpha\beta_{12} + \alpha\gamma_{12} + \beta\gamma_{22} + \alpha\beta\gamma_{122} + \varepsilon_{122}$$
$$ABC_{212} = \mu + \alpha_2 + \beta_1 + \gamma_2 + \alpha\beta_{21} + \alpha\gamma_{22} + \beta\gamma_{12} + \alpha\beta\gamma_{212} + \varepsilon_{212}$$
$$ABC_{332} = \mu + \alpha_3 + \beta_3 + \gamma_2 + \alpha\beta_{33} + \alpha\gamma_{32} + \beta\gamma_{32} + \alpha\beta\gamma_{332} + \varepsilon_{332}$$
$$\overline{C}_2 = \mu \qquad\qquad + \gamma_2 + \overline{\alpha\beta}_{(\gamma_2)} \qquad\qquad + \overline{\alpha\beta\gamma}_{(\gamma_2)} + \bar{\varepsilon}_{(\gamma_2)}$$

since α, β, $\alpha\gamma$, and $\beta\gamma$ drop out due to the restriction that the sum of the treatment effects across any index, holding all other indices constant, equals zero. The subscripts in parenthesis under the two interaction terms indicate that these means involve only those portions of the interaction parameters occurring under level 2 of factor C. Therefore

$$\hat{\gamma}_2 = \overline{C}_2 - \overline{G} = \gamma_2 + \overline{\alpha\beta}_{(\gamma_2)} + \overline{\alpha\beta\gamma}_{(\gamma_2)} + \bar{\varepsilon}_{(\gamma_2)}$$

By assumption, the expected value of $\bar{\varepsilon}_{(\gamma_2)}$ is zero. This leaves the two-way interaction term $\overline{\alpha\beta}_{(\gamma_2)}$ and the three-way interaction term $\overline{\alpha\beta\gamma}_{(\gamma_2)}$. Therefore, unless these terms are zero, the expected value of γ_2 is biased. For the data in Table 4-4, $\overline{\alpha\beta\gamma}_{(\gamma_2)}$ is zero. However,

$$\overline{\alpha\beta}_{(\gamma_2)} = (\alpha\beta_{12} + \alpha\beta_{21} + \alpha\beta_{33})/3$$
$$= (10 + 0 + 20)/3$$
$$= 10$$

and as we see in Table 4-6 our estimate of γ_2 is 10 points higher than it would have been had there not been this particular AB interaction. Note also that γ_3 is underestimated by 10 points but γ_1 is unbiased. This leads to an interesting point, which may or may not be obvious. In estimating the main effect parameters

Table 4-4 Numerical example basic Latin square design with AB interaction

(a) Arrangement of factor levels

	B_1	B_2	B_3
A_1	C_1	C_2	C_3
A_2	C_2	C_3	C_1
A_3	C_3	C_1	C_2

(b) AB interaction values

	B_1	B_2	B_3
A_1	10	10	-20
A_2	0	0	0
A_3	-10	-10	20

(c) Data—three observations per cell

40.22	34.14	-4.52
30.91	30.69	-24.12
39.81	35.85	-20.64

47.27	28.27	26.21
41.48	31.08	21.30
38.78	41.25	20.00

10.22	12.49	36.31
21.56	3.96	22.40
6.78	8.61	10.20

Table 4-5 Analysis of data in Table 4-4 using the Statistical Package for the Social Sciences computer program ANOVA

```
FILE   NONAME   (CREATION DATE = 02/05/77 )
* * * * * * * * * A N A L Y S I S   O F   V A R I A N C E * * * * * * * * * * *
              DEPEND2
        BY  A
            B
            C
* * * * * * * * * * * * * * * * * * * * * * * * * * * * * * * * * * * * * * * *
                         SUM OF                  MEAN                    SIGNIF
SOURCE OF VARIATION      SQUARES      DF        SQUARE        F           OF F
MAIN EFFECTS             6272.599      6       1045.433     20.624        .001
  A                      1779.741      2        889.870     17.555        .001
  B                      2106.154      2       1053.077     20.775        .001
  C                      2386.703      2       1193.352     23.542        .001
2-WAY INTERACTIONS       1908.313      2        954.156     18.823        .001
  A      B               1908.313      2        954.156     18.823        .001

EXPLAINED                8180.911      8       1022.614     20.174        .001
RESIDUAL                  912.422     18         50.690
TOTAL                    9093.333     26        349.744
    27 CASES WERE PROCESSED.
     0 CASES (    0 PCT) WERE MISSING.
LATIN SQUARE ANALYSIS

FILE   NONAME   (CREATION DATE = 02/05/77 )
* * *   M U L T I P L E   C L A S S I F I C A T I O N   A N A L Y S I S   * * *
              DEPEND2
        BY  A
            B
            C
* * * * * * * * * * * * * * * * * * * * * * * * * * * * * * * * * * * * * * * *

GRAND MEAN =     21.61
                                                                  ADJUSTED FOR
                                             ADJUSTED FOR†        INDEPENDENTS
                              UNADJUSTED     INDEPENDENTS         + COVARIATES
VARIABLE + CATEGORY      N    DEV≠N   ETA    DEV≠N    BETA        DEV≠N    BETA
 A
   1                     9    -3.57          -3.57
   2                     9    11.24          11.24
   3                     9    -7.66                  -7.66
                                      .44                  .44

 B
   1                     9     9.17           9.17
   2                     9     2.76           2.76
   3                     9   -11.93         -11.93
                                      .48                  .48
 C
   1                     9      .22            .22
   2                     9   -11.40         -11.40
   3                     9   -11.63         -11.63
                                      .51                  .51

MULTIPLE R SQUARED                                          .690
MULTIPLE R                                                  .831
LATIN SQUARE ANALYSIS
```

† Same as previous two columns since all independent variables are orthogonal.

of factor C all nine AB interaction terms[8] appear exactly once. Therefore the *sum* of the γ's continue to equal zero even in the presence of interactions. However, each γ_i may be biased and for empirical data we have no way of knowing whether the bias is positive or negative.

The biasing effects of interactions on main effect parameter estimates for factors A and B follow the same pattern as illustrated above for factor C. That is, factor A is biased by BC interactions, and factor B is biased by AC interactions, i.e., from interactions involving the other two factors. Three-way interactions exert a biasing effect on all factors.

---

[8] There are, of course, only four independent parameters.

Table 4-6 Known and recovered main effect parameters and sums of squares with and without AB interaction in data

Component of model	Known	Parameters Recovered Without AB interaction	Parameters Recovered With AB interaction	Known	Sums of squares† Recovered Without AB interaction	Sums of squares† Recovered With AB interaction
A_1	−5	−3.57	−3.57			
A_2	10	11.24	11.24	1350	1780	1780
A_3	−5	−7.66	−7.66			
B_1	8	9.17	9.17			
B_2	3	2.76	2.76	1746	2106	2106
B_3	−11	−11.93	−11.93			
C_1	1	0.22	0.22			
C_2	1	1.40	11.40	54	42	2387
C_3	−2	−1.63	−11.63			
G	20	21.61	21.61	10800	12609	12609

† Rounded to nearest whole number.

4-III-1-2 A residual interactions source of variation Although it is not possible to separate the variance due to each interaction it is possible to separate a term which is a function of all treatment effects which are not accounted for by the sum of the main effects. To see how this source of variation is isolated, recall our discussion in the previous section where we noted that in estimating the main effects of factor C each of the nine AB interaction terms appears once. The same is true of the ABC interaction. Therefore if we calculate an AB interaction term exactly *as if* it were a $p \times p$ factorial this term will contain variation due to C, all interactions, and error. By subtracting the sum of squares due factor C we have a residual term composed of the three two-way interaction terms, the one three-way interaction term, and error. The same result occurs if we calculate AC and subtract B or BC and subtract A.

This residual term has $(p-2)(p-1)$ degrees of freedom equal to

$$\mathrm{df}_{AB} - \mathrm{df}_C = (p-1)(p-1) - (p-1)$$
$$= p^2 - 2p + 1 - p + 1$$
$$= p^2 - 3p + 2$$
$$= (p-2)(p-1)$$

A slightly different procedure which leads to the same result is informative. There are $p^2 - 1$ degrees of freedom associated with the variation of the data between the p^2 cells in a Latin square. However, $3(p-1)$ are used to estimate the three main effects leaving

$$(p^2 - 1) - 3(p - 1) = (p - 2)(p - 1)$$

residual degrees of freedom arising from between cell sources of variation other than the grand mean and main effects. Note carefully that $(p - 2)(p - 1)$ is always less than the $(p - 1)(p - 1)$ degrees of freedom that would be required to isolate even a single interaction effect.

As the reader may by now have guessed, the AB interaction term in Table 4-2 is identical to the residual interaction sum of squares. The reason for this somewhat awkward sequencing of material is that when Table 4-2 was originally prepared the existing version of the SPSS procedure ANOVA produced the proper analysis of variance table, without an AB interaction, when the data was input as a $3 \times 3 \times 3$ factorial. Specifically, ANOVA recognized that the inverse of the cross product matrix $(X'X)^{-1}$ did not exist (since interactions cannot be represented in a Latin square design), eliminated all interactions from the design matrix and calculated an $(X'X)^{-1}$ containing only a grand mean and main effects parameters. The moral, of course, is that a computer printout is sometimes more, sometimes less, and sometimes different from what it appears to be. More generally, the reader needs to be wary of taking any computer printout too literally and needs to be aware of the fact that the computer program itself often contains many features which are not contained in published references to the program. This is particularly a problem with programs such as SPSS which are undergoing rapid and extensive development.

4-III-1-3 Expected mean squares When interactions are present in the data, normal procedures[9] for testing the statistical significance of the main effects break down because the mean squares associated with each main effect contain certain interaction terms. Table 4-7 presents the expected mean squares for the Latin square with and without interactions.[10]

4-III-1-4 A test of the no interactions assumption It is clear from Table 4-7 that an appropriate test of the absence of interactions assumption may be made by forming the F ratio from the mean square residual divided by the mean square error. The appropriate degrees of freedom are given in Table 4-7. This test, of course, requires that the number of observations per cell be two or more because a pure error term, i.e., a within-cell source of variation, cannot be defined with one observation per cell. Although we do not recommend having only one observation per cell several procedures have been developed to test the no interactions assumption in this case. The assumptions underlying these tests are rather strenuous. For details see Milliken and Graybill (1972).

---

[9] See Sec. 3-II-5.
[10] The details of the derivation of these expected mean squares assuming interactions is somewhat complex. The interested reader should consult Wilk and Kempthorne (1957) who develop the case generally for random and mixed models as well as for fixed effects models.

Table 4-7 Expected mean squares† for $p \times p$ Latin square with and without presence of interactions

(a) Expected mean squares assuming no interactions

Source of variation	Degrees of freedom	Expected mean square
A	$p-1$	$np\sigma_\alpha^2 + \sigma_\varepsilon^2$
B	$p-1$	$np\sigma_\beta^2 + \sigma_\varepsilon^2$
C	$p-1$	$np\sigma_\gamma^2 + \sigma_\varepsilon^2$

(b) Expected mean squares assuming interactions

Source of variation	Degrees of freedom	Expected mean squares
A	$p-1$	$np\sigma_\alpha^2 + n\sigma_{\beta\gamma}^2 + \dfrac{n(p-2)}{p}\sigma_{\alpha\beta\gamma}^2 + \sigma_\varepsilon^2$
B	$p-1$	$np\sigma_\beta^2 + n\sigma_{\alpha\gamma}^2 + \dfrac{n(p-2)}{p}\sigma_{\alpha\beta\gamma}^2 + \sigma_\varepsilon^2$
C	$p-1$	$np\sigma_\gamma^2 + n\sigma_{\alpha\beta}^2 + \dfrac{n(p-2)}{p}\sigma_{\alpha\beta\gamma}^2 + \sigma_\varepsilon^2$
Residual	$(p-2)(p-1)$	$n\sigma_{\alpha\beta}^2 + n\sigma_{\alpha\gamma}^2 + n\sigma_{\beta\gamma}^2 + \dfrac{n(p-3)}{p}\sigma_{\alpha\beta\gamma}^2 + \sigma_\varepsilon^2$
Error	$p^2(n-1)$	$+ \sigma_\varepsilon^2$

† These expected mean squares are appropriate only for the fixed effects model.

Table 4-8 presents a printout of the BioMedical Computer Program 10V[11] which illustrates the procedure. We have already indicated in Sec. 4-III-1-2 how we could isolate the residual variance due to interactions in the data. Of course this would require two analyses of the data since the inverse of the cross products matrix would not exist if we attempted to directly define a two-way interaction *and* all main effects since the two-way term would also contain the main effects of the other factor, e.g., the *AB* sum of squares contains the *C* sum of squares.

We can, however, use the dummy variable coding procedure discussed in Sec. 3-VI-2-1 to define directly the error variance and let the residual interaction sum of squares "fall out" as a residual.[12] We have labeled the true error term T–E in Table 4-8. The last term, which is automatically labeled ERROR, is actually

---

[11] This program, labeled X64 in earlier editions of the BMD programs, is discussed in detail in Secs. 3-VI-2 and 3-VI-3.

[12] This is done by creating a fourth replication, i.e., subject, source of variation. The dummy variable card for the true error term attributes $(n-1)$ degrees of freedom to the replication factor and p degrees of freedom to any *two* of the factors *A*, *B*, or *C*.

Table 4-8 Analysis of data in Table 4-4 isolating residual sum of squares using BMD10V computer program

```
BMD10V - GENERAL LINEAR HYPOTHESIS (NO. 2) - REVISED MARCH 30, 1973
HEALTH SCIENCES COMPUTING FACILITY, UCLA

PROBLEM CODE. . . . . . . .   LAT-I
NUMBER OF COVARIATES . . .     0
NUMBER OF DUMMY VARIABLE CARDS 5
NUMBER OF OBSERVATIONS . . .   27
NUMBER OF INDICES. . . . . .   4
VARIABLE FORMAT (4F1.0,7X,F6.2)
```

REGRESSION COEFFICIENTS

		HYPOTHESIS				
VAR.	MEAN	A	B	C	T-E	NONE
1	.00000	21.61222	21.61222	21.61222	21.61222	21.61222
2	-3.57444	.00000	-3.57444	-3.57444	-3.57444	-3.57444
3	11.23667	.00000	11.23667	11.23667	11.23667	11.23667
4	9.16889	9.16889	.00000	9.16889	9.16889	9.16889
5	2.76111	2.76111	.00000	2.76111	2.76111	2.76111
6	.22444	.22444	.22444	.00000	.22444	.22444
7	11.40111	11.40111	11.40111	.00000	11.40111	11.40111
8	-.55556	-.55556	-.55556	-.55556	.00000	-.55556
9	5.13889	5.13889	5.13889	5.13889	.00000	5.13889
10	-1.44667	-1.44667	-1.44667	-1.44667	.00000	-1.44667
11	.30667	.30667	.30667	.30667	.00000	.30667
12	-1.36222	-1.36222	-1.36222	-1.36222	.00000	-1.36222
13	-4.96889	-4.96889	-4.96889	-4.96889	.00000	-4.96889
14	2.00667	2.00667	2.00667	2.00667	.00000	2.00667
15	-2.16778	-2.16778	-2.16778	-2.16778	.00000	-2.16778
16	3.23556	3.23556	3.23556	3.23556	.00000	3.23556
17	-2.75556	-2.75556	-2.75556	-2.75556	.00000	-2.75556
18	-1.69778	-1.69778	-1.69778	-1.69778	.00000	-1.69778
19	2.23000	2.23000	2.23000	2.23000	.00000	2.23000
20	3.44333	3.44333	3.44333	3.44333	.00000	3.44333
21	-.12222	-.12222	-.12222	-.12222	.00000	-.12222
22	-.76889	-.76889	-.76889	-.76889	.00000	-.76889
23	-3.85000	-3.85000	-3.85000	-3.85000	.00000	-3.85000
24	.13222	.13222	.13222	.13222	.00000	.13222
25	-1.69444	-1.69444	-1.69444	-1.69444	.00000	-1.69444
TOLERANCE	.42187	.42187	.42187	.42187	.75000	.42187

ANALYSIS OF VARIANCE TABLE

SOURCE	SUM OF SQUARES	D.F.	MEAN SQUARE	F[†]
MEAN	12611.38003	1	12611.38003	13.21731[¶]
A	1779.74082	2	889.87041	.93263
B	2106.15442	2	1053.07721	1.10367
C	2386.70327	2	1193.35163	1.25069
T-E[‡]	912.42193	18	50.69011	.05313
ERROR[§]	1908.31262	2	954.15631	

† This F ratio is not correct. The proper denominator of all F ratios, assuming no interactions, is the mean square for T–E.
‡ "True" error.
§ Residual interactions.
¶ $p_I < .01$.

the residual term we seek. Note also that the sums of the last two sum of squares in Table 4-8 equals the sum of squares error in Table 4-5.

The appropriate F test then is

$$F_{(2,18)} = 954.16/50.69 = 18.82$$

which is significant well beyond the $p_I = 0.01$ level. The size of the residual sum of squares suggests the presence of relatively strong interactions. Unfortunately, we have no way of knowing precisely which terms are involved and therefore no way of knowing which main effects tests of significance and parameter estimates may be effected.

Had the F test of the residual variation been non-significant, F tests of the main effects could proceed using either the mean square error in Table 4-8 or a pooled error term formed by adding the sum of squares for error and residual and dividing by the total number of degrees of freedom, i.e., $np^2 - 3p + 2$.

4-III-1-5 Statistical tests on main effects If the interaction test is significant the researcher faces a dilemma for which there is no completely satisfactory remedy. If the mean square error is used as the denominator for the main effects tests, the true F ratio will be overestimated for main effects confounded by interactions. If the mean square residual is used instead, the true F ratio will tend to be underestimated.

For the data in Table 4-8 none of the main effects are significant at even a $p_1 = 0.25$ level if the mean square residual is used in the denominator of the F ratio. If the true error term is used, however, all factors are significant. This includes factor C which is not significant at even $p_1 = 0.99$ when the AB interaction effect is not present. This occurs, as shown in Table 4-6, because the sum of squares due the AB interaction in the example is included with the sum of squares attributed to factor C. The researcher can, as is evident in Table 4-7, be relatively confident in a non-significant main effect when the true error term is used in the F ratio since interaction effects bias the ratio upwards.

4-III-2 Corrective Procedures when Interactions Exist

4-III-2-1 Conservative F test To avoid rejecting a null hypothesis of no main effects for a factor because of interactions it may be useful to use the mean square residual as the denominator of the F test. This, of course, will tend to result in underestimating the F ratios for main effects which contain no interaction terms or only a portion of the terms in the mean square residual. Individual parameter estimates, however, will continue to be biased and more detailed tests will generally be useless or misleading.

4-III-2-2 Transformations As was noted in Sec. 3-IV, it will often be true that interactions result from the scale of measurement on which the dependent variable is measured. Sometimes it will be possible to find a transformation—e.g., square, square root—which will restore additivity to the data. A successful transformation will be apparent in a non-significant test on the residual term. Of course, there will be the usual dangers associated with any post hoc data search.[13]

4-III-2-3 Design change Although it is most painful to abandon an experiment as a failure, it may be necessary to revert to a full factorial design to fully under-

---

[13] See Sec. 3-V-4.

stand the data. Such a possibility is one of the primary reasons that Latin square designs should be used most cautiously and are probably best avoided when the researcher is exploring unfamiliar ground.

4-IV ADVANCED LATIN SQUARE DESIGNS

In discussing the research uses of the Latin square design we mentioned that the Latin square is often used as a component in more complex experimental designs. In this section we present two such designs to illustrate how this integration might be accomplished. These designs are merely illustrative. The reader who requires a more detailed discussion of the use of Latin squares in complex experimental designs is referred to Winer (1971), Chap. 9, Cox (1958), Chaps. 3, 10, and 13, and Cochran and Cox (1957), Chaps. 4 and 13.

These two examples also present an opportunity for the reader to test his skills at setting up and analyzing a relatively complex data analysis problem. Therefore, we have presented sufficient data for the reader to check his work.

4-IV-1 Design 1

Table 4-9a presents the general plan of the experiment. The response-generating model assumed under this design is

$$y_{ijklm} = \mu + \alpha_i + \beta_j + \gamma_k + \delta_l + \alpha\delta_{il} + \beta\delta_{jl} + \gamma\delta_{kl} + \varepsilon_{ijklm}$$

Table 4-9 First advanced Latin square design and reader test problem

(a) General experimental plan

	D_1			D_2		
	B_1	B_2	B_3	B_1	B_2	B_3
A_1	C_3	C_2	C_1	C_1	C_3	C_2
A_2	C_1	C_3	C_2	C_2	C_1	C_3
A_3	C_2	C_1	C_3	C_3	C_2	C_1

(b) Data—two observations per cell

67	85	34	31	38	45
74	83	3	32	49	41
76	85	15	34	37	56
82	63	14	28	29	49
87	72	16	37	23	31
86	84	16	32	32	41

Table 4-9 Continued

(c) Analysis of variance

Source of variation	Degrees of freedom General	Specific	Mean square	F Ratio
A	$p-1$	2	13.08	<1
B	$p-1$	2	2708.08	44.87
C	$p-1$	2	19.75	<1
D	$q-1$	1	3948.03	65.41
AD	$(p-1)(q-1)$	2	98.03	1.62
BD	$(p-1)(q-1)$	2	5284.53	87.55
CD	$(p-1)(q-1)$	2	275.53	4.56
Residual	$q(p-1)(p-2)$	4	28.56	<1
Error	$p^2q(n-1)$	18	60.36	

(d) Selected polynomial trends and general linear contrasts

Polynomial trends

Trend	Sum of squares	F Ratio†
B_{LIN}	3876.04	64.22
B_{QUAD}	1540.13	25.52
$D_{LIN}*B_{LIN}$	8177.04	135.47
$D_{LIN}*B_{QUAD}$	2392.01	39.63

General linear contrasts

Contrast	Sum of squares	F Ratio†
$\hat{\beta}_1 - \hat{\beta}_2 = 0$	8.17	<1
$\beta\delta_{11} - \beta\delta_{12} = 0$	8.17	<1

† $df_n = 1$, $df_d = 18$.

This design involves two Latin squares to which the levels of a factor D have been randomly assigned. Such a design might be useful where it is known that interaction effects among factors A, B, and C are negligible and the researcher wishes to investigate the effects of an additional variable.

While the model contains the two-way interaction terms involving factor D, all other interactions must be assumed zero. Note, however, that D is biased only by the ABC and ABCD interaction effects. Interactions, should they exist, exert the biasing effects discussed in Sec. 4-III-1. Figure 4-3 schematically presents the pattern of biases. Note that factor D does not influence the pattern because both levels of the factor are always present in parameter estimates.

Table 4-9b presents the data. The analysis of variance proceeds along the lines discussed in Sec. 3-II. The interaction terms for the design matrix X are, of course,

136 THE GENERAL LINEAR MODEL

Components of model	\multicolumn{8}{c	}{Biases from interactions not in model}
	AB	AC	BC	ABC	ABD	ACD	BCD	ABCD
A			*	*			*	*
B		*		*		*		*
C	*			*	*			*
D				*				*
AD			*	*			*	*
BD		*		*		*		*
CD	*			*	*			*
Residual Error	*	*	*	*	*	*	*	*

Note: * indicates the presence of a biasing interaction effect.

Figure 4-3 Schematic of biases due to interaction terms for design 1 in Table 4-9.

Table 4-10 Second advanced Latin square design and reader test problem

(a) General experimental plan

		\multicolumn{3}{c	}{C_1}	\multicolumn{3}{c	}{C_2}
		D_1	D_2	D_3	D_1	D_2	D_3
A_1	B_1	T_1	T_2	T_3	T_4	T_5	T_6
	B_2	T_2	T_3	T_4	T_5	T_6	T_1
	B_3	T_3	T_4	T_5	T_6	T_1	T_2
A_2	B_1	T_4	T_5	T_6	T_1	T_2	T_3
	B_2	T_5	T_6	T_1	T_2	T_3	T_4
	B_3	T_6	T_1	T_2	T_3	T_4	T_5

(b) Data—two observations per cell

157	110	129	117	110	127
133	130	124	131	110	165
80	62	49	63	79	77
66	64	32	75	82	75
97	45	87	95	120	111
109	64	69	103	103	87
105	94	69	109	125	77
123	93	82	125	109	60
102	72	71	82	72	23
116	72	59	67	72	31
151	121	138	115	161	164
142	192	85	97	172	121

Table 4-10 Continued

(c) Analysis of variance

Source of variation	Degrees of freedom General	Specific		Mean square	F Ratio
Row effects	$pq - 1$	5			
A	$(p - 1)$		1	747.56	3.13
B	$(q - 1)$		2	16,468.76	68.96
AB	$(p - 1)(q - 1)$		2	9,279.76	38.86
Column effects	$pq - 1$	5			
C	$(p - 1)$		1	193.39	<1
D	$(q - 1)$		2	2,224.06	9.31
CD	$(p - 1)(q - 1)$		2	1,874.06	7.85
Within-square effects					
T	$(t - 1)$	5		947.02	3.97
Residual	$(pq - 1)(pq - 2)$	20		643.95	2.70†
Error	$(pq)^2(n - 1)$	36		238.81	

(d) Selected polynomial trends

Trend	Sum of squares	F Ratio‡
B_{LIN}	25.52	<1
B_{QUAD}	32,912.01	137.82
T_{LIN}	295.24	1.24
T_{QUAD}	3,916.84	16.40
AB_{LIN}	18,447.52	77.25
AB_{QUAD}	112.01	<1

† The data in fact contain no interaction terms. Note that this test, with $df_n = 20$ and $df_d = 36$, is relatively powerful, i.e., is capable of detecting a small residual effect.

‡ $df_n = 1$, $df_d = 36$.

simply the products of the appropriate main effect columns.[14] Table 4-9, sections (c) and (d), present enough results from the data analyses for the reader to check his work.

4-IV-2 Design 2

Table 4-10a presents the general plan of the experiment. The response-generating model is

$$y_{hijklm} = \mu + \alpha_i + \beta_j + \gamma_k + \delta_l + \tau_m + \alpha\beta_{ij} + \gamma\delta_{kl} + \varepsilon_{hijklm}$$

[14] See Sec. 3-II-3.

The borders of this Latin square are made up of two $p \times q$ factorials. Within the square are $p \times q$ treatments which could, although they are not in this example, represent another $p \times q$ factorial. This design not only controls for variation arising from the main effects of four factors but also controls for the two-way interactions AB and CD. There are, however, 8 two-way, 10 three-way, 5 four-way, and 1 five-way interactions which must be assumed equal to zero. The reader might try to construct a figure similar to Fig. 4-3 which shows precisely which components of the model are biased by which unrepresented interactions.

Table 4-10b presents the data and sections (c) and (d) of the table present sufficient data for the reader to check his work.

4-V SUMMARY

In this chapter we have investigated a class of GLM designs which provide great economy of observations in the investigation of the main effects arising from a set of factors. In addition these designs are often used as components in more complex experimental designs. The efficiency of Latin square designs is achieved at the cost of assuming that the data contain no interaction terms. If this assumption is true the analysis proceeds exactly as discussed in Chap. 3 in the context of full factorial designs. If this assumption is false at least some parameter estimates and tests of significance will be biased and any conclusions reached may be incorrect.

CHAPTER
FIVE

REPEATED MEASURES DESIGNS

5-I Research Uses of Repeated Measures Designs
5-I-1 Economy of Subjects, Time, and Effort
5-I-2 Questions Requiring Repeated Measurements
5-I-3 Controlling for Unique Subject Effects

5-II The Basic Model
5-II-1 The Assumed Underlying (Response-Generating) Structural Model
5-II-2 Assumptions Underlying Repeated Measures Designs
      5-II-2-1 Prior assumptions
      5-II-2-2 Covariance assumption
      5-II-2-3 Random subjects assumption
5-II-3 Significance Tests

5-III The Covariance Assumption
5-III-1 Consequences of Violating the Covariance Assumption
5-III-2 A Test of the Covariance Assumption
5-III-3 Procedures for Correcting for Violations of Covariance Assumption
      5-III-3-1 Adjusted degrees of freedom
      5-III-3-2 Multivariate analysis

5-IV More Complex Repeated Measures Designs
5-IV-1 All-Within Factorial Designs
      5-IV-1-1 Response-generating model
      5-IV-1-2 Expected mean squares and analysis
      5-IV-1-3 ψ for AB interaction
      5-IV-1-4 Orthogonal polynomial trends
5-IV-2 Nested Factorials
      5-IV-2-1 Response-generating model
      5-IV-2-2 Expected mean squares and analysis

5-IV-2-3 Homogeneity of covariance matrices
5-IV-2-4 Compound symmetry and ψ
5-IV-3 Repeated Measures Latin Square
5-IV-3-1 Response-generating model
5-IV-3-2 Expected mean squares
5-IV-3-3 Data analysis

5-V Rules For Constructing Expected Mean Squares

5-VI The Variance Components Model
5-VI-1 Research Uses of the Variance Components Model
5-VI-2 Basic Model and Assumptions
5-VI-3 Estimation of Variance Components
5-VI-4 Tests of Significance

5-VII Summary

In this chapter the properties of a class of General Linear Model (GLM) designs known as repeated measures designs are discussed. The description *"repeated measures"* refers to the fact that each subject is measured under *all* levels of one or more factors. Such repeated measurement presents certain unique research design opportunities. The major difficulty with such designs is that by repeatedly measuring the same subject the observations are not independent which, as noted in Sec. 2-II-3, may seriously distort tests of statistical significance.

Our discussion of repeated measures designs is organized as follows. First, research uses of repeated measures designs are briefly discussed. Second, the basic model for a one-factor repeated measures design, including model assumptions, is presented. Third, the consequences of violating the independence assumption along with potential remedies are discussed. Fourth, the repeated measures principle is extended, with discussion of several complications, to more complex research designs. Fifth, a general procedure for constructing the expected mean squares for any analysis of variance design is presented. And, sixth, a logical extension of the repeated measures design known as the variance components model is outlined.

5-I RESEARCH USES OF REPEATED MEASURES DESIGNS

5-I-1 Economy of Subjects, Time, and Effort

A one-way analysis of variance design with p levels of factor A and n observations per cell requires pn subjects whereas the corresponding repeated measurements design requires only n or $1/p$ as many subjects. In more complex designs the subject savings can be even greater. Thus where subjects are difficult or very expensive to acquire there is a strong incentive to use a repeated measures design. Also, since the different treatment conditions are often administered during a single experimental session, substantial time and effort may be saved when a repeated measures design is used.

As a device for economizing resources it is very important to understand that repeated measures designs place subjects in a very special kind of research context. Three types of effects which arise from the repeated measurement context, and are especially important, are practice, sensitization, and carryover. That is, during trials (as the repeated factor is often generically labeled) subjects may become more (learning) or less (fatigue) proficient at the experimental task; may become sensitized or desensitized to their experimental environment; or may have their performance on later trials affected by carryover effects from earlier trials.

While it is possible to partially allow for these possibilities by certain procedures (e.g., randomly assigning the order in which the treatments are administered to subjects, counterbalancing the order of presentation via a Latin square design, or allowing a sufficient time to elapse between trials) we can never be entirely sure that these procedures have been completely successful. Although we do not believe, as some writers do, that repeated measures designs should never be used merely for reasons of economy, we do suggest that the economy gained should be very substantial when this is the *primary* reason for employing such a design.

5-I-2 Questions Requiring Repeated Measurements

Factors which from one perspective are seen as difficulties to be overcome emerge as important research questions from another perspective. Indeed, many of the most interesting and important research questions addressed by social and behavioral researchers revolve around the basic question of what happens to people as they move through time, space, and circumstances.

Examples abound! To what extent are children desensitized to violence by *repeated* viewing of violent television shows? What sequence of psychological stages does an elderly person *progress through* as his own death becomes imminent? What is the optimal *amount and order* of incarceration, job-training, work-release, etc. for long-term prisoners? Each of these questions inherently requires repeated measurement of the same subject. The decision to investigate such problems forces the researcher to face the special problems presented by repeated measures designs.[1]

5-I-3 Controlling for Unique Subject Effects

One of the difficulties of doing research with human subjects is that each subject tends to be unique in terms of physical and mental capabilities, previous

---

[1] For more details on the research uses of repeated measures designs, including circumstances under which such designs are justified, see Greenwald (1976).

experiences, and current circumstances—to name broadly some of the more obvious differences. In contrast, research with animals often goes to elaborate extremes to secure animals with a similar history—including the sharing of the same parentage for some specified number of generations—and the same, usually sterile, environment.

Human subjects, of course, bring all of their known and unknown characteristics with them as research subjects. And it is to be expected that their responses during the course of an experiment may be influenced, sometimes greatly, by these characteristics. For the known characteristics it may be possible to control either directly, by grouping subjects into homogeneous blocks, or statistically, by the analysis of covariance procedures discussed in the next chapter.

Repeated measures designs, however, allow for partial control over both known and unknown subject effects by treating each subject as a block, i.e., for trial factors each subject's responses may be calculated about the subject's mean response. In effect each subject serves as his own control. Such a use of repeated measures designs is likely to be most productive in situations where the effects of trial factors are expected to be small relative to unique subject effects—a not uncommon occurrence in social and behavioral research.

5-II THE BASIC MODEL

This section presents the basic model for a one factor repeated measures design. The assumptions underlying this model are also presented with special attention given to (1) the independence assumption which will generally be violated and (2) the fixed effects assumption which will be modified. A numerical example, presented in Table 5-1, will be used to facilitate the discussion in this section and in Sec. 5-III, where the independence assumption is investigated in detail. Table 5-1b presents the data analysis using the by now familiar BMD program 10V. Note that computationally the analysis is the same as for a randomized blocks design with one observation per cell. The mathematical models underlying these two designs, however, are quite different.

5-II-1 The Assumed Underlying (Response-Generating) Structural Model

The complete structural model presumed to be responsible for generating the data in a p level, one-factor, repeated measures design with n subjects is

$$y_{ij} = \mu + \pi_i + \alpha_j + \pi\alpha_{ij} + \varepsilon_{ij} \qquad (5\text{-}1)$$

$$\sum_i \pi_i = \sum_j \alpha_j = \sum_i \pi\alpha_{ij} = \sum_j \pi\alpha_{ij} = 0 \qquad (i = 1, n; j = 1, p)$$

The terms in Eq. (5-1) are readily identified: μ, α_j, and ε_{ij} are the grand mean, the deviation in response attributable to subjects being in treatment condition A_j, and the response error of subject i in treatment condition A_j, respectively, i.e., these three terms are defined precisely as in a one factor analysis of variance without repeated measurements; π_i represents the average deviation about the

Table 5-1 Numerical example of a one-factor, repeated measures analysis of variance

(a) Data

	A_1	A_2	A_3	A_4
S_1	13	27	40	62
S_2	45	56	79	93
S_3	8	24	32	61
S_4	39	54	54	65
S_5	44	50	61	78
S_6	30	35	59	87
S_7	35	37	54	73
S_8	42	50	62	76
S_9	23	33	47	69

Factor (column header above $A_1 \ldots A_4$); Subject (row header above $S_1 \ldots S_9$).

(b) Analysis of Variance and Estimated Regression Coefficients

```
BMD10V - GENERAL LINEAR HYPOTHESIS (NO. 2) - REVISED MARCH 30, 1973
HEALTH SCIENCES COMPUTING FACILITY, UCLA

PROBLEM CODE . . . . . . . . .    RM1
NUMBER OF COVARIATES . . . .      -0
NUMBER OF DUMMY VARIABLE CARDS     3
NUMBER OF OBSERVATIONS . . . .    36
NUMBER OF INDICES. . . . . .       2
VARIABLE FORMAT (2F1.0,1X,F2.0)
```

REGRESSION COEFFICIENTS

	HYPOTHESIS			
VAR.	MEAN	A	S	NONE
1	.00000	49.91667	49.91667	49.91667
2	-18.91667	.00000	-18.91667	-18.91667
3	-9.25000	.00000	-9.25000	-9.25000
4	4.30556	.00000	4.30556	4.30556
5	-14.41667	-14.41667	.00000	-14.41667
6	18.33333	18.33333	.00000	18.33333
7	-18.66667	-18.66667	.00000	-18.66667
8	3.08333	3.08333	.00000	3.08333
9	8.33333	8.33333	.00000	8.33333
10	2.83333	2.83333	.00000	2.83333
11	-.16667	-.16667	.00000	-.16667
12	7.58333	7.58333	.00000	7.58333
TOLERANCE	.56250	.56250	.66667	.56250

ANALYSIS OF VARIANCE TABLE

SOURCE	SUM OF SQUARES	D.F.	MEAN SQUARE	F
MEAN	89700.25000	1	89700.25000	2824.79283 †
A	9281.63889	3	3093.87963	97.43082 †
S	4339.00000	8	542.37500	17.08019 †
ERROR	762.11111	24	31.75463	

† $p_1 < 0.01$.

grand mean of subject i over all treatment conditions, and $\pi\alpha_{ij}$ represents the interaction between subject i and treatment condition j. For some purposes it is useful, and common, to assume that $\pi\alpha_{ij}$ is equal to zero, i.e., that the model contains no interactions.

Since the model blocks on subjects there will always be only one observation per cell and, therefore, it will not be possible to separate the variance due $\pi\alpha_{ij}$ and ε_{ij}. For this reason the error sum of squares which results from an analysis of variance of data following the model in Eq. (5-1) is often called a residual error sum of squares or a subject by factor interaction sum of squares. Whatever the label, this term will be the denominator in tests of significance on the model in Eq. (5-1).

5-II-2 Assumptions Underlying Repeated Measures Designs

5-II-2-1 Prior assumptions With the exceptions noted below all of the assumptions made in Sec. 3-II-2 continue to be required. The consequences of violating these assumptions and appropriate corrective actions also apply to repeated measures designs.

5-II-2-2 Covariance assumption In Sec. 2-II-3-1 we noted that a standard assumption of any GLM is that all observations are independent. We also noted that a weaker assumption would suffice for accurate tests of significance but that violation of this weaker assumption can lead to substantial distortion of the reported level of significance.

To be more specific we first define the variance/covariance matrix among the p levels of factor A as[2]

$$\Omega = \begin{bmatrix} \sigma_1^2 & \sigma_{12} & \cdots & \sigma_{1p} \\ \sigma_{21} & \sigma_2^2 & & \\ \vdots & & \ddots & \\ \sigma_{p1} & & & \sigma_p^2 \end{bmatrix} = \begin{bmatrix} \sigma_{11} & \sigma_{12} & \cdots & \sigma_{1p} \\ \sigma_{21} & \sigma_{22} & & \\ \vdots & & \ddots & \\ \sigma_{p1} & & & \sigma_{pp} \end{bmatrix} \quad (5\text{-}2)$$

Independence, of course, requires the expected values of the off-diagonal elements to be zero. However, since the covariance between any two levels of factor A contain the same subject terms π_i for each subject the covariances will tend to be positive unless there are no subject effects.

A somewhat weaker assumption that still allows completely accurate F tests is

$$\Omega = \begin{bmatrix} \sigma_1^2 \rho\sigma_{12} & \cdots & \rho\sigma_{1p} \\ \rho\sigma_{21} & \sigma_2^2 & & \\ & & \ddots & \\ \vdots & & & \\ \rho\sigma_{p1} & & & \sigma_p^2 \end{bmatrix} = \sigma^2 \begin{bmatrix} 1 & \rho & \cdots & \rho \\ \rho & 1 & & \\ \vdots & & \ddots & \vdots \\ & & 1 & \rho \\ \rho & \cdots & \rho & 1 \end{bmatrix} \quad (5\text{-}3)$$

where ρ is the so-called intra-class correlation. In Eq. (5-3) all covariances are equal[3] to a constant which is the product of the within-cell variance and the

---

[2] To simplify the notation the variances and covariances do not carry the subscript ε, e.g. $\sigma_{\varepsilon_1}^2$ is written σ_1^2.

[3] Equation (5-3) also assumes homogeneity of within-cell variances.

intra-class correlation. Such a matrix is said to possess compound symmetry. As we shall see in the next section it is possible to test a sample estimate of Ω for compound symmetry.

Finally, we note that Huynh and Feldt (1970) have shown that the usual F test gives completely accurate results when the variance of the difference between all possible pairs of treatment means

$$\sigma^2_{(\bar{A}_j - \bar{A}_k)} = \frac{1}{n}(\sigma^2_j + \sigma^2_k - 2\sigma_{jk}) \tag{5-4}$$

is constant. A Ω with compound symmetry *always* possesses this property. However, a Ω without compound symmetry may also follow the pattern specified by Eq. (5-4). The practical importance of this is that, as we shall see in the next section, it is possible to calculate a statistic which may be used to adjust the degrees of freedom of the F statistic to correct for inflation of p_1 caused by violation of the assumption specified by Eq. (5-4).

5-II-2-3 Random subjects assumption In repeated measures designs subjects are treated as a blocking variable. Unlike the blocking variables considered in Chaps. 3 and 4, however, subjects are considered to be randomly selected rather than fixed. An immediate consequence of this change in assumption is that while the relations

$$\sum_i \pi_i = \sum_i \pi\alpha_{ij} = 0$$

hold in the population of subjects, in any single sample these terms will generally not sum to zero. Since factor A remains fixed

$$\sum_j \hat{\alpha}_j = \sum_j \hat{\pi\alpha}_{ij} = 0$$

continues to hold for the sample as well as the population data.

To be more specific, the repeated measures design specified by Eq. (5-1) assumes that π_i, $\pi\alpha_{ij}$, and ε_{ij} are normally and independently distributed with expected values

$$E(\pi_i) = E(\pi\alpha_{ij}) = E(\varepsilon_{ij}) = 0$$

and that all three terms are independent.

The consequence of these assumptions is to alter the form of the expected mean squares from the form they would take if subjects were not treated as a random *factor*, as Table 5-2 shows. Specifically, the expected mean square for factor A contains a term due to the interaction between A and S. By definition there is no main subject effect in the expected mean square for factor A since the average subject effect, while generally not zero, is constant across levels of A. Also, since it is not possible to isolate a pure error term in a repeated measures design, it is not possible to test the significance of S unless one is willing to assume that there is no interaction between A and S. Normally, this presents no problems since the researcher will rarely have any interest in such a test. Finally, it is clear from Table 5-2 that the AS mean square provides the proper error term for tests

Table 5-2 Comparison of expected mean squares for a one-factor design with and without repeated measurements

Source of variation	Repeated measurements	
	No	Yes
A	$\sigma_\varepsilon^2 + n\sigma_\alpha^2$	$\sigma_\varepsilon^2 + n\sigma_\alpha^2 + \sigma_{\pi\alpha}^2$
S†		$\sigma_\varepsilon^2 + k\sigma_\pi^2$
Residual (AS)‡	σ_ε^2	$\sigma_\varepsilon^2 + \sigma_{\pi\alpha}^2$

† With no repeated measurements, subjects is not a factor.
‡ With repeated measurements the residual source of variation is identical to the AS interaction.

of significance on factor A, including all a priori and most post hoc tests discussed in Chap. 3. The situation, however, is not so simple for more complex designs, as is discussed more fully in Sec. 5-IV.

5-II-3 Significance Tests

As can be seen from Table 5-1b the analysis of variance takes what by now should be a familiar form. Similarly most of the a priori and post hoc statistical calculations discussed in Chap. 3 may be directly adapted to repeated measures designs.

An exception is polynomial trend analysis. While trend component sum of squares are calculated in the usual way using the procedures presented in Sec. 3-V-3, some modification of the residual or error mean square may be required, depending upon whether or not the term $\pi\alpha_{ij}$ is included in the response-generating model.

Assuming that $\pi\alpha_{ij}$ is included in the model a direct extension of the results in Table 5-2 gives the expected mean square of the linear trend in A as

$$E[\text{MS}_{A(\text{lin})}] = \sigma_\varepsilon^2 + n\sigma_{\alpha(\text{lin})}^2 + \sigma_{\pi\alpha(\text{lin})}^2$$

The last term, however, represents only the linear portion of $\sigma_{\pi\alpha}^2$. Hence using $E(\text{MS}_\text{E})$ as the denominator of the F ratio for testing a linear trend in factor A will result in a downward bias unless $\sigma_{\pi\alpha}^2 = 0$. A similar bias will occur for trends of any order.

It is therefore necessary to partition the error sum of squares into trend components which, to use the linear trend as an example, will have expected mean squares of the form

$$E[\text{MS}_{\text{E}(\text{lin})}] = \sigma_\varepsilon^2 + \sigma_{\pi\alpha(\text{lin})}^2$$

for each trend component in A which is to be tested. Note that the error sum of squares may be partitioned into as many components as there are potential trends, i.e., levels minus one, in the trial factor.

Computationally there are many ways in which the required calculations can be carried out. Conceptually, however, all involve calculating the weighted sum of the observations on the trial factor for each subject with the weights being the orthogonal polynomial trend coefficients.[4] For each subject there will be one such sum for every trend. Using the data for the first subject in Table 5-1 as an example gives

$$y^*_{1(\text{lin})} = -3(13) - 1(27) + 1(40) + 3(62) = 160$$
$$y^*_{1(\text{quad})} = 1(13) - 1(27) - 1(40) + 1(62) = 8 \quad (5\text{-}5)$$
$$y^*_{1(\text{cubic})} = -1(13) + 3(27) - 3(40) + 1(62) = 10$$

Similar scores can be calculated for the remaining eight subjects. The required sum of squares for the linear trend is

$$SS_{E(\text{lin})} = \frac{\sum_{i=1}^{n} \left[y^*_{i(\text{lin})} - \bar{y}^*_{(\text{lin})} \right]}{\sum_{j=1}^{p} C^2_{j(\text{lin})}} \quad (5\text{-}6)$$

with similar formulas applying for higher order trends. As discussed in Sec. 3-V-1, the denominator in Eq. (5-6) is required to return the sum of squares to the original unit of measurement of y. Note that each of the three error terms for the present example has $n - 1 = 8$ degrees of freedom and that $(p - 1)(n - 1) = 3 \times 8 = 24$ equals the total residual degrees of freedom.

A simple procedure for doing a trend analysis for a repeated measures design is as follows. First, transform the observations on the trial factors in a manner similar to Eq. (5-5). Treating each trend as a separate variable, analyze these variables using a simple descriptive program, such as the SPSS procedure FREQUENCIES, which reports variances and means or sums. Using the linear trend as an example, the required residual term will be

$$SS_{E(\text{lin})} = \frac{(n-1)\sigma^2_{y^*(\text{lin})}}{\sum_{j=1}^{p} C^2_{j(\text{lin})}} \quad (5\text{-}7)$$

and the mean square for the linear trend of factor A will be

$$MS_{A(\text{lin})} = \frac{\left[\sum_{i=1}^{n} y^*_{i(\text{lin})} \right]^2}{n \sum_{j=1}^{p} C^2_j} \quad (5\text{-}8)$$

---

[4] These coefficients are presented in App. B, Table B-7.

As an exercise the reader should try to calculate these values for the data in Table 5-1. They are equal to

$$MS_{A(lin)} = 9050.61 \qquad SS_{E(lin)} = 516.25$$
$$MS_{A(quad)} = 220.03 \qquad SS_{E(quad)} = 124.22$$
$$MS_{A(cubic)} = 2.01 \qquad SS_{E(cubic)} = 121.25$$

5-III THE COVARIANCE ASSUMPTION

5-III-1 Consequences of Violating the Covariance Assumption

Box (1954) has shown that the normal effect of violation of the covariance assumption is to produce F ratios which are too large relative to their tabled values. The size of these distortions can be remarkably large, e.g., it is possible to have an actual $p_1 = 0.25$ or larger when using a nominal value of $p_1 = 0.05$. Parameter estimates, however, remain unbiased.

5-III-2 A Test of the Covariance Assumption

Box (1950) provides the following chi-square test, with f_2 degrees of freedom, of the assumption that Ω has compound symmetry

$$\chi^2_{(f_2)} = (1 - C_2) M_2 \tag{5-9}$$

where

$$M_2 = -(n-1) \ln \frac{|\hat{\Omega}|}{|\Omega_0|}$$

$$C_2 = \frac{p(p+1)^2(2p-3)}{6(n-1)(p-1)(p^2+p-4)}$$

$$f_2 = \frac{p^2+p-4}{2}$$

n equals the number of subjects and p equals the number of levels of the trial factor. The vertical lines enclosing $\hat{\Omega}$ and Ω_0 indicate the determinant of these matrices.[5] Ω_0 has a diagonal with all elements equal to the average of the variances in $\hat{\Omega}$ and all off-diagonal elements equal to the average of the covariances in $\hat{\Omega}$, i.e., for sample data, Ω_0 is our best estimate of what the true value of $\hat{\Omega}$ would be *if* Ω did in fact possess compound symmetry. For our example the average variance is 159.41 and the average covariance is 127.66. Note that

$$MS_E = \overline{VAR} - \overline{COV}$$
$$= 159.41 - 127.66$$
$$= 31.75$$

---

[5] The determinant of a matrix is defined in App. A.

and
$$MS_S = \overline{VAR} + (p-1)\overline{COV}$$
$$= 159.41 + 3(127.66)$$
$$= 542.39$$

This indicates that the repeated measures design acquires its greater precision and power *because* the independence assumption is not met.

Table 5-3 illustrates the compound symmetry test for the data in Table 5-1. With a chi-square of 19.57 with 8 degrees of freedom we see that the assumption of compound symmetry is not tenable at the $p_1 = 0.05$ level. Inspection of the

Table 5-3 Covariances, correlations, test of compound symmetry and degrees of freedom adjustment for data in Table 5-1

(a) Covariance matrix

$$\hat{\Omega} = \begin{bmatrix} 185.50 & 153.38 & 167.25 & 100.75 \\ 153.38 & 144.50 & 138.33 & 72.04 \\ 167.25 & 138.33 & 186.44 & 134.18 \\ 100.75 & 72.04 & 134.18 & 121.19 \end{bmatrix}$$

(b) Correlation matrix

$$R_{AA} = \begin{bmatrix} 1.000 & 0.937 & 0.899 & 0.672 \\ 0.937 & 1.000 & 0.843 & 0.544 \\ 0.899 & 0.843 & 1.000 & 0.893 \\ 0.672 & 0.544 & 0.893 & 1.000 \end{bmatrix}$$

(c) Test of compound symmetry $M_2 = -(n-1)\ln\dfrac{|\hat{\Omega}|}{|\Omega_0|}$

$$= -(8)\ln\frac{763{,}056.161}{17{,}359{,}725.865} = -8(-3.0246) = 25.00$$

$$C_2 = \frac{p(p+1)^2(2p-3)}{6(n-1)(p-1)(p^2+p-4)}$$

$$= \frac{4(5)^2(8-3)}{6(8)(3)(16+4-4)} = 0.217$$

$$f_2 = \frac{p^2+p-4}{2} = 16/2 = 8$$

$$\chi^2_{(f_2)} = (1-C_2)M_2$$

$$\chi^2_{(8)} = (1-0.217)25.00 = 19.57$$

(d) Degrees of freedom adjustment

$$\psi = \frac{p^2(\bar{\sigma}_{ii} - \bar{\sigma}_{..})^2}{(p-1)(\Sigma\Sigma\sigma_{ij}^2 - 2p\Sigma\bar{\sigma}_{i.}^2 + p^2\bar{\sigma}_{..}^2)}$$

$$= \frac{4^2(159.41 - 135.59)^2}{3[312{,}692.94 - 8(75{,}128.67) + 16(18{,}384.65)]}$$

$$= 0.520$$

correlation matrix in Table 5-1b shows a clear tendency for adjacent levels of factor A to be most closely correlated with the correlations decreasing with increasing distance between levels of factor A. Such a pattern is particularly likely to occur when the treatment conditions are administered to subjects in order $A_1, A_2, \ldots A_p$.

5-III-3 Procedures for Correcting for Violations of Covariance Assumption

5-III-3-1 Adjusted degrees of freedom There is a formula due to Box (1954) and Geisser and Greenhouse (1958) which may be used to calculate adjusted degrees of freedom for an F test on a repeated factor to account for the upward bias in the value of F caused by violation of the covariance assumption. Specifically, the adjustment factor is

$$\psi = \frac{p^2(\bar{\sigma}_{ii} - \bar{\sigma}_{..})^2}{(p-1)(\Sigma\Sigma\sigma_{ij}^2 - 2p\Sigma\bar{\sigma}_{i.}^2 + p^2\bar{\sigma}_{..}^2)} \quad (5\text{-}10)$$

where

σ_{ij} = elements of $\hat{\Omega}$

$\bar{\sigma}_{i.}$ = mean of row i of $\hat{\Omega}$

$\bar{\sigma}_{ii}$ = mean of diagonal of $\hat{\Omega}$

$\bar{\sigma}_{..}$ = mean of all elements of $\hat{\Omega}$

The normal degrees of freedom are then multiplied by ψ. As can be seen from section (d) of Table 5-3, $\psi = 0.520$ and the degrees of freedom for factor A should be reduced from 3 and 24 to approximately 1.56 and 12.48 for our illustrative data. Since the calculated value of F is 97.4 this adjustment will not change our conclusions regarding factor A at any conventional level of significance.

In their extension of Box's results Geisser and Greenhouse (1958) also showed that the lower bound of ψ is $1/(p-1)$. Greenhouse and Geisser (1959) therefore suggest the following strategy for making significance tests on trial factors. First, if the F test using the lower bounds degrees of freedom is significant conclude that a significant result has been found at the nominal p_1 level. Second, if the F test using the unadjusted degrees of freedom is *not* significant conclude that a significant result has not been found at the nominal p_1 level. Third, if neither of the first two results are obtained, calculate ψ and make the test of significance using the adjusted degrees of freedom at the desired nominal p_1 level.

Two cautionary notes concerning the use of the ψ adjustment are appropriate. First, Box's study investigated correlations among levels of the trial factor ranging from -0.4 to $+0.4$. The degree to which the adjustment is valid outside this range is not known (McCall and Appelbaum 1973). Second, the appropriateness of the adjustment to more complex designs has not been generally investigated (McCall and Appelbaum 1973).

5-III-3-2 Multivariate analysis An alternative to a repeated measures design is to regard each of the observations taken on a subject as a *separate* dependent variable. In such conversions from a univariate to a multivariate model the trial factors disappear. A direct consequence of the omission of these trial factors from the model is that it is no longer necessary to pool errors over the levels of the repeated factors. It is, of course, this pooling in repeated measures designs which necessitates the covariance assumption discussed above.

While a discussion of the multivariate analysis alternatives to the repeated measures design is outside the scope of our topic three general points concerning the relative merits of these two alternative models can be made.[6] First, if all the assumptions underlying both models are met, the univariate repeated measures model will be more powerful than the multivariate alternative. Second, for the one factor design, if $(n - 1)$ is less than p it is not possible to apply the multivariate model. As a practical matter this situation does occur with some frequency in social and behavioral research, necessitating the use of a repeated measures analysis. Third, when the covariance assumption is not met a multivariate model will often be more informative than a repeated measures model.

5-IV MORE COMPLEX REPEATED MEASURES DESIGNS

In this section three more complex repeated measures designs will be discussed. In the process a few new principles and problems will be introduced. The basic principles, however, remain unchanged which allows the three examples presented to double as reader test problems. Therefore, we shall limit our discussion of each design to those aspects which are unique and shall leave the detailed analysis of the data to the reader as an exercise.

5-IV-1 All-Within Factorial Designs

As the name implies all-within designs are research designs where subjects are observed under all combinations of the levels of all experimental factors. Such designs occur frequently in learning and physiological studies where it is often important to observe the same subject under a wide range of conditions. Table 5-4 presents a 3×4 all-within factorial which will be used to illustrate this model. Generalization to models with a larger number of factors is direct.

5-IV-1-1 Response-generating model The underlying structural model presumed to have generated the data in Table 5-4 is

$$y_{ijk} = \mu + \alpha_i + \beta_j + \pi_k + \alpha\beta_{ij} + \alpha\pi_{ik} + \beta\pi_{jk} + \alpha\beta\pi_{ijk} + \varepsilon_{ijk} \qquad (5\text{-}11)$$

$$(i = 1, p; j = 1, q; k = 1, n)$$

---

[6] Good discussions of these multivariate analytical procedures can be found in McCall and Appelbaum (1973) and Cooley and Lohnes (1971).

Table 5-4 Numerical example all within 3 × 4 factorial

(a) Data

Subject	A_1 B_1	B_2	B_3	B_4	A_2 B_1	B_2	B_3	B_4	A_3 B_1	B_2	B_3	B_4
1	150	152	124	130	152	142	140	143	126	138	135	143
2	118	129	103	109	132	119	119	119	111	115	126	139
3	98	95	91	78	100	115	92	86	92	101	97	110
4	88	82	90	65	83	75	82	71	74	56	74	103

(b) Degrees of freedom and expected mean squares

Source of variation	Degrees of freedom Normal	Conservative	Expected mean square
A	$p - 1$	1	$\sigma_\varepsilon^2 + nq\sigma_\alpha^2 + q\sigma_{\alpha\pi}^2$
B	$q - 1$	1	$\sigma_\varepsilon^2 + np\sigma_\beta^2 + p\sigma_{\beta\pi}^2$
AB	$(p - 1)(q - 1)$	1	$\sigma_\varepsilon^2 + n\sigma_{\alpha\beta}^2 + n\sigma_{\alpha\beta\pi}^2$
S	$(n - 1)$	1	$\sigma_\varepsilon^2 + q\sigma_\pi^2$
SA	$(p - 1)(n - 1)$	$(n - 1)$	$\sigma_\varepsilon^2 + q\sigma_{\alpha\pi}^2$
SB	$(q - 1)(n - 1)$	$(n - 1)$	$\sigma_\varepsilon^2 + p\sigma_{\beta\pi}^2$
SAB	$(n - 1)(p - 1)(q - 1)$	$(n - 1)$	$\sigma_\varepsilon^2 + n\sigma_{\alpha\beta\pi}^2$

(c) Analysis of variance

Source of variation	Degrees of freedom Normal	Conservative	Mean square	F Ratio
A	2	1	72.58	1.04
B	3	1	45.72	0.63
AB	6	1	420.47	7.53†
S	3	1	8566.22	
SA	6	3	69.97	
SB	9	3	72.57	
SAB	18	3	55.82	

† $p_1 < 0.01$ using normal or unadjusted degrees of freedom and $p_1 < 0.10$ using conservative test.

where A and B are fixed and S is random. Note that the model specified by Eq. (5-11) is a direct extension of the single-factor repeated measures design considered in Secs. 5-II and 5-III. The major complication is that there will no longer be a single mean square residual or error to serve as the denominator for all F tests of significance.

5-IV-1-2 Expected mean squares and analysis Table 5-4b presents the expected mean squares and the normal and conservative degrees of freedom for this design. Note that there are three residual sources of variation, i.e., MS_{AS} which is the denominator for MS_A, MS_{BS} for MS_B, and MS_{SAB} for MS_{AB}.[7] This pattern of residual variation occurs because the random factor S is completely crossed with factors A and B. The analysis of variance table follows directly from the expected mean squares and is presented in Table 5-4c.[8] Since neither A nor B is significant using the normal degrees of freedom no further analysis seems warranted. Using a $p_1 = 0.05$ level of significance we see that the AB interaction falls into that middle case where it is useful to calculate the adjusted degrees of freedom.

5-IV-1-3 ψ for AB interaction To calculate ψ for the present problem via Eq. (5-10) requires only one minor change: p is changed to $pq = 3 \times 4 = 12$, i.e., tests of significance on the AB interaction are based on a pq by pq variance/covariance matrix. For the data in Table 5-4 this gives

$$= \frac{(12)^2(771.57 - 713.78)^2}{11[79{,}312.875 - (24)(6{,}353{,}504) + (12)^2(713.78)^2]}$$

$$= 0.225$$

Using ψ to adjust the degrees of freedom for the AB interaction results in the calculated F value of 7.53, slightly exceeding the adjusted nominal $F_{(1.35, 4.05)}$ at the $p_1 = 0.05$ level.

In passing, we should note that the calculation of ψ for A or B would involve a p by p, or q by q, $\hat{\Omega}$ matrix, respectively.

5-IV-1-4 Orthogonal polynomial trends The trend analysis for the present all-within design proceeds along the lines discussed in Sec. 5-II-3, especially Eqs. (5-5) to (5-8). The AB interaction may be decomposed into trend components as follows. Using the linear by linear trend as an example, we first obtain the required orthogonal polynomial trend coefficients from the product of linear trend coefficients for factors A and B, i.e.,

		B_1	B_2	B_3	B_4
		-3	-1	1	3
A_1	-1	3	1	-1	-3
A_2	0	0	0	0	0
A_3	1	-3	-1	1	3

---

[7] Actually there are four residual mean squares since MS_s is the denominator for MS_{mean}.
[8] The reader should be warned that, with a few notable exceptions such as the BMD program 08V, most computer analysis of variance programs do not distinguish between fixed and random factors. Many of the F ratios will therefore be formed using the wrong denominator. Since the calculated value of the mean squares, as opposed to the form of their expected values, is not dependent on the distinctions between fixed and random factors the proper F ratios may be quickly formed from any standard printout.

Next, the linear by linear trend score is obtained for each subject, e.g., for subject 1 in Table 5-4

$$y^*_{1(\text{lin by lin})} = 3(150) + 1(152) - 1(124) - 3(130) + 0(152) + 0(142)$$
$$+ 0(140) + 0(143) - 3(126) - 1(138) + 1(135) + 3(143)$$
$$= 136$$

With a slight modification in subscripts the trend mean square and error sum of squares may be calculated via Eqs. (5-8) and (5-6) as

$$MS_{A(\text{lin by lin})} = \frac{\left[\sum_{k=1}^{n} y^*_{k(\text{lin by lin})}\right]^2}{n \sum_{i=1}^{p} \sum_{j=1}^{q} c_{ij}^2}$$

$$= \frac{318096}{4.40} = 1988.10$$

and

$$SS_{E(\text{lin by lin})} = \frac{\sum_{k=1}^{n} \left[y^*_{k(\text{lin by lin})} - \bar{y}^*_{k(\text{lin by lin})}\right]^2}{\sum_{i=1}^{p} \sum_{j=1}^{q} c_{ij}^2}$$

$$= \frac{1428}{40} = 35.70$$

yielding $F_{(1,3)} = 167$, which is significant beyond the $p_1 = 0.01$ level.

As an exercise the reader should complete the trend analysis. The answers are

		Sum of squares[9]	
A	B	Trend	Error
Linear	Linear	1988.00	35.70
Linear	Quadratic	231.13	370.38
Linear	Cubic	16.90	204.30
Quadratic	Linear	264.03	57.50
Quadratic	Quadratic	5.03	145.46
Quadratic	Cubic	17.63	191.50

5-IV-2 Nested Factorials

In this second extension of the one-factor, repeated measures design we consider an example of a factorial design where subjects are observed under all levels of

[9] Each trend component has one degree of freedom and each error component has three degrees of freedom.

some, but not all, factors. Factors on which there are no repeated measures are called group or nesting factors, i.e., subjects are nested under rather than crossed with these factors. Table 5-5a presents data for a two-factor nested factorial which will be used to illustrate nested factorial designs. Note that subjects are observed under all levels of factor B and that the five subjects nested under A_1 are different subjects than the five subjects nested under A_2. Nested designs are, as we shall see, especially useful where the nesting or grouping variables are of minor interest; their main purpose being to reduce error variance.

5-IV-2-1 Response-generating model The structural model presumed to have generated the data in Table 5-5 is

$$y_{ijhk} = \mu + \alpha_i + \pi_{h(i)} + \beta_j + \alpha\beta_{ij} + \beta\pi_{jh(i)} + \varepsilon_{k(ijh)} \tag{5-12}$$

$$(i = 1, p; j = 1, q; h = 1, n; k = 1)$$

where A and B are fixed and S is random. The subscripts in brackets indicate that that component of the model is nested under the factor represented by the bracketed subscript. Note that, as is always true but normally not explicitly noted, the error term ε_k is nested under all factors. Since k always equals one it appears redundant. We shall explain the usefulness of this dummy subscript in Sec. 5-V. Note also that the AS and ABS interactions are not represented in Eq. (5-12) because S is nested under A.

5-IV-2-2 Expected mean squares and analysis Table 5-5b presents the expected mean squares and the normal and conservative degrees of freedom for this design. Note that the total sum of squares has been partitioned into two major components, i.e., between-subjects and within-subjects. This basic partition can be made in any nested design. In designs without repeated measures all sources of variation are between-subjects.

Inspection of Table 5-5b also reveals that the normal and conservative degrees of freedom are the same for tests on between-subject sources of variation. This occurs because of the absence of repeated observations on any between-subject factor. A further consequence of this is that tests of significance on between-subject sources of variation normally are not troubled by violations of the covariance assumption.

For the within-subjects tests the lower bound of ψ is $1/(q-1)$. Multiplying the normal degrees of freedom by $1/(q-1)$ removes that portion of the normal degrees of freedom contributed by the trial factor. Extension of this relationship to more complex nested designs is straightforward. The analysis of variance follows directly from the expected mean squares and is presented in Table 5-5c.

5-IV-2-3 Homogeneity of covariance matrices In a nested design there are different subjects under each level of the nested factor(s). The variance/covariance matrix for trial factors therefore must be pooled over the subject groups created by the nesting factors. Of course, the legitimacy of this pooling rests on the assumption that the pooled matrices are homogeneous.

Table 5-5 Numerical example two-factor factorial design with subjects nested under factor A

(a) Data

		B_1	B_2	B_3	B_4
A_1	S_1	68	45	34	27
	S_2	48	33	37	32
	S_3	30	40	6	25
	S_4	47	26	16	5
	S_5	17	29	28	15
A_2	S_1	74	69	75	54
	S_2	64	68	61	48
	S_3	77	73	44	26
	S_4	69	57	40	41
	S_5	82	33	30	42

(b) Degrees of freedom and expected mean square

Source of variation	Degrees of freedom Normal	Degrees of freedom Conservative	Expected mean square
Between subjects			
A	$p-1$	$p-1$	$\sigma_\varepsilon^2 + \sigma_\pi^2 + nq\sigma_\alpha^2$
S	$p(n-1)$	$p(n-1)$	$\sigma_\varepsilon^2 + \sigma_\pi^2$
Within subjects			
B	$q-1$	1	$\sigma_\varepsilon^2 + \sigma_{\beta\pi}^2 + np\sigma_\beta^2$
AB	$(p-1)(q-1)$	$p-1$	$\sigma_\varepsilon^2 + \sigma_{\beta\pi}^2 + n\sigma_{\alpha\beta}^2$
BS	$p(n-1)(q-1)$	$p(n-1)$	$\sigma_\varepsilon^2 + \sigma_{\beta\pi}^2$

(c) Analysis of variance

Source of variation	Degrees of freedom Normal	Degrees of freedom Conservative	Mean square	F Ratio
Between subjects				
A	1	1	6734.03	21.42†
S	8	8	314.33	
Within subjects				
B	3	1	1327.16	9.54‡
AB	3	1	40.49	<1
$B\dot{S}$	24	8	139.16	

† $p_1 < 0.01$.
‡ $p_1 < 0.01$ using normal degrees of freedom and $p_1 < 0.05$ using conservative degrees of freedom.

Table 5-5 Continued

(d) Tests on model

(i) Homogeneity of covariance matrices¶

$$\hat{\Omega}_1 = \begin{bmatrix} 376.50 & 73.25 & 103.50 & 61.00 \\ 73.25 & 61.30 & 8.10 & 57.40 \\ 103.50 & 8.10 & 168.20 & 58.80 \\ 61.00 & 59.40 & 58.80 & 116.20 \end{bmatrix} \quad \hat{\Omega}_2 = \begin{bmatrix} 48.70 & -60.50 & -59.50 & -25.55 \\ -60.50 & 263.00 & 201.25 & -12.25 \\ -59.50 & 201.25 & 320.50 & 118.00 \\ -25.55 & -12.25 & 118.00 & 109.20 \end{bmatrix}$$

$$\hat{\Omega}_{\text{pooled}} = \begin{bmatrix} 212.60 & 6.38 & 22.00 & 17.73 \\ 6.38 & 162.15 & 104.68 & 23.58 \\ 22.00 & 104.68 & 244.35 & 88.40 \\ 17.73 & 23.58 & 88.40 & 112.70 \end{bmatrix}$$

$$M_1 = N \ln |\hat{\Omega}_{\text{pooled}}| - \Sigma n_i \ln |\hat{\Omega}_i|$$
$$= 10 \ln (474{,}084{,}501) - 5 \ln (89{,}111{,}644) - 5 \ln (1{,}917{,}585)$$
$$= 35.91$$

$$C_1 = \frac{2q^2 + 3q - 1}{6(q+1)(p-1)} \left[\left(\Sigma \frac{1}{n_i} \right) - \frac{1}{N} \right]$$
$$= \frac{2(4)^2 + 3(4) - 1}{6(5)(1)} \left(\frac{4}{10} - \frac{1}{10} \right)$$
$$= 0.430$$

$$f_1 = \frac{q(q+1)(p-1)}{2}$$
$$= \frac{4(5)(1)}{2}$$
$$= 10$$

$$\chi^2_{(f_1)} = (1 - C_1) M_1$$
$$= 0.57(35.91)$$
$$= 20.47$$

(ii) Compound symmetry¶

$$M_2 = -(N - p) \ln \left[\frac{|\hat{\Omega}_{\text{pooled}}|}{|\Omega_0|} \right]$$

$$= -(8) \ln \frac{474{,}084{,}501}{846{,}960{,}383}$$

$$= 4.64$$

$$C_2 = \frac{q(q+1)^2(2q-3)}{6(N-p)(q-1)(q^2+q-4)}$$

$$= \frac{4(5)^2(5)}{6(8)(3)(16)}$$

$$= 0.217$$

¶ N equals total number of subjects.

Table 5-5 Continued

$$f_2 = \frac{q^2 + q - 4}{2}$$

$$= \frac{(4)^2 + 4 - 4}{2}$$

$$= 8$$

$$\chi_2^2 = (1 - C_2)M_2$$

$$= (1 - 0.217)4.64$$

$$= 3.63$$

(e) Adjustment for degrees of freedom

$$\psi = \frac{p^2(\bar{\sigma}_{ii} - \bar{\sigma}_{..})^2}{(p-1)\left(\sum_i \sum_j \sigma_{ij}^2 - 2p\Sigma\bar{\sigma}_{i.}^2 + p\bar{\sigma}_{..}^2\right)}$$

$$= \frac{4^2(182.95 - 78.59)^2}{3[184,234.68 - 2(4)26,554.32 + 4^2(78.59)^2]}$$

$$= 0.822$$

Box (1950) has developed a chi-square test, based on determinants of the variance/covariance matrices, which may be used to test this homogeneity assumption. Table 5-5(d-i) outlines this test and applies it to our example data. As can be seen the chi-square is significant beyond the $p_1 = 0.05$ level which suggests that the variance/covariance matrices are heterogeneous and that the pooling of these matrices is not justified.

Given heterogeneous variance/covariance matrices the test for compound symmetry and the calculation of ψ becomes difficult to justify and may be misleading. The researcher can, of course, use the conservative F test which in this case is significant at the $p_1 = 0.05$ level. The researcher also has the alternative of treating the problem as a multivariate, rather than a univariate, problem.

5-IV-2-4 Compound symmetry and ψ For completeness, sections d(ii) and (e) of Table 5-5 outline the test for compound symmetry of the pooled variance/covariance matrix and calculate ψ. The test is not significant and ψ is relatively close to one. These conclusions, however, may be incorrect given the outcome of the homogeneity of variance/covariance test.

It is interesting to note the following relationships

$$MS_S = \overline{VAR} - \overline{COV} = 182.95 - 43.80 = 139.15$$

and

$$MS_{BS} = \overline{VAR} + (q-1)\overline{COV} = 182.95 + 3(43.80) = 314.33$$

A few simple algebraic calculations will show that if repeated observations on factor B had not been used

$$\mathrm{MS_E} = \overline{\mathrm{VAR}} = 182.95$$

Put another way, repeated measurements, to the extent that $\overline{\mathrm{COV}}$ exceeds zero, tend to *increase* the precision and power of within-subject tests and to *decrease* the precision and power of between-subject tests. It is for this reason that repeated measures designs are generally best avoided when the researcher is especially interested in the nesting factors.

5-IV-3 Repeated Measures Latin Square

In this final example we present a relatively simple Latin Square design with repeated measures to illustrate how the features of two basic classes of GLM designs may be merged and to suggest some of the problems which may thereby arise. Table 5-6 presents data which will be used to illustrate our discussion.

5-IV-3-1 Response-generating model The structural model presumed to have generated the data in Table 5-6 is

$$y_{hijkm} = \mu + \delta_h + \pi_{i(h)} + \alpha_j + \beta_k + \alpha\beta^*_{jk} + \varepsilon_{m(hijk)} \tag{5-13}$$

$$(h, j, k = 1, p; i = 1, n; m = 1)$$

where G, A, and B are fixed, S is random, and * indicates that only partial information is available on the AB interaction. As can be seen from Eq. (5-13) subjects are nested under groups and it is assumed that there are no interactions involving the group factor.

5-IV-3-2 Expected mean squares Table 5-6c gives the expected mean squares and normal and conservative degrees of freedom for the repeated measures Latin square design discussed here. Examination of this section of the table reveals two interesting facts. First the AB* sum of squares is computationally equivalent to the residual sum of squares in the Latin square design which contains all interaction effects in the data. It is only the assumption that the data contain no interactions involving groups which permits isolation of AB*.

Second, it may be shown that

$$\mathrm{SS}_{AB} = \mathrm{SS}_G + \mathrm{SS}_{AB^*}$$

From this perspective the group main effect may be thought of, although it usually is not, as the between-subjects portion of the AB interaction. Thus, depending on the assumptions the researcher is willing to make, it is possible to (1) use AB* as a test of the absence of interaction assumptions as discussed in Sec. 4-III-1-4 or, (2) assuming no interactions involving groups, as a partial test of the presence of an AB interaction, or (3) assuming no main or interaction effects involving groups, test the AB sum of squares for statistical significance directly. Note that in the

160 THE GENERAL LINEAR MODEL

Table 5-6 Numerical example 3 × 3 Latin square with repeated measures on one factor

(a) Structure of Latin square

	A_1	A_2	A_3
G_1	B_2	B_3	B_1
G_2	B_3	B_1	B_2
G_3	B_1	B_2	B_3

(b) Data—three subjects per group

65	44	78
49	42	72
54	18	63
53	56	53
38	61	56
15	71	52
75	80	56
64	70	46
69	22	7

(c) Degrees of freedom and expected mean squares

Source of variation	Degrees of freedom Normal	Degrees of freedom Conservative	Expected mean square
Between-groups	$p-1$	$p-1$	$\sigma_\varepsilon^2 + p\sigma_\pi^2 + np\sigma_\delta^2$
S	$p(n-1)$	$p(n-1)$	$\sigma_\varepsilon^2 + p\sigma_\pi^2$
Within-groups			
A	$p-1$	1	$\sigma_\varepsilon^2 + np\sigma_\alpha^2$
B	$p-1$	1	$\sigma_\varepsilon^2 + np\sigma_\beta^2$
AB*	$(p-1)(p-2)$	1	$\sigma_\varepsilon^2 + np\sigma_{\alpha\beta}^2$
Error	$p(n-1)(p-1)$	$p(n-1)$	σ_ε^2

(d) Analysis of variance

Source of variation	Degrees of freedom Normal	Degrees of freedom Conservative	Mean square	F Ratio
Between-groups	2	2	38.37	<1
S	6	6	470.96	
Within-groups				
A	2	1	12.70	<1
B	2	1	2386.81	14.16†
AB*	2	1	20.22	<1
Error	12	6	168.57	

† $p_1 < .01$ for both normal and conservative F test.

last two cases it is not possible to test our assumptions even partially. More generally, the use of repeated measures in conjunction with Latin squares presents a great many problems for which there often are no readily available remedies. For more details on the use of repeated measurements in Latin square designs the reader is referred to Winer (1971), pp. 711–751.

5-IV-3-3 Data analysis The data analysis plan follows directly from the expected mean squares and is presented in Table 5-6d. Because of the presence of different combinations of the levels of A and B at each level of G no attempt has been made to test the covariance assumption or to compute ψ. We may, however, use the conservative degrees of freedom for within-subjects tests which in the present example is significant for factor B at the $p_1 = 0.01$ level.

5-V RULES FOR CONSTRUCTING EXPECTED MEAN SQUARES

As the complexity of the experimental design increases the complexity of the expected mean square for each source of variation in the model also tends to increase. Therefore, this section presents a simple procedure for generating these expected mean squares for any GLM design. Table 5-7 illustrates the application of these rules using the model for the two-factor nested design discussed in Sec. 5-IV-2.

The first step is to write out the response-generating model in full, indicating with brackets any nesting relationships. For our example, the model is

$$y_{ijhk} = \mu + \alpha_i + \pi_{h(i)} + \beta_j + \alpha\beta_{ij} + \beta\pi_{jh(i)} + \varepsilon_{k(ijh)} \tag{5-14}$$

$$(i = 1, p; j = 1, q; h = 1, n; k = 1)$$

Note that in writing the model the error term is nested under all other factors. As noted previously, this is always true, which is why it is customary to omit the nesting designation when writing the model. For the rules presented here, however, it is important to indicate this relationship. For each term in the model a subscript is said to be: (1) *live* if it is present and not bracketed, (2) *dead* if it is present and bracketed, or (3) *absent* if it is not present at all. Using $\beta\pi_{jh(i)}$ as an example, j and h are live, i is dead, and k is absent.

The second step is to construct a so-called *auxiliary table* such as in Table 5-7. The rows of this table correspond to the components of the model. The columns correspond to the subscripts of each factor with the number of levels of the factor corresponding to that subscript being written below the subscript and an F or R being written above depending on whether the factor is fixed or random.

The third step is to fill in the body of the Auxiliary Table using the following rules:

1. For each row, enter the number of levels of any column (i.e., factor) headed by a subscript which is absent,

162 THE GENERAL LINEAR MODEL

2. For each column, enter a 1 for any cell headed by a dead subscript,
3. For each *random* effect column, enter 1 in the remaining cells,
4. For each *fixed* effect column, enter 0 in the remaining cells.

Table 5-7 Auxiliary table for constructing expected mean squares for nested repeated measures factorial in Table 5-5

Model component	Subscripts†			
	F i_p	F j_q	R h_n	R k_1
α_i	0	q	n	1
$\pi_{h(i)}$	1	q	1	1
β_j	p	0	n	1
$\alpha\beta_{ij}$	0	0	n	1
$\beta\pi_{jh(i)}$	1	0	1	1
$\varepsilon_{k(ijh)}$	1	1	1	1

† F = fixed; R = random.

The final step is to cover the columns corresponding to the live subscripts for a source of variation in the model and, for each row for which these subscripts are either live or dead, to take the product of the visible numbers times the variance of the row effect. Again using $\beta\pi_{jh(i)}$ as an example, we first cover columns j and h and then find those rows which contain the subscripts j, h and i. Only the last two rows in Table 5-7 meet these conditions. Thus the expected mean square for the *BS* source of variation is $\sigma^2_{\beta\pi} + \sigma^2_\varepsilon$. As an exercise the reader should find the remaining expected mean squares for this and the other examples presented in Sec. 5-IV using the procedure outlined above. The reader may check his work against the expected mean squares presented in Tables 5-4, 5-5, and 5-6.

5-VI THE VARIANCE COMPONENTS MODEL

Repeated measures designs are often referred to as mixed effects models because random and fixed factors are both present, i.e., subjects are treated as a random factor while all other factors are fixed.[10] In certain research questions it is appropriate to consider all factors to be random factors. Models with all factors random are variously referred to as random effects, Type II, or variance com-

---

[10] While repeated measures designs are mixed effects models they are logically more similar to fixed effects models than random effects models. This is because all factors, except subjects, are considered fixed. And, as was noted above, the researcher is rarely interested in statistical tests on the subject factor. While there are situations, primarily in the natural sciences, where the researcher is interested in making statistical tests on both fixed and random factors within the same model, these research problems are excluded from our discussion.

ponents models. In this section we shall briefly outline the characteristics of the variance components model giving special attention to how this model differs from the fixed effects model.

Since variance components models are used only rarely in social and behavioral research our discussion will be somewhat cursory, being generally confined to one- or two-factor designs with equal numbers of observations per cell. The reader is warned that, while the variance components model appears from the perspective of this book to be a relatively straightforward extension of the fixed effects model, the mathematical structure of these two models are quite different, much more so than our brief discussion might lead the reader to believe. Two consequences of these differences are especially important. First, the problems which are raised by unbalanced data, i.e., data with unequal numbers of observations per cell, are much more difficult and less easily resolved in the variance components model than in the fixed effects model. Second, in contrast to the fixed effects model, the variance components model is quite sensitive to violation of the model assumptions.[11]

5-VI-1 Research Uses of the Variance Components Model

In the fixed effects model the researcher's interest is in subjects' responses under the specific treatment conditions represented by the levels of each factor. Furthermore, the levels of each factor are selected in a non-random way, usually because the researcher is specifically interested in subjects' responses to the specific treatment conditions presented by the experimental design.

In contrast, in the variance components model the researcher is *not* interested specifically in the treatment effects or in linear combinations, e.g., orthogonal polynomials, of those effects. Rather the researcher is interested in the *variance* of those effects in some specified population of potential treatments. To be valid, however, the specific treatment conditions in the research design must be randomly selected.

In social and behavioral research perhaps the most important use of variance components models is in problems dealing with reliability. For example, in constructing any type of paper-and-pencil, personality trait test an appropriate model might be

$$y_{ij} = \mu + \pi_i + \alpha_j + \varepsilon_{ij} \tag{5-15}$$

where y_{ij} is the response π_i of subject i to a series of questions (α_j's) all purporting to tap the same personality trait, e.g., anxiety. Clearly, the researcher's interest is not in the value of each α_j, since all presumably tap the same personality trait, but in the variance of subjects responses to a random selection of all potential questions related to the personality trait, anxiety. In this example the researcher is interested in minimizing the variance arising from the specific questions and error relative to the total variation in y, i.e., in maximizing the reliability of the test.

---

[11] For more information on this point see Scheffé (1959), Chap. 10, especially Sec. 10-2.

5-VI-2 Basic Model and Assumptions

The structural or response-generating model for any variance components model is exactly the same as for a corresponding fixed effects model. As an example the model for a two-factor design would be

$$y_{ijk} = \mu + \alpha_i + \beta_j + \alpha\beta_{ij} + \varepsilon_{ijk} \tag{5-16}$$

In Eq. (5-16), α, β, $\alpha\beta$, and ε, but not μ which is a fixed constant for all observations, are random variables with variances σ_α^2, σ_β^2, $\sigma_{\alpha\beta}^2$, and σ_ε^2, respectively. The variance of y is presumed to be

$$\sigma_y^2 = \sigma_\alpha^2 + \sigma_\beta^2 + \sigma_{\alpha\beta}^2 + \sigma_\varepsilon^2 \tag{5-17}$$

i.e., the variables are assumed to be independently distributed. Each term in Eq. (5-17) is a variance and is a component of σ_y^2 which accounts for the name of this model.

With the assumptions presented in Sec. 3-II-2, excluding normality and the fixed effects assumptions, it is possible to estimate the variance components in Eq. (5-17). Statistical tests on these estimates, however, require that each variance component be normally, as well as independently, distributed. The reader is again cautioned that the variance components model is very sensitive to violation of the normality assumption.

5-VI-3 Estimation of Variance Components

The procedure for estimating variance components outlined in this section is known as the analysis variance method. Specifically, this method takes the estimated mean squares for each source of variation as they are computed for a fixed effects model and using the general form of the expected mean squares for a random effects model solves for each variance component. For example, the expected mean squares for a one factor random effects model are

$$E(MS_A) = \sigma_\varepsilon^2 + n\sigma_\alpha^2$$

$$E(MS_E) = \sigma_\varepsilon^2$$

therefore, the estimated variance components are

$$\hat{\sigma}_\varepsilon^2 = MS_E$$

and

$$\hat{\sigma}_\alpha^2 = \frac{1}{n}(MS_A - MS_E)$$

More generally, the expected mean squares for a random effects model may be written

$$\dot{E}(m) = P\sigma^2 \tag{5-18}$$

where m is a vector of mean squares, σ^2 a vector of variance components and P a matrix of constants. Using a p by q random effects factorial with n observations per cell as an example yields

$$E(m) = \begin{bmatrix} 1 & nq & 0 & n \\ 1 & 0 & np & n \\ 1 & 0 & 0 & n \\ 1 & 0 & 0 & 0 \end{bmatrix} \begin{bmatrix} \sigma_\varepsilon^2 \\ \sigma_\alpha^2 \\ \sigma_\beta^2 \\ \sigma_{\alpha\beta}^2 \end{bmatrix} \quad (5\text{-}19)$$

From Eqs. (5-18) and (5-19) it follows that our estimates of the variance components may be obtained by

$$\hat{\sigma}^2 = P^{-1}m \quad (5\text{-}20)$$

Equation (5-20) may be used for any random effects model with balanced data but will generally not work for unbalanced data. Searle (1971, Chaps. 10 and 11) discusses procedures for estimating variance components for unbalanced data.

Unfortunately, there is nothing in Eq. (5-20) which prevents the estimated variance components from being negative. Since a variance component is by definition positive this is an obviously unsatisfactory state of affairs, which becomes even more unsatisfactory if the researcher is interested in ratios of the variance components. Searle (1971, pp. 406–408) outlines several courses of action which might be taken if one or more elements of σ^2 is negative including:

1. Accepting the estimate but regarding it as an indication that the true value is zero.
2. Changing the estimated value to zero which is intuitively plausible but which alters desirable properties of the estimates such as unbiasedness and minimum variance.
3. Collecting more data in the hope that the negative component will disappear.

Searle also notes and provides references to the following four procedures which may be used to avoid negative variance components:

1. Pooling minimal mean squares with predecessors.
2. Re-specifying the response-generating model.
3. Using maximum likelihood estimators.
4. Using Bayesian estimators.

5-VI-4 Tests of Significance

Hypotheses in the variance components model concern variances, e.g., $H_0: \sigma_\alpha^2 = 0$. It is precisely because the hypotheses concern variances, rather than treatment effects, that the significance tests depend so much upon the normality assumptions discussed above.

The form of the F ratios necessary to test each hypothesis follows directly from the general form of the expected mean squares which may be constructed using the rules presented in Sec. 5-V. Unlike the fixed effects model, however, F

166 THE GENERAL LINEAR MODEL

tests involving random effects models follow the central F distribution even if the null hypothesis is not true. For example, the F test for a one-way design is

$$F = \left[1 + \frac{\sigma_\alpha^2}{\sigma_\varepsilon^2}\right] F_{[p-1, p(n-1)]}$$

Thus the calculated F statistic is a multiple of the tabled central F distribution whether σ_α^2 is zero or not. Therefore, the power of the test $\sigma_\alpha^2 = 0$ against some

Table 5-8 Summary of most important equations in Chap. 5

Compound symmetry

$$\Omega = \sigma_\varepsilon^2 \begin{bmatrix} 1 & \rho & \cdots & \rho \\ \rho & 1 & & \vdots \\ \vdots & & 1 & \rho \\ \rho & \cdots & \rho & 1 \end{bmatrix}$$

Constant variance of treatment differences

$$\sigma_{\bar{A}_j - \bar{A}_k}^2 = \frac{1}{n}(\sigma_j^2 + \sigma_k^2 - 2\sigma_{jk})$$

Chi-square test of compound symmetry

$$\chi^2_{(f_2)} = (1 - C_2) M_2$$

where

$$M_2 = -(n-1) \ln \frac{|\hat{\Omega}|}{|\hat{\Omega}_0|}$$

$$C_2 = \frac{p(p+1)^2(2p-3)}{6(n-1)(p-1)(p^2+p-4)}$$

$$f_2 = \frac{p^2 + p - 4}{2}$$

Adjustment factor for violation of constant variance of treatment differences assumption

$$\psi = \frac{p^2(\bar{\sigma}_{ii} - \bar{\sigma}_{..})^2}{(p-1)(\Sigma\Sigma\sigma_{ij}^2 - 2p\Sigma\bar{\sigma}_{i.} + p^2\bar{\sigma}_{..}^2)}$$

Chi-square homogeneity of covariance matrices test

$$\chi^2_{(f_1)} = (1 - C_1) M_1$$

where

$$M_1 = N \ln |\hat{\Omega}_{\text{pooled}}| - \Sigma n_i \ln |\hat{\Omega}_i|$$

$$C_1 = \frac{2q^2 + 3q - 1}{6(q+1)(p-1)} \left(\sum \frac{1}{n_i}\right) - \frac{1}{N}$$

$$f_1 = \frac{q(q+1)(p-1)}{2}$$

Estimated variance components—analysis of variance method for balanced data

$$\hat{\sigma}^2 = P^{-1} m$$

alternative specified by the ratio $\sigma_\alpha^2/\sigma_\varepsilon^2$ is equal to

$$\Pr(F) > \frac{F_{[p-1,\,p(n-1),\,p_1]}}{\left[1 + \dfrac{\sigma_\alpha^2}{\sigma_\varepsilon^2}\right]}$$

For a further discussion of the variance components model and certain problems when it is extended to more complex designs the reader is referred to Searle (1971, Chaps. 9, 10, and 11) and Winer (1971, Secs. 3-17, 5-15, and 5-25).

5-VII SUMMARY

The GLM designs investigated in this chapter provide great economy in subjects, and often in experimental effort. More importantly, the nature of many important social and behavioral research problems require, by their very nature, the use of repeated measurement on the same subject. In such circumstances there is reason to believe that the observations are not independent and much of this chapter has been directed to dealing with the potentially severe consequences of this problem. Finally, the characteristics of the variance components or random effects model were very briefly examined. The reader was cautioned, however, that the mathematical structure of this model differs more from the fixed effects model, with a number of important theoretical and practical implications, than our cursory examination would suggest. Table 5-8 presents a summary of the most important formulas discussed in this chapter.

CHAPTER
SIX

ANALYSIS OF COVARIANCE

6-I Research Uses of Covariance Designs
6-I-1 Reduction of Mean Square Error
6-I-2 Matching Subject Groups
6-I-3 Investigating Nature of Treatment Effects
6-I-4 Analysis of Variance With Missing Data

6-II The Basic Model
6-II-1 Assumed Underlying (Response-Generating) Structural Model
    6-II-1-1 Model 1—homogeneous regression slopes
    6-II-1-2 Model 2—heterogeneous regression slopes
6-II-2 Assumptions Underlying the Analysis of Covariance
    6-II-2-1 Prior assumptions
    6-II-2-2 Additional assumptions
6-II-3 Partitioning the Variation in y
    6-II-3-1 Partitioning y, x_c, and their cross products
    6-II-3-2 Regression slopes and correlations
    6-II-3-3 The ANCOVA partition of the sum of squares
    6-II-3-4 Alternative partitions of the sum of squares
6-II-4 Adjusted Treatment Means
6-II-5 GLM Matrix Approach
6-II-6 Significance Tests
    6-II-6-1 The ANCOVA table
    6-II-6-2 General linear contrasts
    6-II-6-3 Adjusted treatment means

6-III Assumptions Underlying the Analysis of Covariance
6-III-1 Assumptions Concerning Errors
6-III-2 Treatments Do Not Affect Covariate
      6-III-2-1 Consequences of violating assumption
      6-III-2-2 Detecting assumption violation
      6-III-2-3 Corrective procedures
6-III-3 Homogeneity of Regression Slopes
      6-III-3-1 A numerical example
      6-III-3-2 Consequences of violating assumption
      6-III-3-3 Detecting assumption violation
      6-III-3-4 Corrective procedures
6-III-4 Linear Regression
      6-III-4-1 Consequences of violating assumption
      6-III-4-2 Detecting assumption violation
      6-III-4-3 Corrective procedures
6-III-5 Covariate Measured Without Error
      6-III-5-1 Consequences of violating assumption
      6-III-5-2 Detecting assumption violation
      6-III-5-3 Corrective procedures

6-IV A Comparison of Covariance Analysis and Randomized Blocks

6-V Advanced Covariance Designs
6-V-1 Factorial ANCOVA With One Covariate
6-V-2 Factorial ANCOVA With Two Covariates

6-VI Summary

Previous chapters have considered a variety of analysis of variance designs which increase both the precision of parameter estimates and the power of statistical tests, i.e., randomized blocks, Latin squares, and repeated measures designs. All of these designs involve the "direct" control of sources of variation. Specifically, subjects are grouped into homogeneous blocks and variation associated with the block effect(s) is removed from the error sum of squares.

This chapter considers a variety of General Linear Model (GLM) designs known as the analysis of covariance (ANCOVA) which are used to "statistically" control sources of variation in the data by removing from the dependent variable y a term of the form βx_c.[1] The variable x_c is a covariate or, as it is sometimes called, a concomitant variable which is believed to be associated, i.e., to covary,

---

[1] The subscript c in x_c indicates that we are referencing that column of the design matrix X containing the covariate. In this and the next chapter we shall use bold face type to reference a variable in a specific set of empirical data and regular type to reference a variable more generally.

with y and β is a regression coefficient, estimated from the data, which relates changes in x_c to changes in y.

It may be useful to think of covariance analysis as creating a new dependent variable

$$y^* = y - \beta x_c \qquad (6\text{-}1)$$

where y^* represents the "residual" portion of y which cannot be accounted for by the covariate x_c.[2] The variation in y^* can then be partitioned via the analysis of variance procedures discussed in earlier chapters.[3] In actual practice only a single set of computations is required.

The covariate, although it may be nominally scaled, is usually intervally or ratio scaled.[4] Thus covariance analyses typically contain a mixture of the nominally-scaled variables associated with analysis of variance and the intervally- and ratio-scaled variables associated with regression analysis. In this sense ANCOVA is the meeting, and more importantly the joining, point under the GLM umbrella of analysis of variance and regression techniques.

ANCOVA is also the meeting point of analysis of variance and regression analysis in another important sense. The designs considered in previous chapters have been restricted to equal numbers of observations per cell and categorical independent variables which are represented in the design matrix as contrasts between factor levels. This has meant the independent variables are orthogonal and therefore the variation in y can be partitioned into components which are uniquely attributable to each source of variation in the model. In general, however, the covariate will tend to be correlated with the other independent variables in the data even if the researcher assumes, as he sometimes does, that the covariate is uncorrelated with these variables in the *population*. This raises the problem so familiar to users of regression techniques of how to partition the variation in y. As we shall see, ANCOVA and regression analysis handle this partitioning problem in quite different ways. These differences are required not by any fundamental mathematical or statistical considerations but rather because ANCOVA users normally attempt to *interpret* the treatment effects, after adjustment for the covariate, in the same fashion as they are interpreted in analysis of variance with equal numbers of observations per cell rather than in the less definitive sense in which the effects of a set of correlated independent variables are interpreted in regression analysis.

Moreover, the assumptions generally made in conjunction with covariance analysis—principally homogeneity of regression slopes within cells and absence of treatment effects on the covariate—are made not so much for statistical reasons as to make the covariance analysis conceptually valid and/or interpretable.

---

[2] Although the functional form relating y^* and x_c in Eq. (6-1) is linear this is only a convenience not a requirement as we shall discuss more fully in Sec. 6-III-4.

[3] There are a number of other terms such as σ_e^2 for which it is useful to compare values before and after adjustment for the covariate. In these cases we shall use an asterisk, as in Eq. (6-1), to indicate that the value of the term has been adjusted for any effects of the covariate.

[4] See Sec. 1-IV for a discussion of the characteristics of different scales of measurement.

Indeed, our major concern when we discuss violations of the ANCOVA assumptions will not be their effects on statistical tests but rather their effects on the validity of the interpretations we may wish to make on the basis of our data analyses. It is especially in this congruence between the researcher's data analysis objectives and the characteristics of the ANCOVA procedure that many of the most substantial interpretative problems in ANCOVA arise.

The remainder of this chapter is divided into five sections. The first discusses some of the research uses of the ANCOVA procedure. The second develops the basic model. The third discusses the assumptions underlying ANCOVA and the consequences of violating these assumptions. The fourth reviews the relative advantages and disadvantages of randomized blocks designs versus covariance designs. The last section describes extensions of the basic model to more complex ANCOVA designs and presents reader test problems.

6-I RESEARCH USES OF COVARIANCE DESIGNS

In 1957, the journal *Biometrics* ran a special issue on the ANCOVA. The first two articles in this issue discussed the nature and uses of ANCOVA (Cochran, 1957) and the interpretation of treatment means which have been adjusted for one or more covariates (Smith, 1957). In this and the next two sections we shall at times rely rather heavily on these two articles. A careful reading of this issue of *Biometrics* is suggested for anyone considering using covariance analysis.

6-I-1 Reduction of Mean Square Error

Cochran (1957) notes that the relationship between the mean square errors in the analysis of variance σ_ε^2 and covariance $\sigma_\varepsilon^2 *$ is about

$$\sigma_\varepsilon^2 * = \sigma_\varepsilon^2 (1 - \rho^2) \left(\frac{df_E}{df_E - 1} \right) \tag{6-2}$$

where df_E is the degrees of freedom for σ_ε^2 and ρ is the correlation between the covariate and the dependent variable. Thus, for ρ above 0.3 or 0.4, the covariance adjustment may result in a rather substantial reduction in the mean square error and therefore considerably more precise parameter estimates and powerful statistical tests.

In this case the ANCOVA model is being used in the same way as a randomized blocks or a Latin square design would be used to reduce error variance. Generally this use assumes that there is no relationship between the covariate and the treatment factors in the experiment. This can normally be insured by measuring the covariate(s) before applying the treatments and then randomly assigning treatments to subjects.

A broad class of social and behavioral research problems for which the covariance procedure is particularly useful for reducing the mean square error occurs where the researcher is interested in the change between pre- and post-treatment levels of some dependent variable, e.g., attitudes or unit sales, as a function of the experimental treatments, e.g., different persuasive messages or different pricing levels. In these situations the pre-treatment level of the dependent variable serves as the covariate. Since the correlation between the covariate and dependent variable is often very high in situations such as this the reduction in the mean square error is often very substantial.

To illustrate the flexibility of the ANCOVA procedure it may be useful to contrast the above procedure with the use of difference scores between pre- and post-treatment levels of the dependent variable. If x_c is the pre-treatment level and y the post-treatment level of the dependent variable, what is analyzed in an analysis of difference scores is a new variable

$$z = y - x_c \qquad (6\text{-}3)$$

Equation (6-3) clearly shows the implied assumption that $\beta = 1$. Further, it is implicitly assumed that $\beta = 1$ within each cell of the research design. Often these implicit assumptions are not tested, although they may be, when difference scores are used as the dependent variable.

The ANCOVA also provides a procedure for making covariance adjustments when the covariate and dependent variable are measured on different scales. For example, in the attitude and sales examples given above the covariates might have been level of subjects' intelligence and level of in-store product promotion, respectively. In cases such as these it is generally not possible to specify a priori the value of β. The ANCOVA procedure thus provides a flexible procedure for estimating β from the data. It also tends to explicate the assumptions made, and as we shall see, provides a set of procedures for testing these assumptions.

6-1-2 Matching Subject Groups

In social and behavioral research the researcher is often forced to work with intact groups, e.g., classes of school children, production units, and/or is prohibited from randomly assigning levels of the independent variable(s) to subjects. To the extent that the covariate and dependent variable are related and the group means on the covariate differ, comparisons between any two groups i and j will contain a bias equal to $\beta(\bar{x}_{c_i} - \bar{x}_{c_j})$. The ANCOVA provides a procedure for removing this bias.

In effect ANCOVA "matches" all subject groups on the covariate. Unlike physical matching, which requires us to find one or more blocks of subjects with the same set of covariate values, i.e., blocking variable values, the covariate matching is "statistical" and equates all groups to the mean value of the covariate. Thus we are able to remove the effects of the covariate from the dependent variable without having to find equal numbers of subjects for each value or range of values the covariate may take.

This statistical matching of subject groups is perhaps the use for which the ANCOVA model is most frequently employed in social and behavioral research. Unlike the previous use, however, this use of ANCOVA is fraught with potential interpretative and statistical difficulties. First, situations where ANCOVA is used to remove a source of variation over which the researcher cannot gain direct control are the same situations where all the problems presented by associative, as opposed to causal, models typically occur.[5] That is, we can never be sure that some biasing effect other than the covariate has not been overlooked.

Second, in statistically matching groups to the mean of the covariate we are asking a "what if" type of question for which there may be no empirical counterpart. For example, one of our statistically defined groups may own 0.8 houses, have 2.3 children, and/or have 0.5 of a wife employed full time. This average, of course, will not correspond to any specific subject group. Thus, it is often not clear to what population our conclusions might apply.

Third, certain statistical problems occur when subject groups differ on the covariate. These problems increase as the differences between group covariate means increase. Somewhat ironically, it is precisely those situations where groups differ substantially on the covariate in which ANCOVA is most likely to be used to statistically match subject groups. More will be said about these problems in Secs. 6-II and 6-III.

In concluding this section we should note that the covariate adjustment continues to reduce the mean square error precisely as described in the previous section when ANCOVA is used to statistically match subject groups.

6-I-3 Investigating Nature of Treatment Effects

In some research problems it may be of interest to know whether the treatment(s) exerts its effect directly on the dependent variable or through some intervening variable, i.e., the covariate. This question may be investigated by comparing the results of an analysis of variance with an ANCOVA. To the extent that a significant treatment effect is found in the former analysis, but not the latter, there is at least the suggestion that the treatment is exercising its effect on the dependent variable via the covariate. For example, it might be possible to use such a procedure to determine whether relative changes in attitude following a series of persuasive communications was due to differential learning of messages contained in these communications. For further details on this use of ANCOVA, including difficulties of interpretation, the reader is referred to Smith (1957).

6-I-4 Analysis of Variance With Missing Data

Sometimes it will happen, even in a true experiment, that one or more observations will be lost for reasons essentially unrelated to the research. In such cases the ANCOVA procedure may be used to compute accurate treatment means and tests of significance. This is done by assigning any value (e.g., 0) to the missing datum point and constructing a dummy covariate where the covariate takes any value (e.g., 1) other than zero for the missing observation and zero

[5] See Sec. 3-VII-2.

elsewhere. If more than one observation is missing the above procedure may be extended. There will be one covariate for each missing value. The standard ANCOVA computations will give the correct analysis of variance results.[6]

6-II THE BASIC MODEL

Table 6-1 presents a numerical example which will be used to facilitate the discussion in this section. The artificially contrived data is for a one factor ANCOVA with seven observations per cell.

6-II-1 Assumed Underlying (Response-Generating) Structural Model

It will simplify our later discussion to introduce two slightly different ANCOVA models. The first model, which is normally presented as *the* covariance model, assumes homogeneity of regression slopes within cells. The second does not. The second model is often introduced as a vehicle, when compared against the first model, for testing the homogeneity of regression slopes assumption. The point we wish to make at the outset is that mathematically and statistically the second model is as valid as the first. It does, however, present certain additional interpretation problems.

6-II-1-1 Model 1—homogeneous regression slopes The complete structural model assumed to be responsible for generating data for a one factor ANCOVA, such as that in Table 6-1, is

$$y_{ij} = \mu + \alpha_i + \beta(x_{c_{ij}} - \bar{x}_c) + \varepsilon_{ij} \qquad (6\text{-}4)$$

$$\sum_i \alpha_i = 0$$

$$(i = 1, p; j = 1, n)$$

Although not required the covariate has been, as is common practice, centered to a mean of zero. This coding scheme keeps the grand mean of y free of the effects of the mean of the covariate since the sum of the deviations of a variable about its mean equals zero.

Moving the covariate term to the left, Eq. (6-4) can be rewritten

$$y_{ij} - \beta(x_{c_{ij}} - \bar{x}_c) = \mu + \alpha_i + \varepsilon_{ij} \qquad (6\text{-}5)$$

The right side of Eq. (6-5) is, of course, simply the equation for a one-factor analysis of variance. The left side of the equation indicates that it is that residual portion of y which cannot be explained by the covariate which is being partitioned into a series of additive components which are attributable to the different sources

---

[6] This procedure was first presented by Bartlett in 1937 [cited in Cochran (1957)]. More recently this use of ANCOVA has been discussed by Coons (1957, pp. 387–405).

Table 6-1 Numerical example one-factor analysis of covariance

	Factor					
	A_1		A_2		A_3	
x_c	y	x_c	y	x_c	y
12	19	12	22	11	18
7	13	15	28	6	21
10	10	14	24	9	24
8	9	12	27	10	21
8	12	10	24	15	28
5	6	8	16	7	15
13	18	5	21	13	21
Marginal means	9.00	12.43	10.86	23.14	10.14	21.14
Grand means					10.00	18.90

of variation postulated by the response-generating model. The response-generating models for more complex designs are designated in precisely the same way.

6-II-1-2 Model 2—heterogeneous regression slopes If we are not willing to assume that the relationship between y and x_c is the same within each cell of the research design the appropriate response-generating model for the one way ANCOVA becomes

$$y_{ij} = \mu + \alpha_i + \beta_i(x_{c_{ij}} - \bar{x}_c) + \varepsilon_{ij} \qquad (6\text{-}6)$$

$$\sum_i \alpha_i = 0$$

$$(i = 1, p; j = 1, n)$$

Although more complex and somewhat more difficult to handle statistically, Eq. (6-6) is just as valid a response-generating model as is Eq. (6-4).[7] Our other comments in the preceding section apply equally to the case with heterogeneous regressions. Finally, as we shall see in Sec. 6-III-3-3, the difference between the sum of squares explained by Eqs. (6-6) and (6-4) may be used to test the homogeneity of regression slopes assumption.

6-II-2 Assumptions Underlying the Analysis of Covariance

6-II-2-1 Prior assumptions All of the assumptions discussed in Sec. 3-II-2 in the context of the full factorial design continue to hold. The consequences of violating these assumptions and the appropriate remedies also apply to the ANCOVA model.

---

[7] For a discussion of this point see Maxwell and Cramer (1975).

6-II-2-2 Additional assumptions The following additional assumptions, although not absolutely required, are usually included as part of the ANCOVA model:

1. Treatments have no affect on the covariate.
2. The regression slope coefficients β_i are equal for all treatment group populations.
3. The true relationship between y and x_c within each treatment group population is linear.
4. The covariate is measured without error.

Each of these assumptions, along with certain of those assumptions referred to in Sec. 6-II-2-1, are investigated in detail in Sec. 6-III.

6-II-3 Partitioning the Variation in y

In this section we will use the data in Table 6-1 to illustrate how the variation in y is partitioned and attributed to each component in the ANCOVA model. As noted in the introduction, this partitioning of the variation in y is complicated by the fact that the covariate will normally be correlated with the other independent variables in the model. The result is that the variance in y explained by x_c and the other independent variables will overlap, i.e., will not be orthogonal. Covariance analysis handles this problem in a standard way. Specifically, the variation due the covariate is *extracted* first and then the remaining variation is uniquely attributed to the remaining components in the model.[8]

6-II-3-1 Partitioning y, x_c, and their cross products In discussing the interrelationships among the variables in the ANCOVA model it is useful to begin by partitioning (via one-way analyses of variance) y, x_c, and their cross products. Section (*a*) of Table 6-2 gives the partitions both generally and for the data in Table 6-1. The notation adopted in Table 6-2(*b-i*) for referring to the various sum of squares is somewhat different from that employed in the rest of this text. We use these symbols here because they are rather standard in the statistical literature and may therefore be helpful to the reader wishing to pursue the ANCOVA model further.

The procedures for partitioning y and x_c should be obvious. The cross products between these variables may be partitioned as follows:

$$T_{yx} = n \sum_{i=1}^{p} (\bar{x}_{c_i} - \bar{x}_c)(\bar{y}_i - \bar{y})$$

$$E_{yx} = \sum_{j=1}^{n} \sum_{i=1}^{p} (x_{c_{ij}} - \bar{x}_{c_i})(y_{ij} - \bar{y}_i)$$

$$S_{yx} = T_{yx} + E_{yx}$$

---

[8] We are, of course, continuing to assume that all independent variables, other than the covariate, are orthogonal. Chapter 7 examines the general regression model where all independent variables may be correlated.

Table 6-2 Partition of sum of squares and cross products, regressions, and correlations for data in Table 6-1

(a) Sum of squares and cross products

(i) General

Source of variation	Degrees of freedom	y	x_c	yx_c
A	$p-1$	T_{yy}	T_{xx}	T_{yx}
Error	$p(n-1)$	E_{yy}	E_{xx}	E_{yx}
Total		S_{yy}	S_{xx}	S_{yx}

(ii) Specific

Source of variation	Degrees of freedom	y	x_c	yx_c
A	2	454.38†	12.29	73.00
Error	18	333.43	181.71	173.00
Total	20	787.81	194.00	246.00

(b) Regression slope coefficients‡

Within-cell = $\hat{\beta}_w = E_{yx}/E_{xx} = 173.00/181.71 = 0.952$
Between-cell = $\hat{\beta}_t = T_{yx}/T_{xx} = 73.00/12.29 = 5.940$
Total = $\hat{\beta}_s = S_{yx}/S_{xx} = 246.00/194.00 = 1.268$

(c) Correlations between y and x_c‡

Within-cell = $r_w = E_{yx}/(E_{yy}^{\frac{1}{2}}E_{xx}^{\frac{1}{2}}) = 173/(333.43^{\frac{1}{2}})(181.71^{\frac{1}{2}}) = 0.703$
Between-cell = $r_t = T_{yx}/(T_{yy}^{\frac{1}{2}}T_{xx}^{\frac{1}{2}}) = 73/(454.38^{\frac{1}{2}})(12.29^{\frac{1}{2}}) = 0.977$
Total = $r_s = S_{yx}/(S_{yy}^{\frac{1}{2}}S_{xx}^{\frac{1}{2}}) = 246/(787.81^{\frac{1}{2}})(194.00^{\frac{1}{2}}) = 0.629$

Note: For simplicity the subscript for the covariate has been dropped in the symbols for the sum of squares.
† Significant at $p_1 = 0.05$.
‡ The simple formulas for the regression slopes and correlations apply because all sum of squares are computed about their respective means.

A few simple calculations reveal that factor A is significantly related to y but not to x_c. The non-significant result indicates that the frequently made assumption that the treatments do not effect the covariate is tenable.

6-II-3-2 Regression slopes and correlations As section (b) of Table 6-2 indicates it is possible to compute three estimates, only two of which are independent, of the regression slope coefficient β which relates changes in x_c to changes in y.

The first of these, $\hat{\beta}_w$, is the most important as it is this estimate of β which is used to adjust the treatment means for differences in the covariate means among groups. Note that $\hat{\beta}_w$ is estimated from error sum of squares. This means that $\hat{\beta}_w$ has been estimated by pooling the three separate regressions between y and x_c at each level of factor A. Thus, $\hat{\beta}_w$ is free of any treatment effects on the covariate.

Similarly it is possible to fit a linear regression between y and x_c to the means of y and x_c at each level of factor A. For the present data, $\hat{\beta}_t$ is over six times as large as $\hat{\beta}_w$. Such large discrepancies, either under or over, are quite likely because $\hat{\beta}_t$ is usually based on a smaller number of degrees of freedom[9] than is $\hat{\beta}_w$ and thus tends to have a relatively larger sampling error. Of course, $\hat{\beta}_s$ provides no additional information since it equals

$$\frac{T_{yx} + E_{yx}}{T_{xx} + E_{xx}}$$

Section (c) of Table 6-2 presents the correlations corresponding to the regression coefficients in section (b). These correlations, being standardized measures of the relationship between y and x_c contain no information not present in the regression slopes. They do, however, present this information in a manner which is easier to assimilate. The within-cell correlation indicates that y and x_c are substantially correlated. The between-cell correlation is extremely large but is based on only one degree of freedom.

6-II-3-3 The ANCOVA partition of the sum of squares Table 6-3 presents the ANCOVA for the data in Table 6-1 using the SPSS program ANOVA. This program was briefly described in Sec. 4-II-4-1. We will not repeat that discussion here but will simply note that a covariate may be added to the design specified on the procedure card by adding the SPSS keyword WITH followed by the variable name of the covariate. For the present example the procedure card is

$$\text{ANOVA} \qquad \text{D} \quad \text{BY A(1, 3) WITH C}$$

where D is the dependent variable, A is factor A, and C is the covariate.

The sum of squares in Table 6-3 can be related to the data in Table 6-2 as follows. First, note that the total sum of squares for y is 787.10 in both tables. The error sum of squares may be calculated in two equivalent ways, i.e.,

$$\begin{aligned} E_{yy}^* &= E_{yy} - \hat{\beta}_w E_{xy} \\ &= 333.43 - (0.952)173 \\ &= 333.43 - 164.70 \\ &= 168.73 \end{aligned} \qquad (6\text{-}7)$$

---

[9] The degrees of freedom for $\hat{\beta}_w$ and $\hat{\beta}_t$ are $p(n-2) = 3(5) = 15$ and $p - 2 = 1$, respectively.

or

$$E_{yy}^* = (1 - r_w^2)E_{yy}$$
$$= (0.506)333.43 \qquad (6\text{-}8)$$
$$= 168.72$$

where the asterisk indicates a sum of squares which has been adjusted for the covariate. Thus, the error sum of squares is reduced in proportion to the square of the within-cell correlation r_w. In this example the reduction is almost 50 percent. Since only one degree of freedom is lost to the covariate the estimated mean square error for the ANCOVA is

$$\hat{\sigma}_\varepsilon^{2*} = \hat{\sigma}_\varepsilon^2 (1 - r_w^2) \left[\frac{p(n-1)}{p(n-1)-1} \right]$$
$$= 18.52 \times (0.506)(1.059) \qquad (6\text{-}9)$$
$$= 9.92$$

Table 6-3 Analysis of data in Table 6-1 using the Statistical Package for the Social Sciences computer program ANOVA

```
ONE WAY ANALYSIS OF COVARIANCE
FILE    NONAME   (CREATION DATE = 02/05/77 )
* * * * * * * * * * * A N A L Y S I S   O F   V A R I A N C E * * * * * * * * * * *
                    D
                 BY A
                 WITH C
* * * * * * * * * * * * * * * * * * * * * * * * * * * * * * * * * * * * * *
                                SUM OF              MEAN                 SIGNIF
SOURCE OF VARIATION             SQUARES      DF     SQUARE      F        OF F
COVARIATES                      311.938       1     311.938    31.430    .001
     C                          311.938       1     311.938    31.430    .001
MAIN EFFECTS                    307.146       2     153.573    15.473    .001
     A                          307.146       2     153.573    15.473    .001

EXPLAINED                       619.085       3     206.362    20.792    .001
RESIDUAL                        168.725      17       9.925
TOTAL                           787.810      20      39.390

COVARIATE          BETA
C                  1.268
     21 CASES WERE PROCESSED.
      0 CASES (    0 PCT) WERE MISSING.
ONE WAY ANALYSIS OF COVARIANCE
FILE    NONAME   (CREATION DATE = 02/05/77 )
* * *   M U L T I P L E   C L A S S I F I C A T I O N   A N A L Y S I S   * * *
                    D
                 BY A
                 WITH C
* * * * * * * * * * * * * * * * * * * * * * * * * * * * * * * * * * * * * *
GRAND MEAN =    18.90
                                                ADJUSTED FOR       ADJUSTED FOR
                                                INDEPENDENTS       INDEPENDENTS
                                  UNADJUSTED                       + COVARIATES
VARIABLE + CATEGORY       N       DEV≠N   ETA   DEV≠N      BETA    DEV≠N    BETA
A
     1                    7        -6.48                           -5.52
     2                    7         4.24                            3.42
     3                    7         2.24                            2.10
                                           .76                              .64
MULTIPLE R SQUARED                                                          .786
MULTIPLE R                                                                  .886
```

The treatment sum of squares in the ANCOVA is called the reduced treatment sum of squares and designated T^*_{yyR}. It can be shown that

$$\begin{aligned} T^*_{yyR} &= T_{yy} + \hat{\beta}_w E_{yx} - \hat{\beta}_s S_{yx} \\ &= T_{yy} + \hat{\beta}_w E_{yx} - \hat{\beta}_s (E_{yx} + T_{yx}) \\ &= T_{yy} + (\hat{\beta}_w - \hat{\beta}_s) E_{yx} - \hat{\beta}_s T_{yx} \end{aligned} \quad (6\text{-}10)$$

Note from Eq. (6-10) that if the homogeneity of regression assumption is met the second term, $(\hat{\beta}_w - \hat{\beta}_s)E_{yx}$, is zero. Similarly, if the assumption that the treatment has no effect on the covariate is met the third term is zero since T_{yx} is zero. When both of these assumptions are met $T^*_{yyR} = T_{yy}$. Of course, for empirical data, T^*_{yyR} will differ somewhat from T_{yy} because of sampling error.

For the present example

$$\begin{aligned} T^*_{yyR} &= 454.38 + (0.952 - 1.268)173 - (1.268)73 \\ &= 454.38 - 54.668 - 92.564 \\ &= 307.15 \end{aligned}$$

In this particular case the covariate removed approximately 32 percent of the treatment sum of squares from T_{yy}. Close inspection of Eq. (6-10), however, reveals that the covariate adjustment may also result in the "reduced" sum of squares T^*_{yyR} being greater than T_{yy}, e.g., when $\hat{\beta}_w = \hat{\beta}_s$ and $\hat{\beta}_s$ and T_{yx} have opposite signs.

A point which may not be obvious is that T^*_{yyR} is not equal to the sum of squared deviations calculated about the treatment means after adjustment for the covariate. The latter is usually designated T^*_{yyA}, and is related to T^*_{yyR} as follows

$$T^*_{yyR} = T^*_{yyA} - (\hat{\beta}_t - \hat{\beta}_w)^2 \frac{T^2_{xx}}{T_{xx} + E_{xx}} \quad (6\text{-}11)$$

Since the second term on the right-hand side of Eq. (6-11) is never negative T^*_{yyR} must be less than or equal to T^*_{yyA}. The difference between these terms represents the adjustment necessary because of sampling errors in the estimation of β.

Finally, the sum of squares attributable to the covariate is

$$\begin{aligned} S_{xx} &= \frac{S^2_{yx}}{S_{yy}S_{xx}} S_{yy} \\ &= r^2_s S_{yy} \end{aligned} \quad (6\text{-}12)$$

where the subscript for x has been omitted. For the present example this is

$$\begin{aligned} &= (0.629) \times 787.81 \\ &= 311.69 \end{aligned}$$

which is, within rounding error, equal to 311.938. The multiplier r^2_s is the proper term because the ANCOVA partitioning process extracts the variation in y

ANALYSIS OF COVARIANCE **181**

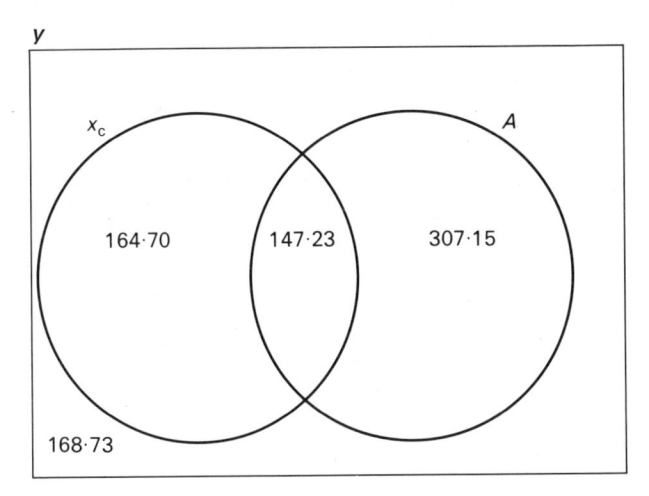

[Venn diagram with two overlapping circles labeled x_c and A. Left circle: 164.70; overlap: 147.23; right circle: 307.15; outside: 168.73. The whole is bounded in a rectangle labeled y.]

Figure 6-1 Schematic illustration of partition of the sum of squares of y for one-factor ANCOVA in Table 6-1.

attributable to x_c first. Note that in the middle of Table 6-3 that it is $\hat{\beta}_s$ which is reported as BETA. As we shall see in Sec. 6-II-4, however, it is still $\hat{\beta}_w$ which is used to adjust the treatment means for differences on the covariate between subject groups.

6-II-3-4 Alternative partitions of the sum of squares Figure 6-1 schematically illustrates the partition of the example data. Generally, this partition holds for any one factor ANCOVA. The crucial element in Figure 6-1 is the overlap of 147.23, i.e., the amount by which the sum of squares of factor A is reduced, between factor A and x_c. The point we wish to emphasize is that the allocation of this overlapping variation is a judgmental problem.

Covariance analysis by extracting x_c first effectively allocates the jointly determined variation in y to x_c. We could, however, just as legitimately, remove factor A first and then extract x_c. This latter partition would assign the overlapping variation to factor A. A third alternative, which is the general regression approach considered in the next chapter, would be *not* to attribute this joint variation to either factor A or x_c but to test whether the variation uniquely attributable to factor A and/or x_c is statistically significant.

6-II-4 Adjusted Treatment Means

Table 6-4 shows how the treatment means of factor A are adjusted for differences among groups on the covariate. First, the difference between the group mean $\bar{x}_{c_i}$ and the total mean $\bar{x}_c$ of the covariate is found for each group. Second, multiply these differences by $\hat{\beta}_w$. This gives the amount of the adjustment which is then subtracted from $\bar{y}_i$ to give the adjusted treatment means $\bar{y}_i^*$.

182 THE GENERAL LINEAR MODEL

Table 6-4 Relationships among treatment means, covariate, and adjusted treatment means for data in Table 6-1

$\bar{y}_i$	$\bar{x}_{c_i}$	$(\bar{x}_{c_i} - \bar{x}_c)$	$\hat{\beta}$	$\hat{\beta}(\bar{x}_{c_i} - \bar{x}_c)$	$\bar{y}_i^*$†	$(\bar{y}_i - \bar{y})$	$(\bar{y}_i^* - \bar{y})$
12.43	9.00	−1.00	0.952	−0.956	13.38	−6.47	−5.52
23.14	10.86	0.86	0.952	0.819	22.32	4.24	3.42
21.14	10.14	0.14	0.952	0.133	21.01	2.24	2.11
18.90	10.00	0		0	18.90	0	0

† $\bar{y}_i^* = \bar{y}_i - \hat{\beta}(\bar{x}_{c_i} - \bar{x}_c)$.

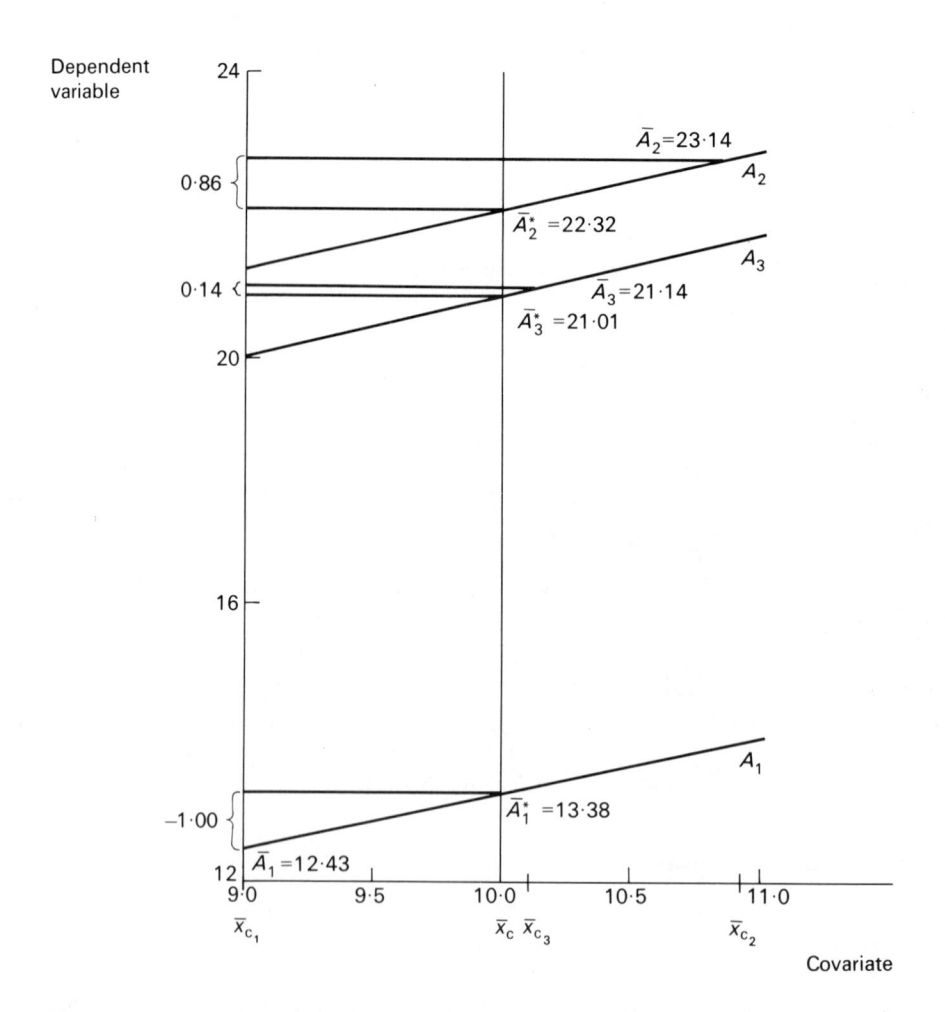

Figure 6-2 Graphical illustration of covariance procedure for adjusting treatment means using data in Table 6-4.

ANALYSIS OF COVARIANCE **183**

Figure 6-2 illustrates these relationships. We see from this figure that the adjustment process extrapolates all groups to the mean of the covariate. To put it another way, we are determining what the treatment means *would have been* had all groups had covariate means equal to the grand mean of the covariate.

6-II-5 GLM Matrix Approach

In this section we will relate the ANCOVA model to its GLM foundation and illustrate how the correlation between x_c and factor A is dealt with in partitioning the variation in y. Table 6-5 presents an analysis of the example data using the matrix techniques discussed in Chaps. 1 and 3. The computations are exactly the same as described in those chapters.

Table 6-5 Analysis of data in Table 6-1 using general matrix methods

(*a*) Structural model

$$y_{ij} = \mu + \alpha_i + \beta x_{c_{ij}} + \varepsilon_{ij}$$
$$\sum \alpha_i = 0$$
$$(i = 1, p; j = 1, n)$$

(*b*) Matrix representation of structural model

$$_N y_1 = {_N}X_m {_m}\theta_1 + {_N}\varepsilon_1$$

(*c*) Data†

$$X = \begin{bmatrix} 1 & 1 & 0 & 2 \\ 1 & 1 & 0 & -3 \\ 1 & 1 & 0 & 0 \\ 1 & 1 & 0 & -2 \\ 1 & 1 & 0 & -2 \\ 1 & 1 & 0 & -5 \\ 1 & 1 & 0 & 3 \\ 1 & 0 & 1 & 2 \\ 1 & 0 & 1 & 5 \\ 1 & 0 & 1 & 4 \\ 1 & 0 & 1 & 2 \\ 1 & 0 & 1 & 0 \\ 1 & 0 & 1 & -2 \\ 1 & 0 & 1 & -5 \\ 1 & -1 & -1 & 1 \\ 1 & -1 & -1 & -4 \\ 1 & -1 & -1 & -1 \\ 1 & -1 & -1 & 0 \\ 1 & -1 & -1 & 5 \\ 1 & -1 & -1 & -3 \\ 1 & -1 & -1 & 3 \end{bmatrix} \quad y = \begin{bmatrix} 19 \\ 13 \\ 10 \\ 9 \\ 12 \\ 6 \\ 18 \\ 22 \\ 28 \\ 24 \\ 27 \\ 24 \\ 16 \\ 21 \\ 18 \\ 21 \\ 24 \\ 21 \\ 28 \\ 15 \\ 21 \end{bmatrix}$$

Table 6-5 Continued

(d) Cross products

$$X'X = \begin{bmatrix} 21 & 0 & 0 & 0 \\ 0 & 14 & 7 & -8 \\ 0 & 7 & 14 & 5 \\ 0 & -8 & 5 & 194 \end{bmatrix} \quad X'y = \begin{bmatrix} 397 \\ -61 \\ 14 \\ 246 \end{bmatrix}$$

(e) Inverse of $X'X$

$$(X'X)^{-1} = \begin{bmatrix} 0.048 & 0.000 & 0.000 & 0.000 \\ 0.000 & 0.101 & -0.052 & 0.006 \\ 0.000 & -0.052 & 0.099 & -0.005 \\ 0.000 & 0.006 & -0.005 & 0.006 \end{bmatrix}$$

(f) Parameter estimates

$$\hat{\theta} = \begin{bmatrix} \hat{\mu} \\ \hat{\alpha}_1 \\ \hat{\alpha}_2 \\ \hat{\beta} \end{bmatrix} = (X'X)^{-1}X'y = \begin{bmatrix} 18.905 \\ -5.524 \\ 3.422 \\ 0.952 \end{bmatrix}$$

(g) Explained and error variance

$$\begin{aligned} SS_R = \hat{\theta}'X'y = &\ (\ 18.905 \cdot\ 397) = \ 7505.29 \\ &+(-5.524 \cdot -61) \quad +336.96 \\ &+(\ \ 3.422 \cdot\ \ 14) \quad\ \ +47.91 \\ &+(\ \ 0.952 \cdot\ 246) \quad +234.19 \\ &\hline \\ &\qquad\qquad\qquad\qquad\ \ 8124.35 \end{aligned}$$

$$SS_E = y'y - \hat{\theta}'X'y = 8293.08 - 8124.35 = 168.73$$

† Note that the covariate, column 4 in the design matrix X, has been centered to a mean of zero. This recoding of x_c keeps the mean of y free from the confounding effects of the mean of x_c.

The interpretations of the numbers in Table 6-5 are also the same with the following exceptions. In section (d) of this table, column 4 and row 4 contain the numbers -8 and 5 which indicates that x_c is correlated with the levels of factor A. x_c is orthogonal to the grand mean μ because we have centered x_c to a mean of zero. Recoding x_c has no other substantive effects on the data analysis.

Section (f) of Table 6-5 is particularly important as it shows that the parameter estimates of $\hat{\alpha}_1$ and $\hat{\alpha}_2$, and $\hat{\beta}$ are the adjusted treatment effects and the within-cell regression coefficient, respectively. Adding the appropriate $\hat{\alpha}$'s to $\hat{\mu}$ gives the adjusted treatment means calculated in the previous section.

Finally, we need to consider the partitioning of the explained sum of squares in Table 6-5g. $\hat{\theta}'X'y$ gives the correct *total* sum of squares explained by the model in section (a) of the table. Also, because $\hat{\mu}$ is orthogonal to the remaining terms in the model, the first component in $\hat{\theta}'X'y$ is uniquely attributable to $\hat{\mu}$. The remaining three terms, however, are correlated and the last three numbers which are added to give SS_R may *not* be interpreted as uniquely attributable to factor A or x_c. We may, however, make the standard ANCOVA partition rather easily by deleting the two terms representing factor A from the model and repeating the calculations in Table 6-5 for this reduced model. Since we are no longer distinguishing levels of factor A we know that the estimated β will be the total regression coefficient $\hat{\beta}_s$. The term $\hat{\mu}$ will remain the same, while $X'X$ will be the same as previously calculated except that the second and third rows and columns are deleted. Thus, the explained variance is

$$SS_R = \hat{\theta}'X'y = (18.905, 1.268)\begin{pmatrix} 397 \\ 246 \end{pmatrix}$$

$$= 7505.29 + 311.93$$

$$= 7817.22$$

The second term in the summation is the variation due the covariate when it is extracted first and the difference between the total sum of squares and this sum is $8293.08 - 7817.22 = 475.86$. Since this difference includes the error sum of squares

$$SS_{\tilde{R}}^{*} = T_{yyR}^{*} = 475.86 - 168.73 = 307.13$$

which is, within rounding error, the reduced sum of squares attributable to factor A calculated above.

6-II-6 Significance Tests

6-II-6-1 The ANCOVA table Tests of significance and power are computed in the usual way as described in Secs. 3-II-5 and 3-II-6.

6-II-6-2 General linear contrasts General linear contrasts and polynomial trends are calculated in the same manner as described in Sec. 3-V.

6-II-6-3 Adjusted treatment means Although no new principles are involved there is a somewhat different way in which adjusted treatment means may be statistically tested which can be used when $(X'X)^{-1}$ is not readily available and which reveals one of the difficulties of covariance analysis.

To begin with the estimated square of the standard error of an adjusted treatment mean is

$$\hat{\sigma}^2_{(\bar{y}_i^*)} = \hat{\sigma}_\varepsilon^{2*}\left[\frac{1}{n_i} + \frac{(\bar{x}_{c_i} - \bar{x}_c)^2}{E_{xx}}\right] \tag{6-13}$$

Similarly, the squared standard error of the difference between any two adjusted treatment means is

$$\hat{\sigma}^2_{(\bar{y}_i^* - \bar{y}_j^*)} = \hat{\sigma}_\varepsilon^{2*}\left[\frac{1}{n_i} + \frac{1}{n_j} + \frac{(\bar{x}_{c_i} - \bar{x}_{c_j})^2}{E_{xx}}\right] \tag{6-14}$$

For example, to test the hypothesis that $\bar{y}_1^* = \bar{y}_2^*$ we form the F ratio[10]

$$F_{(1,N-m)} = \frac{(\bar{y}_1^* - \bar{y}_2^*)^2}{\hat{\sigma}^2_{(\bar{y}_1^* - \bar{y}_2^*)}}$$

$$F_{(1,17)} = \frac{(13.38 - 22.32)^2}{9.93 \left[\frac{1}{7} + \frac{1}{7} + \frac{(9.00 - 10.86)^2}{181.71} \right]} \quad (6\text{-}15)$$

$$= 26.47$$

which is significant well beyond $p_1 = 0.001$. Note that we get the same result using the t test described in Sec. 3-V-1, i.e.,

$$t_{(N-m)} = \frac{l - l_H}{\sigma_\varepsilon^* [C'(X'X)^{-1}C]^{\frac{1}{2}}}$$

$$t_{(17)} = \frac{-8.94}{(9.93)^{\frac{1}{2}} \left[(1 \quad -1) \begin{pmatrix} 0.101 & -0.052 \\ -0.052 & 0.099 \end{pmatrix} \begin{pmatrix} 1 \\ -1 \end{pmatrix} \right]^{\frac{1}{2}}}$$

$$= -5.15$$

since

$$t_{(N-m)} = [F_{(1,N-m)}]^{\frac{1}{2}} \quad (6\text{-}16)$$

An examination of the last term in Eqs. (6-13) and (6-14) reveals one of the major statistical problems which may occur in covariance analysis. Specifically, the greater the difference between the covariate means among groups the larger this term will be and the greater will be the standard error. This means the standard error for tests of significance is being increased to account for the fact that the adjusted treatment means have been extrapolated on the basis of the covariate. To take an extreme example, if the range of observations in two groups of equal size was 8–12 and 18–22 the adjusted treatment means would be for two statistically defined groups each with a covariate mean of 15. Thus the ANCOVA would project or extrapolate the two treatment means into a region of x_c for which there are no observations. The F test then could have relatively low power not because the adjusted treatment means were necessarily very similar but rather because the differences among covariate means were relatively large.

6-III ASSUMPTIONS UNDERLYING THE ANALYSIS OF COVARIANCE

Compared with the analysis of variance, considerably less is known about the effects of violations of the assumptions underlying the ANCOVA model. Enough

---

[10] The data necessary for this test is presented in Tables 6-2 to 6-5.

is known, however, to suggest the general nature of the consequences of violating these assumptions. Also, there are certain tests that can be made to determine if these assumptions have been violated and, in some cases, procedures are available which can at least partially, if not completely, compensate for the effects of these assumption violations.

6-III-1 Assumptions Concerning Errors

The F test rests upon the assumptions that errors associated with each y value are independently and normally distributed with constant variance. In Sec. 2-II these assumptions were investigated in detail and it was concluded that the analysis of variance is:

1. Relatively insensitive to even substantial departures from normality.
2. Somewhat more sensitive to departures from homogeneous variances, especially when there are unequal numbers of observations per cell.
3. Very sensitive to violations of the independence assumption.

Since the independence assumption is only likely to be substantially violated in specific situations, e.g., repeated measures designs, the general conclusion was reached that F tests are relatively insensitive to violations of assumptions concerning the distribution of errors.

It has been generally assumed by researchers that violations of error distribution assumptions produce similar consequences in the ANCOVA and analysis of variance. Glass, et al. (1972) find some support for this statement. In addition they note that there is limited evidence to suggest:

1. That non-normality in the covariate increases the sensitivity of the F test to non-normality in y.
2. That heterogeneity in the variances of the covariate across treatment levels of a factor increases the sensitivity of the F test to heterogeneous variances in y.

Glass, et al. go on to note that the studies upon which the above conclusions were based involved rather stringent assumptions which limit the usefulness of the precise numerical results regarding probability statements obtained in these studies.

6-III-2 Treatments Do Not Affect Covariate

6-III-2-1 Consequences of violating assumption
When the treatment factor and the covariate are correlated the ANCOVA procedure adjusts the sum of squares due to the treatment as well as the error sum of squares. Depending on the characteristics of the data discussed in Sec. 6-II-3-3, this adjustment may be positive or negative. This adjustment, however, often raises a number of interpretative problems.

To take an example, assume a researcher is interested in the relative effectiveness of several different teaching methods. During the course of the experiment the researcher also measures student study time. In analyzing the data the researcher finds a significant difference among teaching methods but wonders whether this difference is due to differences in study time. The researcher therefore conducts a covariance analysis and finds that, when the effects of study time are removed, there are no significant differences among teaching methods. Any conclusion that teaching methods were not differentially effective, however, would very likely be incorrect since it is quite likely that the treatments themselves affected the covariate. It might be the case, for example, that certain teaching methods produce higher levels of motivation and thereby encourage students to spend more time on their studies. Such an analysis suggests, although it does not prove, the mechanism through which the teaching methods were differentially effective.

It is also likely that when the treatment affects the covariate the regressions relating y to x_c will be heterogeneous. This problem is investigated in Sec. 6-III-3. Here we will simply note that the major effect of heterogeneous regressions is to complicate interpretation of the data.

6-III-2-2 Detecting assumption violation Violation of this assumption may be tested via an analysis of variance on the covariate. A significant result indicates that the treatment(s) has effected the covariate. Of course, this test is not required when the covariate is measured before administration of the treatments and the treatments are randomly assigned to subjects.

6-III-2-3 Corrective procedures Once the experiment is completed there is really nothing which can be done to correct any problems arising from treatment effects on the covariate. The researcher should, of course, take care not to misinterpret his data. In replications, however, it may be possible to measure the covariate before administration of the treatments and to assign treatments to subjects randomly, thereby insuring that treatments have no opportunity to affect the covariate.

6-III-3 Homogeneity of Regression Slopes

In Sec. 6-II-1 it was noted that it is mathematically and statistically correct to posit an ANCOVA model with heterogeneous regression slopes. Most ANCOVA users, however, routinely assume—sometimes implicitly—homogeneous regressions. This situation is due partly to the widely held, but erroneous, belief that homogeneous regressions are a requirement of the ANCOVA model and partly to avoid the difficulties of interpreting the data when regressions are heterogeneous. Because of the frequency of its assumption and the interpretative difficulties which arise in the face of heterogeneous regressions we shall investigate this assumption in some depth, illustrating our discussion with a numerical example.

6-III-3-1 A numerical example Table 6-6 presents data which will be used to illustrate the ANCOVA with heterogeneous regressions. The covariate—here coded with its mean centered to zero—is the same as in Table 6-1. The variable y has been altered to produce different within-cell regressions. The coding for μ, α_1, and α_2 should require no explanation. The last two terms represent the interactions between factor A and x_c and, as we shall see, allow for heterogeneity of within-cell regressions. Note that this coding procedure for interactions between factor A and x_c is exactly the same as discussed in Sec. 3-II-3-1 for coding interactions between factors, e.g., $\beta_{A1C} = x_c \alpha_1$.

In matrix terms the model with homogeneous regressions is

$$_N y_1 = {_N} X_m {_m} \theta_1 + {_N} \varepsilon_1 \qquad (6\text{-}17)$$

$$(N = 21; m = 4)$$

and the model with heterogeneous regressions is

$$_N y_1 = {_N} X_m {_m} \theta_1 + {_N} \varepsilon_1 \qquad (6\text{-}18)$$

$$(N = 21; m = 6)$$

Table 6-6 Numerical example of one-factor analysis of covariance with heterogeneous regressions

Factor	y	x_c	μ	α_1	α_2	β_{A1C}	β_{A2C}
A_1	24	2	1	1	0	2	0
	4	−3	1	1	0	−3	0
	14	0	1	1	0	0	0
	14	−2	1	1	0	−2	0
	19	−2	1	1	0	−2	0
	9	−5	1	1	0	−5	0
	24	3	1	1	0	3	0
A_2	22	2	1	0	1	0	2
	28	5	1	0	1	0	5
	24	4	1	0	1	0	4
	27	2	1	0	1	0	2
	24	0	1	0	1	0	0
	16	−2	1	0	1	0	−2
	21	−5	1	0	1	0	−5
A_3	13	1	1	−1	−1	−1	−1
	18	−4	1	−1	−1	4	4
	20	−1	1	−1	−1	1	1
	16	0	1	−1	−1	0	0
	21	5	1	−1	−1	−5	−5
	12	−3	1	−1	−1	3	3
	15	3	1	−1	−1	−3	−3

190 THE GENERAL LINEAR MODEL

For convenience we shall call the model in Eq. (6-17) the reduced model and the model in Eq. (6-18) the full model. The only difference between these models is that the full model contains, in addition to the variables in the reduced model, the last two variables in Table 6-6, which represent the interactions between factor A and x_c. Note that Eqs. (6-17) and (6-18) are the matrix equivalents of the ANCOVA models presented in Sec. 6-II-1 and labeled Eqs. (6-4) and (6-6), respectively.

Table 6-7 presents the data analysis for both the reduced and full models using the SPSS procedure ANOVA in sections (a) and (b), respectively. The analysis of the reduced model is the same as presented in Sec. 6-II-3-3 except that the dependent variable is labeled DH to indicate the presence of heterogeneous regressions.

Table 6-7 Analysis of covariance of data in Table 6-6 with heterogeneous regressions using Statistical Package for the Social Sciences computer program ANOVA

```
(a)   ANCOVA Assuming Homogeneous Regressions--Reduced Model

ONE WAY ANALYSIS OF COVARIANCE
                         ANOVA           DH BY A(1,3) WITH C
                         STATISTICS      ALL
                0042500 CM REQUIRED FOR ANOVA
ONE WAY ANALYSIS OF COVARIANCE
FILE   NONAME  (CREATION DATE = 02/05/77 )
* * * * * * * * * * A N A L Y S I S   O F   V A R I A N C E * * * * * * * * * *
                  DH
               BY A
               WITH C
* * * * * * * * * * * * * * * * * * * * * * * * * * * * * * * * * * * * * *
                                SUM OF                      MEAN              SIGNIF
SOURCE OF VARIATION             SQUARES      DF             SQUARE       F    OF F
COVARIATES                      270.314       1             270.314   14.335  .001
   C                            270.314       1             270.314   14.335  .001
MAIN EFFECTS                    157.781       2              78.890    4.184  .033
   A                            157.781       2              78.890    4.184  .033
EXPLAINED                       428.095       3             142.698    7.567  .002
RESIDUAL                        320.571      17              18.857
TOTAL                           748.667      20              37.433

COVARIATE          BETA†
C              1.180    1.900
      21 CASES WERE PROCESSED.
       0 CASES (    0 PCT) WERE MISSING.
ONE WAY ANALYSIS OF COVARIANCE
FILE   NONAME  (CREATION DATE = 02/05/77 )
* * *   M U L T I P L E   C L A S S I F I C A T I O N   A N A L Y S I S   * * *
                  DH
               BY A
               WITH C
* * * * * * * * * * * * * * * * * * * * * * * * * * * * * * * * * * * * * *
GRAND MEAN =    18.33
                                                ADJUSTED FOR    ADJUSTED FOR
                                                INDEPENDENTS    INDEPENDENTS
                                 UNADJUSTED                     + COVARIATES
VARIABLE + CATEGORY       N      DEV≠N    ETA   DEV≠N    BETA   DEV≠N    BETA
A
     1                    7      -2.90                          -1.90
     2                    7       4.81                           3.95
     3                    7      -1.90                          -2.05
                                         .57                            .47
MULTIPLE R SQUARED                                                      .572
MULTIPLE R                                                              .756
```

Table 6-7 Continued

(b) ANCOVA Assuming Heterogeneous Regressions—Full Model

```
                    ANOVA        DH BY A(1,3) WITH C,A1C,A2C
                    STATISTICS   ALL
          0042600 CM REQUIRED FOR ANOVA

ONE WAY ANALYSIS OF COVARIANCE
FILE  NONAME  (CREATION DATE = 02/09/77 )
        * * *  A N A L Y S I S  O F  V A R I A N C E  * * * * * * * * * *
              DH
           BY A
         WITH C
              A1C
              A2C
* * * * * * * * * * * * * * * * * * * * * * * * * * * * * * * * * * * *
                              SUM OF              MEAN                 SIGNIF
SOURCE OF VARIATION           SQUARES     DF     SQUARE       F         OF F
COVARIATES                    391.314      3    130.438     18.872     .001
  C                           285.833      1    285.833     18.442     .001
  A1C                         102.484      1    102.484      6.969     .019
  A2C                           2.189      1      2.189       .149     .705
MAIN EFFECTS                  136.823      2     68.411      4.653     .027
  A                           136.823      2     68.411      4.653     .027

EXPLAINED                     528.136      5    105.627      7.185     .001
RESIDUAL                      220.531     15     14.702
TOTAL                         748.667     20     37.433

COVARIATE        BETA¹
C                1.228     1.097
A1C              1.189     1.091
A2C              -.147     -.299

 21 CASES WERE PROCESSED.
  0 CASES ( 0 PCT) WERE MISSING.

ONE WAY ANALYSIS OF COVARIANCE
FILE   NONAME   (CREATION DATE = 02/09/77 )
* * *    M U L T I P L E   C L A S S I F I C A T I O N   A N A L Y S I S   * * *
              DH
           BY A
         WITH C
              A1C
              A2C
* * * * * * * * * * * * * * * * * * * * * * * * * * * * * * * * * * * *
GRAND MEAN =    18.33
                                                                ADJUSTED FOR
                                               ADJUSTED FOR     INDEPENDENTS
                                UNADJUSTED     INDEPENDENTS    + COVARIATES
VARIABLE + CATEGORY       N    DEV'N    ETA   DEV'N     BETA   DEV'N    BETA
A
  1                       7    -2.90                           -1.20
  2                       7     4.81                            3.64
  3                       7    -1.90                           -2.43
                                        .57                             .44
MULTIPLE R SQUARED                                                      .705
MULTIPLE R                                                              .840
```

† The first column of BETA coefficients is for the total data $\hat{\beta}_s$. The second column is for the within-cell regressions $\hat{\beta}_w$, which may be obtained by inserting a card "OPTIONS 9" between the ANOVA and STATISTICS cards.

In section (b) of Table 6-7, C represents the covariate and A1C and A2C represent the interactions between factor A and x_c. With the within-cell BETA coefficients for C, A1C, and A2C, the individual within-cell regression slopes may be recovered as follows

$$\hat{\beta}_1 = \hat{\beta} + \hat{\beta}_{A1C} \qquad = 1.097 + 1.091 \qquad = 2.188$$

$$\hat{\beta}_2 = \hat{\beta} + \hat{\beta}_{A2C} \qquad = 1.097 - 0.299 \qquad = 0.798$$

$$\hat{\beta}_3 = \hat{\beta} - \hat{\beta}_{A1C} - \hat{\beta}_{A2C} = 1.097 - 1.091 + 0.299 = 0.305$$

Note that this procedure is completely analogous to the recovery of treatment

Table 6-8 Relationships among treatment means, covariates, and adjusted treatment means for data in Tables 6-6 and 6-7

$\bar{y}_i$	$\bar{x}_{c_i}$†	$(\bar{x}_{c_i} - \bar{x}_c)$	$\hat{\beta}_i$‡	$\hat{\beta}_i(\bar{x}_{c_i} - \bar{x}_c)$	$\bar{y}_i^*$§	$(\bar{y}_i - \bar{y})$	$(\bar{y}_i^* - \bar{y}^*)$
15.43	9.00	−1.00	2.188	−2.188	17.62	−2.90	−1.20
23.14	10.86	0.86	0.798	0.686	22.45	4.81	3.64
16.43	10.14	0.14	0.305	0.043	16.39	−1.90	−2.43
18.33	10.00	0	1.097	−0.486	18.82	0	0

† Measured on original scale.
‡ Within-cell regression coefficient; last entry is average regression coefficient over three levels of factor A.
§ $\bar{y}_i^* = \bar{y}_i - \hat{\beta}_i(\bar{x}_{c_i} - \bar{x}_c)$.

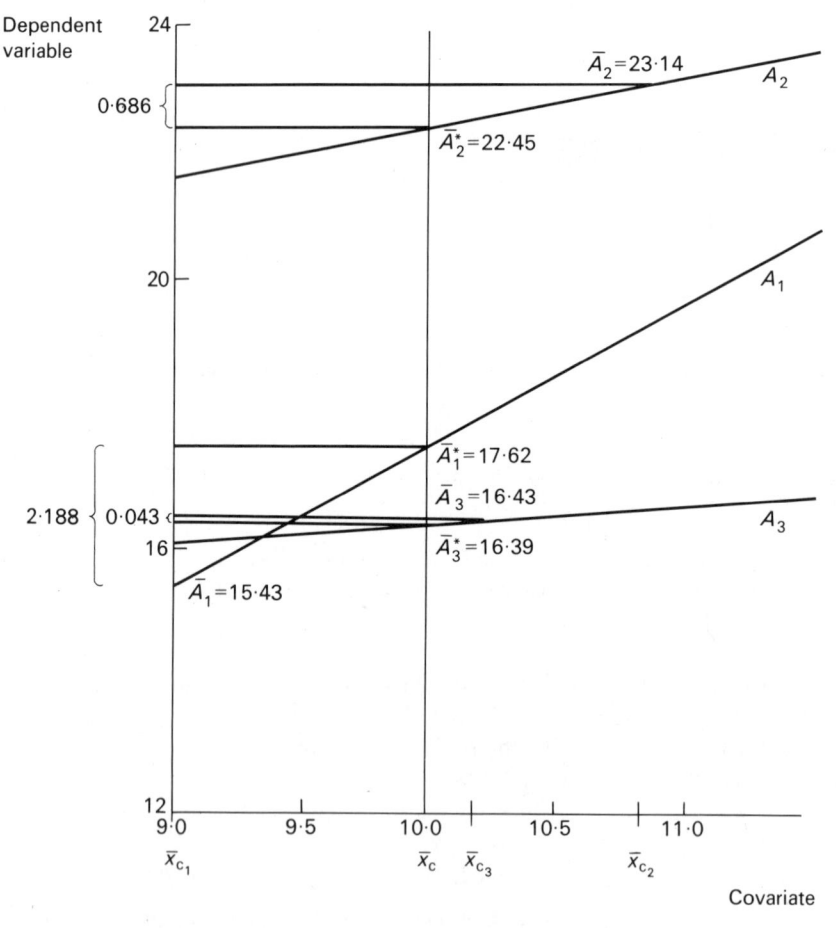

Figure 6-3 Graphical illustration of analysis of covariance with heterogeneous regressions for data in Table 6-8.

means in the factorial analysis of variance,[11] e.g., $\hat{\beta}_{A1C}$ represents the deviation of the regression slope in level 1 of factor A from the average regression slope $\hat{\beta}$. The same is true for $\hat{\beta}_{A2C}$; and since $\hat{\beta}_{A1C}$ and $\hat{\beta}_{A2C}$ are deviations from $\hat{\beta}$, it follows that $\hat{\beta}_3$ equals $\hat{\beta}$ plus the negative of the sum of $\hat{\beta}_{A1C}$ and $\hat{\beta}_{A2C}$. In a similar way we may define the intercepts of the within-cell regressions with the y axis as follows

$$\hat{\beta}_{01} = \hat{\mu} + \hat{\alpha}_1 \quad\quad = 18.33 - 1.20 \quad\quad = 17.63$$
$$\hat{\beta}_{02} = \hat{\mu} + \hat{\alpha}_2 \quad\quad = 18.33 + 3.64 \quad\quad = 22.45$$
$$\hat{\beta}_{03} = \hat{\mu} + \hat{\alpha}_1 - \hat{\alpha}_2 = 18.33 + 1.20 - 3.64 = 16.39$$

Since $\bar{x}_c = 0$, these intercepts are also the adjusted treatment means.

Table 6-8 summarizes the relationships among the variables of interest in the ANCOVA with heterogeneous regressions. Figure 6-3 presents this data graphically. Note that this table and figure are the same as Table 6-5 and Figure 6-2 except that $\hat{\beta}$ has been allowed to vary across levels of factor A.

The next three sections will use the data presented in Tables 6-7 and 6-8 and Figure 6-3 to discuss the consequences of violating the homogeneity of regression assumption, procedures for detecting such violations, and possible remedies.

6-III-3-2 Consequences of violating assumption The major effect of heterogeneous regressions is that, as is clearly shown in Figure 6-3, the differences among treatment means will be different for each value of x_c. Indeed, at some point, the regression lines will cross, reversing the rank order of the adjusted treatment effects. The point at which any two regression lines i and j cross, Z_{ij}, is equal to

$$Z_{ij} = \frac{(\bar{y}_i - \bar{y}_j) + (\hat{\beta}_j \bar{x}_{c_j} - \hat{\beta}_i \bar{x}_{c_i})}{(\hat{\beta}_j - \hat{\beta}_i)} \tag{6-19}$$

For example, using the data in Table 6-8, we find that[12]

$$Z_{13} = \frac{-1 + 0.305(10.14) - 2.188(9.00)}{-1.883} = 9.35$$

Similarly, we can calculate $Z_{12} = 13.39$ and $Z_{23} = -2.30$. Note, however, that only Z_{13} is within the range of the covariate for both levels of factor A.

The problem is similar to, but more complex than, the interpretation of main effects given interactions in a factorial design. Comparisons among treatment means which have been adjusted to the mean of the covariate are valid only at that specific level of x_c. Furthermore, since this adjustment involves a statistical extrapolation when group covariate means differ the comparisons may not be among conditions which have any empirical counterpart.[13] That is, there may be

---

[11] See Sec. 3-II-3-2.
[12] For x_c centered to zero mean $Z_{13} = 9.35 - 10.00 = -0.65$.
[13] This problem was discussed in some detail in Secs. 6-I-2 and 6-III-2-1.

no actual subject groups in the population to which the statistical conclusions can be generalized.

Finally, regarding the effects on the F test of assuming a homogeneous model when in fact a heterogeneous model is correct we note the conclusions of Glass, et al. (1972, p. 277) that:

1. The F test is fairly robust with respect to violation of the homogeneity assumption.
2. Heterogeneity of regressions produces smaller type I errors.

They further note that the studies upon which these conclusions are based involved a fairly restrictive set of assumptions which may greatly limit the generality of these conclusions.

6-III-3-3 Detecting assumption violation Violation of the homogeneity assumption may be tested via the following F statistic

$$F_{(m_F - m_R, N - m_F)} = \frac{(SS_F - SS_R)/(m_F - m_R)}{(SS_T - SS_F)/(N - m_F)} \qquad (6\text{-}20)$$

where SS_T is the total sum of squares; SS_F and SS_R are the sum of squares due the regressions for the full and reduced models respectively; m_F and m_R are the corresponding degrees of freedom; and N is the total number of observations.

For the data in Table 6-8 the F value is

$$F_{(2,15)} = \frac{(528.136 - 428.096)/(6 - 4)}{(748.667 - 528.136)/(21 - 6)} = 3.40$$

Since $F_{(2,15,0.05)} = 2.79$ we can reject the assumption of homogeneous regressions at the $p_1 = 0.05$ level of significance.

6-III-3-4 Corrective procedures Given the interpretative difficulties which are inherent in an ANCOVA model with heterogeneous regressions the researcher should at least consider the possibility of converting the covariate into a blocking variable in either the present or future studies. If this is not possible or desirable the only alternative is to adopt a model with heterogeneous regressions and to specifically investigate the nature of treatment slope interactions.

6-III-4 Linear Regression

The usual ANCOVA assumption that the relationship between y and x_c is linear is a special case of the assumption in Sec. 1-III-3 that the response-generating model is correctly specified. Strictly speaking, the ANCOVA model does not require linearity in the relationship between y and x_c. Indeed, it is possible to construct and statistically test a model which assumes neither linearity nor homogeneity of the regressions across cells in the research design. The interpretation of such a model would be most difficult to say the least. If the homogeneity assumption is met, however, differences between the treatment means will be constant across all levels of x_c irrespective of the form of the regression which relates x_c to y.

6-III-4-1 Consequences of violating assumption Incorrect specification of the form of the regression between y and x_c generally biases parameter estimates in an unknown direction and biases upward the error sum of squares. Tests of significance on the components of the model thus tend to be conservative.

6-III-4-2 Detecting assumption violation It is possible to partition the reduced treatment sum of squares into two components which may be used to test the linearity assumption. Using the notation developed in Sec. 6-II-3 these components are

$$S_3 = T_{yy} - \hat{\beta}_t T_{yx} \tag{6-21}$$

$$S_4 = \hat{\beta}_t T_{yx} + \hat{\beta}_w E_{yx} - \hat{\beta}_s S_{yx} \tag{6-22}$$

S_3 is the variation of the treatments about the between-treatment regression line.[14] Assuming that the true regression is linear, this is an independent estimate of the error sum of squares with $(p-2)$ degrees of freedom. Therefore, an appropriate test of the linearity assumption is

$$F_{[p-2, p(n-1)-1]} = \frac{S_3/(p-2)}{SS_E^*/[p(n-1)-1]} \tag{6-23}$$

where p is the number of treatments and SS_E^* is the error sum of squares from the covariance analysis. This test, however, presumes homogeneity of regressions and therefore is appropriate only after the homogeneity assumption has been validated.

For example, the linearity test of the data in Table 6-1[15] is

$$F_{(1,15)} = \frac{20.76/1}{168.73/15} = 1.84$$

which is not significant at the $p_1 = 0.05$ level.

Since computer programs typically do not provide the values for T_{yx}, E_{yx}, and S_{yx} the following procedure is often useful as a rough test of the linearity assumption. Specifically, this procedure involves fitting an ANCOVA model containing all the usual terms *plus* higher order polynomial terms for the covariate, i.e., x_c^2, x_c^3, etc. Usually the addition of a quadratic and possibly a cubic term will be sufficient to reveal any non-linearity in the relationship between y and x_c. The higher order covariate terms can then be tested against the hypothesis

---

[14] Symbols S_3 and S_4 are, in the context of the ANCOVA, fairly standard. S_1 and S_2, which are not presented here, are used to test the assumption of homogeneity of regression. The F test for homogeneity of regressions presented in Sec. 6-III-3-3 leads to the same result.

[15] The required data is contained in Tables 6-2 and 6-3.

Table 6-9 Analysis of covariance of data in Table 6-1 with addition of quadratic and cubic covariate terms

```
ONE WAY ANALYSIS OF COVARIANCE
                   ANOVA         D BY A(1,3) WITH C,CSQ,CCUBE
                   STATISTICS    ALL
                   FINISH
          0042600 CM REQUIRED FOR ANOVA

ONE WAY ANALYSIS OF COVARIANCE
FILE  NONAME  (CREATION DATE = 02/05/77 )
* * * * * * * * * * A N A L Y S I S   O F   V A R I A N C E * * * * * * * * * *
                D
             BY A
           WITH C
                CSQ
                CCUBE
* * * * * * * * * * * * * * * * * * * * * * * * * * * * * * * * * * * * *
                                  SUM OF              MEAN               SIGNIF
SOURCE OF VARIATION               SQUARES     DF      SQUARE       F     OF F
COVARIATES                        334.503      3     111.501    10.307   .001
  C                                55.502      1      55.502     5.131   .039
  CSQ                              22.565      1      22.565     2.086   .169
  CCUBE                              .000      1        .000      .000   .997
MAIN EFFECTS                      291.041      2     145.520    13.452   .001
  A                               291.041      2     145.520    13.452   .001

EXPLAINED                         625.544      5     125.109    11.565   .001
RESIDUAL                          162.266     15      10.818
TOTAL                             787.810     20      39.390
```

that their true value is zero using the procedures discussed in Secs. 3-II-5-3 and 3-V-1.

As an example, Table 6-9 presents an ANCOVA of the data in Table 6-1 with quadratic and cubic terms added. Note that neither x_c^2 nor x_c^3 is significantly different from zero. Although the SPSS procedure ANOVA does not provide such a test, strictly speaking, for reasons which are discussed in the next chapter, we should *simultaneously* test the hypotheses that x_c^2 and x_c^3 are equal to zero. In the present instance such a test is not significant at the $p_1 = 0.05$ level.

6-III-4-3 Corrective procedures Once the data is in hand the only corrective procedure for a violation of the linearity assumption is the substitution of the appropriate functional form which relates y and x_c. Often simple scatter plots of the data will suggest the proper form. Because of the increased likelihood of heterogeneity of regressions when the linearity assumption is violated, separate plots should be made for each cell in the research design.

In replication studies it may be wise to consider converting the covariate into a blocking variable when the relationship between y and x_c is non-linear. The rationale for this change follows the logic presented in Sec. 3-II-2-1. By coding the covariate as a p level blocking variable $(p-1)$ of the means are allowed to move freely. Thus, the practical effect of blocking is to allow the relationship between y and x_c to follow any functional form which can be represented by a polynomial of degree $(p-1)$. A polynomial of even a relatively low degree is quite flexible and will closely fit a wide range of true relationships. For details and an example the reader is referred to Sec. 3-II-2-1.

6-III-5 Covariate Measured without Error

In the typical use of the ANCOVA the experimenter establishes levels of the experimental factors which can usually be assumed to be free of errors of measurement. The variable x_c, however, will often represent a characteristic of subjects, such as intelligence or previous level of performance on a task, and is measured subject to error. Thus the question of the effects of errors of measurement assumes special prominence in the ANCOVA.

6-III-5-1 Consequences of violating assumption The effect of errors of measurement is to reduce the absolute value of the slope coefficient. Specifically, if x_c is composed of a true and an error component

$$x_c = \chi_c + \varepsilon$$

and the true values of the covariate and the error component are normally and independently distributed then the expected value of the estimated slope is

$$E(\hat{\beta}) = \beta\left(\frac{\sigma_\chi^2}{\sigma_\chi^2 + \sigma_\varepsilon^2}\right) \tag{6-24}$$

where β is the true population slope and the term in parenthesis is the reliability with which the covariate is measured.

Thus the expected value of the adjusted treatment means will be equal to

$$\alpha_i - \alpha_j + \beta(1 - R)(\mu_{x_i} - \mu_{x_j})$$

where R is the reliability of the covariate and $(\mu_{x_i} - \mu_{x_j})$ is the population difference between group covariate means. Thus to the extent that μ_{x_i} and μ_{x_j} differ, unreliability in the measurement of the covariate will result in only a partial adjustment of the treatment means for differences among groups on the covariate.

6-III-5-2 Detecting assumption violation Broadly stated the question of reliability is the question of the consistency with which something is measured. The detection of unreliability therefore requires at least two measurements which may be compared. As a general rule in a typical covariance experiment the researcher will not have such data. For details on the concept and measurement of reliability the reader should consult more specific references, e.g., Ghiselli (1964).

6-III-5-3 Corrective procedures Assuming that at least a moderate degree of unreliability has been detected or is presumed to be present in the covariate the researcher may wish to find a more accurate and statistically efficient way of estimating β. Cochran (1968) briefly discusses, and provides references to, procedures which have been developed for situations when two estimates of the magnitude of the covariate are available. Since this rarely happens in applied work we shall not pursue these methods further.

According to Johnston (1972, p. 283): "There are two main types of estimator (of β) described in the literature; one type is based on instrumental variables of various kinds and the other on maximum likelihood methods buttressed with fairly strong assumptions about the covariance matrix of the measurement errors." Because of the stringency of the assumptions and the greater complexity of the procedure we shall not pursue maximum likelihood methods further.

An especially simple instrumental variable procedure is to rank the covariate values and then divide the subjects into three equal groups. The regression slope is then

$$\hat{\beta} = \frac{\bar{Y}_3 - \bar{Y}_1}{\bar{X}_3 - \bar{X}_1}$$

where group one contains the lowest and group three the highest scores on the covariate. Group two is omitted. With such an external estimate of β one degree of freedom would be lost from the error sum of squares. For further details on the use of instrumental variables in the context of errors of measurement see Johnston (1972, pp. 278–291).

6-IV A COMPARISON OF COVARIANCE ANALYSIS AND RANDOMIZED BLOCKS

At various points in this chapter it has been suggested that problems encountered in the ANCOVA procedure, e.g., non-linearity in the relationship between y and x_c or heterogeneity of regression slopes, may be overcome by converting the covariate into a blocking variable. Therefore, before considering more complex ANCOVA models, it is appropriate to summarize the relative advantages and disadvantages of these two GLM models.

Covariance analysis has three advantages when compared with randomized blocks:

1. Covariance analysis can often be used to control statistically for variables which the researcher has not included in his original research plan.
2. Covariance analysis can be used where it is difficult or impossible to form homogeneous blocks of subjects.
3. Feldt (1958) has shown that, given the assumptions underlying the ANCOVA model are true, the ANCOVA design is more precise than the randomized blocks design when the correlation between y and x_c is greater than 0.6.

In contrast, four advantages may be cited for randomized blocks in comparison with covariance analysis:

1. The randomized blocks design allows assessment of the effects of group differences on a concomitant variable without having to extrapolate treatment means to the mean of the concomitant variable. That is, comparisons among treatment means are made between experimentally defined groups in randomized blocks designs as opposed to statistically defined "groups" in covariance analysis.

2. Since a design with b blocks allows any relationship between y and x_c which can be fitted by a polynomial of degree $(b-1)$ the randomized blocks design is often preferable to a covariance design when the relationship between y and x_c is non-linear.
3. Feldt (1958) has also suggested that the randomized blocks design is more precise than the covariance design when the correlation between y and x_c is less than 0.4. Correlations below 0.4 are quite common in social and behavioral research.
4. Finally, the covariance design requires more assumptions and is generally more difficult to interpret than a corresponding randomized blocks design.

A comparison of the relative advantages and disadvantages of covariance and randomized blocks designs leads to two major conclusions. First, research problems do occur where the covariance design is preferable to randomized blocks designs, e.g., where it is not possible to construct homogeneous blocks. Second, where it is possible to construct homogeneous blocks of equal size and randomly assign treatments to blocks the blocking design is generally superior to the covariance design.

6-V ADVANCED COVARIANCE DESIGNS

The covariance model may be extended beyond the basic model developed in Sec. 6-II in two ways. First, the covariance model may be extended to more complex analysis of variance designs. Second, the covariance model may be extended to the case of multiple covariates. Both of these extensions are relatively direct and require no new basic principles. We shall therefore briefly outline a covariance analysis for a 2×3 factorial, first with one covariate and then with two. The detailed analysis of these examples is left to the reader as a test problem.

6-V-1 Factorial ANCOVA with One Covariate

The model for a two-factor ANCOVA is

$$y_{ijk} = \mu + \alpha_i + \beta_j + \alpha\beta_{ij} + \theta_1(x_{c_{ijk}} - \bar{x}_c) + \varepsilon_{ijk} \tag{6-25}$$
$$(i = 1, p; j = 1, q; k = 1, n)$$

Equation (6-25) is a direct extension of the one-factor ANCOVA developed in Sec. 6-II and that discussion, as well as the discussion in Sec. 6-III of the assumptions underlying the ANCOVA model, applies in its entirety to the present factorial ANCOVA.

Table 6-10 presents a numerical example together with selected analyses of the data which will facilitate our discussion. Note especially section (c) of Table 6-10, which partitions y, x_c, and their cross products. Using a slight variation of the notation previously developed, e.g., T_{yy} is broken into the orthogonal

Table 6-10 Numerical example two-factor factorial analysis of covariance

(a) Data

		B_1		B_2		B_3	
		x_c	y	x_c	y	x_c	y
A_1		22	114	6	135	11	27
		11	138	4	120	19	26
		10	127	5	137	14	37
		24	106	13	116	3	34
A_2		2	106	13	84	22	72
		3	114	5	81	15	100
		18	77	20	54	20	73
		10	81	20	85	23	87

(b) Analysis of covariance

Source of variation	Degrees of freedom General	Degrees of freedom Specific	Sum of squares	F Ratio
Main effects	$p + q - 2$	3	8630.28	27.51†
A	$p - 1$	1	150.76	1.44
B	$q - 1$	2	8594.34	41.10†
AB	$(p - 1)(q - 1)$	2	12921.41	61.79†
Covariate	r	1	1422.25	13.60†
error	$pq(n - 1) - r$	17	1777.50	

(c) Partitions of sum of squares of y, x_c, and cross products

Source of variation	y	Cross products	x_c
A	$A_{yy} = 442.04$	$A_{xy} = -124.46$	$A_{xx} = 35.04$
B	$B_{yy} = 12291.08$	$B_{xy} = -1036.29$	$B_{xx} = 108.58$
AB	$AB_{yy} = 11599.08$	$AB_{xy} = 672.21$	$AB_{xx} = 358.08$
Error	$E_{yy} = 3199.75$	$E_{xy} = -997.25$	$E_{xx} = 699.25$

(d) Tests on model

(i) Homogeneity

$$F_{(5,12)} = \frac{(26{,}135.56 - 25{,}754.46)/(11 - 6)}{(27{,}531.96 - 26{,}135.56)/(23 - 11)} = 0.65$$

(ii) Linearity‡

$$F_{(2,15)} = \frac{(1777.50 - 1719.02)/2}{1719.02/15} = 0.26$$

Table 6-10 Continued

(e) Polynomial trends and selected post hoc contrasts§

B_{LIN}	7967.55	$AB_{LIN\ by\ LIN}$	7518.11
B_{QUAD}	980.96	$AB_{LIN\ by\ QUAD}$	3339.88
$\hat{\beta}_1 - \hat{\beta}_2$		309.34	
$\hat{\beta}_1 - 2\hat{\beta}_2 + \hat{\beta}_3$		8122.33	

† $p_1 < 0.01$.
‡ Tested against model with square and cubic terms.
§ All values are sums of squares with one degree of freedom.

components A_{yy}, B_{yy}, and AB_{yy}, the reduced sum of squares for factor A is

$$A^*_{yyR} = (A_{yy} + E_{yy}) - \frac{(A_{xy} + E_{xy})^2}{(A_{xx} + E_{xx})} - E^*_{yy}$$

$$= (442.04 + 3199.75) - \frac{(-124.46 - 997.25)^2}{(35.04 + 699.25)} - 1777.50 \qquad (6\text{-}26)$$

$$= 150.76$$

B^*_{yyR} and AB^*_{yyR} may be calculated via Eq. (6-26) by an appropriate substitution of terms for A_{yy}, A_{xy}, and A_{xx}. Although superficially different, Eq. (6-26) is structurally identical to Eqs. (6-10) and (6-11) which were used to calculate the reduced sum of squares for the one factor ANCOVA. Note also that the error sum of squares

$$E^*_{yy} = E_{yy} - \frac{E^2_{xy}}{E_{xx}}$$

is calculated exactly as in a one-factor ANCOVA.

An important aspect of Eq. (6-26) is that the adjustment for the covariate is made separately for each source of variation in the analysis of variance table. Because of this procedure the relationship between y and x_c will differ for different sources of variation. Note especially in section (b) of Table 6-10 that the adjusted sum of squares for main effects is different from the adjusted sum of squares for factors A and B. The reason for this is that the main effects line in section (b) reflects the average relationship between y and x_c for factor A and for factor B. In terms of Eq. (6-26) the main effects line may be reproduced by substituting $(A_{yy} + B_{yy})$, $(A_{xy} + B_{xy})$, and $(A_{xx} + B_{xx})$ at the appropriate points.

Table 6-10, sections (d) and (e) test the homogeneity and linearity assumptions and present polynomial trends and selected post hoc analyses. The homogeneity test is exactly the same as developed in Sec. 6-III-3-3 for the one-factor ANCOVA except that in the heterogeneous regression slope model x_c interacts with the B and the AB effects as well as the A effects. Polynomial trends and post hoc

Table 6-11 Numerical example two-factor factorial analysis of covariance with two covariates

(a) Data

		B_1			Factor B_2			B_3	
	x_{c_1}	x_{c_2}	y	x_{c_1}	x_{c_2}	y	x_{c_1}	x_{c_2}	y
A_1	22	19	153	6	17	156	11	20	45
	11	13	156	4	3	136	19	18	59
	10	11	149	5	1	116	14	6	36
	24	10	135	13	25	159	3	9	55
A_2	2	9	119	13	2	75	22	15	107
	3	11	141	5	24	128	15	13	115
	18	14	125	20	3	82	20	12	111
	10	10	130	20	9	100	23	9	102

(b) Analysis of covariance

Source of variation	Degrees of freedom General	Specific	Sum of squares	F Ratio
Main effects	$p + q - 2$	3	13263.60	75.21†
A	$(p - 1)$	1	50.79	0.86
B	$(q - 1)$	2	13081.47	111.26†
AB	$(p - 1)(q - 1)$	2	11966.94	101.78†
Covariates	r	2	2865.89	24.38†
Covariate 1	1	1	348.84	5.93‡
Covariate 2	1	1	2649.21	45.06†
Error	$pq(n - 1) - r$	16	940.61	

(c) Homogeneity test

$$F_{(10,6)} = \frac{(30220.40 - 29821.22)/(17 - 7)}{(30761.83 - 30220.40)/(23 - 17)} = 0.44$$

(d) Polynomial trends and selected post hoc contrasts§

B_{LIN}	12811.14	$AB_{LIN\ by\ LIN}$	5683.63
B_{QUAD}	608.37	$AB_{LIN\ by\ QUAD}$	4273.24
$\hat{\beta}_1 - \hat{\beta}_2$		1259.27	
$\hat{\beta}_1 - 2\hat{\beta}_2 + \hat{\beta}_3$		11388.28	

† $p_1 < 0.01$.
‡ $p_1 < 0.05$.
§ All values are sums of squares with 1 degree of freedom.

contrasts are calculated exactly as discussed in Chap. 3. Note, however, that the reduced sum of squares for $B_{\text{LIN}} + B_{\text{QUAD}}$ does not equal the reduced sum of squares for factor B. The reason for this is the same as discussed in the above paragraph for the failure of the adjusted sum of squares for factors A and B to equal the main effects adjusted sum of squares.

6-V-2 Factorial ANCOVA with Two Covariates

The model for a two-factor ANCOVA with two covariates is

$$y_{ijk} = \mu + \alpha_i + \beta_j + \alpha\beta_{ij} + \theta_1(x_{c_{1ijk}} - \bar{x}_{c_1}) + \theta_2(x_{c_{2ijk}} - \bar{x}_{c_2}) + \varepsilon_{ijk} \quad (6\text{-}27)$$
$$(i = 1, p; j = 1, q; k = 1, n)$$

Except for the addition of a second covariate, Eq. (6-27) is identical to Eq. (6-25). Not surprisingly then the analysis is almost identical with the exception that in place of the assumption of homogeneous regression *lines* we now change the assumption to homogeneous regression *planes*. Table 6-11 presents relevant data with sufficient answers to serve as a reader test problem. We should note, however, that since most ANCOVA computer programs handle only a few covariates it will probably be necessary to use a general regression program, as described in the next chapter, to generate the analysis necessary to test the homogeneity assumption.

Table 6-12 Summary of most important equations in Chap. 6

Reduced mean square error

$$\sigma_\varepsilon^{2*} = \sigma_\varepsilon^2 (1 - \rho^2)\left(\frac{\mathrm{df}_E}{\mathrm{df}_E - 1}\right)$$

Squared standard error of adjusted treatment mean

$$\hat{\sigma}_{(\bar{y}_i^*)}^2 = \sigma_\varepsilon^{2*}\left[\frac{1}{n_i} + \frac{(\bar{x}_{c_i} - \bar{x}_c)^2}{E_{xx}}\right]$$

Squared standard error of difference between adjusted treatment means

$$\hat{\sigma}_{(\bar{y}_i^* - \bar{y}_j^*)}^2 = \sigma_\varepsilon^{2*}\left[\frac{1}{n_i} + \frac{1}{n_j} + \frac{(\bar{x}_{c_i} - \bar{x}_{c_j})^2}{E_{xx}}\right]$$

F test of homogeneity assumption

$$F_{(m_F - m_R, N - m_F)} = \frac{(SS_F - SS_R)/(m_F - m_R)}{(SS_T - SS_F)/(N - m_F)}$$

F test of linearity assumption

$$F_{[p-2, p(n-1)-1]} = \frac{S_3/(p-2)}{SS_E^*/[p(n-1)-1]}$$

6-VI SUMMARY

Covariance analysis is both a powerful and delicate analytical tool. Used skillfully it allows the researcher to probe certain types of questions in certain types of situations where it is not possible to gain "direct" control over sources of variation which would otherwise inflate error variance and possibly bias parameter estimates. But covariance analysis is always a delicate instrument subject to a host of influences such as heterogeneity of regression, extrapolation instabilities, and measurement errors which threaten to render the analysis useless or, even worse, misleading. It is for this reason that covariance analysis is best regarded as the last, rather than the first, analytical strategy. Table 6-12 presents a summary of the most important equations developed in this chapter.

CHAPTER
SEVEN

GENERAL REGRESSION ANALYSIS

7-I Research Uses of General Regression Analysis

7-I-1 Construction of "Causal" Models
7-I-2 Prediction

7-II The Basic Model

7-II-1 The Assumed Underlying (Response-Generating) Structural Model
7-II-2 An Alternative Formulation of the Response-Generating Model
7-II-3 Assumptions Underlying Regression Analysis

7-III Some Procedures for Interpreting the Regression Equation

7-III-1 A Numerical Example
7-III-2 Beta Weights
7-III-3 $R^2_{y_{12}\ldots k}$
7-III-4 R^2 and Beta Weights
7-III-5 Semipartial and Partial Correlations
       7-III-5-1 Semipartial correlation
       7-III-5-2 Partial correlation
       7-III-5-3 Formulas for k independent variables
7-III-6 $\hat{\beta}r_{yx}$
       7-III-6-1 Direct relationships
       7-III-6-2 Indirect relationships—suppressor variables
       7-III-6-3 Traditional suppression
       7-III-6-4 Negative suppression
       7-III-6-5 Reciprocal suppression
7-III-7 Regression Structure Coefficients
7-III-8 Orthogonalization of Independent Variables
       7-III-8-1 Hierarchial models
       7-III-8-2 Factors
       7-III-8-3 Overlap variables

7-IV Problems Associated With Multicollinearity

7-IV-1 A Numerical Example
7-IV-2 Standard Errors of Parameter Estimates
       7-IV-2-1 Stability of parameter estimates
       7-IV-2-2 Statistical tests on the regression equation
7-IV-3 Sensitivity to Model Specification
7-IV-4 Restricted Range of Independent Variables
7-IV-5 A Test for Multicollinearity
7-IV-6 Corrective Procedures

7-V Some Comments on Stepwise Regression Techniques

7-VI Summary

In this chapter our focus shifts from data analysis techniques and procedures *normally* associated with the analysis of experimental data to techniques and procedures *normally* associated with the analysis of data obtained via non-experimental procedures, e.g., data obtained from observational or survey research studies. The word normally has been emphasized because the problems addressed in this chapter require no new basic mathematical or statistical concepts. Parameter estimates, tests of statistical significance, power calculations, general linear contrasts and so on continue to be made using the procedures described in previous chapters.

What has changed is the character of the data to be analyzed. In a way which is fully comparable to the analysis of data following a Latin square, repeated measures, or covariance design, the general regression model discussed here presents procedures for the analysis of data with special characteristics and forces us to confront directly the difficulties which tend to arise in the analysis of such data.

Specifically, this chapter is addressed to the analysis of data in which there are no restrictions on the pattern of intercorrelations which may exist among the independent variables. With the opportunity to analyze such data come special statistical and interpretative problems which are similar to, but generally more complex than, those previously encountered in the discussion of covariance designs. Fundamentally, these problems arise from the inability to partition the variation in the dependent variable which is explained by the full model into components which are *uniquely* attributable to each independent variable in the assumed response-generating model. This inability to uniquely partition the variation in y is, of course, a consequence of the intercorrelations among the independent variables. Techniçal, such intercorrelated data are said to exhibit multicollinearity. As we shall see, the degree of difficulty of the statistical and interpretative problems which arise in the analysis of such data is largely a function of the degree of multicollinearity among the independent variables. It is then the primary task of this chapter to explicate, and where possible to suggest procedures for alleviating, the statistical and interpretative problems which tend to occur in the analysis of data exhibiting multicollinearity among the independent variables.

This chapter is divided into five major sections. Section one briefly discusses research uses of general regression analysis with emphasis on the analysis of non-experimental data. Section two develops the basic model. Section three, which is the most important section, discusses a number of procedures for interpreting the regression equation with correlated predictors. Section four discusses certain problems associated with correlated predictors. Finally, section five briefly comments on a widely used and misused set of regression procedures known as Stepwise Regression.

7-I RESEARCH USES OF GENERAL REGRESSION ANALYSIS

The title of this chapter includes the word "general" to indicate that any of the designs discussed in Chaps. 3 through 6 could be subsumed under the models discussed in this concluding chapter. Thus, although the discussion here will primarily be carried on in the context of non-experimental data, our remarks will be generally relevant to the analysis of data produced by any of the research designs previously discussed which involve correlated factors. Of course, the special problems investigated under each of those designs will be compounded by the problems associated with correlated experimental factors.

In a broad sense then the research uses of general regression analysis include the research uses of all the GLMs previously discussed. Therefore, we shall confine our remarks in this section to uses of regression analysis not previously discussed with special emphasis on the analysis of non-experimental data.

7-I-1 Construction of "Causal" Models

In Sec. 3-VII-2 the logical and procedural differences between causal and associative models were discussed. In a footnote to that section, it was also noted that the distinction between these two types of models is not as clear-cut as our few words on the subject might have indicated. A full discussion of these two broad categories of models and the gradations between them would lead us far beyond the bounds of our topic into the areas of model building and philosophy of science.[1]

What needs to be emphasized here is that even in non-experimental research the researcher typically selects variables for investigation on the more or less well-founded belief that these variables *are* causally related. That the procedures

---

[1] An excellent text, in the context of behavioral and social research, on these topics is Kaplan (1964). The problem of making causal inferences from non-experimental data is discussed by Blalock (1961) and more recently, in the context of computer data analysis, by Nie, et al. (1975).

available in such research provide a less firm foundation upon which to build causal models is cause for concern and caution but not for the complete abandonment of the construction of such causal models. The techniques discussed in this chapter provide important mathematical and statistical tools which aid in the construction of causal models of social and behavioral phenomena where true experimentation is not feasible.

In this context a point made in Sec. 3-II-2-7 bears repeating. The goal of social and behavioral research is frequently to generalize obtained research findings to a larger population. Even where it is possible to assign treatment conditions randomly, and thereby produce uncorrelated factors, the variables represented by these factors will normally be correlated in this larger population. A complete causal model which can be accurately generalized to this population, therefore, requires knowledge of the intercorrelations among the variables of interest.

7-I-2 Prediction

In certain areas the problem of *immediate* concern is the prediction of some variable(s). The focus of such inquiries is the accuracy with which the dependent variable can be predicted. Whether the independent variables are in fact the proximate cause of the state of the dependent variable or only a concomitant or surrogate measure of such variables is of distinctly secondary concern in such investigations.

Examples of such prediction-oriented investigations are numerous: college grades are predicted by SAT scores; level of unemployment by a bewildering array of economic and non-economic variables...ad infinitum. It is to be emphasized that predictive models are generally inferior to causal models, even for purposes of prediction, when the independent variables are in fact concomitant or surrogate representations of the true causal influences. This inferiority is due to the indirect and generally tenuous link which predictive models tend to establish between the dependent variable and the causative factors and the fact that changes in the level of these causal variables are normally reflected with relatively high error variance in the predictor variables.

Despite these limitations, predictive models are often extremely useful. This is especially true when the predictions are made for relatively short time periods and/or for a relatively narrow range of conditions. The regression procedures discussed in this chapter are especially well suited for the construction and validation of such predictive models.

7-II THE BASIC MODEL

In this section the basic regression model is discussed. The assumptions underlying this model are also presented. Since relatively little that is new is involved this section is very brief and contains no numerical examples. Section 7-III will present several numerical examples which will be used to illustrate different procedures for interpreting the estimated regression equation.

7-II-1 The Assumed Underlying (Response-Generating) Structural Model

The complete structural model assumed to be responsible for generating the data in a regression model with k independent variables is

$$y_i = \theta_0 + \theta_1 x_{i1} + \theta_2 x_{i2} + \cdots + \theta_k x_{ik} + \varepsilon_i \tag{7-1}$$

$$(i = 1, N)$$

θ_0 is the population value of y when all independent variables are equal to zero. θ_0 is called the intercept, i.e., that point where the regression plane crosses the y axis. Note that θ_0 is generally not equal to the grand mean of y.

7-II-2 An Alternative Formulation of the Response-Generating Model

Inspection of Eq. (7-1) indicates that the value of θ_1 tells us how much the value of y will change for a 1-unit change in x_1. A similar interpretation holds for $\theta_2 \ldots \theta_k$. Since the independent variables will generally have different standard deviations, i.e., will be measured in different units of measurement, the values of the different values in the parameter vector $\boldsymbol{\theta}$ are not directly comparable.

Therefore, it is very useful to convert all variables, including y, to standard deviates with unit variance. This may be done before parameter estimates are made. Equation (7-1), however, may be rewritten as

$$y_i = \beta_0 + \beta_1 \frac{\sigma_y}{\sigma_1} x_{i1} + \beta_2 \frac{\sigma_y}{\sigma_2} x_{i2} + \cdots + \beta_k \frac{\sigma_y}{\sigma_k} x_{ik} + \varepsilon_i \tag{7-2}$$

where σ is the standard deviation of the variable indicated by the subscript. Each β_i—generally called a beta weight to distinguish it from the corresponding raw regression coefficient θ_i—measures the number of standard deviations y will change when x_i increases by one standard deviation. Thus the β's may be directly compared with one another. Note also that, given the standard deviations of the variables, we may easily convert raw regression coefficients to beta weights (or vice versa) since

$$\beta_i \frac{\sigma_y}{\sigma_i} = \theta_i$$

or

$$\beta_i = \theta_i \frac{\sigma_i}{\sigma_y}$$

Implicit in Eqs. (7-1) and (7-2) is the assumption that the data were drawn from a single population, i.e., there are no subscripts in the model indicating that subjects were drawn from distinct populations. Furthermore, we shall assume in this chapter that all independent variables are at least intervally scaled. If the assumption that subjects were drawn from a single population is not tenable it would be necessary to represent different subject groups in the usual manner via categorical variables. In this case our discussion in Chap. 6 regarding heterogeneity of regression slopes would apply in its entirety to the present class of GLM models.

The estimated beta weights may be derived directly from the equation

$$\hat{\beta} = R_{xx}^{-1} r_{xy} \tag{7-3}$$

where R_{xx} is the matrix of intercorrelations among the independent variables and r_{xy} is the vector of correlations between y and each independent variable.[2] Except for the change in the scales of measurement, Eq. (7-3) is mathematically identical to

$$\hat{\theta} = (X'X)^{-1} X'y \tag{7-4}$$

as all of the models discussed in this book are invariant with respect to changes in the mean or standard deviation of any variable.[3] Since the parameters in $\hat{\theta}$ are no longer interpretable as deviations among subject group means we shall generally find inspection of $\hat{\beta}$ more revealing than inspection of $\hat{\theta}$, despite their structural equivalence. In a similar vein we shall, as is general practice, find it more useful to examine correlations among variables rather than cross products and sums of squares. While such changes tend to orient us to different aspects of the data they involve no fundamental mathematical or statistical changes from the procedures discussed in the first six chapters.

7-II-3 Assumptions Underlying Regression Analysis

All of the assumptions discussed in Sec. 3-II-2 apply to the regression model. Two points, however, do merit special consideration.

First, the fixed effects assumption implies that the independent variables are measured without error. For data obtained via survey or observational procedures this assumption will often be violated. Since this problem has already been discussed in Sec. 6-III-5 in the context of analysis of covariance designs we shall not pursue the problem further here. The interested reader is referred to Chap. 6 of this book and Johnston (1972), Chap. 9.

Second, the absence of multicollinearity among the independent variables has *not* been assumed, except in the very unlikely case in which two independent variables are perfectly correlated. In this instance R_{xx}^{-1} and $(X'X)^{-1}$ would not exist and we would be forced to drop at least one of the variables from the model. This is not to say that substantial problems do not occur in the presence of multicollinearity—they clearly do, and the next two sections are devoted to a discussion of these problems.

---

[2] Inclusion of the intercept as the first term in $\hat{\beta}$ does not affect Eq. (7-3).
[3] See Sec. 1-IV for a discussion of this point.

Table 7-1 Data for numerical example: regression analysis with three independent variables

y	x_1	x_2	x_3	y	x_1	x_2	x_3
−1.71	−0.84	−1.07	−0.26	−0.39	−0.05	−2.68	−2.79
0.06	−0.30	−0.38	−1.12	0.83	1.66	0.15	−1.32
−0.02	−0.57	−0.39	−0.52	0.96	1.00	0.35	0.64
−2.24	−2.76	0.52	1.63	−0.88	−1.08	0.09	2.12
−0.72	0.01	0.68	0.64	−1.06	−1.30	−1.28	−0.67
−1.10	−2.21	−0.07	0.70	0.06	−0.13	−0.90	−1.05
−0.11	−1.04	0.80	0.96	−1.21	−1.71	−0.17	0.74
1.16	−0.05	1.33	−0.58	2.27	0.10	0.77	−0.04
1.45	1.32	2.06	0.99	1.22	0.34	0.86	0.18
−0.50	0.42	−0.86	−0.71	−1.23	−0.70	−1.96	−1.25
−0.52	−1.44	−0.63	0.47	0.59	0.00	0.18	0.09
−0.89	−0.10	0.14	0.57	1.37	1.03	0.39	−0.11
1.30	0.47	1.62	1.44	1.12	−0.34	−1.19	−1.11
0.98	−0.20	0.90	1.41	0.56	−0.80	−1.37	−1.40
0.26	0.15	0.46	0.22	0.02	0.71	−0.61	−0.61

7-III SOME PROCEDURES FOR INTERPRETING THE REGRESSION EQUATION

This section reviews a number of different procedures which may be useful in interpreting the regression equation. Each of these procedures examines the structure of the regression equation from a somewhat different perspective and therefore tends to focus the researcher's attention on different aspects of the data which are reflected in the regression equation. The need for such a variety of interpretative aids is a direct function of the multicollinearity among the independent variables and the consequent inability to separate the explained variation in y into components uniquely attributable to each independent variable. It should be emphasized that the different procedures discussed here are complementary rather than competitive.

7-III-1 A Numerical Example

Table 7-1 presents artificial data which will be used to facilitate our discussion. This sample data was generated from a hypothetical population where each variable has a mean of zero, a standard deviation of one, and the following matrix R of intercorrelations among the variables.[4]

---

[4] This data set was generated via the IMSL computer program subroutine GGNRM. This program allows the user to generate an $_NX_k$ matrix of k multivariate normal deviates with an arbitrary variance/covariance structure specified by the user. For details the reader is referred to the International Mathematical and Statistical Library, Vol. 1, Edition 5, 1975, Inc. of Houston, Texas. Other programs which produce similar data are available on many computer systems.

$$R = \begin{bmatrix} r_{yy} & r_{yx_1} & r_{yx_2} & r_{yx_3} \\ r_{x_1y} & r_{x_1x_1} & r_{x_1x_2} & r_{x_1x_3} \\ r_{x_2y} & r_{x_2x_1} & r_{x_2x_2} & r_{x_2x_3} \\ r_{x_3y} & r_{x_3x_1} & r_{x_3x_2} & r_{x_3x_3} \end{bmatrix} = \begin{bmatrix} 1 & 0.7 & 0.5 & 0 \\ 0.7 & 1 & 0.4 & 0 \\ 0.5 & 0.4 & 1 & 0.7 \\ 0 & 0 & 0.7 & 1 \end{bmatrix}$$

This particular pattern of intercorrelations has, as we shall see, been chosen to illustrate certain complexities which often arise in the analysis of intercorrelated data. To simplify the notation we shall from this point on use only the numerical column index of X when referencing specific independent variables, e.g., $r_{x_1x_2}$ will be given as r_{12}, the x's being understood.

Table 7-2 presents an analysis of the data in Table 7-1. Section (a) of Table 7-2

Table 7-2 Analysis of data in Table 7-1 using the Statistical Package for the Social Sciences computer program procedure REGRESSION

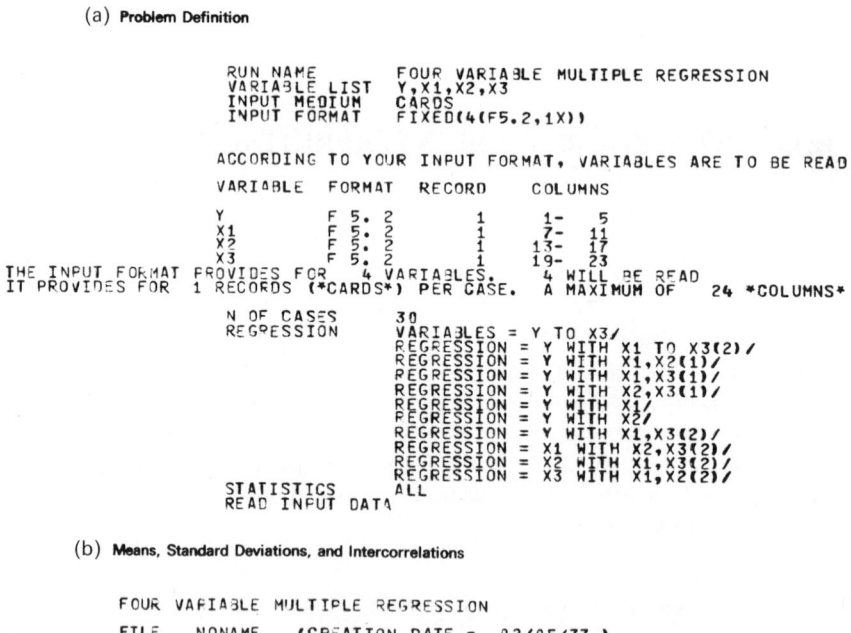

(a) **Problem Definition**

```
                    RUN NAME        FOUR VARIABLE MULTIPLE REGRESSION
                    VARIABLE LIST   Y,X1,X2,X3
                    INPUT MEDIUM    CARDS
                    INPUT FORMAT    FIXED(4(F5.2,1X))

                    ACCORDING TO YOUR INPUT FORMAT, VARIABLES ARE TO BE READ
                    VARIABLE   FORMAT   RECORD      COLUMNS

                    Y          F  5. 2      1        1-   5
                    X1         F  5. 2      1        7-  11
                    X2         F  5. 2      1       13-  17
                    X3         F  5. 2      1       19-  23
THE INPUT FORMAT PROVIDES FOR    4 VARIABLES.    4 WILL BE READ
IT PROVIDES FOR  1 RECORDS (*CARDS*) PER CASE.   A MAXIMUM OF    24 *COLUMNS*

                    N OF CASES         30
                    REGRESSION         VARIABLES = Y TO X3/
                                       REGRESSION = Y WITH X1 TO X3(2)/
                                       REGRESSION = Y WITH X1,X2(1)/
                                       REGRESSION = Y WITH X1,X3(1)/
                                       REGRESSION = Y WITH X2,X3(1)/
                                       REGRESSION = Y WITH X1/
                                       REGRESSION = Y WITH X2/
                                       REGRESSION = Y WITH X1,X3(2)/
                                       REGRESSION = X1 WITH X2,X3(2)/
                                       REGRESSION = X2 WITH X1,X3(2)/
                                       REGRESSION = X3 WITH X1,X2(2)/
                    STATISTICS         ALL
                    READ INPUT DATA
```

(b) **Means, Standard Deviations, and Intercorrelations**

```
        FOUR VARIABLE MULTIPLE REGRESSION
        FILE   NONAME   (CREATION DATE = 02/05/77 )
        * * * * * * * * * * * * * * * * * * * *   M U L

        VARIABLE           MEAN         STANDARD DEV    CASES

        Y                 .0543           1.0852         30
        X1               -.3577            .9345         30
        X2               -.0753           1.0554         30
        X3               -.0087           1.0856         30


        CORRELATION COEFFICIENTS.

        A VALUE OF 99.00000 IS PRINTED
        IF A COEFFICIENT CANNOT BE COMPUTED.


        X1                .70017
        X2                .45806          .27014
        X3               -.11037         -.16849         .69808
                            Y               X1             X2
```

Table 7-2 Continued

(c) Parameter Estimates and Significance Tests

```
FOUR VARIABLE MULTIPLE REGRESSION
FILE    NONAME   (CREATION DATE = 02/05/77.)
* * * * * * * * * * * * * * * * * * * *   M U L T I P L E
DEPENDENT VARIABLE..    Y
MEAN RESPONSE          .05433      STD. DEV.        1.08520
VARIABLE(S) ENTERED ON STEP NUMBER    1..   X1
                                            X3
                                            X2

MULTIPLE R          .82686       ANALYSIS OF VARIANCE      DF
R SQUARE            .68370       REGRESSION                 3.
ADJUSTED R SQUARE   .64720       RESIDUAL                  26.
STD DEVIATION       .64457       COEFF OF VARIABILITY    1186.3 PCT

ANALYSIS OF VARIANCE    SUM OF SQUARES    MEAN SQUARE      F      SIGNIFICANCE
REGRESSION                  23.34974        7.78325    18.73328      .000
RESIDUAL                    10.80240         .41548

-------------------- VARIABLES IN THE EQUATION --------------------
VARIABLE           B            STD ERROR B          F             BETA
                                                  ------------   ----------
                                                  SIGNIFICANCE   ELASTICITY

X1              .47394457        .15551175       9.2861384       .4081343
                                                    .005        -3.11989
X3             -.55451611        .18000395       9.4899578      -.5547418
                                                    .005         .08845
X2              .75584539        .18956903      15.897585        .7350636
                                                    .000        -1.04798
(CONSTANT)      .27598206        .12779485       4.6637472
                                                    .040
```

(d) Ninety-five Percent Confidence Intervals and Variance/Covariance Matrix

```
COEFFICIENTS AND CONFIDENCE INTERVALS.
VARIABLE      B           STD ERROR B        T         95.0 PCT CONFIDENCE INTERVAL
X1         .47394457       .15551175      3.0476447     .15428559   ,   .79360356
X3        -.55451611       .18000395     -3.0805775    -.92451953   ;  -.18451270
X2         .75584539       .18956903      3.9871775     .36618066   ,  1.1455101
CONSTANT   .27598206       .12779485      2.1595711     .13295983E-01,  .53866813
FOUR VARIABLE MULTIPLE REGRESSION
FILE    NONAME   (CREATION DATE = 02/05/77.)
* * * * * * * * * * * * * * * * * * * *   M U L T I P L E
DEPENDENT VARIABLE..    Y

VARIANCE/COVARIANCE MATRIX OF THE UNNORMALIZED REGRESSION COEFFICIENTS.

X1         .02418
X2        -.01620       .03594
X3         .01450      -.02674       .03240
            X1           X2           X3
```

presents information which describes the problem. The only significant change from SPSS data analysis of GLMs presented in earlier chapters is the use of the procedure REGRESSION instead of ANOVA. The first line in the procedure paragraph defines the variables included in the analysis. The remaining five lines define five different regression equations. The number in parentheses following each desired regression equation indicates whether all independent variables are to be entered simultaneously (an even number) or in a stepwise manner (an odd number). Stepwise regression analysis is discussed in Sec. 7-V.

Section (b) of Table 7-2 presents variable means, standard deviations, and intercorrelations. The specific values, being for sample data, are not precisely the same as for the population described in the first paragraph of this section.

Sections (c) and (d) of Table 7-2 present the data analysis for the first regression equation requested in section (a). Although the format of the printout is somewhat different the numerical results should by now be familiar. The overall significance of the regression equation is tested via the usual analysis of variance, i.e., via the statistical significance of the *total* sum of squares explained by the regression equation. Note that the standard error of $\hat{\theta}_i$ is simply the square root of the ith diagonal element of the variance/covariance matrix in Table 7-2d, e.g.,

$$\hat{\sigma}_{\theta_1} = (0.02418)^{\frac{1}{2}} = 0.1555$$

The variance/covariance matrix is, of course, equal to $\sigma_\varepsilon^2 (X'X)^{-1}$. Note that this matrix is defined for the raw regression coefficients rather than the beta weights. Therefore, while it will be more convenient to interpret the beta weight, statistical tests are most easily made on the raw regression coefficients. This is only a computational convenience since $\hat{\beta}_i$ and $\hat{\theta}_i$ carry the same information.

7-III-2 Beta Weights

As we noted earlier the magnitude of $\hat{\beta}_i$ may be interpreted as the number of standard deviations $\hat{y}$ (the expected value of y) will increase for a one standard deviation increase in x_i. Implicit in this definition of $\hat{\beta}_i$ is that all other independent variables remain constant. Geometrically, $\hat{\beta}_i$ specifies the slope of the regression plane along the x_i axis. Since x_i passes through the origin of the geometric space all other independent variables are held constant. It is for this reason that $\hat{\beta}_i$ is more fully and properly called a *partial* beta weight, i.e., the effects of all other independent variables have been removed or partialed out of the relationship between y and x_i.[5] In our present example an increase of one standard deviation in x_1 gives rise to an increase of 0.408 standard deviations in the expected value of y with all other independent variables held constant. It is this partialing effect which accounts for the fact that the β estimated in the covariance model is the pooled within-cell regression coefficient, i.e., the between-cell effects have been partialed out. Note that β as defined in Chap. 6 is a raw regression coefficient not a beta weight as defined here.

7-III-3 $R^2_{y \cdot 12 \ldots k}$

$R_{y \cdot 12 \ldots k}$ is called the multiple correlation coefficient, the subscripts indicating the variables involved. For simplicity we shall normally drop the subscripts since it will usually be clear which variables are involved. A useful way to interpret R is to think of it as a simple correlation between y and $\hat{y}$, i.e., the correlation between

---

[5] A more complete notation for β_i would be $\beta_{i \cdot 12 \ldots (i) \ldots k}$, which indicates that the effects of all independent variables to the right of the first subscript dot have been, except for (i), removed out of β_i.

the original values of the dependent variable and the corresponding values of y estimated from

$$\hat{y} = X\hat{\beta}$$

Since $\hat{y}$ is based on a linear combination of the independent variables, R, unlike a true simple correlation, is always greater than or equal to zero. R^2 is then the proportion of variance in y explained by the regression equation, i.e., the sum of squares explained by the model divided by the total sum of squares.[6] Since the explained sum of squares contains error variance it is useful to know that an unbiased estimate of R^2 is

$$R_{adj}^2 = 1 - (1 - R^2)\frac{N-1}{N-k-1} \qquad (7\text{-}5)$$

where N is the number of subjects and k the number of independent variables.

7-III-4 R^2 and Beta Weights

Since $\hat{\beta}_i$ specifies the relationship between x_i and $\hat{y}$ only when all other x_j are held constant it is not surprising to find that R^2 is based upon the intercorrelations among the independent variables as well as the beta weights.

More specifically it may be shown that

$$R^2 = \sum_{i=1}^{k} \hat{\beta}_i^2 + \sum_{i=1}^{k}\sum_{j=i+1}^{k} 2r_{ij}\hat{\beta}_i\hat{\beta}_j \qquad (7\text{-}6)$$

Note that the second term in Eq. (7-6) involves all possible pairs of the independent variables. Even for a relatively small number of independent variables this will require a substantial number of terms. Of course, when all values of r_{ij} are zero this last set of terms vanishes and R^2 equals the sum of the squared beta weights, which are statistically, if not substantially, quite easy to interpret. Note also that in this special case

$$R^2 = \sum_{i=1}^{k} r_{yi}^2$$

and that

$$\hat{\beta}_i = r_{yi}$$

For the present example

$$R^2 = (0.408)^2 + (0.735)^2 + (-0.555)^2 + 2(0.270)(0.408)(0.735)$$
$$+ 2(-0.168)(0.408)(-0.555) + 2(0.698)(0.735)(-0.555)$$
$$= 0.166 + 0.540 + 0.308 + 0.162 + 0.076 - 0.570$$
$$= 0.682$$

---

[6] As noted in Sec. 1-III-5-4 the sum of squares due the mean of y is usually omitted from the numerator and the denominator of R^2. That is, y is usually assumed to be intervally scaled, but not ratio scaled. For a discussion of this latter point see Sec. 3-II-5-2.

Two things of importance are revealed by this example. First, the sum of the squared beta weights may be greater than R^2. They may also be less. Second, terms of the form $2r_{ij}\hat{\beta}_i\hat{\beta}_j$ may be negative. Since a negative variance is not possible it is clear that Eq. (7-6) may not serve as a scheme for partitioning variance.

7-III-5 Semipartial and Partial Correlations

Two variables which facilitate interpretation of the regression equation are the semipartial and partial correlations. For simplicity we shall develop these concepts for two independent variables and then extend them to the general case of k independent variables.

Figure 7-1 presents the problem graphically. Each circle represents a variable with unit variance. Area a is the proportion of the variance in y attributable to x_1 after the effects of x_2 have been removed from x_1. Area b is the "portion of the variance" in y attributable to the joint influence of x_1 and x_2. The quotation marks have been used because area b may be negative. Thus, while a useful heuristic, Figure 7-1 is not entirely correct. Finally, area d is the residual variation in y which is not explained, either singularly or jointly, by x_1 and x_2.

7-III-5-1 Semipartial correlation The semipartial correlation of independent variable x_i is the correlation between y and x_i after the effects of all other independent variables have been removed or partialed from x_i, i.e., the semipartial for x_i is the correlation between y and that residual portion of x_i which cannot be explained by the other independent variables. This coefficient is called a *semi-partial* because the effects of the other independent variables are removed from x_i but not from y.

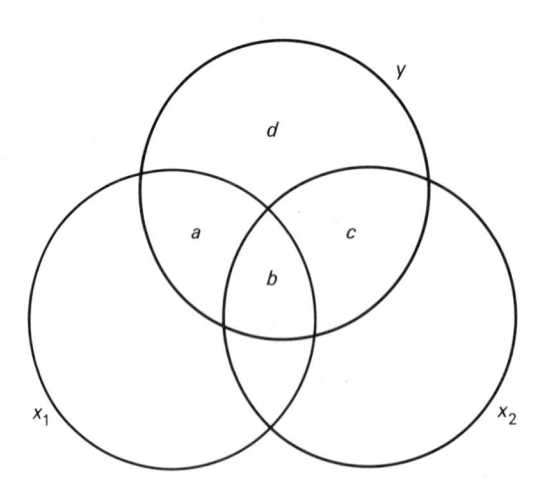

Figure 7-1 Schematic diagram to illustrate semipartial and partial correlations for two independent variables. (Note that this schematic is not totally correct since area b can be negative.)

The squared semipartial for x_i then is the proportion of the variance of y accounted for by x_i after the effects of all other independent variables have been removed from x_i. In Figure 7-1 the squared semipartial is represented by area a for x_1 and area c for x_2.

Mathematically, the semipartial correlation for the two variable case is defined as

$$sr_{y(i \cdot j)} = \frac{r_{yi} - r_{yj}r_{ij}}{(1 - r_{ij}^2)^{\frac{1}{2}}} \tag{7-7}$$

the notation $(i \cdot j)$ indicating that the effects of x_j have been removed from x_i but not from y. As an example, using the data in Tables 7-1 and 7-2, omitting x_3,

$$sr_{y(1 \cdot 2)} = \frac{0.700 - (0.458)(0.270)}{(1 - 0.270)^{\frac{1}{2}}} = 0.599$$

Thus approximately 36 percent of the variance in y is accounted for by x_1 after the effects of x_2 have been removed from x_1. The reader should try calculating $sr_{y(2 \cdot 1)}$, which is equal to 0.279.

7-III-5-2 Partial correlation In the partial correlation coefficient for x_i the effects of all other independent variables are removed from both x_i and y. In Figure 7-1 the partial correlation for x_1 is

$$pr_{y1 \cdot 2} = \left(\frac{a}{a+d}\right)^{\frac{1}{2}} = \frac{r_{y1} - r_{y2}r_{12}}{(1 - r_{y2}^2)^{\frac{1}{2}}(1 - r_{12}^2)^{\frac{1}{2}}} \tag{7-8}$$

$$= \frac{0.700 - (0.458)(0.270)}{(1 - 0.458^2)^{\frac{1}{2}}(1 - 0.270^2)^{\frac{1}{2}}}$$

$$= 0.673$$

Note the absence of parentheses in $pr_{y1 \cdot 2}$: this indicates that x_2 has been partialed out of both x_1 and y. By interchanging r_{y1} and r_{y2} we can calculate the partial correlation for x_2 as

$$pr_{y2 \cdot 1} = \left(\frac{c}{c+d}\right)^{\frac{1}{2}} = \frac{0.458 - (0.700)(0.270)}{(1 - 0.700^2)^{\frac{1}{2}}(1 - 0.270^2)^{\frac{1}{2}}} = 0.391$$

In words, the squared partial for x_1 tells us that approximately 45 percent of the variation in y which is *not* accounted for by x_2 is due that portion of x_1 which is free of the effects of x_2. The squared partial for x_2 may be similarly interpreted. Note that the partial correlation of a variable is always greater than or equal to the corresponding semipartial.

7-III-5-3 Formulas for k independent variables Finally, we note that the semipartial and partial correlations may be calculated for any x_i in the case of k independent variables as follows

$$sr_i = \hat{\beta}_i [1 - R_{i \cdot 12 \ldots (i) \ldots k}^2]^{\frac{1}{2}} \tag{7-9}$$

218 THE GENERAL LINEAR MODEL

and

$$\text{pr}_i = \frac{\text{sr}_i}{[1 - R^2_{y \cdot 12\ldots(i)\ldots k}]^{\frac{1}{2}}} \quad (7\text{-}10)$$

For simplicity the complex subscripting has been omitted from sr_i and pr_i. The term R^2 in Eq. (7-9) is the squared multiple correlation between x_i and all other independent variables. The term R^2 in Eq. (7-10) is the squared multiple correlation between y and all independent variables except x_i. In both equations the subscript (i) indicates the omission of variable x_i. The interpretation of sr_i and pr_i in the case of k independent variables is precisely the same as for two independent variables.

For our example data these correlations are

$$\text{sr}_1 = 0.336 \quad \text{pr}_1 = 0.513$$
$$\text{sr}_2 = 0.440 \quad \text{pr}_2 = 0.616$$
$$\text{sr}_3 = -0.340 \quad \text{pr}_3 = -0.517$$

Squaring each sr_i indicates that the contributions of x_1 and x_3 to R^2, after removal of the effects of all other independent variables, are approximately equal and about half the magnitude of x_2. Note also that

$$\Sigma \, \text{sr}_i^2 \neq R^2$$

In the present example $\Sigma \, \text{sr}_i^2$ is about 62 percent of the magnitude of R^2. As we shall see, however, $\Sigma \, \text{sr}_i^2$ may be greater than R^2 under certain special conditions.

7-III-6 $\hat{\beta} r_{yx_i}$

In Chap. 1 it was noted that the explained sum of squares is equal to $\hat{\theta}'X'y$. Since R^2 is $\hat{\theta}'X'y$ standardized to a base of one, a simple replacement of variables yields

$$R^2 = \hat{\beta}' r_{yx} \quad (7\text{-}11)$$

where r_{yx} is a vector of correlations between y and each independent variable. These correlations are often called zero order correlations, indicating that no variables have been partialed out, or validity coefficients. The individual terms of the form $\hat{\beta}_i r_{yx_i}$ in Eq. (7-11) are often referred to as contributions to prediction or weighted validity coefficients. As Conger (1974) notes, however, the designation "contribution to prediction" cannot be correct since it is quite possible for $\hat{\beta}_i$ to be relatively large and $\hat{\beta}_i r_{yx_i}$ to be zero or even negative.

Despite the fact that Eq. (7-11) cannot serve as a unique variance-partitioning scheme, examination of the weighted validity coefficients against their respective beta weights will reveal certain aspects of the structure of the regression equation. In the remainder of this discussion we shall assume $r_{yx} \geq 0$ for all x_i. This restriction simplifies our discussion without altering its substance since $r_{yx_i} < 0$ can be made positive by reflecting the x_i axis, i.e., by multiplying x_i by -1. The sign of

r_{ij} will change if x_i or x_j is reflected and will remain unchanged if *both* x_i and x_j are reflected. We should also note that our discussion will be exact for two independent variables but only approximate for k independent variables. For more on this latter point the reader is referred to Conger (1974).

7-III-6-1 Direct relationships In the simplest case all x_i are orthogonal and $\hat{\beta}_i r_{yx_i} = r_{yx_i}^2$. Note in this case that the beta weights are simply the zero order correlations. Similarly, when

$$0 < \hat{\beta} < r_{yx_i}$$

and, consequently

$$0 < \hat{\beta}_i r_{yx_i} < r_{yx_i}^2$$

x_i will be partially redundant with at least one other independent variable in the regression equation in its prediction of variation in y. In both of these cases the relationships between y and x_i are direct in that y and x_i have a positive validity coefficient.

7-III-6-2 Indirect relationships—suppressor variables When $\hat{\beta}_i$ falls outside the range of 0 to r_{yx_i} the presence of suppressor variables in the regression equation is indicated. A suppressor variable x_j is a variable which removes, i.e., suppresses, variance in some other variable x_i which is unrelated to the variation in y. A suppressor variable[7] is characterized by a $\hat{\beta}_j$ which is large relative to $\hat{\beta}_j r_{yx_j}$, i.e., has a very small validity coefficient relative to $\hat{\beta}_j$. Conger (1974) has identified three different types of suppressor variables which we now proceed to discuss. This discussion also gives us an opportunity to present three numerical examples which may serve as reader test problems.

7-III-6-3 Traditional suppression Formally, traditional suppression occurs when $r_{yx_i} > 0$, $r_{yx_j} = 0$, and $r_{ij} \neq 0$. Since x_j is not correlated with y, any correlation it has with x_i must be with that portion of x_i which is unrelated to y. By removing this variation from x_i the overall correlation $R_{y \cdot ij}$ is increased. For empirical data it is only required that r_{yx_j} be small.

Using the data in Tables 7-1 and 7-2 as an example

$$R^2 = \hat{\beta} r_{yx} = [0.408, 0.735, -0.555] \begin{bmatrix} 0.700 \\ 0.458 \\ -0.110 \end{bmatrix}$$

$$= 0.286 + 0.337 + 0.061$$

$$= 0.683$$

---

[7] Although it is common to designate one of the two variables involved as the "suppressor," suppression is, as we shall see, a fully symmetrical relationship, i.e., if x_i suppresses x_j, then we may also say that x_j suppresses x_i.

220 THE GENERAL LINEAR MODEL

which suggests that x_3 is acting as a suppressor variable. The fact that $r_{23} = 0.698$, while r_{12} and r_{13} are relatively small, suggests that x_3 is suppressing irrelevant variance in x_2. Inspection of the known population correlations in Sec. 7-III-1, indicates that this is in fact what is occuring.

Two things about this example are noteworthy. First, the sign of $\hat{\beta}_3$ is opposite the sign of r_{23}. This is a characteristic of traditional suppression. Second, the semipartial correlation sr_3 will be non-zero with sign opposite r_{23} as inspection of Eq. (7-7), for the two independent variable case, reveals. As noted in Sec. 7-III-5-3, $sr_3 = -0.340$. It is in this sense that suppression is fully symmetrical; for although our attention tends to be drawn to the x_i with the positive validity coefficient we may just as legitimately focus on the x_j with the zero validity coefficient after it has been freed from the suppressing effects of x_i.

Table 7-3 Numerical example negative suppression and reader test problem

(a) Data

y	x_1	x_2	x_3	y	x_1	x_2	x_3
−1.71	−0.84	−0.36	−0.27	−0.39	−0.05	−1.82	−1.53
0.06	−0.30	−0.59	−0.94	0.83	−0.66	−1.06	−0.64
−0.02	−0.57	−0.79	−0.08	0.96	1.00	0.48	1.23
−2.24	−2.76	−0.46	0.18	−0.88	−1.08	−0.27	2.21
−0.72	0.01	1.03	−0.71	−1.06	−1.30	−1.39	−0.33
−1.10	−2.21	−1.23	0.66	0.06	−0.13	−0.85	−0.38
−0.11	−1.04	−0.22	0.77	−1.21	−1.71	−0.79	0.46
1.16	−0.05	0.16	−0.70	2.27	0.10	−0.92	1.91
1.45	1.32	1.73	0.43	1.22	0.34	0.10	0.71
−0.50	0.42	0.06	−0.89	−1.23	−0.70	−1.26	−0.90
−0.52	−1.44	−1.39	1.29	0.59	0.00	−0.28	0.67
−0.89	−0.10	0.65	−0.41	1.37	1.03	0.25	0.66
1.30	0.47	0.73	1.70	1.12	−0.34	−2.00	1.22
0.98	−0.20	−0.18	2.30	0.56	−0.80	−2.16	0.54
0.26	0.15	0.30	0.08	0.02	0.71	0.15	−0.50

(b) Selected regression results

$$R^2 = 0.7208$$

$$\beta = \begin{pmatrix} 0.890 \\ -0.319 \\ 0.424 \end{pmatrix} \quad r_{yx} = \begin{pmatrix} 0.700 \\ 0.203 \\ 0.381 \end{pmatrix}$$

$$R_{xx} = \begin{bmatrix} 1 & 0.559 & -0.028 \\ 0.559 & 1 & 0.057 \\ -0.028 & 0.057 & 1 \end{bmatrix}$$

$$sr = \begin{pmatrix} 0.736 \\ -0.264 \\ 0.423 \end{pmatrix} \quad pr = \begin{pmatrix} 0.813 \\ -0.447 \\ 0.625 \end{pmatrix}$$

Table 7-4 Numerical example reciprocal suppression and reader test problem

(a) Data

y	x_1	x_2	y	x_1	x_2
−1.71	−0.42	−1.34	0.96	−1.53	2.81
0.85	0.47	0.11	0.43	1.52	−0.99
−0.43	−1.36	0.61	−0.50	0.68	−1.41
−0.78	−0.71	−0.36	−0.11	−0.51	−0.61
−2.24	−2.56	1.14	−0.31	0.92	−1.47
−0.04	−0.65	0.86	0.74	0.90	0.05
1.15	0.14	0.24	1.30	0.11	1.74
−2.01	−0.38	−1.35	0.84	1.27	−0.93
−0.11	−1.22	1.45	0.57	1.69	−0.59
0.05	1.03	−1.42	−0.05	0.31	−0.37

(b) Selected regression results

$$R^2 = 0.411 \qquad R_{xx} = \begin{bmatrix} 1 & -0.616 \\ -0.616 & 1 \end{bmatrix}$$

$$\hat{\beta} = \begin{pmatrix} 0.800 \\ 0.610 \end{pmatrix} \qquad \text{sr} = \begin{pmatrix} 0.630 \\ 0.481 \end{pmatrix}$$

$$r_{yx} = \begin{pmatrix} 0.424 \\ 0.118 \end{pmatrix} \qquad \text{pr} = \begin{pmatrix} 0.634 \\ 0.531 \end{pmatrix}$$

7-III-6-4 Negative suppression Formally, negative suppression is defined by the condition $r_{yi} < r_{yj}r_{ij}$, where x_i is arbitrarily defined as the variable with the smaller validity coefficient and $r_{ij} > 0$. That is, while x_i is correlated with y its primary function in the regression equation is the suppression of irrelevant variation in x_j.

Table 7-3 presents data which exhibits negative suppression. Selected results of the data analysis are presented to (1) illustrate the characteristic features of negative suppression, and (2) serve as check points for readers wishing to test their understanding of the regression analysis procedures discussed thus far.

Note that in section (b) of Table 7-3 that the sign of $\hat{\beta}_2$, the variable with the smaller validity coefficient, is negative. This pattern is characteristic of "negative" suppression. Note also that $\hat{\beta}_1$ exceeds r_{y1}, indicating that the suppression relationship exists between x_1 and x_2.[8] Examination of the intercorrelation matrix reinforces this conclusion as we clearly see that x_3 is essentially unrelated to x_1 or x_2.

7-III-6-5 Reciprocal suppression Formally, reciprocal suppression occurs when $r_{y1} > 0$, $r_{y2} > 0$, and $r_{12} < 0$. The negative correlation between x_1 and x_2, in the

---

[8] While $\hat{\beta}_3$ exceeds r_{y3} it does so by only a nominal amount.

presence of positive correlations of y with both x_1 and x_2, indicates that x_1 is suppressing irrelevant variation in x_2 and vice versa; hence the name "reciprocal" suppression.

Table 7-4 presents an example of reciprocal suppression as well as a reader test problem. Note that $\hat{\beta}_1 > r_{y1}$, $\hat{\beta}_2 > r_{y2}$, and that

$$r_{y1}^2 + r_{y2}^2 < R_{y\cdot 12}^2 < sr_1^2 + sr_2^2$$

All of these interrelationships are characteristic of data exhibiting reciprocal suppression.

7-III-7 Regression Structure Coefficients

In Sec. 7-III-3 we noted that $R_{y\cdot 12\ldots k}^2$ could be interpreted as the correlation between y and $\hat{y}$ the expected value of y estimated from k independent variables. In Sec. 1-III-5 it was shown that the correlation between two vectors, e.g., y and $\hat{y}$, is equal to the cosine of the angle between these vectors: r_{yx} gives these correlations for y and each x_i. A simple extension of these concepts leads us to ask what are the correlations between the estimated value of y and each x_i. Such correlations between a set of observed variables and a variable, e.g., $\hat{y}$, estimated from these observed variables are generally called structure coefficients.

Deriving these structure coefficients is relatively easy and instructive. We begin by assuming that all variables are standardized. Since R^2 is the variance in y explained by X it follows that multiplication of $\hat{y}$ by $1/R$ converts $\hat{y}$ into a standardized variable with unit variance. Therefore the correlations we seek are

$$r_{x\hat{y}} = \frac{1}{N} X'\hat{y} \frac{1}{R}$$

Since $\hat{y} = X\beta$, we have

$$r_{x\hat{y}} = \frac{1}{N} X'X\beta \frac{1}{R}$$

$$= R_{xx}\beta \frac{1}{R}$$

However,

$$\beta = R_{xx}^{-1} r_{yx}$$

which yields

$$r_{x\hat{y}} = R_{xx} R_{xx}^{-1} r_{yx} \frac{1}{R}$$

$$= I r_{yx} \frac{1}{R} \qquad (7\text{-}12)$$

$$= r_{xy} \frac{1}{R}$$

That is, the structure coefficients we seek are simply the zero order correlations between y and x_i divided by the standard deviation of $\hat{y}$, the multiple correlation coefficient R.

Note that $r_{x_i\hat{y}}$ is always greater than $r_{x_i y}$ except in the limiting case where R equals one. This is not surprising since error variance in y has been removed from $\hat{y}$. Note also that $r_{x\hat{y}}$ puts almost no emphasis on the beta weights. This is quite important since, as we shall see in the next section, the beta weights can be extremely unstable between samples of data. It is especially this latter point which makes the inspection of $r_{x\hat{y}}$ so valuable an interpretative tool.

7-III-8 Orthogonalization of Independent Variables

In concluding our discussion of procedures for aiding the researcher in interpreting a regression equation we will briefly discuss three broad categories of techniques through which the researcher may make his independent variables uncorrelated. We emphasize brief since an extended discussion of these techniques would quickly lead us beyond the bounds of our topic into the areas of theory construction and multivariate statistics.[9]

7-III-8-1 Hierarchial models In this method of orthogonalizing the independent variable x_1 is entered into the regression first. Next $x_{2 \cdot 1}$ is entered, where the subscripts indicate that x_1 has been partialed out of x_2. The proportion of variance of y explained by the regression equation then is

$$R^2_{y12\ldots k} = R^2_{y \cdot 1} + R^2_{y(2 \cdot 1)} + R^2_{y \cdot (3 \cdot 12)} + \cdots + R^2_{y \cdot (k \cdot 12 \ldots k-1)}$$

That is, the variables are entered into the model in a hierarchial order. Each x_i, beyond the first, has the effect of all x_j with lower subscripts removed, i.e., x_i has been redefined, and orthogonalized, to be a partial of order $(i - 1)$.

The difficult question, of course, is the order in which the x_i's are to be entered. Broadly speaking, this may be done in three ways. First, the order may be determined statistically using a criterion such as entering that variable which results in the largest increase in R^2. Such procedures are generally called stepwise regression and are discussed later. Second, the researcher may be guided by a theoretical model which assigns greater importance or causal priority to some variables than to others. Third, in prediction studies where the x_i are highly intercorrelated it is often desirable to assign priority to independent variables which are most readily available.

7-III-8-2 Factors Mathematically, it is possible to transform k correlated variables into k variables which are uncorrelated. Such constructed variables are called factors. A regression analysis may then be conducted using the factors in place

---

[9] Multivariate statistics involve the analysis of data containing multiple dependent variables as well as multiple independent variables. Two text on this complex topic to which the reader is referred are Cooley and Lohnes (1971) and Van de Geer (1971).

of the independent variables. Since the factors are orthogonal, the squared beta weights will be equal to the validity coefficients and

$$R^2 = \sum_{i=1}^{p} \beta_i^2 = \sum_{i=1}^{p} r_{yf_i}^2 \qquad (7\text{-}13)$$

Note that the validity coefficients in this equation refer to the correlations between y and each constructed factor. Note also that the summation is over p factors rather than k variables. The importance of this is that when variables are very highly correlated there is reason to presume they are measuring the same thing. In such a case it may be possible to express the k variables in terms of a relatively few factors. Thus, there will be, at most, k factors and often p will be substantially less than k.

An important point to understand is that a regression equation calculated with k factors will explain exactly the same proportion of the variation in y as a regression equation calculated with the k independent variables from which those factors are constructed. Whether the factors result in a more interpretable regression equation essentially depends upon whether the factors themselves are interpretable in terms of the variables from which they are constructed. In empirical data it sometimes happens that the factors are very easy to interpret; often, however, this is not so. To discuss factor analysis in greater depth would take us far beyond the bounds of our topic and so our cursory discussion of this topic must be concluded here. The reader is warned, however, that the application of factor analysis techniques is fraught with difficulties and requires a substantial understanding of the technique for its proper use as a data analysis tool.[10]

7-III-8-3 Overlap variables Finally, we note that it is possible to separate out that portion of each independent variable which overlaps with the other independent variables in the data set and to construct a set of variables to represent these overlaps. All of the resulting variables will be orthogonal and the regression equation may be computed upon these constructed independent variables in the usual way. These required procedures are similar to, but more complex than, the factor analytic procedure discussed above. For further details, and references, the reader is referred to Gorsuch (1973).

7-IV PROBLEMS ASSOCIATED WITH MULTICOLLINEARITY

This section extends the discussion of Sec. 7-III by discussing certain problems which are closely related to the degree of multicollinearity among the independent

---

[10] A readable discussion of the basic principles upon which factor analysis is based is contained in Chaps. 4 and 5 of Cooley and Lohnes (1971). Gorsuch (1973) discusses factor analytic procedures in the context of analyzing correlated independent variables, providing an example and additional references to the literature on this problem.

GENERAL REGRESSION ANALYSIS **225**

variables. We shall also present a test for multicollinearity and suggest certain possible corrective procedures. We should again emphasize that, except for the unlikely case where $(X'X)^{-1}$ does not exist the absence of multicollinearity is *not* an assumption of the GLM.

7-IV-1 A Numerical Example

Table 7-5 presents data which will be used to facilitate our discussion. Sufficient results are shown in section (b) of the table to illustrate the problems discussed in this section and to serve as check points for readers wishing to analyze the data as a test problem.

Table 7-5 Numerical example: high multicollinearity among independent variables

(a) Data

y	x_1	x_2	x_3	y	x_1	x_2	x_3
−1.71	−0.30	−0.67	−0.77	−0.39	0.19	−1.53	−1.44
0.06	−0.43	−0.53	−0.80	0.83	−1.42	−0.86	−1.04
−0.02	−0.75	−0.74	−0.67	0.96	0.72	0.69	1.27
−2.24	−2.26	−1.16	−1.67	−0.88	−0.89	−0.53	0.18
−0.72	0.47	0.74	0.13	−1.06	−1.07	−1.49	−1.46
−1.10	−2.25	−1.53	−1.47	0.06	−0.21	−0.70	−0.58
−0.11	−1.32	−0.38	−0.34	−1.21	−1.52	−1.11	−1.10
1.16	−0.80	0.27	−0.21	2.27	−1.30	−0.42	0.52
1.45	0.84	1.82	1.67	1.22	−0.32	0.31	0.56
1.50	0.88	0.06	−0.13	−1.23	−0.15	−1.30	−1.32
−0.52	−1.59	−1.45	−0.85	0.59	−0.38	−0.15	0.18
−0.89	0.44	0.39	0.02	1.37	0.51	0.57	0.98
1.30	−0.21	0.85	1.30	1.12	−1.17	−1.53	−0.50
0.98	−0.89	−0.05	0.79	0.56	−1.43	−1.81	−1.11
0.26	0.03	0.31	0.25	0.02	0.93	0.25	0.24

(b) Selected regression results

$$R^2_{y \cdot 123} = 0.565\dagger \qquad r_{yx} = \begin{pmatrix} 0.219 \\ 0.457 \\ 0.679 \end{pmatrix}$$

$$R_{xx} = \begin{bmatrix} 1 & 0.697 & 0.589 \\ 0.697 & 1 & 0.885 \\ 0.589 & 0.885 & 1 \end{bmatrix} \qquad \hat{\sigma}_\theta = \begin{pmatrix} 0.217 \\ 0.380 \\ 0.331 \end{pmatrix}$$

$$\hat{\beta} = \begin{pmatrix} -0.125 \\ -0.564 \\ 1.252\dagger \end{pmatrix} \qquad \hat{\sigma}_\beta = \begin{pmatrix} 0.181 \\ 0.314 \\ 0.279 \end{pmatrix}$$

† $p_1 < 0.001$.

7-IV-2 Standard Errors of Parameter Estimates

In Sec. 3-II-5-2 we noted that the standard error of the estimate of any single parameter in $\hat{\theta}$ is equal to $\hat{\sigma}_\varepsilon(C_{ii})^{\frac{1}{2}}$ where C_{ii} is the ith diagonal element of $(X'X)^{-1}$. There is an alternative expression for the standard error of a parameter estimate which is very revealing of the statistical problems associated with multicollinearity. Specifically,

$$\hat{\sigma}_{\theta_i} = \frac{\hat{\sigma}_y}{\hat{\sigma}_{x_i}} \left(\frac{1 - R^2_{y \cdot 12\ldots k}}{N - k - 1} \right)^{\frac{1}{2}} \cdot \left(\frac{1}{1 - R^2_{i \cdot 12\ldots(i)\ldots k}} \right)^{\frac{1}{2}} \quad (7\text{-}14)$$

or, assuming the variables are standardized,

$$\hat{\sigma}_{\beta_i} = \left(\frac{1 - R^2_{y \cdot 12\ldots k}}{N - k - 1} \right)^{\frac{1}{2}} \left(\frac{1}{1 - R^2_{i \cdot 12\ldots(i)\ldots k}} \right)^{\frac{1}{2}} \quad (7\text{-}15)$$

Examination of Eqs. (7-14) and (7-15) reveals that as the multiple correlation between x_i and all other independent variables approaches 1 the standard error of $\hat{\sigma}_{\beta_i}$ approaches infinity. Using x_2 as an example we have

$$\hat{\sigma}_{\beta_2} = \left(\frac{1 - 0.565}{26} \right)^{\frac{1}{2}} \cdot \left(\frac{1}{1 - 0.831} \right)^{\frac{1}{2}}$$

$$= (0.1293)(2.432)$$

$$= 0.314$$

For this example $\hat{\sigma}_{\beta_2}$ is almost two and one half times as large as it would have been had x_2 been uncorrelated with x_1 and x_3, all other things being equal. This result has two general consequences, which are considered in the following two sections.

7-IV-2-1 Stability of parameter estimates The first consequence revealed by Eqs. (7-14) and (7-15) is that parameter estimates will be increasingly unstable as multicollinearity increases. Such instability will not only make it more difficult to interpret the beta weights it will also tend to make them not statistically significant even when they are relatively large. For example, the 95 percent confidence interval for $\hat{\beta}_2$ is

$$-1.211 < \hat{\beta}_2 < 0.083$$

which is not significant since the interval includes zero. Had $R^2_{y \cdot 123}$ been the same, and x_2 uncorrelated with x_1 and x_3, the 95 percent confidence interval for $\hat{\beta}_2$ would have been

$$-0.830 < \hat{\beta}_2 < -0.300$$

which is significant at $p_1 = 0.05$ level.

7-IV-2-2 Statistical tests on the regression equation The second consequence referred to in Sec. 7-IV-2 is that in making statistical tests of individual regression coefficients and subsets of regression coefficients we encounter a number of possible results which are superficially paradoxical. For example, we have already seen that a large beta weight may be non-significant because of instability in parameter estimates caused by high multicollinearity. Indeed it is possible to have R^2 significant—i.e., for the entire regression equation to be significant—but none of the $\hat{\beta}_i$ significant at any given probability level. More generally, Geary and Leser (1968, p. 20) suggest that six different patterns of results may be distinguished:

1. R^2 and all $\hat{\beta}_i$ significant.
2. R^2 and some but not all $\hat{\beta}_i$ significant.
3. R^2 but none of the $\hat{\beta}_i$ significant.
4. All $\hat{\beta}_i$ significant but not R^2.
5. Some $\hat{\beta}_i$ significant but not R^2.
6. Neither R^2 nor any $\hat{\beta}_i$ significant.

In commenting on Geary and Leser (1968), Cramer (1972) makes a number of points which have important implications for conducting statistical tests on the regression equation. First, he notes that a test of the hypothesis $R^2 = 0$ is equivalent to a test that *all* $\hat{\beta}_i = 0$. Cramer therefore notes the usual prescription that when the hypothesis $R^2 = 0$ is not rejected, i.e., cases four, five, and six, detailed statistical tests on components of the regression equation are generally unwarranted. Second, he points out that in comparing the significance of R^2 and any single $\hat{\beta}_j$ two different models are being compared, i.e., one in which all $\hat{\beta}_i$ may be different from zero versus one in which all $\hat{\beta}_i$ except $\hat{\beta}_j$ may be different from zero. The reason for this, of course, is that the value of $\hat{\beta}_j$ may depend not only on the relationship between y and x_j but also on the relationship between x_j and all other independent variables included in the regression equation.

More generally, because of the very complex relationships among variables which may exist in a model with correlated independent variables, statistical tests on individual parameters or subsets of parameters are often misleading. Cramer argues strongly that in such cases it is imperative that the researcher carefully formulate the alternate models which he believes are relevant and that statistical tests should be confined to comparisons between such models.

Such comparisons between models are particularly important in case two and, to a lesser extent, three where it is possible that at least some independent variables may be omitted from the regression equation without significantly affecting the results. If we use R_F^2 to indicate the proportion of variance in y explained by the full regression equation with k independent variables and R_R^2 the corresponding term for a regression equation based on a p variable subset of those k independent variables an appropriate test of the two models is

$$F_{(k-p, N-k-1)} = \frac{(R_F^2 - R_R^2)/(k - p)}{(1 - R_F^2)/(N - k - 1)} \qquad (7\text{-}16)$$

For example, inspection of the data in Table 7-5 suggests that variables x_1 and x_2 might be dropped from the model without substantial impact. Making the proper substitutions in Eq. (7-16) gives

$$F_{(2,26)} = \frac{(0.565 - 0.461)/2}{(1 - 0.565)/26} = 3.10$$

which is not significant at the $p_1 = 0.05$ level, thereby confirming the hypothesis that x_1 and x_2 may be dropped without adversely affecting the model.

7-IV-3 Sensitivity to Model Specification

In Secs. 1-III-3 and 3-II-2-2 we noted that a failure to include relevant independent variables in the model would not affect parameter estimates when the independent variables are uncorrelated. Since each $\hat{\beta}_i$ depends partially on the interrelationships among all independent variables it should by now be clear that the omission of a relevant independent variable from the model will tend to bias parameter estimates of those variables left in the model. The point we wish to make here is that these biases may be extreme in the presence of high multicollinearity.

Using the data in Table 7-5 as example, we find $\hat{\beta}_1 = -0.277$ and $\hat{\beta}_3 = 0.842$ when x_2 is omitted from the model, i.e., the value of $\hat{\beta}_1$ is more than doubled and the value of β_3 is reduced by almost a third when the model is incorrectly specified by the omission of x_2. If x_3 is omitted we obtain $\hat{\beta}_1 = -0.194$ and $\hat{\beta}_2 = 0.592$, i.e., the value of $\hat{\beta}_2$ is relatively large and approximately equal to the *negative* of its true value. It is results such as these which make it crucial that research using regression analysis be guided by sound theory. We shall have somewhat more to say about the role of theory in Sec. 7-V.

7-IV-4 Restricted Range of Independent Variables

Similarly, we have at numerous points discussed the hazards of estimating y outside the range of our independent variables. In the context of correlated independent variables much of the total space included in the range of each independent variable considered individually will be empty. Indeed, the proportion of empty space increases directly with increasing multicollinearity among the independent variables. Predictions of y in such empty portions of the geometric space may be extremely unreliable and inaccurate.

7-IV-5 A Test for Multicollinearity

Farrar and Glauber (1967) have developed a three-step statistical procedure for detecting multicollinearity and isolating the variables involved. First, they note that an appropriate test that all pairs of independent variables are uncorrelated is

$$\chi^2_{[1/2k(k-1)]} = -[N - 1 - 1/6(2k + 5)] \ln |R| \qquad (7\text{-}17)$$

where $\chi^2_{[1/2k(k-1)]}$ is a chi-square with $1/2k(k-1)$ degrees of freedom and $\ln |R|$

is the natural logarithm of the determinant[11] of the correlation matrix among the independent variables.[12]

Should the chi-square be significant each variable may be tested for multi-collinearity by calculating the following F values

$$F_{(k-1, N-k)} = \frac{R^2_{i \cdot 12\ldots(i)\ldots k}}{1 - R^2_{i \cdot 12\ldots(i)\ldots k}} \cdot \frac{N-k}{k-1} \qquad (7\text{-}18)$$

for each independent variable where $R^2_{i \cdot 12\ldots(i)\ldots k}$ is the squared multiple correlation between x_i and all other independent variables.

For each x_i for which the F test specified by Eq. (7-18) is significant the specific independent variables responsible for producing the multicollinearity via their correlation with x_i may be identified through the following t values:

$$t_{(N-k)} = \frac{\mathrm{pr}_{ij \cdot 12\ldots(i,j)\ldots k}(N-k)^{\frac{1}{2}}}{(1 - \mathrm{pr}^2_{ij \cdot 12\ldots(i,j)\ldots k})^{\frac{1}{2}}} \qquad (7\text{-}19)$$

where $\mathrm{pr}_{ij \cdot 12\ldots(i,j)\ldots k}$ is the partial correlation of x_i and x_j holding all other independent variables constant. Note carefully that the correlations in Eqs. (7-18) and (7-19) involve *only* the independent variables.

Using the data in Table 7-5 the chi-square test for multicollinearity is 59.80 with 3 degrees of freedom which is, not surprisingly, highly significant. The F values, with 2 and 27 degrees of freedom, for x_1, x_2, and x_3 are 629.36, 66.38, and 49.29, respectively. The t values, with 27 degrees of freedom, are

	x_1	x_2	x_3
x_1	—	2.74	−0.43
x_2	2.74	—	5.24
x_3	−0.43	5.24	—

Except for the partial correlation between x_1 and x_3 all t values are highly significant. Thus multicollinearity can be substantially reduced by dropping x_2 from the model without a substantial decrease in R^2, which drops from 0.565 to 0.511.

7-IV-6 Corrective Procedures

In a formal sense there is no need to correct for multicollinearity. For a variety of reasons, however, it is often desirable to reduce the degree of multicollinearity among the independent variables in our data. Since most of these procedures have been discussed above we shall simply summarize the possible corrective procedures.

---

[11] The determinant of a matrix is defined and briefly discussed in App. A.

[12] Geometrically, this test is equivalent to a test that the space defined by the k independent variables is spherical.

First, special care should be taken in interpreting the regression equation. This includes computation and evaluation of the statistics discussed above, e.g., semipartial and partial correlations, standard errors of regression coefficients, etc.

Second, it may be possible to delete certain variables from the model. Here the procedure of Farrar and Glauber (1967) is very useful for identifying likely candidates for omission. Of course, selecting the variables to be omitted must be carried out not only on statistical grounds but also requires a judgement on the part of the researcher which must be based on theoretical and pragmatic considerations.

Third, it is always mathematically possible to orthogonalize the independent variables. Whether it is useful to do so is essentially an empirical question which can be answered only in the context of a particular research inquiry.

Finally, it may be possible to reduce multicollinearity by acquiring additional data. This is likely to be most useful in situations where circumstances forced the researcher to initially acquire the data from a narrow range of subjects or under a limited range of circumstances.

7-V SOME COMMENTS ON STEPWISE REGRESSION TECHNIQUES

Over the last two decades the increasingly widespread accessibility of high speed computers has made possible the general use of a range of data analysis techniques heretofore unavailable because of the sheer computational effort involved. In addition, the existence of readily accessible, easy to use computer programs has encouraged many researchers to use procedures they are not entirely familiar with. In this concluding section we shall briefly comment on one such procedure which has been widely used and abused in social and behavioral research, namely, stepwise regression.

The procedures referred to by the general label *stepwise* regression, which are well described by Draper and Smith (1966, Chap. 6), all involve the selection of a subset of p independent variables which are in some sense "best" from a larger set k. "Best" is usually defined in terms of changes in R^2. In the most usual forward selection procedure variables are added one at a time until R^2 fails to increase by a significant amount. At each step that variable not already included in the regression equation which has the largest partial correlation with y is entered into the model. In a reverse procedure, called backward selection, that variable in the equation which contributes least to R^2 is eliminated from the model.[13] More recent computer programs also provide for the reexamination of variables entered (in forward regression) or eliminated (in backward regression) at each step of the regression. The process stops when R^2 fails to change by an

---

[13] Due to suppressor effects, p variable regression equations arrived at via forward and backward selection will not necessarily contain the same p independent variables or yield the same R^2.

amount determined either explicitly or implicitly by the user of the stepwise program.

Despite its frequent use, stepwise regression suffers from certain liabilities which have made many researchers, e.g., Cooley and Lohnes (1971, p. 57), question whether these procedures are useful at all in social and behavioral research. In broad terms these objections to stepwise procedures seem to be of two distinct types.

The first type of objection is essentially statistical. Specifically, stepwise regression has an enormous capacity to simply capitalize on chance in searching the data for the best regression equation. The extent of this capitalization depends on a variety of factors, the most important of which are the number of independent variables searched and the extent of multicollinearity in the data. Furthermore, as Pope and Webster (1972) note, normal statistical tests are not appropriate since all standard sampling distributions—e.g., t, F—assume that the independent variables included in the model have been selected without reference to the data.

The second type of objection centers around the fact that in using stepwise procedures the researcher surrenders his judgement to the computer. In this vein the inclusion of a variable which increases R^2 by 0.2105 will always be preferred to the inclusion of a variable which will increase R^2 by 0.2104, no matter what theoretical or pragmatic arguments there might be for inclusion of one variable in the regression model as opposed to the other.

The judgement of some researchers that stepwise regression should be totally avoided may be unduly harsh. Future research may uncover theoretical sampling distributions which are relevant to stepwise regression. And it seems reasonable to regard theoretically and/or intuitively plausible relationships which are established via such procedures as hypotheses which are as worthy of investigation as those established in other ways. Nevertheless, stepwise regression analysis should be used most cautiously and should generally be confined to studies with relatively large sample sizes.[14]

7-VI SUMMARY

This chapter has examined the characteristics of GLM designs with no restrictions on the pattern of intercorrelations among the independent variables. Although the discussion occurred in the context of intervally-scaled, non-experimental data the material presented is generally relevant to the designs discussed in earlier chapters when the experimental factors are correlated. An important point is that GLM designs do not require the absence of multicollinearity: rather, the major effect of multicollinearity is to complicate the problem of interpreting the regression

---

[14] Cohen and Cohen (1975, p. 104) recommend at least 40 observations per independent variable in the initial data set. This contrasts with a usual recommendation which is closer to 10 to one when all independent variables are included in the model.

232 THE GENERAL LINEAR MODEL

equation and it has been the major task of this chapter to present techniques and procedures which facilitate that process of interpretation. Table 7-6 summarizes the most important equations presented in this chapter.

Table 7-6 Summary of most important equations in Chap. 7

Regression equation

$$y_i = \beta_0 + \beta_1 \left(\frac{\sigma_y}{\sigma_1}\right) x_1 + \beta_2 \left(\frac{\sigma_y}{\sigma_2}\right) x_2 + \cdots + \beta_k \left(\frac{\sigma_y}{\sigma_k}\right) x_k + \varepsilon_i$$

Adjusted R^2

$$R^2_{adj} = 1 - (1 - R^2) \frac{N-1}{N-k-1}$$

R^2 and beta weights

$$R^2 = \sum_{i=1}^{k} \hat{\beta}_i^2 + \sum_{i=1}^{k} \sum_{j=i+1}^{k} 2 r_{ij} \hat{\beta}_i \hat{\beta}_j$$

Semi-partial correlation
  Two independent variables

$$sr_{y(i \cdot j)} = \frac{r_{yi} - r_{yj} r_{ij}}{(1 - r_{ij}^2)^{\frac{1}{2}}}$$

  k independent variables

$$sr_i = \hat{\beta}_i (1 - R^2_{i \cdot 12\ldots(i)\ldots k})^{\frac{1}{2}}$$

Partial correlation
  Two independent variables

$$pr_{yi \cdot j} = \frac{r_{yi} - r_{yj} r_{ij}}{(1 - r_{yj}^2)^{\frac{1}{2}} (1 - r_{ij}^2)^{\frac{1}{2}}}$$

  k independent variables

$$pr_i = \frac{sr_i}{(1 - R^2_{y \cdot 12\ldots(i)\ldots k})^{\frac{1}{2}}}$$

βr_{yx}

$$R^2 = \beta' r_{yx}$$

Regression structure coefficients

$$r_{x\hat{y}} = r_{xy} \frac{1}{R}$$

Standard error of parameter estimates

$$\hat{\sigma}_{\theta_i} = \frac{\hat{\sigma}_y}{\hat{\sigma}_{x_i}} \left(\frac{1 - R^2_{y \cdot 12\ldots k}}{N - k - 1}\right)^{\frac{1}{2}} \cdot \left(\frac{1}{1 - R^2_{i \cdot 12\ldots(i)\ldots k}}\right)^{\frac{1}{2}}$$

Farrar and Glauber multicollinearity test

$$\chi^2_{[1/2k(k-1)]} = -[N - 1 - \tfrac{1}{6}(2k + 5)] \ln |\mathbf{R}|$$

$$F_{(k-1, N-k)} = \frac{R^2_{i \cdot 12\ldots(i)\ldots k}}{1 - R^2_{i \cdot 12\ldots(i)\ldots k}} \cdot \frac{N-k}{k-1}$$

$$t_{(N-k)} = \frac{pr_{ij \cdot 12\ldots(i,j)\ldots k}(N-k)^{\frac{1}{2}}}{(1 - pr^2_{ij \cdot 12\ldots(i,j)\ldots k})^{\frac{1}{2}}}$$

POSTSCRIPT

We have seen the General Linear Model (GLM) formulated in a great many specific forms. As one of our major professed goals was to emphasize the commonality underlying all GLM designs it seems fitting that we should conclude this book by reemphasizing that theme.

What cannot be stressed too strongly is the fact that in all of its special formulations the GLM remains constant. The assumptions underlying the model, procedures for estimating parameters and testing hypotheses, tests for assumption violations and possible corrective actions—all remain unchanged as we have proceeded from chapter to chapter. What has changed, e.g., from Latin squares to repeated measures designs, is the *character* of the data to be analyzed. In discussing Latin square designs it is not that the GLM cannot deal with interactions among the factors in the area of inquiry, for clearly the *model* can. It is rather that the *data* has been collected in such a way that the interaction effects, if present, cannot be disentangled for that specific set of data. Similarly, in not focusing in all chapters on the lack of independence among observations (except in the chapter on repeated measures designs) we were not suggesting that correlated observations do not present a potential problem in these formulations of the GLM, for Chap. 2 clearly showed this not to be true. Rather, we noted that *good research design* procedures would normally lead to the collection of *data* in which the observations are independent.

Put more generally, specific substantive questions and data acquisition procedures present the researcher with data exhibiting a unique set of characteristics. The challenges to the researcher are to choose a specific variant of the GLM which properly reflects the substantive questions posed and the nature of the data collected towards resolving those questions, and then to specify and conduct an appropriate a priori and post hoc analysis of the data. Skillfully and knowledgeably used GLM procedures, augmented by high speed computers, present the social and behavioral researcher with a most powerful set of analytical tools which can aid him greatly in the pursuit of substantive knowledge within his field of interest.

APPENDIX
A

REVIEW OF SOME BASIC MATRIX ALGEBRA

A-I-1 Definitions
A-I-2 Basic Matrix Operations
      A-I-2-1 Addition and subtraction
      A-I-2-2 Scalar multiplication
      A-I-2-3 Matrix multiplication
      A-I-2-4 Transposition
A-I-3 Matrix Inversion
A-I-4 Determinant of a Matrix

The purpose of this appendix is briefly to review the basic concepts and operations of matrix algebra which are utilized in this book.

A-I-1 Definitions

A matrix is a collection of ordered numbers. Each number is an element of the matrix which is ordered in the matrix by its row and column position. For example, the following matrix

$$A = \begin{bmatrix} a_{11} & a_{12} & a_{13} \\ a_{21} & a_{22} & a_{33} \end{bmatrix}$$

is a 2 row by 3 column matrix. Matrix A is said to be of order 2 by 3. By definition two matrices are equal if, and only if, the elements in each corresponding pair of elements are the same. Thus a p by q matrix can never be equal to a q by p matrix unless $p = q$.

A matrix of order p by 1 is called a column *vector*. Similarly a 1 by p matrix is called a row vector. Since vectors are simply matrices with one row or one column all of the rules applicable to matrices are applicable to vectors.

Finally, we note that in matrix parlance a single number, which is not an element of some matrix, is called a scalar.

A-I-2 Basic Matrix Operations

A-I-2-1 Addition and subtraction Two matrices may be added if, and only if, they are of the same order. Specifically, if two p by q matrices A and B are added to give a new matrix C then each element in C is of the form $c_{ij} = a_{ij} + b_{ij}$. If B is subtracted from A then $c_{ij} = a_{ij} - b_{ij}$. The matrix C, of course, is always of the same order as A and B.

A-I-2-2 Scalar multiplication If A is a p by q matrix and d is a scalar then in the scalar multiplication of A by d each element of A is multiplied by d.

A-I-2-3 Matrix multiplication A p by q matrix A may be multiplied by a k by m matrix B if and only if $q = k$. The resulting matrix $C = A \cdot B$ will be of order p by m. Matrix multiplication is said to be row by column. That is each element of C is defined by the relation

$$c_{ij} = a_{i1}b_{1j} + a_{i2}b_{2j} + \cdots + a_{iq}b_{kj}$$

$$= \sum_{h=1}^{q,k} a_{ih}b_{hj}$$

i.e., c_{ij} is equal to the sum of the products of each pair of elements in row i of A and column j of B.

Note that in matrix multiplication AB will generally not be equal to BA. In fact in many situations BA will not be defined, given that AB is defined, since the number of columns of B will not equal the number of rows of A. Thus the order of the matrices is important for matrix multiplication and it is customary to speak of pre- or post-multiplication of a matrix, e.g., for AB, matrix B post-multiplies A or equivalently A pre-multiplies B.

A-I-2-4 Transposition The transposition of a matrix requires the interchanging of rows and columns. If A is a p by q matrix its transpose will be a q by p matrix A', the prime indicating the transpose of A. For example, if

$$A = \begin{bmatrix} a_{11} & a_{12} & a_{13} \\ a_{21} & a_{22} & a_{23} \end{bmatrix}$$

then

$$A' = \begin{bmatrix} a_{11} & a_{21} \\ a_{12} & a_{22} \\ a_{13} & a_{23} \end{bmatrix}$$

Note that $A'A$ and AA' are always defined and square, i.e., have the same number of rows and columns.

A-I-3 Matrix Inversion

The matrix analog of division is called matrix inversion. The inverse of a matrix A is denoted A^{-1} and has the property

$$AA^{-1} = A^{-1}A = I$$

where I is an identity matrix with ones on the diagonal and zeros elsewhere. The inverse is defined *only* for square matrices.

A-I-4 Determinant of a Matrix

Every square matrix may be characterized by a single number which is called its determinant. The determinant of a matrix A of order p is designated by $|A|$ and is defined as the sum of the alternatively signed products of the elements of A formed from permutations of the integers 1 to p. There are p factorial ($p!$) products, each with p elements, entering the summation. For a matrix of order 2

$$|A| = a_{11}a_{22} - a_{12}a_{21}$$

and for a matrix of order 3

$$|A| = a_{11}a_{22}a_{33} - a_{11}a_{23}a_{32} + a_{12}a_{23}a_{31}$$
$$- a_{12}a_{21}a_{33} + a_{13}a_{21}a_{32} - a_{13}a_{22}a_{31}$$

Any good book on matrix algebra will describe several methods of computing the determinant. Fortunately, most computer centers have very simple programs which will perform the tedious calculations.

While determinants play a very important role in matrix algebra generally, our interest in them is very specific and limited. First, if $|A| = 0$ the inverse of A does not exist. For the models discussed in this book, it is assumed that the inverse of certain matrices exist or equivalently that the determinants of these matrices are not zero. Second, the determinant of a dispersion, variance/covariance, or correlation matrix is the multivariate generalization of the variance of a variable and plays a role in certain of the statistical tests discussed in this book.

APPENDIX
B

STATISTICAL TABLES

B-1 t Distribution
B-2 F Distribution
B-3 Chi-Square Distribution
B-4 Non-Central F Distribution
B-5 F_{max} Distribution
B-6 Curves of Constant Power for Tests on Main Effects
B-7 Orthogonal Polynomial Coefficients

Table B-1 t Distribution†

df_E					p_1‡				
	0.25	0.10	0.05	0.025	0.01	0.005	0.0025	0.001	0.0005
1	1.000	3.078	6.314	12.706	31.821	63.657	127.32	318.31	636.62
2	0.816	1.886	2.920	4.303	6.965	9.925	14.089	22.327	31.598
3	0.765	1.638	2.353	3.182	4.541	5.841	7.453	10.214	12.924
4	0.741	1.533	2.132	2.776	3.747	4.604	5.598	7.173	8.610
5	0.727	1.476	2.015	2.571	3.365	4.032	4.773	5.893	6.869
6	0.718	1.440	1.943	2.447	3.143	3.707	4.317	5.208	5.959
7	0.711	1.415	1.895	2.365	2.998	3.499	4.029	4.785	5.408
8	0.706	1.397	1.860	2.306	2.896	3.355	3.833	4.501	5.041
9	0.703	1.383	1.833	2.262	2.821	3.250	3.690	4.297	4.781
10	0.700	1.372	1.812	2.228	2.764	3.169	3.581	4.144	4.587
11	0.697	1.363	1.796	2.201	2.718	3.106	3.497	4.025	4.437
12	0.695	1.356	1.782	2.179	2.681	3.055	3.428	3.930	4.318
13	0.694	1.350	1.771	2.160	2.650	3.012	3.372	3.852	4.221
14	0.692	1.345	1.761	2.145	2.624	2.977	3.326	3.787	4.140
15	0.691	1.341	1.753	2.131	2.602	2.947	3.286	3.733	4.073
16	0.690	1.337	1.746	2.120	2.583	2.921	3.252	3.686	4.015
17	0.689	1.333	1.740	2.110	2.567	2.898	3.222	3.646	3.965
18	0.688	1.330	1.734	2.101	2.552	2.878	3.197	3.610	3.922
19	0.688	1.328	1.729	2.093	2.539	2.861	3.174	3.579	3.883
20	0.687	1.325	1.725	2.086	2.528	2.845	3.153	3.552	3.850
21	0.686	1.323	1.721	2.080	2.518	2.831	3.135	3.527	3.819
22	0.686	1.321	1.717	2.074	2.508	2.819	3.119	3.505	3.792
23	0.685	1.319	1.714	2.069	2.500	2.807	3.104	3.485	3.767
24	0.685	1.318	1.711	2.064	2.492	2.797	3.091	3.467	3.745
25	0.684	1.316	1.708	2.060	2.485	2.787	3.078	3.450	3.725
26	0.684	1.315	1.706	2.056	2.479	2.779	3.067	3.435	3.707
27	0.684	1.314	1.703	2.052	2.473	2.771	3.057	3.421	3.690
28	0.683	1.313	1.701	2.048	2.467	2.763	3.047	3.408	3.674
29	0.683	1.311	1.699	2.045	2.462	2.756	3.038	3.396	3.659
30	0.683	1.310	1.697	2.042	2.457	2.750	3.030	3.385	3.646
40	0.681	1.303	1.684	2.021	2.423	2.704	2.971	3.307	3.551
60	0.679	1.296	1.671	2.000	2.390	2.660	2.915	3.232	3.460
120	0.677	1.289	1.658	1.980	2.358	2.617	2.860	3.160	3.373
∞	0.674	1.282	1.645	1.960	2.326	2.567	2.807	3.090	3.291

† This table is abridged from Table 12 in Pearson and Hartley (1966). Reproduced with the kind permission of the trustees of *Biometrika*. The columns for $p_1 = 0.10$, 0.01, and 0.0005 are taken from Fisher and Yates, *Statistical Tables for Biological, Agricultural, and Medical Research*, 6th ed., 1974, Harlow: Longman.

‡ p_1 is for a one-tailed test.

Table B-2 F Distribution

$1-p_1$					df$_N$, degrees of freedom for numerator								$1-p_1$
	1	2	3	4	5	6	7	8	9	10	11	12	
1 0.0005	0.0^662	0.0^350	0.0^238	0.0^294	0.016	0.022	0.027	0.032	0.036	0.039	0.042	0.045	0.0005
0.001	0.0^525	0.0^210	0.0^260	0.013	0.021	0.028	0.034	0.039	0.044	0.048	0.051	0.054	0.001
0.005	0.0^462	0.0^251	0.018	0.032	0.044	0.054	0.062	0.068	0.073	0.078	0.082	0.085	0.005
0.010	0.0^325	0.010	0.029	0.047	0.062	0.073	0.082	0.089	0.095	0.100	0.104	0.107	0.010
0.025	0.0^215	0.026	0.057	0.082	0.100	0.113	0.124	0.132	0.139	0.144	0.149	0.153	0.025
0.05	0.0^262	0.054	0.099	0.130	0.151	0.167	0.179	0.188	0.195	0.201	0.207	0.211	0.05
0.10	0.025	0.117	0.181	0.220	0.246	0.265	0.279	0.289	0.298	0.304	0.310	0.315	0.10
0.25	0.172	0.389	0.494	0.553	0.591	0.617	0.637	0.650	0.661	0.670	0.680	0.684	0.25
0.50	1.00	1.50	1.71	1.82	1.89	1.94	1.98	2.00	2.03	2.04	2.05	2.07	0.50
0.75	5.83	7.50	8.20	8.58	8.82	8.98	9.10	9.19	9.26	9.32	9.36	9.41	0.75
0.90	39.9	49.5	53.6	55.8	57.2	58.2	58.9	59.4	59.9	60.2	60.5	60.7	0.90
0.95	161	200	216	225	230	234	237	239	241	242	243	244	0.95
0.975	648	800	864	900	922	937	948	957	963	969	973	977	0.975
0.99	405^1	500^1	540^1	562^1	576^1	586^1	593^1	598^1	602^1	606^1	608^1	611^1	0.99
0.995	162^2	200^2	216^2	225^2	231^2	234^2	237^2	239^2	241^2	242^2	243^2	244^2	0.995
0.999	406^3	500^3	540^3	562^3	576^3	586^3	593^3	598^3	602^3	606^3	609^3	611^3	0.999
0.9995	162^4	200^4	216^4	225^4	231^4	234^4	237^4	239^4	241^4	242^4	243^4	244^4	0.9995
2 0.0005	0.0^650	0.0^350	0.0^242	0.011	0.020	0.029	0.037	0.044	0.050	0.056	0.061	0.065	0.0005
0.001	0.0^520	0.0^210	0.0^268	0.016	0.027	0.037	0.046	0.054	0.061	0.067	0.072	0.077	0.001
0.005	0.0^450	0.0^250	0.020	0.038	0.055	0.069	0.081	0.091	0.099	0.106	0.112	0.118	0.005
0.01	0.0^320	0.010	0.032	0.056	0.075	0.092	0.105	0.116	0.125	0.132	0.139	0.144	0.01
0.025	0.0^213	0.026	0.062	0.094	0.119	0.138	0.153	0.165	0.175	0.183	0.190	0.196	0.025
0.05	0.0^250	0.053	0.105	0.144	0.173	0.194	0.211	0.224	0.235	0.244	0.251	0.257	0.05
0.10	0.020	0.111	0.183	0.231	0.265	0.289	0.307	0.321	0.333	0.342	0.350	0.356	0.10
0.25	0.133	0.333	0.439	0.500	0.540	0.568	0.588	0.604	0.616	0.626	0.633	0.641	0.25
0.50	0.667	1.00	1.13	1.21	1.25	1.28	1.30	1.32	1.33	1.34	1.35	1.36	0.50
0.75	2.57	3.00	3.15	3.23	3.28	3.31	3.34	3.35	3.37	3.38	3.39	3.39	0.75
0.90	8.53	9.00	9.16	9.24	9.29	9.33	9.35	9.37	9.38	9.39	9.40	9.41	0.90
0.95	18.5	19.0	19.2	19.2	19.3	19.3	19.4	19.4	19.4	19.4	19.4	19.4	0.95
0.975	38.5	39.0	39.2	39.2	39.3	39.3	39.4	39.4	39.4	39.4	39.4	39.4	0.975
0.99	98.5	99.0	99.2	99.2	99.3	99.3	99.4	99.4	99.4	99.4	99.4	99.4	0.99
0.995	198	199	199	199	199	199	199	199	199	199	199	199	0.995
0.999	998	999	999	999	999	999	999	999	999	999	999	999	0.999
0.9995	200^1	200^1	200^1	200^1	200^1	200^1	200^1	200^1	200^1	200^1	200^1	200^1	0.9995
3 0.0005	0.0^646	0.0^350	0.0^244	0.012	0.023	0.033	0.043	0.052	0.060	0.067	0.074	0.079	0.0005
0.001	0.0^519	0.0^210	0.0^271	0.018	0.030	0.042	0.053	0.063	0.072	0.079	0.086	0.093	0.001
0.005	0.0^446	0.0^250	0.021	0.041	0.060	0.077	0.092	0.104	0.115	0.124	0.132	0.138	0.005
0.01	0.0^319	0.010	0.034	0.060	0.083	0.102	0.118	0.132	0.143	0.153	0.161	0.168	0.01
0.025	0.0^212	0.026	0.065	0.100	0.129	0.152	0.170	0.185	0.197	0.207	0.216	0.224	0.025
0.05	0.0^246	0.052	0.108	0.152	0.185	0.210	0.230	0.246	0.259	0.270	0.279	0.287	0.05
0.10	0.019	0.109	0.185	0.239	0.276	0.304	0.325	0.342	0.356	0.367	0.376	0.384	0.10
0.25	0.122	0.317	0.424	0.489	0.531	0.561	0.582	0.600	0.613	0.624	0.633	0.641	0.25
0.50	0.585	0.881	1.00	1.06	1.10	1.13	1.15	1.16	1.17	1.18	1.19	1.20	0.50
0.75	2.02	2.28	2.36	2.39	2.41	2.42	2.43	2.44	2.44	2.44	2.45	2.45	0.75
0.90	5.54	5.46	5.39	5.34	5.31	5.28	5.27	5.25	5.24	5.23	5.22	5.22	0.90
0.95	10.1	9.55	9.28	9.12	9.01	8.94	8.89	8.85	8.81	8.79	8.76	8.74	0.95
0.075	17.4	16.0	15.4	15.1	14.9	14.7	14.6	14.5	14.5	14.4	14.4	14.3	0.975
0.99	34.1	30.8	29.5	28.7	28.2	27.9	27.7	27.5	27.3	27.2	27.1	27.1	0.99
0.995	55.6	49.8	47.5	46.2	45.4	44.8	44.4	44.1	43.9	43.7	43.5	43.4	0.995
0.999	167	149	141	137	135	133	132	131	130	129	129	128	0.999
0.9995	266	237	225	218	214	211	209	208	207	206	204	204	0.9995

df$_E$, degrees of freedom for denominator

Read 0.0^356 as 0.00056, 200^1 as 2,000, 162^4 as 1,620,000, and so on.

Table B-2 Continued

$1 - p_1$				df_N, degrees of freedom for numerator								$1 - p_1$	
	15	20	24	30	40	50	60	100	120	200	500	∞	
0.0005	0.051	0.058	0.062	0.066	0.069	0.072	0.074	0.077	0.078	0.080	0.081	0.083	0.0005	1
0.001	0.060	0.067	0.071	0.075	0.079	0.082	0.084	0.087	0.088	0.089	0.091	0.092	0.001
0.005	0.093	0.101	0.105	0.109	0.113	0.116	0.118	0.121	0.122	0.124	0.126	0.127	0.005
0.01	0.115	0.124	0.128	0.132	0.137	0.139	0.141	0.145	0.146	0.148	0.150	0.151	0.01
0.025	0.161	0.170	0.175	0.180	0.184	0.187	0.189	0.193	0.194	0.196	0.198	0.199	0.025
0.05	0.220	0.230	0.235	0.240	0.245	0.248	0.250	0.254	0.255	0.257	0.259	0.261	0.05
0.10	0.325	0.336	0.342	0.347	0.353	0.356	0.358	0.362	0.364	0.366	0.368	0.370	0.10
0.25	0.698	0.712	0.719	0.727	0.734	0.738	0.741	0.747	0.749	0.752	0.754	0.756	0.25
0.50	2.09	2.12	2.13	2.15	2.16	2.17	2.17	2.18	2.18	2.19	2.19	2.20	0.50
0.75	9.49	9.58	9.63	9.67	9.71	9.74	9.76	9.78	9.80	9.82	9.84	9.85	0.75
0.90	61.2	61.7	62.0	62.3	62.5	62.7	62.8	63.0	63.1	63.2	63.3	63.3	0.90
0.95	246	248	249	250	251	252	252	253	253	254	254	254	0.95
0.975	985	993	997	100^1	101^1	101^1	101^1	101^1	101^1	102^1	102^1	102^1	0.975
0.99	616^1	621^1	623^1	626^1	629^1	630^1	631^1	633^1	634^1	635^1	636^1	637^1	0.99
0.995	246^2	248^2	249^2	250^2	251^2	252^2	253^2	253^2	254^2	254^2	254^2	255^2	0.995
0.999	616^3	621^3	623^3	626^3	629^3	630^3	631^3	633^3	634^3	635^3	636^3	637^3	0.999
0.9995	246^4	248^4	249^4	250^4	251^4	252^4	252^4	253^4	253^4	253^4	254^4	254^4	0.9995
0.0005	0.076	0.088	0.094	0.101	0.108	0.113	0.116	0.122	0.124	0.127	0.130	0.132	0.0005	2
0.001	0.088	0.100	0.107	0.114	0.121	0.126	0.129	0.135	0.137	0.140	0.143	0.145	0.001
0.005	0.130	0.143	0.150	0.157	0.165	0.169	0.173	0.179	0.181	0.184	0.187	0.189	0.005
0.01	0.157	0.171	0.178	0.186	0.193	0.198	0.201	0.207	0.209	0.212	0.215	0.217	0.01
0.025	0.210	0.224	0.232	0.239	0.247	0.251	0.255	0.261	0.263	0.266	0.269	0.271	0.025
0.05	0.272	0.286	0.294	0.302	0.309	0.314	0.317	0.324	0.326	0.329	0.332	0.334	0.05
0.10	0.371	0.386	0.394	0.402	0.410	0.415	0.418	0.424	0.426	0.429	0.433	0.434	0.10
0.25	0.657	0.672	0.680	0.689	0.697	0.702	0.705	0.711	0.713	0.716	0.719	0.721	0.25
0.50	1.38	1.39	1.40	1.41	1.42	1.42	1.43	1.43	1.43	1.44	1.44	1.44	0.50
0.75	3.41	3.43	3.43	3.44	3.45	3.45	3.46	3.47	3.47	3.48	3.48	3.48	0.75
0.90	9.42	9.44	9.45	9.46	9.47	9.47	9.47	9.48	9.48	9.49	9.49	9.49	0.90
0.95	19.4	19.4	19.5	19.5	19.5	19.5	19.5	19.5	19.5	19.5	19.5	19.5	0.95
0.975	39.4	39.4	39.5	39.5	39.5	39.5	39.5	39.5	39.5	39.5	39.5	39.5	0.975
0.99	99.4	99.4	99.5	99.5	99.5	99.5	99.5	99.5	99.5	99.5	99.5	99.5	0.99
0.995	199	199	199	199	199	199	199	199	199	199	199	200	0.995
0.999	999	999	999	999	999	999	999	999	999	999	999	999	0.999
0.9995	200^1	200^1	200^1	200^1	200^1	200^1	200^1	200^1	200^1	200^1	200^1	200^1	0.9995
0.0005	0.093	0.109	0.117	0.127	0.136	0.143	0.147	0.156	0.158	0.162	0.166	0.169	0.0005	3
0.001	0.107	0.123	0.132	0.142	0.152	0.158	0.162	0.171	0.173	0.177	0.181	0.184	0.001
0.005	0.154	0.172	0.181	0.191	0.201	0.207	0.211	0.220	0.222	0.227	0.231	0.234	0.005
0.01	0.185	0.203	0.212	0.222	0.232	0.238	0.242	0.251	0.253	0.258	0.262	0.264	0.01
0.025	0.241	0.259	0.269	0.279	0.289	0.295	0.299	0.308	0.310	0.314	0.318	0.321	0.025
0.05	0.304	0.323	0.332	0.342	0.352	0.358	0.363	0.370	0.373	0.377	0.382	0.384	0.05
0.10	0.402	0.420	0.430	0.439	0.449	0.455	0.459	0.467	0.469	0.474	0.476	0.480	0.10
0.25	0.658	0.675	0.684	0.693	0.702	0.708	0.711	0.719	0.721	0.724	0.728	0.730	0.25
0.50	1.21	1.23	1.23	1.24	1.25	1.25	1.25	1.26	1.26	1.26	1.27	1.27	0.50
0.75	2.46	2.46	2.46	2.47	2.47	2.47	2.47	2.47	2.47	2.47	2.47	2.47	0.75
0.90	5.20	5.18	5.18	5.17	5.16	5.15	5.15	5.14	5.14	5.14	5.14	5.13	0.90
0.95	8.70	8.66	8.63	8.62	8.59	8.58	8.57	8.55	8.55	8.54	8.53	8.53	0.95
0.975	14.3	14.2	14.1	14.1	14.0	14.0	14.0	14.0	13.9	13.9	13.9	13.9	0.975
0.99	26.9	26.7	26.6	26.5	26.4	26.4	26.3	26.2	26.2	26.2	26.1	26.1	0.99
0.995	43.1	42.8	42.6	42.5	42.3	42.2	42.1	42.0	42.0	41.9	41.9	41.8	0.995
0.999	127	126	126	125	125	125	124	124	124	124	124	123	0.999
0.9995	203	201	200	199	199	198	198	197	197	197	196	196	0.9995

df_E, degrees of freedom for denominator

Table B-2 Continued

$1-p_1$				df_N, degrees of freedom for numerator									$1-p_1$
	1	2	3	4	5	6	7	8	9	10	11	12	

df_E, degrees of freedom for denominator

4

$1-p_1$	1	2	3	4	5	6	7	8	9	10	11	12	$1-p_1$
0.0005	$0.0^6 44$	$0.0^3 50$	$0.0^2 46$	0.013	0.024	0.036	0.047	0.057	0.066	0.075	0.082	0.089	0.0005
0.001	$0.0^5 18$	$0.0^2 10$	$0.0^2 73$	0.019	0.032	0.046	0.058	0.069	0.079	0.089	0.097	0.104	0.001
0.005	$0.0^4 44$	$0.0^2 50$	0.022	0.043	0.064	0.083	0.100	0.114	0.126	0.137	0.145	0.153	0.005
0.01	$0.0^3 18$	0.010	0.035	0.063	0.088	0.109	0.127	0.143	0.156	0.167	0.176	0.185	0.01
0.025	$0.0^2 11$	0.026	0.066	0.104	0.135	0.161	0.181	0.198	0.212	0.224	0.234	0.243	0.025
0.05	$0.0^2 44$	0.052	0.110	0.157	0.193	0.221	0.243	0.261	0.275	0.288	0.298	0.307	0.05
0.10	0.018	0.108	0.187	0.243	0.284	0.314	0.338	0.356	0.371	0.384	0.394	0.403	0.10
0.25	0.117	0.309	0.418	0.484	0.528	0.560	0.583	0.601	0.615	0.627	0.637	0.645	0.25
0.50	0.549	0.828	0.941	1.00	1.04	1.06	1.08	1.09	1.10	1.11	1.12	1.13	0.50
0.75	1.81	2.00	2.05	2.06	2.07	2.08	2.08	2.08	2.08	2.08	2.08	2.08	0.75
0.90	4.54	4.32	4.19	4.11	4.05	4.01	3.98	3.95	3.94	3.92	3.91	3.90	0.90
0.95	7.71	6.94	6.59	6.39	6.26	6.16	6.09	6.04	6.00	5.96	5.94	5.91	0.95
0.975	12.2	10.6	9.98	9.60	9.36	9.20	9.07	8.98	8.90	8.84	8.79	8.75	0.975
0.99	21.2	18.0	16.7	16.0	15.5	15.2	15.0	14.8	14.7	14.5	14.4	14.4	0.99
0.995	31.3	26.3	24.3	23.2	22.5	22.0	21.6	21.4	21.1	21.0	20.8	20.7	0.995
0.999	74.1	61.2	56.2	53.4	51.7	50.5	49.7	49.0	48.5	48.0	47.7	47.4	0.999
0.9995	106	87.4	80.1	76.1	73.6	71.9	70.6	69.7	68.9	68.3	67.8	67.4	0.9995

5

$1-p_1$	1	2	3	4	5	6	7	8	9	10	11	12	$1-p_1$
0.0005	$0.0^6 43$	$0.0^3 50$	$0.0^2 47$	0.014	0.025	0.038	0.050	0.061	0.070	0.081	0.089	0.096	0.0005
0.001	$0.0^5 17$	$0.0^2 10$	$0.0^2 75$	0.019	0.034	0.048	0.062	0.074	0.085	0.095	0.104	0.112	0.001
0.005	$0.0^4 43$	$0.0^2 50$	0.022	0.045	0.067	0.087	0.105	0.120	0.134	0.146	0.156	0.165	0.005
0.01	$0.0^3 17$	0.010	0.035	0.064	0.091	0.114	0.134	0.151	0.165	0.177	0.188	0.197	0.01
0.025	$0.0^2 11$	0.025	0.067	0.107	0.140	0.167	0.189	0.208	0.223	0.236	0.248	0.257	0.025
0.05	$0.0^2 43$	0.052	0.111	0.160	0.198	0.228	0.252	0.271	0.287	0.301	0.313	0.322	0.05
0.10	0.017	0.108	0.188	0.247	0.290	0.322	0.347	0.367	0.383	0.397	0.408	0.418	0.10
0.25	0.113	0.305	0.415	0.483	0.528	0.560	0.584	0.604	0.618	0.631	0.641	0.650	0.25
0.50	0.528	0.799	0.907	0.965	1.00	1.02	1.04	1.05	1.06	1.07	1.08	1.09	0.50
0.75	1.69	1.85	1.88	1.89	1.89	1.89	1.89	1.89	1.89	1.89	1.89	1.89	0.75
0.90	4.06	3.78	3.62	3.52	3.45	3.40	3.37	3.34	3.32	3.30	3.28	3.27	0.90
0.95	6.61	5.79	5.41	5.19	5.05	4.95	4.88	4.82	4.77	4.74	4.71	4.68	0.95
0.975	10.0	8.43	7.76	7.39	7.15	6.98	6.85	6.76	6.68	6.62	6.57	6.52	0.975
0.99	16.3	13.3	12.1	11.4	11.0	10.7	10.5	10.3	10.2	10.1	9.96	9.89	0.99
0.995	22.8	18.3	16.5	15.6	14.9	14.5	14.2	14.0	13.8	13.6	13.5	13.4	0.995
0.999	47.2	37.1	33.2	31.1	29.7	28.8	28.2	27.6	27.2	26.9	26.6	26.4	0.999
0.9995	63.6	49.8	44.4	41.5	39.7	38.5	37.6	36.9	36.4	35.9	35.6	35.2	0.9995

6

$1-p_1$	1	2	3	4	5	6	7	8	9	10	11	12	$1-p_1$
0.0005	$0.0^6 43$	$0.0^3 50$	$0.0^2 47$	0.014	0.026	0.039	0.052	0.064	0.075	0.085	0.094	0.103	0.0005
0.001	$0.0^5 17$	$0.0^2 10$	$0.0^2 75$	0.020	0.035	0.050	0.064	0.078	0.090	0.101	0.111	0.119	0.001
0.005	$0.0^4 43$	$0.0^2 50$	0.022	0.045	0.069	0.090	0.109	0.126	0.140	0.153	0.164	0.174	0.005
0.01	$0.0^3 17$	0.010	0.036	0.066	0.094	0.118	0.139	0.157	0.172	0.186	0.197	0.207	0.01
0.025	$0.0^2 11$	0.025	0.068	0.109	0.143	0.172	0.195	0.215	0.231	0.246	0.258	0.268	0.025
0.05	$0.0^2 43$	0.052	0.112	0.162	0.202	0.233	0.259	0.279	0.296	0.311	0.324	0.334	0.05
0.10	0.017	0.107	0.189	0.249	0.294	0.327	0.354	0.375	0.392	0.406	0.418	0.429	0.10
0.25	0.111	0.302	0.413	0.481	0.524	0.561	0.586	0.606	0.622	0.635	0.645	0.654	0.25
0.50	0.515	0.780	0.886	0.942	0.977	1.00	1.02	1.03	1.04	1.05	1.05	1.06	0.50
0.75	1.62	1.76	1.78	1.79	1.79	1.78	1.78	1.78	1.77	1.77	1.77	1.77	0.75
0.90	3.78	3.46	3.29	3.18	3.11	3.05	3.01	2.98	2.96	2.94	2.92	2.90	0.90
0.95	5.99	5.14	4.76	4.53	4.39	4.28	4.21	4.15	4.10	4.06	4.03	4.00	0.95
0.975	8.81	7.26	6.60	6.23	5.99	5.82	5.70	5.60	5.52	5.46	5.41	5.37	0.975
0.99	13.7	10.9	9.78	9.15	8.75	8.47	8.26	8.10	7.98	7.87	7.79	7.72	0.99
0.995	18.6	14.5	12.9	12.0	11.5	11.1	10.8	10.6	10.4	10.2	10.1	10.0	0.995
0.999	35.5	27.0	23.7	21.9	20.8	20.0	19.5	19.0	18.7	18.4	18.2	18.0	0.999
0.9995	46.1	34.8	30.4	28.1	26.6	25.6	24.9	24.3	23.9	23.5	23.2	23.0	0.9995

Table B-2 Continued

$1-p_1$	15	20	24	30	40	50	60	100	120	200	500	∞	$1-p_1$	df_E
0.0005	0.105	0.125	0.135	0.147	0.159	0.166	0.172	0.183	0.186	0.191	0.196	0.200	0.0005	4
0.001	0.121	0.141	0.152	0.163	0.176	0.183	0.188	0.200	0.202	0.208	0.213	0.217	0.001	
0.005	0.172	0.193	0.204	0.216	0.229	0.237	0.242	0.253	0.255	0.260	0.266	0.269	0.005	
0.01	0.204	0.226	0.237	0.249	0.261	0.269	0.274	0.285	0.287	0.293	0.298	0.301	0.01	
0.025	0.263	0.284	0.296	0.308	0.320	0.327	0.332	0.342	0.346	0.351	0.356	0.359	0.025	
0.05	0.327	0.349	0.360	0.372	0.384	0.391	0.396	0.407	0.409	0.413	0.418	0.422	0.05	
0.10	0.424	0.445	0.456	0.467	0.478	0.485	0.490	0.500	0.502	0.508	0.510	0.514	0.10	
0.25	0.664	0.683	0.692	0.702	0.712	0.718	0.722	0.731	0.733	0.737	0.740	0.743	0.25	
0.50	1.14	1.15	1.16	1.16	1.17	1.18	1.18	1.18	1.18	1.19	1.19	1.19	0.50	
0.75	2.08	2.08	2.08	2.08	2.08	2.08	2.08	2.08	2.08	2.08	2.08	2.08	0.75	
0.90	3.87	3.84	3.83	3.82	3.80	3.80	3.79	3.78	3.78	3.77	3.76	3.76	0.90	
0.95	5.86	5.80	5.77	5.75	5.72	5.70	5.69	5.66	5.66	5.65	5.64	5.63	0.95	
0.975	8.66	8.56	8.51	8.46	8.41	8.38	8.36	8.32	8.31	8.29	8.27	8.26	0.975	
0.99	14.2	14.0	13.9	13.8	13.7	13.7	13.7	13.6	13.6	13.5	13.5	13.5	0.99	
0.995	20.4	20.2	20.0	19.9	19.8	19.7	19.6	19.5	19.5	19.4	19.4	19.3	0.995	
0.999	46.8	46.1	45.8	45.4	45.1	44.9	44.7	44.5	44.4	44.3	44.1	44.0	0.999	
0.9995	66.5	65.5	65.1	64.6	64.1	63.8	63.6	63.2	63.1	62.9	62.7	62.6	0.9995	
0.0005	0.115	0.137	0.150	0.163	0.177	0.186	0.192	0.205	0.209	0.216	0.222	0.226	0.0005	5
0.001	0.132	0.155	0.167	0.181	0.195	0.204	0.210	0.223	0.227	0.233	0.239	0.244	0.001	
0.005	0.186	0.210	0.223	0.237	0.251	0.260	0.266	0.279	0.282	0.288	0.294	0.299	0.005	
0.01	0.219	0.244	0.257	0.270	0.285	0.293	0.299	0.312	0.315	0.322	0.328	0.331	0.01	
0.025	0.280	0.304	0.317	0.330	0.344	0.353	0.359	0.370	0.374	0.380	0.386	0.390	0.025	
0.05	0.345	0.369	0.382	0.395	0.408	0.417	0.422	0.432	0.437	0.442	0.448	0.452	0.05	
0.10	0.440	0.463	0.476	0.488	0.501	0.508	0.514	0.524	0.527	0.532	0.538	0.541	0.10	
0.25	0.669	0.690	0.700	0.711	0.722	0.728	0.732	0.741	0.743	0.748	0.752	0.755	0.25	
0.50	1.10	1.11	1.12	1.12	1.13	1.13	1.14	1.14	1.14	1.15	1.15	1.15	0.50	
0.75	1.89	1.88	1.88	1.88	1.88	1.88	1.87	1.87	1.87	1.87	1.87	1.87	0.75	
0.90	3.24	3.21	3.19	3.17	3.16	3.15	3.14	3.13	3.12	3.12	3.11	3.10	0.90	
0.95	4.62	4.56	4.53	4.50	4.46	4.44	4.43	4.41	4.40	4.39	4.37	4.36	0.95	
0.975	6.43	6.33	6.28	6.23	6.18	6.14	6.12	6.08	6.07	6.05	6.03	6.02	0.975	
0.99	9.72	9.55	9.47	9.38	9.29	9.24	9.20	9.13	9.11	9.08	9.04	9.02	0.99	
0.995	13.1	12.9	12.8	12.7	12.5	12.5	12.4	12.3	12.3	12.2	12.2	12.1	0.995	
0.999	25.9	25.4	25.1	24.9	24.6	24.4	24.3	24.1	24.1	23.9	23.8	23.8	0.999	
0.9995	34.6	33.9	33.5	33.1	32.7	32.5	32.3	32.1	32.0	31.8	31.7	31.6	0.9995	
0.0005	0.123	0.148	0.162	0.177	0.193	0.203	0.210	0.225	0.229	0.236	0.244	0.249	0.0005	6
0.001	0.141	0.166	0.180	0.195	0.211	0.222	0.229	0.243	0.247	0.255	0.262	0.267	0.001	
0.005	0.197	0.224	0.238	0.253	0.269	0.279	0.286	0.301	0.304	0.312	0.318	0.324	0.005	
0.01	0.232	0.258	0.273	0.288	0.304	0.313	0.321	0.334	0.338	0.346	0.352	0.357	0.01	
0.025	0.293	0.320	0.334	0.349	0.364	0.375	0.381	0.394	0.398	0.405	0.412	0.415	0.025	
0.05	0.358	0.385	0.399	0.413	0.428	0.437	0.444	0.457	0.460	0.467	0.472	0.476	0.05	
0.10	0.453	0.478	0.491	0.505	0.519	0.526	0.533	0.546	0.548	0.556	0.559	0.564	0.10	
0.25	0.675	0.696	0.707	0.718	0.729	0.736	0.741	0.751	0.753	0.758	0.762	0.765	0.25	
0.50	1.07	1.08	1.09	1.10	1.10	1.11	1.11	1.11	1.12	1.12	1.12	1.12	0.50	
0.75	1.76	1.76	1.75	1.75	1.75	1.75	1.74	1.74	1.74	1.74	1.74	1.74	0.75	
0.90	2.87	2.84	2.82	2.80	2.78	2.77	2.76	2.75	2.74	2.73	2.73	2.72	0.90	
0.95	3.94	3.87	3.84	3.81	3.77	3.75	3.74	3.71	3.70	3.69	3.68	3.67	0.95	
0.975	5.27	5.17	5.12	5.07	5.01	4.98	4.96	4.92	4.90	4.88	4.86	4.85	0.975	
0.99	7.56	7.40	7.31	7.23	7.14	7.09	7.06	6.99	6.97	6.93	6.90	6.88	0.99	
0.995	9.81	9.59	9.47	9.36	9.24	9.17	9.12	9.03	9.00	8.95	8.91	8.88	0.995	
0.999	17.6	17.1	16.9	16.7	16.4	16.3	16.2	16.0	16.0	15.9	15.8	15.7	0.999	
0.9995	22.4	21.9	21.7	21.4	21.1	20.9	20.7	20.5	20.4	20.3	20.2	20.1	0.9995	

df_N, degrees of freedom for numerator

df_E, degrees of freedom for denominator

Table B-2 Continued

df_E	$1 - p_1$	1	2	3	4	5	6	7	8	9	10	11	12	$1 - p_1$
7	0.0005	$0.0^6 42$	$0.0^3 50$	$0.0^2 48$	0.014	0.027	0.040	0.053	0.066	0.078	0.088	0.099	0.108	0.0005
	0.001	$0.0^5 17$	$0.0^2 10$	$0.0^2 76$	0.020	0.035	0.051	0.067	0.081	0.093	0.105	0.115	0.125	0.001
	0.005	$0.0^4 42$	$0.0^2 50$	0.023	0.046	0.070	0.093	0.113	0.130	0.145	0.159	0.171	0.181	0.005
	0.01	$0.0^3 17$	0.010	0.036	0.067	0.096	0.121	0.143	0.162	0.178	0.192	0.205	0.216	0.01
	0.025	$0.0^2 10$	0.025	0.068	0.110	0.146	0.176	0.200	0.221	0.238	0.253	0.266	0.277	0.025
	0.05	$0.0^2 42$	0.052	0.113	0.164	0.205	0.238	0.264	0.286	0.304	0.319	0.332	0.343	0.05
	0.10	0.017	0.107	0.190	0.251	0.297	0.332	0.359	0.381	0.399	0.414	0.427	0.438	0.10
	0.25	0.110	0.300	0.412	0.481	0.528	0.562	0.588	0.608	0.624	0.637	0.649	0.658	0.25
	0.50	0.506	0.767	0.871	0.926	0.960	0.983	1.00	1.01	1.02	1.03	1.04	1.04	0.50
	0.75	1.57	1.70	1.72	1.72	1.71	1.71	1.70	1.70	1.69	1.69	1.69	1.68	0.75
	0.90	3.59	3.26	3.07	2.96	2.88	2.83	2.78	2.75	2.72	2.70	2.68	2.67	0.90
	0.95	5.59	4.74	4.35	4.12	3.97	3.87	3.79	3.73	3.68	3.64	3.60	3.57	0.95
	0.975	8.07	6.54	5.89	5.52	5.29	5.12	4.99	4.90	4.82	4.76	4.71	4.67	0.975
	0.99	12.2	9.55	8.45	7.85	7.46	7.19	6.99	6.84	6.72	6.62	6.54	6.47	0.99
	0.995	16.2	12.4	10.9	10.0	9.52	9.16	8.89	8.68	8.51	8.38	8.27	8.18	0.995
	0.999	29.2	21.7	18.8	17.2	16.2	15.5	15.0	14.6	14.3	14.1	13.9	13.7	0.999
	0.9995	37.0	27.2	23.5	21.4	20.2	19.3	18.7	18.2	17.8	17.5	17.2	17.0	0.9995
8	0.0005	$0.0^5 42$	$0.0^3 50$	$0.0^2 48$	0.014	0.027	0.041	0.055	0.068	0.081	0.092	0.102	0.112	0.0005
	0.001	$0.0^5 17$	$0.0^2 10$	$0.0^2 76$	0.020	0.036	0.053	0.068	0.083	0.096	0.109	0.120	0.130	0.001
	0.005	$0.0^4 42$	$0.0^2 50$	0.027	0.047	0.072	0.095	0.115	0.133	0.149	0.164	0.176	0.187	0.005
	0.01	$0.0^3 17$	0.010	0.036	0.068	0.097	0.123	0.146	0.166	0.183	0.198	0.211	0.222	0.01
	0.025	$0.0^2 10$	0.025	0.069	0.111	0.148	0.179	0.204	0.226	0.244	0.259	0.273	0.285	0.025
	0.05	$0.0^2 42$	0.052	0.113	0.166	0.208	0.241	0.268	0.291	0.310	0.326	0.339	0.351	0.05
	0.10	0.017	0.107	0.190	0.253	0.299	0.335	0.363	0.386	0.405	0.421	0.435	0.445	0.10
	0.25	0.109	0.298	0.411	0.481	0.529	0.563	0.589	0.610	0.627	0.640	0.654	0.661	0.25
	0.50	0.499	0.757	0.860	0.915	0.948	0.971	0.988	1.00	1.01	1.02	1.02	1.03	0.50
	0.75	1.54	1.66	1.67	1.66	1.66	1.65	1.64	1.64	1.64	1.63	1.63	1.62	0.75
	0.90	3.46	3.11	2.92	2.81	2.73	2.67	2.62	2.59	2.56	2.54	2.52	2.50	0.90
	0.95	5.32	4.46	4.07	3.84	3.69	3.58	3.50	3.44	3.39	3.35	3.31	3.28	0.95
	0.975	7.57	6.06	5.42	5.05	4.82	4.65	4.53	4.43	4.36	4.30	4.24	4.20	0.975
	0.99	11.3	8.65	7.59	7.01	6.63	6.37	6.18	6.03	5.91	5.81	5.73	5.67	0.99
	0.995	14.7	11.0	9.60	8.81	8.30	7.95	7.69	7.50	7.34	7.21	7.10	7.01	0.995
	0.999	25.4	18.5	15.8	14.4	13.5	12.9	12.4	12.0	11.8	11.5	11.4	11.2	0.999
	0.9995	31.6	22.8	19.4	17.6	16.4	15.7	15.1	14.6	14.3	14.0	13.8	13.6	0.9995
9	0.0005	$0.0^6 41$	$0.0^3 50$	$0.0^2 48$	0.015	0.027	0.042	0.056	0.070	0.083	0.094	0.105	0.115	0.0005
	0.001	$0.0^5 17$	$0.0^2 10$	$0.0^2 77$	0.021	0.037	0.054	0.070	0.085	0.099	0.112	0.123	0.134	0.001
	0.005	$0.0^4 42$	$0.0^2 50$	0.023	0.047	0.073	0.096	0.117	0.136	0.153	0.168	0.181	0.192	0.005
	0.01	$0.0^3 17$	0.010	0.037	0.068	0.098	0.125	0.149	0.169	0.187	0.202	0.216	0.228	0.01
	0.025	$0.0^2 10$	0.025	0.069	0.112	0.150	0.181	0.207	0.230	0.248	0.265	0.279	0.291	0.025
	0.05	$0.0^2 40$	0.052	0.113	0.167	0.210	0.244	0.272	0.296	0.315	0.331	0.345	0.358	0.05
	0.10	0.017	0.107	0.191	0.254	0.302	0.338	0.367	0.390	0.410	0.426	0.441	0.452	0.10
	0.25	0.108	0.297	0.410	0.480	0.529	0.564	0.591	0.612	0.629	0.643	0.654	0.664	0.25
	0.50	0.494	0.749	0.852	0.906	0.939	0.962	0.978	0.990	1.00	1.01	1.01	1.02	0.50
	0.75	1.51	1.62	1.63	1.63	1.62	1.61	1.60	1.60	1.59	1.59	1.58	1.58	0.75
	0.90	3.36	3.01	2.81	2.69	2.61	2.55	2.51	2.47	2.44	2.42	2.40	2.38	0.90
	0.95	5.12	4.26	3.86	3.63	3.48	3.37	3.29	3.23	3.18	3.14	3.10	3.07	0.95
	0.975	7.21	5.71	5.08	4.72	4.48	4.32	4.20	4.10	4.03	3.96	3.91	3.87	0.975
	0.99	10.6	8.02	6.99	6.42	6.06	5.80	5.61	5.47	5.35	5.26	5.18	5.11	0.99
	0.995	13.6	10.1	8.72	7.96	7.47	7.13	6.88	6.69	6.54	6.42	6.31	6.23	0.995
	0.999	22.9	16.4	13.9	12.6	11.7	11.1	10.7	10.4	10.1	9.89	9.71	9.57	0.999
	0.9995	28.0	19.9	16.8	15.1	14.1	13.3	12.8	12.4	12.1	11.8	11.6	11.4	0.9995

df_N, degrees of freedom for numerator

df_E, degrees of freedom for denominator

Table B-2 Continued

$1-p_1$	15	20	24	30	40	50	60	100	120	200	500	∞	$1-p_1$	
					df_N, degrees of freedom for numerator									
0.0005	0.130	0.157	0.172	0.188	0.206	0.217	0.225	0.242	0.246	0.255	0.263	0.268	0.0005	7
0.001	0.148	0.176	0.191	0.208	0.225	0.237	0.245	0.261	0.266	0.274	0.282	0.288	0.001	
0.005	0.206	0.235	0.251	0.267	0.285	0.296	0.304	0.319	0.324	0.332	0.340	0.345	0.005	
0.01	0.241	0.270	0.286	0.303	0.320	0.331	0.339	0.355	0.358	0.366	0.373	0.379	0.01	
0.025	0.304	0.333	0.348	0.364	0.381	0.392	0.399	0.413	0.418	0.426	0.433	0.437	0.025	
0.05	0.369	0.398	0.413	0.428	0.445	0.455	0.461	0.476	0.479	0.485	0.493	0.498	0.05	
0.10	0.463	0.491	0.504	0.519	0.534	0.543	0.550	0.562	0.566	0.571	0.578	0.582	0.10	
0.25	0.679	0.702	0.713	0.725	0.737	0.745	0.749	0.760	0.762	0.767	0.772	0.775	0.25	
0.50	1.05	1.07	1.07	1.08	1.08	1.09	1.09	1.10	1.10	1.10	1.10	1.10	0.50	
0.75	1.68	1.67	1.67	1.66	1.66	1.66	1.65	1.65	1.65	1.65	1.65	1.65	0.75	
0.90	2.63	2.59	2.58	2.56	2.54	2.52	2.51	2.50	2.49	2.48	2.48	2.47	0.90	
0.95	3.51	3.44	3.41	3.38	3.34	3.32	3.30	3.27	3.27	3.25	3.24	3.23	0.95	
0.975	4.57	4.47	4.42	4.36	4.31	4.28	4.25	4.21	4.20	4.18	4.16	4.14	0.975	
0.99	6.31	6.16	6.07	5.99	5.91	5.86	5.82	5.75	5.74	5.70	5.67	5.65	0.99	
0.995	7.97	7.75	7.65	7.53	7.42	7.35	7.31	7.22	7.19	7.15	7.10	7.08	0.995	
0.999	13.3	12.9	12.7	12.5	12.3	12.2	12.1	11.9	11.9	11.8	11.7	11.7	0.999	
0.9995	16.5	16.0	15.7	15.5	15.2	15.1	15.0	14.7	14.7	14.6	14.5	14.4	0.9995	
0.0005	0.136	0.164	0.181	0.198	0.218	0.230	0.239	0.257	0.262	0.271	0.281	0.287	0.0005	8
0.001	0.155	0.184	0.200	0.218	0.238	0.250	0.259	0.277	0.282	0.292	0.300	0.306	0.001	
0.005	0.214	0.244	0.261	0.279	0.299	0.311	0.319	0.337	0.341	0.351	0.358	0.364	0.005	
0.01	0.250	0.281	0.297	0.315	0.334	0.346	0.354	0.372	0.376	0.385	0.392	0.398	0.01	
0.025	0.313	0.343	0.360	0.377	0.395	0.407	0.415	0.431	0.435	0.442	0.450	0.456	0.025	
0.05	0.379	0.409	0.425	0.441	0.459	0.469	0.477	0.493	0.496	0.505	0.510	0.516	0.05	
0.10	0.472	0.500	0.515	0.531	0.547	0.556	0.563	0.578	0.581	0.588	0.595	0.599	0.10	
0.25	0.684	0.707	0.718	0.730	0.743	0.751	0.756	0.767	0.769	0.775	0.780	0.783	0.25	
0.50	1.04	1.05	1.06	1.07	1.07	1.07	1.08	1.08	1.08	1.09	1.09	1.09	0.50	
0.75	1.62	1.61	1.60	1.60	1.59	1.59	1.59	1.58	1.58	1.58	1.58	1.58	0.75	
0.90	2.46	2.42	2.40	2.38	2.36	2.35	2.34	2.32	2.32	2.31	2.30	2.29	0.90	
0.95	3.22	3.15	3.12	3.08	3.04	3.02	3.01	2.97	2.97	2.95	2.94	2.93	0.95	
0.975	4.10	4.00	3.95	3.89	3.84	3.81	3.78	3.74	3.73	3.70	3.68	3.67	0.975	
0.99	5.52	5.36	5.28	5.20	5.12	5.07	5.03	4.96	4.95	4.91	4.88	4.86	0.99	
0.995	6.81	6.61	6.50	6.40	6.29	6.22	6.18	6.09	6.06	6.02	5.98	5.95	0.995	
0.999	10.8	10.5	10.3	10.1	9.92	9.80	9.73	9.57	9.54	9.46	9.39	9.34	0.999	
0.9995	13.1	12.7	12.5	12.2	12.0	11.8	11.8	11.6	11.5	11.4	11.4	11.3	0.9995	
0.0005	0.141	0.171	0.188	0.207	0.228	0.242	0.251	0.270	0.276	0.287	0.297	0.303	0.0005	9
0.001	0.160	0.191	0.208	0.228	0.249	0.262	0.271	0.291	0.296	0.307	0.316	0.323	0.001	
0.005	0.220	0.253	0.271	0.290	0.310	0.324	0.332	0.351	0.356	0.366	0.376	0.382	0.005	
0.01	0.257	0.289	0.307	0.326	0.346	0.358	0.368	0.386	0.391	0.400	0.410	0.415	0.01	
0.025	0.320	0.352	0.370	0.388	0.408	0.420	0.428	0.446	0.450	0.459	0.467	0.473	0.025	
0.05	0.386	0.418	0.435	0.452	0.471	0.483	0.490	0.508	0.510	0.518	0.526	0.532	0.05	
0.10	0.479	0.509	0.525	0.541	0.558	0.568	0.575	0.588	0.594	0.602	0.610	0.613	0.10	
0.25	0.687	0.711	0.723	0.736	0.749	0.757	0.762	0.773	0.776	0.782	0.787	0.791	0.25	
0.50	1.03	1.04	1.05	1.05	1.06	1.06	1.07	1.07	1.07	1.08	1.08	1.08	0.50	
0.75	1.57	1.56	1.56	1.55	1.55	1.54	1.54	1.53	1.53	1.53	1.53	1.53	0.75	
0.90	2.34	2.30	2.28	2.25	2.23	2.22	2.21	2.19	2.18	2.17	2.17	2.16	0.90	
0.95	3.01	2.94	2.90	2.86	2.83	2.80	2.79	2.76	2.75	2.73	2.72	2.71	0.95	
0.975	3.77	3.67	3.61	3.56	3.51	3.47	3.45	3.40	3.39	3.37	3.35	3.33	0.975	
0.99	4.96	4.81	4.73	4.65	4.57	4.52	4.48	4.42	4.40	4.36	4.33	4.31	0.99	
0.995	6.03	5.83	5.73	5.62	5.52	5.45	5.41	5.32	5.30	5.26	5.21	5.19	0.995	
0.999	9.24	8.90	8.72	8.55	8.37	8.26	8.19	8.04	8.00	7.93	7.86	7.81	0.999	
0.9995	11.0	10.6	10.4	10.2	9.94	9.80	9.71	9.53	9.49	9.40	9.32	9.26	0.9995	

df_E, degrees of freedom for denominator

Table B-2 Continued

df_E	$1-p_1$	1	2	3	4	5	6	7	8	9	10	11	12	$1-p_1$
10	0.0005	0.0^641	0.0^350	0.0^249	0.015	0.028	0.043	0.057	0.071	0.085	0.097	0.108	0.119	0.0005
	0.001	0.0^517	0.0^210	0.0^277	0.021	0.037	0.054	0.071	0.087	0.101	0.114	0.126	0.137	0.001
	0.005	0.0^441	0.0^250	0.023	0.048	0.073	0.098	0.119	0.139	0.156	0.171	0.185	0.197	0.005
	0.01	0.0^317	0.010	0.037	0.069	0.100	0.127	0.151	0.172	0.190	0.206	0.220	0.233	0.01
	0.025	0.0^210	0.025	0.069	0.113	0.151	0.183	0.210	0.233	0.252	0.269	0.283	0.296	0.025
	0.05	0.0^241	0.052	0.114	0.168	0.211	0.246	0.275	0.299	0.319	0.336	0.351	0.363	0.05
	0.10	0.017	0.106	0.191	0.255	0.303	0.340	0.370	0.394	0.414	0.430	0.444	0.457	0.10
	0.25	0.107	0.296	0.409	0.480	0.529	0.565	0.592	0.613	0.631	0.645	0.657	0.667	0.25
	0.50	0.490	0.743	0.845	0.899	0.932	0.954	0.971	0.983	0.992	1.00	1.01	1.01	0.50
	0.75	1.49	1.60	1.60	1.59	1.59	1.58	1.57	1.56	1.56	1.55	1.55	1.54	0.75
	0.90	3.28	2.92	2.73	2.61	2.52	2.46	2.41	2.38	2.35	2.32	2.30	2.28	0.90
	0.95	4.96	4.10	3.71	3.48	3.33	3.22	3.14	3.07	3.02	2.98	2.94	2.91	0.95
	0.975	6.94	5.46	4.83	4.47	4.24	4.07	3.95	3.85	3.78	3.72	3.66	3.62	0.975
	0.99	10.0	7.56	6.55	5.99	5.64	5.39	5.20	5.06	4.94	4.85	4.77	4.71	0.99
	0.995	12.8	9.43	8.08	7.34	6.87	6.54	6.30	6.12	5.97	5.85	5.75	5.66	0.995
	0.999	21.0	14.9	12.6	11.3	10.5	9.92	9.52	9.20	8.96	8.75	8.58	8.44	0.999
	0.9995	25.5	17.9	15.0	13.4	12.4	11.8	11.3	10.9	10.6	10.3	10.1	9.93	0.9995
11	0.0005	0.0^641	0.0^350	0.0^249	0.015	0.028	0.043	0.058	0.072	0.086	0.099	0.111	0.121	0.0005
	0.001	0.0^516	0.0^210	0.0^278	0.021	0.038	0.055	0.072	0.088	0.103	0.116	0.129	0.140	0.001
	0.005	0.0^440	0.0^250	0.023	0.048	0.074	0.099	0.121	0.141	0.158	0.174	0.188	0.200	0.005
	0.01	0.0^316	0.010	0.037	0.069	0.100	0.128	0.153	0.175	0.193	0.210	0.224	0.237	0.01
	0.025	0.0^210	0.025	0.069	0.114	0.152	0.185	0.212	0.236	0.256	0.273	0.288	0.301	0.025
	0.05	0.0^241	0.052	0.114	0.168	0.212	0.248	0.278	0.302	0.323	0.340	0.355	0.368	0.05
	0.10	0.017	0.106	0.192	0.256	0.305	0.342	0.373	0.397	0.417	0.435	0.448	0.461	0.10
	0.25	0.107	0.295	0.408	0.481	0.529	0.565	0.592	0.614	0.633	0.645	0.658	0.667	0.25
	0.50	0.486	0.739	0.840	0.893	0.926	0.948	0.964	0.977	0.986	0.994	1.00	1.01	0.50
	0.75	1.47	1.58	1.58	1.57	1.56	1.55	1.54	1.53	1.53	1.52	1.52	1.51	0.75
	0.90	3.23	2.86	2.66	2.54	2.45	2.39	2.34	2.30	2.27	2.25	2.23	2.21	0.90
	0.95	4.84	3.98	3.59	3.36	3.20	3.09	3.01	2.95	2.90	2.85	2.82	2.79	0.95
	0.975	6.72	5.26	4.63	4.28	4.04	3.88	3.76	3.66	3.59	3.53	3.47	3.43	0.975
	0.99	9.65	7.21	6.22	5.67	5.32	5.07	4.89	4.74	4.63	4.54	4.46	4.40	0.99
	0.995	12.2	8.91	7.60	6.88	6.42	6.10	5.86	5.68	5.54	5.42	5.32	5.24	0.995
	0.999	19.7	13.8	11.6	10.3	9.58	9.05	8.66	8.35	8.12	7.92	7.76	7.62	0.999
	0.9995	23.6	16.4	13.6	12.2	11.2	10.6	10.1	9.76	9.48	9.24	9.04	8.88	0.9995
12	0.0005	0.0^641	0.0^350	0.0^249	0.015	0.028	0.044	0.058	0.073	0.087	0.101	0.113	0.124	0.0005
	0.001	0.0^516	0.0^210	0.0^278	0.021	0.038	0.056	0.073	0.089	0.104	0.118	0.131	0.143	0.001
	0.005	0.0^439	0.0^250	0.023	0.048	0.075	0.100	0.122	0.143	0.161	0.177	0.191	0.204	0.005
	0.01	0.0^316	0.010	0.037	0.070	0.101	0.130	0.155	0.176	0.196	0.212	0.227	0.241	0.01
	0.025	0.0^210	0.025	0.070	0.114	0.153	0.186	0.214	0.238	0.259	0.276	0.292	0.305	0.025
	0.05	0.0^241	0.052	0.114	0.169	0.214	0.250	0.280	0.305	0.325	0.343	0.358	0.372	0.05
	0.10	0.016	0.106	0.192	0.257	0.306	0.344	0.375	0.400	0.420	0.438	0.452	0.466	0.10
	0.25	0.106	0.295	0.408	0.480	0.530	0.566	0.594	0.616	0.633	0.649	0.662	0.671	0.25
	0.50	0.484	0.735	0.835	0.888	0.921	0.943	0.959	0.972	0.981	0.989	0.995	1.00	0.50
	0.75	1.46	1.56	1.56	1.55	1.54	1.53	1.52	1.51	1.51	1.50	1.50	1.49	0.75
	0.90	3.18	2.81	2.61	2.48	2.39	2.33	2.28	2.24	2.21	2.19	2.17	2.15	0.90
	0.95	4.75	3.89	3.49	3.26	3.11	3.00	2.91	2.85	2.80	2.75	2.72	2.69	0.95
	0.975	6.55	5.10	4.47	4.12	3.89	3.73	3.61	3.51	3.44	3.37	3.32	3.28	0.975
	0.99	9.33	6.93	5.95	5.41	5.06	4.82	4.64	4.50	4.39	4.30	4.22	4.16	0.99
	0.995	11.8	8.51	7.23	6.52	6.07	5.76	5.52	5.35	5.20	5.09	4.99	4.91	0.995
	0.999	18.6	13.0	10.8	9.63	8.89	8.38	8.00	7.71	7.48	7.29	7.14	7.01	0.999
	0.9995	22.2	15.3	12.7	11.1	10.4	9.74	9.28	8.94	8.66	8.43	8.24	8.08	0.9995

df_N, degrees of freedom for numerator

df_E, degrees of freedom for denominator

Table B-2 Continued

$1-p_1$	\multicolumn{11}{c}{df_N, degrees of freedom for numerator}	$1-p_1$	
	15	20	24	30	40	50	60	100	120	200	500	∞		
0.0005	0.145	0.177	0.195	0.215	0.238	0.251	0.262	0.282	0.288	0.299	0.311	0.319	0.0005	10
0.001	0.164	0.197	0.216	0.236	0.258	0.272	0.282	0.303	0.309	0.321	0.331	0.338	0.001	
0.005	0.226	0.260	0.279	0.299	0.321	0.334	0.344	0.365	0.370	0.380	0.391	0.397	0.005	
0.01	0.263	0.297	0.316	0.336	0.357	0.370	0.380	0.400	0.405	0.415	0.424	0.431	0.01	
0.025	0.327	0.360	0.379	0.398	0.419	0.431	0.441	0.459	0.464	0.474	0.483	0.488	0.025	
0.05	0.393	0.426	0.444	0.462	0.481	0.493	0.502	0.518	0.523	0.532	0.541	0.546	0.05	
0.10	0.486	0.516	0.532	0.549	0.567	0.578	0.586	0.602	0.605	0.614	0.621	0.625	0.10	
0.25	0.691	0.714	0.727	0.740	0.754	0.762	0.767	0.779	0.782	0.788	0.793	0.797	0.25	
0.50	1.02	1.03	1.04	1.05	1.05	1.06	1.06	1.06	1.06	1.07	1.07	1.07	0.50	
0.75	1.53	1.52	1.52	1.51	1.51	1.50	1.50	1.49	1.49	1.49	1.48	1.48	0.75	
0.90	2.24	2.20	2.18	2.16	2.13	2.12	2.11	2.09	2.08	2.07	2.06	2.06	0.90	
0.95	2.85	2.77	2.74	2.70	2.66	2.64	2.62	2.59	2.58	2.56	2.55	2.54	0.95	
0.975	3.52	3.42	3.37	3.31	3.26	3.22	3.20	3.15	3.14	3.12	3.09	3.08	0.975	
0.99	4.56	4.41	4.33	4.25	4.17	4.12	4.08	4.01	4.00	3.96	3.93	3.91	0.99	
0.995	5.47	5.27	5.17	5.07	4.97	4.90	4.86	4.77	4.75	4.71	4.67	4.64	0.995	
0.999	8.13	7.80	7.64	7.47	7.30	7.19	7.12	6.98	6.94	6.87	6.81	6.76	0.999	
0.9995	9.56	9.16	8.96	8.75	8.54	8.42	8.33	8.16	8.12	8.04	7.96	7.90	0.9995	
0.0005	0.148	0.182	0.201	0.222	0.246	0.261	0.271	0.293	0.299	0.312	0.324	0.331	0.0005	11
0.001	0.168	0.202	0.222	0.243	0.266	0.282	0.292	0.313	0.320	0.332	0.343	0.353	0.001	
0.005	0.231	0.266	0.286	0.308	0.330	0.345	0.355	0.376	0.382	0.394	0.403	0.412	0.005	
0.01	0.268	0.304	0.324	0.344	0.366	0.380	0.391	0.412	0.417	0.427	0.439	0.444	0.01	
0.025	0.332	0.368	0.386	0.407	0.429	0.442	0.450	0.472	0.476	0.485	0.495	0.503	0.025	
0.05	0.398	0.433	0.452	0.469	0.490	0.503	0.513	0.529	0.535	0.543	0.552	0.559	0.05	
0.10	0.490	0.524	0.541	0.559	0.578	0.588	0.595	0.614	0.617	0.625	0.633	0.637	0.10	
0.25	0.694	0.719	0.730	0.744	0.758	0.767	0.773	0.780	0.788	0.794	0.799	0.803	0.25	
0.50	1.02	1.03	1.03	1.04	1.05	1.05	1.05	1.06	1.06	1.06	1.06	1.06	0.50	
0.75	1.50	1.49	1.49	1.48	1.47	1.47	1.47	1.46	1.46	1.46	1.45	1.45	0.75	
0.90	2.17	2.12	2.10	2.08	2.05	2.04	2.03	2.00	2.00	1.99	1.98	1.97	0.90	
0.95	2.72	2.65	2.61	2.57	2.53	2.51	2.49	2.46	2.45	2.43	2.42	2.40	0.95	
0.975	3.33	3.23	3.17	3.12	3.06	3.03	3.00	2.96	2.94	2.92	2.90	2.88	0.975	
0.99	4.25	4.10	4.02	3.94	3.86	3.81	3.78	3.71	3.69	3.66	3.62	3.60	0.99	
0.995	5.05	4.86	4.76	4.65	4.55	4.49	4.45	4.36	4.34	4.29	4.25	4.23	0.995	
0.999	7.32	7.01	6.85	6.68	6.52	6.41	6.35	6.21	6.17	6.10	6.04	6.00	0.999	
0.9995	8.52	8.14	7.94	7.75	7.55	7.43	7.35	7.18	7.14	7.06	6.98	6.93	0.9995	
0.0005	0.152	0.186	0.206	0.228	0.253	0.269	0.280	0.305	0.311	0.323	0.337	0.345	0.0005	12
0.001	0.172	0.207	0.228	0.250	0.275	0.291	0.302	0.326	0.332	0.344	0.357	0.365	0.001	
0.005	0.235	0.272	0.292	0.315	0.339	0.355	0.365	0.388	0.393	0.405	0.417	0.424	0.005	
0.01	0.273	0.310	0.330	0.352	0.375	0.391	0.401	0.422	0.428	0.441	0.450	0.458	0.01	
0.025	0.337	0.374	0.394	0.416	0.437	0.450	0.461	0.481	0.487	0.498	0.508	0.514	0.025	
0.05	0.404	0.439	0.458	0.478	0.499	0.513	0.522	0.541	0.545	0.556	0.565	0.571	0.05	
0.10	0.496	0.528	0.546	0.564	0.583	0.595	0.604	0.621	0.625	0.633	0.641	0.647	0.10	
0.25	0.695	0.721	0.734	0.748	0.762	0.771	0.777	0.789	0.792	0.799	0.804	0.808	0.25	
0.50	1.01	1.02	1.03	1.03	1.04	1.04	1.05	1.05	1.05	1.05	1.06	1.06	0.50	
0.75	1.48	1.47	1.46	1.45	1.45	1.44	1.44	1.43	1.43	1.43	1.42	1.42	0.75	
0.90	2.11	2.06	2.04	2.01	1.99	1.97	1.96	1.94	1.93	1.92	1.91	1.90	0.90	
0.95	2.62	2.54	2.51	2.47	2.43	2.40	2.38	2.35	2.34	2.32	2.31	2.30	0.95	
0.975	3.18	3.07	3.02	2.96	2.91	2.87	2.85	2.80	2.79	2.76	2.74	2.72	0.975	
0.99	4.01	3.86	3.78	3.70	3.62	3.57	3.54	3.47	3.45	3.41	3.38	3.36	0.99	
0.995	4.72	4.53	4.43	4.33	4.23	4.17	4.12	4.04	4.01	3.97	3.93	3.90	0.995	
0.999	6.71	6.40	6.25	6.09	5.93	5.83	5.76	5.63	5.59	5.52	5.46	5.42	0.999	
0.9995	7.74	7.37	7.18	7.00	6.80	6.68	6.61	6.45	6.41	6.33	6.25	6.20	0.9995	

df_E, degrees of freedom for denominator

248 THE GENERAL LINEAR MODEL

Table B-2 Continued

df_E, degrees of freedom for denominator

df_E	$1-p_1$	1	2	3	4	5	6	7	8	9	10	11	12	$1-p_1$
15	0.0005	0.0^641	0.0^350	0.0^249	0.015	0.029	0.045	0.061	0.076	0.091	0.105	0.117	0.129	0.0005
	0.001	0.0^516	0.0^210	0.0^279	0.021	0.039	0.057	0.075	0.092	0.108	0.123	0.137	0.149	0.001
	0.005	0.0^439	0.0^250	0.023	0.049	0.076	0.102	0.125	0.147	0.166	0.183	0.198	0.212	0.005
	0.01	0.0^316	0.010	0.037	0.070	0.103	0.132	0.158	0.181	0.202	0.219	0.235	0.249	0.01
	0.025	0.0^210	0.025	0.070	0.116	0.156	0.190	0.219	0.244	0.265	0.284	0.300	0.315	0.025
	0.05	0.0^241	0.051	0.115	0.170	0.216	0.254	0.285	0.311	0.333	0.351	0.368	0.382	0.05
	0.10	0.016	0.106	0.192	0.258	0.309	0.348	0.380	0.406	0.427	0.446	0.461	0.475	0.10
	0.25	0.105	0.293	0.407	0.480	0.531	0.568	0.596	0.618	0.637	0.652	0.667	0.676	0.25
	0.50	0.478	0.726	0.826	0.878	0.911	0.933	0.948	0.960	0.970	0.977	0.984	0.989	0.50
	0.75	1.43	1.52	1.52	1.51	1.49	1.48	1.47	1.46	1.46	1.45	1.44	1.44	0.75
	0.90	3.07	2.70	2.49	2.36	2.27	2.21	2.16	2.12	2.09	2.06	2.04	2.02	0.90
	0.95	4.54	3.68	3.29	3.06	2.90	2.79	2.71	2.64	2.59	2.54	2.51	2.48	0.95
	0.975	6.20	4.76	4.15	3.80	3.58	3.41	3.29	3.20	3.12	3.06	3.01	2.96	0.975
	0.99	8.68	6.36	5.42	4.89	4.56	4.32	4.14	4.00	3.89	3.80	3.73	3.67	0.99
	0.995	10.8	7.70	6.48	5.80	5.37	5.07	4.85	4.67	4.54	4.42	4.33	4.25	0.995
	0.999	16.6	11.3	9.34	8.25	7.57	7.09	6.74	6.47	6.26	6.08	5.93	5.81	0.999
	0.9995	19.5	13.2	10.8	9.48	8.66	8.10	7.68	7.36	7.11	6.91	6.75	6.60	0.9995
20	0.0005	0.0^640	0.0^350	0.0^250	0.015	0.029	0.046	0.063	0.079	0.094	0.109	0.123	0.136	0.0005
	0.001	0.0^516	0.0^210	0.0^279	0.022	0.039	0.058	0.077	0.095	0.112	0.128	0.143	0.156	0.001
	0.005	0.0^439	0.0^250	0.023	0.050	0.077	0.104	0.129	0.151	0.171	0.190	0.206	0.221	0.005
	0.01	0.0^316	0.010	0.037	0.071	0.105	0.135	0.162	0.187	0.208	0.227	0.244	0.259	0.01
	0.025	0.0^210	0.025	0.071	0.117	0.158	0.193	0.224	0.250	0.273	0.292	0.310	0.325	0.025
	0.05	0.0^240	0.051	0.115	0.172	0.219	0.258	0.290	0.318	0.340	0.360	0.377	0.393	0.05
	0.10	0.016	0.106	0.193	0.260	0.312	0.353	0.385	0.412	0.435	0.454	0.472	0.485	0.10
	0.25	0.104	0.292	0.407	0.480	0.531	0.569	0.598	0.622	0.641	0.656	0.671	0.681	0.25
	0.50	0.472	0.718	0.816	0.868	0.900	0.922	0.938	0.950	0.959	0.966	0.972	0.977	0.50
	0.75	1.40	1.49	1.48	1.47	1.45	1.44	1.43	1.42	1.41	1.40	1.39	1.39	0.75
	0.90	2.97	2.59	2.38	2.25	2.16	2.09	2.04	2.00	1.96	1.94	1.91	1.89	0.90
	0.95	4.35	3.49	3.10	2.87	2.71	2.60	2.51	2.45	2.39	2.35	2.31	2.28	0.95
	0.975	5.87	4.46	3.86	3.51	3.29	3.13	3.01	2.91	2.84	2.77	2.72	2.68	0.975
	0.99	8.10	5.85	4.94	4.43	4.10	3.87	3.70	3.56	3.46	3.37	3.29	3.23	0.99
	0.995	9.94	6.99	5.82	5.17	4.76	4.47	4.26	4.09	3.96	3.85	3.76	3.68	0.995
	0.999	14.8	9.95	8.10	7.10	6.46	6.02	5.69	5.44	5.24	5.08	4.94	4.82	0.999
	0.9995	17.2	11.4	9.20	8.02	7.28	6.76	6.38	6.08	5.85	5.66	5.51	5.38	0.9995
24	0.0005	0.0^640	0.0^350	0.0^250	0.015	0.030	0.046	0.064	0.080	0.096	0.112	0.126	0.139	0.0005
	0.001	0.0^516	0.0^210	0.0^279	0.022	0.040	0.059	0.079	0.097	0.115	0.131	0.146	0.160	0.001
	0.005	0.0^440	0.0^250	0.023	0.050	0.078	0.106	0.131	0.154	0.175	0.193	0.210	0.226	0.005
	0.01	0.0^316	0.010	0.038	0.072	0.106	0.137	0.165	0.189	0.211	0.231	0.249	0.264	0.01
	0.025	0.0^210	0.025	0.071	0.117	0.159	0.195	0.227	0.253	0.277	0.297	0.315	0.331	0.025
	0.05	0.0^240	0.051	0.116	0.173	0.221	0.260	0.293	0.321	0.345	0.365	0.383	0.399	0.05
	0.10	0.016	0.106	0.193	0.261	0.313	0.355	0.388	0.416	0.439	0.459	0.476	0.491	0.10
	0.25	0.104	0.291	0.406	0.480	0.532	0.570	0.600	0.623	0.643	0.659	0.671	0.684	0.25
	0.50	0.469	0.714	0.812	0.863	0.895	0.917	0.932	0.944	0.953	0.961	0.967	0.972	0.50
	0.75	1.39	1.47	1.46	1.44	1.43	1.41	1.40	1.39	1.38	1.38	1.37	1.36	0.75
	0.90	2.93	2.54	2.33	2.19	2.10	2.04	1.98	1.94	1.91	1.88	1.85	1.83	0.90
	0.95	4.26	3.40	3.01	2.78	2.62	2.51	2.42	2.36	2.30	2.25	2.21	2.18	0.95
	0.975	5.72	4.32	3.72	3.38	3.15	2.99	2.87	2.78	2.70	2.64	2.59	2.54	0.975
	0.99	7.82	5.61	4.72	4.22	3.90	3.67	3.50	3.36	3.26	3.17	3.09	3.03	0.99
	0.995	9.55	6.66	5.52	4.89	4.49	4.20	3.99	3.83	3.69	3.59	3.50	3.42	0.995
	0.999	14.0	9.34	7.55	6.59	5.98	5.55	5.23	4.99	4.80	4.64	4.50	4.39	0.999
	0.9995	16.2	10.6	8.52	7.39	6.68	6.18	5.82	5.54	5.31	5.13	4.98	4.85	0.9995

df_N, degrees of freedom for numerator

Table B-2 Continued

$1-p_1$	\multicolumn{11}{c}{df_N, degrees of freedom for numerator}	$1-p_1$	
	15	20	24	30	40	50	60	100	120	200	500	∞		
0.0005	0.159	0.197	0.220	0.244	0.272	0.290	0.303	0.330	0.339	0.353	0.368	0.377	0.0005	15
0.001	0.181	0.219	0.242	0.266	0.294	0.313	0.325	0.352	0.360	0.375	0.388	0.398	0.001	
0.005	0.246	0.286	0.308	0.333	0.360	0.377	0.389	0.415	0.422	0.435	0.448	0.457	0.005	
0.01	0.284	0.324	0.346	0.370	0.397	0.413	0.425	0.450	0.456	0.469	0.483	0.490	0.01	
0.025	0.349	0.389	0.410	0.433	0.458	0.474	0.485	0.508	0.514	0.526	0.538	0.546	0.025	
0.05	0.416	0.454	0.474	0.496	0.519	0.535	0.545	0.565	0.571	0.581	0.592	0.600	0.05	
0.10	0.507	0.542	0.561	0.581	0.602	0.614	0.624	0.641	0.647	0.658	0.667	0.672	0.10	
0.25	0.701	0.728	0.742	0.757	0.772	0.782	0.788	0.802	0.805	0.812	0.818	0.822	0.25	
0.50	1.00	1.01	1.02	1.02	1.03	1.03	1.03	1.04	1.04	1.04	1.04	1.05	0.50	
0.75	1.43	1.41	1.41	1.40	1.39	1.39	1.38	1.38	1.37	1.37	1.36	1.36	0.75	
0.90	1.97	1.92	1.90	1.87	1.85	1.83	1.82	1.79	1.79	1.77	1.76	1.76	0.90	
0.95	2.40	2.33	2.39	2.25	2.20	2.18	2.16	2.12	2.11	2.10	2.08	2.07	0.95	
0.975	2.86	2.76	2.70	2.64	2.59	2.55	2.52	2.47	2.46	2.44	2.41	2.40	0.975	
0.99	3.52	3.37	3.29	3.21	3.13	3.08	3.05	2.98	2.96	2.92	2.89	2.87	0.99	
0.995	4.07	3.88	3.79	3.69	3.59	3.52	3.48	3.39	3.37	3.33	3.29	3.26	0.995	
0.999	5.54	5.25	5.10	4.95	4.80	4.70	4.64	4.51	4.47	4.41	4.35	4.31	0.999	
0.9995	6.27	5.93	5.75	5.58	5.40	5.29	5.21	5.06	5.02	4.94	4.87	4.83	0.9995	
0.0005	0.169	0.211	0.235	0.263	0.295	0.316	0.331	0.364	0.375	0.391	0.408	0.422	0.0005	20
0.001	0.191	0.233	0.258	0.286	0.318	0.339	0.354	0.386	0.395	0.413	0.429	0.441	0.001	
0.005	0.258	0.301	0.327	0.354	0.385	0.405	0.419	0.448	0.457	0.474	0.490	0.500	0.005	
0.01	0.297	0.340	0.365	0.392	0.422	0.441	0.455	0.483	0.491	0.508	0.521	0.532	0.01	
0.025	0.363	0.406	0.430	0.456	0.484	0.503	0.514	0.541	0.548	0.562	0.575	0.585	0.025	
0.05	0.430	0.471	0.493	0.518	0.544	0.562	0.572	0.595	0.603	0.617	0.629	0.637	0.05	
0.10	0.520	0.557	0.578	0.600	0.623	0.637	0.648	0.671	0.675	0.685	0.694	0.704	0.10	
0.25	0.708	0.736	0.751	0.767	0.784	0.794	0.801	0.816	0.820	0.827	0.835	0.840	0.25	
0.50	0.989	1.00	1.01	1.01	1.02	1.02	1.02	1.03	1.03	1.03	1.03	1.03	0.50	
0.75	1.37	1.36	1.35	1.34	1.33	1.33	1.32	1.31	1.31	1.30	1.30	1.29	0.75	
0.90	1.84	1.79	1.77	1.74	1.71	1.69	1.68	1.65	1.64	1.63	1.62	1.61	0.90	
0.95	2.20	2.12	2.08	2.04	1.99	1.97	1.95	1.91	1.90	1.88	1.86	1.84	0.95	
0.975	2.57	2.46	2.41	2.35	2.29	2.25	2.22	2.17	2.16	2.13	2.10	2.09	0.975	
0.99	3.09	2.94	2.86	2.78	2.69	2.64	2.61	2.54	2.52	2.48	2.44	2.42	0.99	
0.995	3.50	3.32	3.22	3.12	3.02	2.96	2.92	2.83	2.81	2.76	2.72	2.69	0.995	
0.999	4.56	4.29	4.15	4.01	3.86	3.77	3.70	3.58	3.54	3.48	3.42	3.38	0.999	
0.9995	5.07	4.75	4.58	4.42	4.24	4.15	4.07	3.93	3.90	3.82	3.75	3.70	0.9995	
0.0005	0.174	0.218	0.244	0.274	0.309	0.331	0.349	0.384	0.395	0.416	0.434	0.449	0.0005	24
0.001	0.196	0.241	0.268	0.298	0.332	0.354	0.371	0.405	0.417	0.437	0.455	0.469	0.001	
0.005	0.264	0.310	0.337	0.367	0.400	0.422	0.437	0.469	0.479	0.498	0.515	0.527	0.005	
0.01	0.304	0.350	0.376	0.405	0.437	0.459	0.473	0.505	0.513	0.529	0.546	0.558	0.01	
0.025	0.370	0.415	0.441	0.468	0.498	0.518	0.531	0.562	0.568	0.585	0.599	0.610	0.025	
0.05	0.437	0.480	0.504	0.530	0.558	0.575	0.588	0.613	0.622	0.637	0.649	0.659	0.05	
0.10	0.527	0.566	0.588	0.611	0.635	0.651	0.662	0.685	0.691	0.704	0.715	0.723	0.10	
0.25	0.712	0.741	0.757	0.773	0.791	0.802	0.809	0.825	0.829	0.837	0.844	0.850	0.25	
0.50	0.983	0.994	1.00	1.01	1.01	1.02	1.02	1.02	1.02	1.02	1.03	1.03	0.50	
0.75	1.35	1.33	1.32	1.31	1.30	1.29	1.29	1.28	1.28	1.27	1.27	1.26	0.75	
0.90	1.78	1.73	1.70	1.67	1.64	1.62	1.61	1.58	1.57	1.56	1.54	1.53	0.90	
0.95	2.11	2.03	1.98	1.94	1.89	1.86	1.84	1.80	1.79	1.77	1.75	1.73	0.95	
0.975	2.44	2.33	2.27	2.21	2.15	2.11	2.08	2.02	2.01	1.98	1.95	1.94	0.975	
0.99	2.89	2.74	2.66	2.58	2.49	2.44	2.40	2.33	2.31	2.27	2.24	2.21	0.99	
0.995	3.25	3.06	2.97	2.87	2.77	2.70	2.66	2.57	2.55	2.50	2.46	2.43	0.995	
0.999	4.14	3.87	3.74	3.59	3.45	3.35	3.29	3.16	3.14	3.07	3.01	2.97	0.999	
0.9995	4.55	4.25	4.09	3.93	3.76	3.66	3.59	3.44	3.41	3.33	3.27	3.22	0.9995	

df_E, degrees of freedom for denominator

Table B-2 Continued

df_E	$1-p_1$	\multicolumn{12}{c}{df_N, degrees of freedom for numerator}	$1-p_1$
		1	2	3	4	5	6	7	8	9	10	11	12	
30	0.0005	0.0⁶40	0.0³50	0.0²50	0.015	0.030	0.047	0.065	0.082	0.098	0.114	0.129	0.143	0.0005
	0.001	0.0⁵16	0.0²10	0.0²80	0.022	0.040	0.060	0.080	0.099	0.117	0.134	0.150	0.164	0.001
	0.005	0.0⁴40	0.0²50	0.024	0.050	0.079	0.107	0.133	0.156	0.178	0.197	0.215	0.231	0.005
	0.01	0.0³16	0.010	0.038	0.072	0.107	0.138	0.167	0.192	0.215	0.235	0.254	0.270	0.01
	0.025	0.0²10	0.025	0.071	0.118	0.161	0.197	0.229	0.257	0.281	0.302	0.321	0.337	0.025
	0.05	0.0²40	0.051	0.116	0.174	0.222	0.263	0.296	0.325	0.349	0.370	0.389	0.406	0.05
	0.10	0.016	0.106	0.193	0.262	0.315	0.357	0.391	0.420	0.443	0.464	0.481	0.497	0.10
	0.25	0.103	0.290	0.406	0.480	0.532	0.571	0.601	0.625	0.645	0.661	0.676	0.688	0.25
	0.50	0.466	0.709	0.807	0.858	0.890	0.912	0.927	0.939	0.948	0.955	0.961	0.966	0.50
	0.75	1.38	1.45	1.44	1.42	1.41	1.39	1.38	1.37	1.36	1.35	1.35	1.34	0.75
	0.90	2.88	2.49	2.28	2.14	2.05	1.98	1.93	1.88	1.85	1.82	1.79	1.77	0.90
	0.95	4.17	3.32	2.92	2.69	2.53	2.42	2.33	2.27	2.21	2.16	2.13	2.09	0.95
	0.975	5.57	4.18	3.59	3.25	3.03	2.87	2.75	2.65	2.57	2.51	2.46	2.41	0.975
	0.99	7.56	5.39	4.51	4.02	3.70	3.47	3.30	3.17	3.07	2.98	2.91	2.84	0.99
	0.995	9.18	6.35	5.24	4.62	4.23	3.95	3.74	3.58	3.45	3.34	3.25	3.18	0.995
	0.999	13.3	8.77	7.05	6.12	5.53	5.12	4.82	4.58	4.39	4.24	4.11	4.00	0.999
	0.9995	15.2	9.90	7.90	6.82	6.14	5.66	5.31	5.04	4.82	4.65	4.51	4.38	0.9995
40	0.0005	0.0⁶40	0.0³50	0.0²50	0.016	0.030	0.048	0.066	0.084	0.100	0.117	0.132	0.147	0.0005
	0.001	0.0⁵16	0.0²10	0.0²80	0.022	0.042	0.061	0.081	0.101	0.119	0.137	0.153	0.169	0.001
	0.005	0.0⁴40	0.0²50	0.024	0.051	0.080	0.108	0.135	0.159	0.181	0.201	0.220	0.237	0.005
	0.01	0.0³16	0.010	0.038	0.073	0.108	0.140	0.169	0.195	0.219	0.240	0.259	0.276	0.01
	0.025	0.0³99	0.025	0.071	0.119	0.162	0.199	0.232	0.260	0.285	0.307	0.327	0.344	0.025
	0.05	0.0²40	0.051	0.116	0.175	0.224	0.265	0.299	0.329	0.354	0.376	0.395	0.412	0.05
	0.10	0.016	0.106	0.194	0.263	0.317	0.360	0.394	0.424	0.448	0.469	0.488	0.504	0.10
	0.25	0.103	0.290	0.405	0.480	0.533	0.572	0.603	0.627	0.647	0.664	0.680	0.691	0.25
	0.50	0.463	0.705	0.802	0.854	0.885	0.907	0.922	0.934	0.943	0.950	0.956	0.961	0.50
	0.75	1.36	1.44	1.42	1.40	1.39	1.37	1.36	1.35	1.34	1.33	1.32	1.31	0.75
	0.90	2.84	2.44	2.23	2.09	2.00	1.93	1.87	1.83	1.79	1.76	1.73	1.71	0.90
	0.95	4.08	3.23	2.84	2.61	2.45	2.34	2.25	2.18	2.12	2.08	2.04	2.00	0.95
	0.975	5.42	4.05	3.46	3.13	2.90	2.74	2.62	2.53	2.45	2.39	2.33	2.29	0.975
	0.99	7.31	5.18	4.31	3.83	3.51	3.29	3.12	2.99	2.89	2.80	2.73	2.66	0.99
	0.995	8.83	6.07	4.98	4.37	3.99	3.71	3.51	3.35	3.22	3.12	3.03	2.95	0.995
	0.999	12.6	8.25	6.60	5.70	5.13	4.73	4.44	4.21	4.02	3.87	3.75	3.64	0.999
	0.9995	14.4	9.25	7.33	6.30	5.64	5.19	4.85	4.59	4.38	4.21	4.07	3.95	0.9995
60	0.0005	0.0⁶40	0.0³50	0.0²51	0.016	0.031	0.048	0.067	0.085	0.103	0.120	0.136	0.152	0.0005
	0.001	0.0⁵16	0.0²10	0.0²80	0.022	0.041	0.062	0.083	0.103	0.122	0.140	0.157	0.174	0.001
	0.005	0.0⁴40	0.0²50	0.024	0.051	0.081	0.110	0.137	0.162	0.185	0.206	0.225	0.243	0.005
	0.01	0.0³16	0.010	0.038	0.073	0.109	0.142	0.172	0.199	0.223	0.245	0.265	0.283	0.01
	0.025	0.0³99	0.025	0.071	0.120	0.163	0.202	0.235	0.264	0.290	0.313	0.333	0.351	0.025
	0.05	0.0²40	0.051	0.116	0.176	0.226	0.267	0.303	0.333	0.359	0.382	0.402	0.419	0.05
	0.10	0.016	0.106	0.194	0.264	0.318	0.362	0.398	0.428	0.453	0.475	0.493	0.510	0.10
	0.25	0.102	0.289	0.405	0.480	0.534	0.573	0.604	0.629	0.650	0.667	0.680	0.695	0.25
	0.50	0.461	0.701	0.798	0.849	0.880	0.901	0.917	0.928	0.937	0.945	0.951	0.956	0.50
	0.75	1.35	1.42	1.41	1.38	1.37	1.35	1.33	1.32	1.31	1.30	1.29	1.29	0.75
	0.90	2.79	2.39	2.18	2.04	1.95	1.87	1.82	1.77	1.74	1.71	1.68	1.66	0.90
	0.95	4.00	3.15	2.76	2.53	2.37	2.25	2.17	2.10	2.04	1.99	1.95	1.92	0.95
	0.975	5.29	3.93	3.34	3.01	2.79	2.63	2.51	2.41	2.33	2.27	2.22	2.17	0.975
	0.99	7.08	4.98	4.13	3.65	3.34	3.12	2.95	2.82	2.72	2.63	2.56	2.50	0.99
	0.995	8.49	5.80	4.73	4.14	3.76	3.49	3.29	3.13	3.01	2.90	2.82	2.74	0.995
	0.999	12.0	7.76	6.17	5.31	4.76	4.37	4.09	3.87	3.69	3.54	3.43	3.31	0.999
	0.9995	13.6	8.65	6.81	5.82	5.20	4.76	4.44	4.18	3.98	3.82	3.69	3.57	0.9995

Table B-2 Continued

$1-p_1$	\multicolumn{12}{c}{df_N, degrees of freedom for numerator}	$1-p_1$	
	15	20	24	30	40	50	60	100	120	200	500	∞		
0.0005	0.179	0.226	0.254	0.287	0.325	0.350	0.369	0.410	0.420	0.444	0.467	0.483	0.0005	30
0.001	0.202	0.250	0.278	0.311	0.348	0.373	0.391	0.431	0.442	0.465	0.488	0.503	0.001	
0.005	0.271	0.320	0.349	0.381	0.416	0.441	0.457	0.495	0.504	0.524	0.543	0.559	0.005	
0.01	0.311	0.360	0.388	0.419	0.454	0.476	0.493	0.529	0.538	0.559	0.575	0.590	0.01	
0.025	0.378	0.426	0.453	0.482	0.515	0.535	0.551	0.585	0.592	0.610	0.625	0.639	0.025	
0.05	0.445	0.490	0.516	0.543	0.573	0.592	0.606	0.637	0.644	0.658	0.676	0.685	0.05	
0.10	0.534	0.575	0.598	0.623	0.649	0.667	0.678	0.704	0.710	0.725	0.735	0.746	0.10	
0.25	0.716	0.746	0.763	0.780	0.798	0.810	0.818	0.835	0.839	0.848	0.856	0.862	0.25	
0.50	0.978	0.989	0.994	1.00	1.01	1.01	1.01	1.02	1.02	1.02	1.02	1.02	0.50	
0.75	1.32	1.30	1.29	1.28	1.27	1.26	1.26	1.25	1.24	1.24	1.23	1.23	0.75	
0.90	1.72	1.67	1.64	1.61	1.57	1.55	1.54	1.51	1.50	1.48	1.47	1.46	0.90	
0.95	2.01	1.93	1.89	1.84	1.79	1.76	1.74	1.70	1.68	1.66	1.64	1.62	0.95	
0.975	2.31	2.20	2.14	2.07	2.01	1.97	1.94	1.88	1.87	1.84	1.81	1.79	0.975	
0.99	2.70	2.55	2.47	2.39	2.30	2.25	2.21	2.13	2.11	2.07	2.03	2.01	0.99	
0.995	3.01	2.82	2.73	2.63	2.52	2.46	2.42	2.32	2.30	2.25	2.21	2.18	0.995	
0.999	3.75	3.49	3.36	3.22	3.07	2.98	2.92	2.79	2.76	2.69	2.63	2.59	0.999	
0.9995	4.10	3.80	3.65	3.48	3.32	3.22	3.15	3.00	2.97	2.89	2.82	2.78	0.9995	
0.0005	0.185	0.236	0.266	0.301	0.343	0.373	0.393	0.441	0.453	0.480	0.504	0.525	0.0005	40
0.001	0.209	0.259	0.290	0.326	0.367	0.396	0.415	0.461	0.473	0.500	0.524	0.545	0.001	
0.005	0.279	0.331	0.362	0.396	0.436	0.463	0.481	0.524	0.534	0.559	0.581	0.599	0.005	
0.01	0.319	0.371	0.401	0.435	0.473	0.498	0.516	0.556	0.567	0.592	0.613	0.628	0.01	
0.025	0.387	0.437	0.466	0.498	0.533	0.556	0.573	0.610	0.620	0.641	0.662	0.674	0.025	
0.05	0.454	0.502	0.529	0.558	0.591	0.613	0.627	0.658	0.669	0.685	0.704	0.717	0.05	
0.10	0.542	0.585	0.609	0.636	0.664	0.683	0.696	0.724	0.731	0.747	0.762	0.772	0.10	
0.25	0.720	0.752	0.769	0.787	0.806	0.819	0.828	0.846	0.851	0.861	0.870	0.877	0.25	
0.50	0.972	0.983	0.989	0.994	1.00	1.00	1.01	1.01	1.01	1.01	1.02	1.02	0.50	
0.75	1.30	1.28	1.26	1.25	1.24	1.23	1.22	1.21	1.21	1.20	1.19	1.19	0.75	
0.90	1.66	1.61	1.57	1.54	1.51	1.48	1.47	1.43	1.42	1.41	1.39	1.38	0.90	
0.95	1.92	1.84	1.79	1.74	1.69	1.66	1.64	1.59	1.58	1.55	1.53	1.51	0.95	
0.975	2.18	2.07	2.01	1.94	1.88	1.83	1.80	1.74	1.72	1.69	1.66	1.64	0.975	
0.99	2.52	2.37	2.29	2.20	2.11	2.06	2.02	1.94	1.92	1.87	1.83	1.80	0.99	
0.995	2.78	2.60	2.50	2.40	2.30	2.23	2.18	2.09	2.06	2.01	1.96	1.93	0.995	
0.999	3.40	3.15	3.01	2.87	2.73	2.64	2.57	2.44	2.41	2.34	2.28	2.23	0.999	
0.9995	3.68	3.39	3.24	3.08	2.92	2.82	2.74	2.60	2.57	2.49	2.41	2.37	0.9995	
0.0005	0.192	0.246	0.278	0.318	0.365	0.398	0.421	0.478	0.493	0.527	0.561	0.585	0.0005	60
0.001	0.216	0.270	0.304	0.343	0.389	0.421	0.444	0.497	0.512	0.545	0.579	0.602	0.001	
0.005	0.287	0.343	0.376	0.414	0.458	0.488	0.510	0.559	0.572	0.602	0.633	0.652	0.005	
0.01	0.328	0.383	0.416	0.453	0.495	0.524	0.545	0.592	0.604	0.633	0.658	0.679	0.01	
0.025	0.396	0.450	0.481	0.515	0.555	0.581	0.600	0.641	0.654	0.680	0.704	0.720	0.025	
0.05	0.463	0.514	0.543	0.575	0.611	0.633	0.652	0.690	0.700	0.719	0.746	0.759	0.05	
0.10	0.550	0.596	0.622	0.650	0.682	0.703	0.717	0.750	0.758	0.776	0.793	0.806	0.10	
0.25	0.725	0.758	0.776	0.796	0.816	0.830	0.840	0.860	0.865	0.877	0.888	0.896	0.25	
0.50	0.967	0.978	0.983	0.989	0.994	0.998	1.00	1.00	1.01	1.01	1.01	1.01	0.50	
0.75	1.27	1.25	1.24	1.22	1.21	1.20	1.19	1.17	1.17	1.16	1.15	1.15	0.75	
0.90	1.60	1.54	1.51	1.48	1.44	1.41	1.40	1.36	1.35	1.33	1.31	1.29	0.90	
0.95	1.84	1.75	1.70	1.65	1.59	1.56	1.53	1.48	1.47	1.44	1.41	1.39	0.95	
0.975	2.06	1.94	1.88	1.82	1.74	1.70	1.67	1.60	1.58	1.54	1.51	1.48	0.975	
0.99	2.35	2.20	2.12	2.03	1.94	1.88	1.84	1.75	1.73	1.68	1.63	1.60	0.99	
0.995	2.57	2.39	2.29	2.19	2.08	2.01	1.96	1.86	1.83	1.78	1.73	1.69	0.995	
0.999	3.08	2.83	2.69	2.56	2.41	2.31	2.25	2.11	2.09	2.01	1.93	1.89	0.999	
0.9995	3.30	3.02	2.87	2.71	2.55	2.45	2.38	2.23	2.19	2.11	2.03	1.98	0.9995	

Table B-2 Continued

$1-p_1$				df_N, degrees of freedom for numerator									$1-p_1$
	1	2	3	4	5	6	7	8	9	10	11	12	

df_E, degrees of freedom for denominator

120
$1-p_1$	1	2	3	4	5	6	7	8	9	10	11	12	$1-p_1$
0.0005	0.0^640	0.0^350	0.0^251	0.016	0.031	0.049	0.067	0.087	0.105	0.123	0.140	0.156	0.005
0.001	0.0^516	0.0^210	0.0^281	0.023	0.042	0.063	0.084	0.105	0.125	0.144	0.162	0.179	0.001
0.005	0.0^439	0.0^250	0.024	0.051	0.081	0.111	0.139	0.165	0.189	0.211	0.230	0.249	0.005
0.01	0.0^316	0.010	0.038	0.074	0.110	0.143	0.174	0.202	0.227	0.250	0.271	0.290	0.01
0.025	0.0^399	0.025	0.072	0.120	0.165	0.204	0.238	0.268	0.295	0.318	0.340	0.359	0.025
0.05	0.0^239	0.051	0.117	0.177	0.227	0.270	0.306	0.337	0.364	0.388	0.408	0.427	0.05
0.10	0.016	0.105	0.194	0.265	0.320	0.365	0.401	0.432	0.458	0.480	0.500	0.518	0.10
0.25	0.102	0.288	0.405	0.481	0.534	0.574	0.606	0.631	0.652	0.670	0.685	0.699	0.25
0.50	0.458	0.697	0.793	0.844	0.875	0.896	0.912	0.923	0.932	0.939	0.945	0.950	0.50
0.75	1.34	1.40	1.39	1.37	1.35	1.33	1.31	1.30	1.29	1.28	1.27	1.26	0.75
0.90	2.75	2.35	2.13	1.99	1.90	1.82	1.77	1.72	1.68	1.65	1.62	1.60	0.90
0.95	3.92	3.07	2.68	2.45	2.29	2.18	2.09	2.02	1.96	1.91	1.87	1.83	0.95
0.975	5.15	3.80	3.23	2.89	2.67	2.52	2.39	2.30	2.22	2.16	2.10	2.05	0.975
0.99	6.85	4.79	3.95	3.48	3.17	2.96	2.79	2.66	2.56	2.47	2.40	2.34	0.99
0.995	8.18	5.54	4.50	3.92	3.55	3.28	3.09	2.93	2.81	2.71	2.62	2.54	0.995
0.999	11.4	7.32	5.79	4.95	4.42	4.04	3.77	3.55	3.38	3.24	3.12	3.02	0.999
0.9995	12.8	8.10	6.34	5.39	4.79	4.37	4.07	3.82	3.63	3.47	3.34	3.22	0.9995

∞
$1-p_1$	1	2	3	4	5	6	7	8	9	10	11	12	$1-p_1$
0.0005	0.0^639	0.0^350	0.0^251	0.016	0.032	0.050	0.069	0.088	0.108	0.127	0.144	0.161	0.0005
0.001	0.0^516	0.0^210	0.0^281	0.023	0.042	0.063	0.085	0.107	0.128	0.148	0.167	0.185	0.001
0.005	0.0^439	0.0^250	0.024	0.052	0.082	0.113	0.141	0.168	0.193	0.216	0.236	0.256	0.005
0.01	0.0^316	0.010	0.038	0.074	0.111	0.145	0.177	0.206	0.232	0.256	0.278	0.298	0.01
0.025	0.0^398	0.025	0.072	0.121	0.166	0.206	0.241	0.272	0.300	0.325	0.347	0.367	0.025
0.05	0.0^239	0.051	0.117	0.178	0.229	0.273	0.310	0.342	0.369	0.394	0.417	0.436	0.05
0.10	0.016	0.105	0.195	0.266	0.322	0.367	0.405	0.436	0.463	0.487	0.508	0.525	0.10
0.25	0.102	0.288	0.404	0.481	0.535	0.576	0.608	0.634	0.655	0.674	0.690	0.703	0.25
0.50	0.455	0.693	0.789	0.839	0.870	0.891	0.907	0.918	0.927	0.934	0.939	0.945	0.50
0.75	1.32	1.39	1.37	1.35	1.33	1.31	1.29	1.28	1.27	1.25	1.24	1.24	0.75
0.90	2.71	2.30	2.08	1.94	1.85	1.77	1.72	1.67	1.63	1.60	1.57	1.55	0.90
0.95	3.84	3.00	2.60	2.37	2.21	2.10	2.01	1.94	1.88	1.83	1.79	1.75	0.95
0.975	5.02	3.69	3.12	2.79	2.57	2.41	2.29	2.19	2.11	2.05	1.99	1.94	0.975
0.99	6.63	4.61	3.78	3.32	3.02	2.80	2.64	2.51	2.41	2.32	2.25	2.18	0.99
0.995	7.88	5.30	4.28	3.72	3.35	3.09	2.90	2.74	2.62	2.52	2.43	2.36	0.995
0.999	10.8	6.91	5.42	4.62	4.10	3.74	3.47	3.27	3.10	2.96	2.84	2.74	0.999
0.9995	12.1	7.60	5.91	5.00	4.42	4.02	3.72	3.48	3.30	3.14	3.02	2.90	0.9995

Table B-2 Continued

$1 - p_1$	15	20	24	30	40	50	60	100	120	200	500	∞	$1 - p_1$	
				df_N, degrees of freedom for numerator										
0.0005	0.199	0.256	0.293	0.338	0.390	0.429	0.458	0.524	0.543	0.578	0.614	0.676	0.0005	120
0.001	0.223	0.282	0.319	0.363	0.415	0.453	0.480	0.542	0.568	0.595	0.631	0.691	0.001	
0.005	0.297	0.356	0.393	0.434	0.484	0.520	0.545	0.605	0.623	0.661	0.702	0.733	0.005	
0.01	0.338	0.397	0.433	0.474	0.522	0.556	0.579	0.636	0.652	0.688	0.725	0.755	0.01	
0.025	0.406	0.464	0.498	0.536	0.580	0.611	0.633	0.684	0.698	0.729	0.762	0.789	0.025	
0.05	0.473	0.527	0.559	0.594	0.634	0.661	0.682	0.727	0.740	0.767	0.785	0.819	0.05	
0.10	0.560	0.609	0.636	0.667	0.702	0.726	0.742	0.781	0.791	0.815	0.838	0.855	0.10	
0.25	0.730	0.765	0.784	0.805	0.828	0.843	0.853	0.877	0.884	0.897	0.911	0.923	0.25	
0.50	0.961	0.972	0.978	0.983	0.989	0.992	0.994	1.00	1.00	1.00	1.01	1.01	0.50	
0.75	1.24	1.22	1.21	1.19	1.18	1.17	1.16	1.14	1.13	1.12	1.11	1.10	0.75	
0.90	1.55	1.48	1.45	1.41	1.37	1.34	1.32	1.27	1.26	1.24	1.21	1.19	0.90	
0.95	1.75	1.66	1.61	1.55	1.50	1.46	1.43	1.37	1.35	1.32	1.28	1.25	0.95	
0.975	1.95	1.82	1.76	1.69	1.61	1.56	1.53	1.45	1.43	1.39	1.34	1.31	0.975	
0.99	2.19	2.03	1.95	1.86	1.76	1.70	1.66	1.56	1.53	1.48	1.42	1.38	0.99	
0.995	2.37	2.19	2.09	1.98	1.87	1.80	1.75	1.64	1.61	1.54	1.48	1.43	0.995	
0.999	2.78	2.53	2.40	2.26	2.11	2.02	1.95	1.82	1.76	1.70	1.62	1.54	0.999	
0.9995	2.96	2.67	2.53	2.38	2.21	2.11	2.01	1.88	1.84	1.75	1.67	1.60	0.9995	
0.0005	0.207	0.270	0.311	0.360	0.422	0.469	0.505	0.599	0.624	0.704	0.804	1.00	0.0005	∞
0.001	0.232	0.296	0.338	0.386	0.448	0.493	0.527	0.617	0.649	0.719	0.819	1.00	0.001	
0.005	0.307	0.372	0.412	0.460	0.518	0.559	0.592	0.671	0.699	0.762	0.843	1.00	0.005	
0.01	0.349	0.413	0.452	0.499	0.554	0.595	0.625	0.699	0.724	0.782	0.858	1.00	0.01	
0.025	0.418	0.480	0.517	0.560	0.611	0.645	0.675	0.741	0.763	0.813	0.878	1.00	0.025	
0.05	0.484	0.543	0.577	0.617	0.663	0.694	0.720	0.781	0.797	0.840	0.896	1.00	0.05	
0.10	0.570	0.622	0.652	0.687	0.726	0.752	0.774	0.826	0.838	0.877	0.919	1.00	0.10	
0.25	0.736	0.773	0.793	0.816	0.842	0.860	0.872	0.901	0.910	0.932	0.957	1.00	0.25	
0.50	0.956	0.967	0.972	0.978	0.983	0.987	0.989	0.993	0.994	0.997	0.999	1.00	0.50	
0.75	1.22	1.19	1.18	1.16	1.14	1.13	1.12	1.09	1.08	1.07	1.04	1.00	0.75	
0.90	1.49	1.42	1.38	1.34	1.30	1.26	1.24	1.18	1.17	1.13	1.08	1.00	0.90	
0.95	1.67	1.57	1.52	1.46	1.39	1.35	1.32	1.24	1.22	1.17	1.11	1.00	0.95	
0.975	1.83	1.71	1.64	1.57	1.48	1.43	1.39	1.30	1.27	1.21	1.13	1.00	0.975	
0.99	2.04	1.88	1.79	1.70	1.59	1.52	1.47	1.36	1.32	1.25	1.15	1.00	0.99	
0.995	2.19	2.00	1.90	1.79	1.67	1.59	1.53	1.40	1.36	1.28	1.17	1.00	0.995	
0.999	2.51	2.27	2.13	1.99	1.84	1.73	1.66	1.49	1.45	1.34	1.21	1.00	0.999	
0.9995	2.65	2.37	2.22	2.07	1.91	1.79	1.71	1.53	1.48	1.36	1.22	1.00	0.9995	

df_E, degrees of freedom for denominator

This table was originally compiled by W. J. Dixon and F. J. Massey, Jr. and is reproduced with the kind permission of the publishers of the following sources: Hald (1952), Merrington and Thompson (1943), Colcord and Deming (1936), and Dixon and Massey (1969).

Table B-3 Chi-Square Distribution†

df_E	\multicolumn{8}{c}{p_1}
	0.500	0.250	0.100	0.050	0.025	0.010	0.005	0.001
1	0.454936	1.32330	2.70554	3.84146	5.02389	6.63490	7.87944	10.828
2	1.38629	2.77259	4.60517	5.99146	7.37776	9.21034	10.5966	13.816
3	2.36597	4.10834	6.25139	7.81473	9.34840	11.3449	12.8382	16.266
4	3.35669	5.38527	7.77944	9.48773	11.1433	13.2767	14.8603	18.467
5	4.35146	6.62568	9.23636	11.0705	12.8325	15.0863	16.7496	20.515
6	5.34812	7.84080	10.6446	12.5916	14.4494	16.8119	18.5476	22.458
7	6.34581	9.03715	12.0170	14.0671	16.0128	18.4753	20.2777	24.322
8	7.34412	10.2189	13.3616	15.5073	17.5345	20.0902	21.9550	26.125
9	8.34283	11.3888	14.6837	16.9190	19.0228	21.6660	23.5894	27.877
10	9.34182	12.5489	15.9872	18.3070	20.4832	23.2093	25.1882	29.588
11	10.3410	13.7007	17.2750	19.6751	21.9200	24.7250	26.7568	31.264
12	11.3403	14.8454	18.5493	21.0261	23.3367	26.2170	28.2995	32.909
13	12.3398	15.9839	19.8119	22.3620	24.7356	27.6882	29.8195	34.528
14	13.3393	17.1169	21.0641	23.6848	26.1189	29.1412	31.3194	36.123
15	14.3389	18.2451	22.3071	24.9958	27.4884	30.5779	32.8013	37.697
16	15.3385	19.3689	23.5418	26.2962	28.8454	31.9999	34.2672	39.252
17	16.3382	20.4887	24.7690	27.5871	30.1910	33.4087	35.7185	40.790
18	17.3379	21.6049	25.9894	28.8693	31.5264	34.8053	37.1565	42.312
19	18.3377	22.7178	27.2036	30.1435	32.8523	36.1909	38.5823	43.820
20	19.3374	23.8277	28.4120	31.4104	34.1696	37.5662	39.9968	45.315
21	20.3372	24.9348	29.6151	32.6706	35.4789	38.9322	41.4011	46.797
22	21.3370	26.0393	30.8133	33.9244	36.7807	40.2894	42.7957	48.268
23	22.3369	27.1413	32.0069	35.1725	38.0756	41.6384	44.1813	49.728
24	23.3367	28.2412	33.1962	36.4150	39.3641	42.9798	45.5585	51.179
25	24.3366	29.3389	34.3816	37.6525	40.6465	44.3141	46.9279	52.618
26	25.3365	30.4346	35.5632	38.8851	41.9232	45.6417	48.2899	54.052
27	26.3363	31.5284	36.7412	40.1133	43.1945	46.9629	49.6449	55.476
28	27.3362	32.6205	37.9159	41.3371	44.4608	48.2782	50.9934	56.892
29	28.3361	33.7109	39.0875	42.5570	45.7223	49.5879	52.3356	58.301
30	29.3360	34.7997	40.2560	43.7730	46.9792	50.8922	53.6720	59.703
40	39.3353	45.6160	51.8051	55.7585	59.3417	63.6907	66.7760	73.402
50	49.3349	56.3336	63.1671	67.5048	71.4202	76.1539	79.4900	86.661
60	59.3347	66.9815	74.3970	79.0819	83.2977	88.3794	91.9517	99.607
70	69.3345	77.5767	85.5270	90.5312	95.0232	100.425	104.215	112.317
80	79.3343	88.1303	96.5782	101.879	106.629	112.329	116.321	124.839
90	89.3342	98.6499	107.565	113.145	118.136	124.116	128.299	137.208
100	99.3341	109.141	118.498	124.342	129.561	135.807	140.169	149.449

† This table is abridged from Table 8 in Pearson and Hartley (1966). Reproduced with the kind permission of the trustees of *Biometrika*.

Table B-4 Non-Central F Distribution†

(a) $p_{\text{I}} = 0.05$

df_N	df_E	ϕ‡ 0.5	1.0	1.2	1.4	1.6	1.8	2.0	2.2	2.6	3.0
1	2	0.9271	0.8617	0.8256	0.7847	0.7402	0.6927	0.6432	0.5926	0.4915	0.3950
	4	0.9141	0.8048	0.7415	0.6694	0.5910	0.5095	0.4284	0.3509	0.2169	0.1198
	6	0.9077	0.7768	0.7010	0.6153	0.5238	0.4315	0.3431	0.2629	0.1374	0.0611
	8	0.9040	0.7610	0.6784	0.5858	0.4883	0.3916	0.3015	0.2223	0.1054	0.0413
	10	0.9017	0.7510	0.6642	0.5675	0.4666	0.3680	0.2775	0.1997	0.0890	0.0322
	12	0.9000	0.7440	0.6544	0.5551	0.4521	0.3524	0.2620	0.1854	0.0793	0.0272
	14	0.8988	0.7390	0.6474	0.5462	0.4418	0.3414	0.2513	0.1756	0.0728	0.0240
	16	0.8979	0.7351	0.6420	0.5394	0.4341	0.3333	0.2433	0.1685	0.0683	0.0219
	18	0.8972	0.7321	0.6379	0.5342	0.4281	0.3270	0.2373	0.1631	0.0649	0.0203
	20	0.8966	0.7297	0.6345	0.5300	0.4233	0.3220	0.2325	0.1589	0.0623	0.0192
	22	0.8961	0.7277	0.6317	0.5265	0.4194	0.3180	0.2287	0.1555	0.0603	0.0183
	24	0.8957	0.7260	0.6294	0.5236	0.4161	0.3146	0.2255	0.1527	0.0586	0.0175
	26	0.8954	0.7246	0.6274	0.5212	0.4134	0.3118	0.2228	0.1504	0.0573	0.0169
	28	0.8951	0.7233	0.6258	0.5192	0.4111	0.3094	0.2206	0.1485	0.0561	0.0165
	30	0.8948	0.7223	0.6243	0.5173	0.4090	0.3073	0.2186	0.1468	0.0551	0.0160
	40	0.8939	0.7185	0.6192	0.5110	0.4020	0.3001	0.2119	0.1410	0.0518	0.0147
	60	0.8930	0.7147	0.6140	0.5047	0.3949	0.2930	0.2053	0.1354	0.0487	0.0134
	120	0.8920	0.7108	0.6087	0.4983	0.3879	0.2859	0.1988	0.1300	0.0457	0.0123
	∞	0.8910	0.7070	0.6036	0.4920	0.3810	0.2791	0.1926	0.1248	0.0430	0.0112
2	2	0.9324	0.8814	0.8527	0.8201	0.7840	0.7451	0.7038	0.6608	0.5722	0.4837
	4	0.9201	0.8239	0.7657	0.6976	0.6219	0.5414	0.4598	0.3804	0.2400	0.1353
	6	0.9129	0.7891	0.7135	0.6257	0.5303	0.4330	0.3396	0.2554	0.1264	0.0520
	8	0.9083	0.7672	0.6810	0.5821	0.4769	0.3729	0.2773	0.1955	0.0821	0.0273
	10	0.9052	0.7523	0.6592	0.5536	0.4430	0.3361	0.2408	0.1624	0.0609	0.0175
	12	0.9030	0.7417	0.6438	0.5336	0.4197	0.3115	0.2173	0.1419	0.0490	0.0126
	14	0.9013	0.7337	0.6323	0.5189	0.4028	0.2941	0.2010	0.1281	0.0416	0.0099
	16	0.9000	0.7274	0.6234	0.5077	0.3901	0.2812	0.1892	0.1183	0.0367	0.0082
	18	0.8989	0.7225	0.6164	0.4988	0.3802	0.2713	0.8102	0.1110	0.0331	0.0071
	20	0.8980	0.7184	0.6107	0.4917	0.3723	0.2634	0.1732	0.1054	0.0305	0.0063
	22	0.8973	0.7150	0.6059	0.4858	0.3658	0.2570	0.1675	0.1009	0.0285	0.0057
	24	0.8967	0.7122	0.6019	0.4808	0.3603	0.2517	0.1629	0.0973	0.0269	0.0052
	26	0.8961	0.7097	0.5985	0.4767	0.3558	0.2472	0.1590	0.0943	0.0256	0.0048
	28	0.8957	0.7076	0.5956	0.4730	0.3518	0.2434	0.1558	0.0918	0.0245	0.0045
	30	0.8953	0.7058	0.5930	0.4699	0.3484	0.2401	0.1530	0.0896	0.0236	0.0043
	40	0.8938	0.6992	0.5839	0.4588	0.3365	0.2288	0.1434	0.0824	0.0207	0.0035
	60	0.8923	0.6924	0.5746	0.4476	0.3247	0.2177	0.1341	0.0756	0.0181	0.0029
	120	0.8908	0.6855	0.5651	0.4364	0.3129	0.2069	0.1253	0.0692	0.0157	0.0024
	∞	0.8892	0.6785	0.5556	0.4251	0.3013	0.1963	0.1168	0.0632	0.0137	0.0019
3	2	0.9342	0.8882	0.8623	0.8327	0.7998	0.7640	0.7260	0.6861	0.6030	0.5187
	4	0.9221	0.8302	0.7735	0.7064	0.6311	0.5505	0.4683	0.3880	0.2453	0.1384
	6	0.9144	0.7909	0.7134	0.6226	0.5235	0.4225	0.3264	0.2407	0.1132	0.0435
	8	0.9092	0.7643	0.6733	0.5683	0.4570	0.3482	0.2504	0.1694	0.0639	0.0184
	10	0.9056	0.7454	0.6453	0.5314	0.4134	0.3019	0.2059	0.1307	0.0419	0.0098
	12	0.9028	0.7314	0.6249	0.5050	0.3831	0.2709	0.1776	0.1074	0.0305	0.0061
	14	0.9007	0.7207	0.6093	0.4853	0.3611	0.2490	0.1583	0.0922	0.0238	0.0042
	16	0.8990	0.7122	0.5972	0.4701	0.3443	0.2328	0.1444	0.0817	0.0196	0.0031
	18	0.8976	0.7054	0.5874	0.4581	0.3313	0.2204	0.1340	0.0740	0.0167	0.0025
	20	0.8965	0.6997	0.5794	0.4483	0.3208	0.2106	0.1259	0.0682	0.0146	0.0020
	22	0.8955	0.6950	0.5728	0.4402	0.3122	0.2026	0.1195	0.0637	0.0131	0.0017
	24	0.8947	0.6909	0.5671	0.4333	0.3051	0.1961	0.1143	0.0601	0.0119	0.0015
	26	0.8940	0.6875	0.5623	0.4275	0.2990	0.1907	0.1100	0.0571	0.0110	0.0013
	28	0.8934	0.6845	0.5581	0.4225	0.2938	0.1860	0.1064	0.0547	0.0103	0.0012
	30	0.8928	0.6818	0.5544	0.4182	0.2894	0.1820	0.1033	0.0526	0.0097	0.0011
	40	0.8909	0.6723	0.5414	0.4028	0.2738	0.1684	0.0930	0.0458	0.0078	0.0008
	60	0.8888	0.6624	0.5279	0.3872	0.2583	0.1552	0.0833	0.0397	0.0062	0.0006
	120	0.8866	0.6522	0.5142	0.3716	0.2431	0.1425	0.0743	0.0342	0.0049	0.0004
	∞	0.8843	0.6415	0.5000	0.3557	0.2280	0.1304	0.0659	0.0293	0.0038	0.0003

† This table is abridged from Tiku (1967) with the kind permission of the editor of the *Journal of the American Statistical Association*.

‡ $\phi = [\lambda/(df_N + 1)]^{\frac{1}{2}}$ where λ is the non-centrality parameter and df_N is the number of degrees of freedom in the numerator of the F-test. Tabled number is p_{II} and power is $1 - p_{\text{II}}$.

Table B-4 Continued

df_N	df_E	\multicolumn{10}{c}{ϕ}
		0.5	1.0	1.2	1.4	1.6	1.8	2.0	2.2	2.6	3.0
4	2	0.9351	0.8917	0.8672	0.8391	0.8079	0.7738	0.7375	0.6993	0.6193	0.5374
	4	0.9232	0.8332	0.7771	0.7103	0.6350	0.5542	0.4714	0.3905	0.2466	0.1389
	6	0.9151	0.7906	0.7112	0.6178	0.5158	0.4122	0.3143	0.2282	0.1030	0.0375
	8	0.9094	0.7602	0.6649	0.5549	0.4389	0.3271	0.2286	0.1493	0.0515	0.0132
	10	0.9052	0.7378	0.6315	0.5110	0.3876	0.2736	0.1788	0.1076	0.0301	0.0059
	12	0.9020	0.7208	0.6066	0.4791	0.3516	0.2380	0.1475	0.0833	0.0199	0.0032
	14	0.8995	0.7076	0.5875	0.4550	0.3253	0.2129	0.1266	0.0680	0.0143	0.0019
	16	0.8975	0.6970	0.5723	0.4363	0.3054	0.1945	0.1118	0.0577	0.0109	0.0013
	18	0.8958	0.6883	0.5600	0.4214	0.2898	0.1804	0.1009	0.0503	0.0087	0.0009
	20	0.8945	0.6811	0.5498	0.4092	0.2774	0.1695	0.0926	0.0449	0.0073	0.0007
	22	0.8933	0.6750	0.5413	0.3991	0.2672	0.1607	0.0861	0.0408	0.0062	0.0006
	24	0.8923	0.6698	0.5341	0.3907	0.2587	0.1535	0.0808	0.0376	0.0054	0.0005
	26	0.8914	0.6653	0.5279	0.3834	0.2516	0.1475	0.0765	0.0349	0.0049	0.0004
	28	0.8906	0.6614	0.5225	0.3772	0.2455	0.1424	0.0730	0.0328	0.0044	0.0003
	30	0.8899	0.6579	0.5178	0.3718	0.2402	0.1381	0.0700	0.0311	0.0040	0.0003
	40	0.8874	0.6454	0.5009	0.3526	0.2219	0.1234	0.0601	0.0254	0.0029	0.0002
	60	0.8848	0.6322	0.4833	0.3332	0.2040	0.1095	0.0511	0.0206	0.0021	0.0001
	120	0.8819	0.6183	0.4652	0.3136	0.1865	0.0965	0.0431	0.0164	0.0015	0.0001
	∞	0.8789	0.6038	0.4466	0.2940	0.1695	0.0844	0.0360	0.0130	0.0011	0.0000
5	2	0.9356	0.8939	0.8702	0.8431	0.8128	0.7798	0.7445	0.7074	0.6293	0.5490
	4	0.9238	0.8349	0.7791	0.7124	0.6369	0.5558	0.4727	0.3914	0.2467	0.1386
	6	0.9154	0.7897	0.7087	0.6131	0.5088	0.4033	0.3044	0.2181	0.0952	0.0333
	8	0.9093	0.7561	0.6573	0.5432	0.4237	0.3099	0.2115	0.1342	0.0430	0.0100
	10	0.9048	0.7308	0.6193	0.4933	0.3660	0.2509	0.1579	0.0909	0.0227	0.0038
	12	0.9012	0.7111	0.5904	0.4566	0.3254	0.2118	0.1249	0.0665	0.0136	0.0018
	14	0.8983	0.6956	0.5679	0.4287	0.2957	0.1845	0.1033	0.0516	0.0090	0.0010
	16	0.8960	0.6829	0.5499	0.4069	0.2732	0.1646	0.0883	0.0418	0.0064	0.0006
	18	0.8941	0.6725	0.5352	0.3895	0.2557	0.1496	0.0774	0.0351	0.0048	0.0004
	20	0.8924	0.6638	0.5231	0.3753	0.2417	0.1380	0.0693	0.0303	0.0038	0.0003
	22	0.8910	0.6564	0.5129	0.3635	0.2303	0.1288	0.0630	0.0267	0.0031	0.0002
	24	0.8898	0.6501	0.5042	0.3536	0.2209	0.1213	0.0580	0.0240	0.0026	0.0001
	26	0.8888	0.6445	0.4967	0.3451	0.2129	0.1151	0.0540	0.0218	0.0022	0.0001
	28	0.8878	0.6397	0.4901	0.3379	0.2062	0.1099	0.0507	0.0201	0.0019	0.0001
	30	0.8870	0.6354	0.4844	0.3315	0.2003	0.1055	0.0479	0.0186	0.0017	0.0001
	40	0.8840	0.6198	0.4638	0.3091	0.1803	0.0908	0.0390	0.0142	0.0011	0.0000
	60	0.8807	0.6033	0.4423	0.2864	0.1609	0.0772	0.0313	0.0106	0.0007	0.0000
	120	0.8771	0.5857	0.4201	0.2638	0.1422	0.0649	0.0247	0.0078	0.0004	0.0000
	∞	0.8733	0.5671	0.3971	0.2412	0.1245	0.0538	0.0192	0.0056	0.0003	0.0000
6	2	0.9360	0.8953	0.8722	0.8457	0.8161	0.7839	0.7493	0.7129	0.6361	0.5569
	4	0.9242	0.8361	0.7803	0.7136	0.6380	0.5567	0.4733	0.3916	0.2464	0.1381
	6	0.9156	0.7887	0.7063	0.6090	0.5028	0.3959	0.2962	0.2100	0.0893	0.0301
	8	0.9092	0.7525	0.6506	0.5332	0.4109	0.2958	0.1978	0.1225	0.0369	0.0080
	10	0.9042	0.7245	0.6086	0.4782	0.3480	0.2325	0.1417	0.0784	0.0177	0.0026
	12	0.9003	0.7024	0.5761	0.4373	0.3036	0.1908	0.1077	0.0544	0.0097	0.0011
	14	0.8972	0.6847	0.5506	0.4061	0.2711	0.1619	0.0859	0.0401	0.0059	0.0005
	16	0.8946	0.6702	0.5301	0.3816	0.2465	0.1412	0.0710	0.0312	0.0039	0.0003
	18	0.8924	0.6582	0.5132	0.3621	0.2275	0.1257	0.0605	0.0252	0.0028	0.0002
	20	0.8905	0.6480	0.4992	0.3461	0.2124	0.1139	0.0528	0.0210	0.0021	0.0001
	22	0.8889	0.6394	0.4874	0.3328	0.2001	0.1045	0.0469	0.0179	0.0016	0.0001
	24	0.8875	0.6319	0.4773	0.3216	0.1900	0.0970	0.0423	0.0157	0.0013	0.0001
	26	0.8863	0.6253	0.4686	0.3121	0.1815	0.0908	0.0387	0.0139	0.0011	0.0000
	28	0.8852	0.6196	0.4610	0.3039	0.1744	0.0857	0.0357	0.0125	0.0009	0.0000
	30	0.8843	0.6145	0.4543	0.2968	0.1682	0.0814	0.0333	0.0114	0.0008	0.0000
	40	0.8807	0.5960	0.4302	0.2717	0.1471	0.0672	0.0256	0.0081	0.0004	0.0000
	60	0.8768	0.5760	0.4050	0.2464	0.1270	0.0545	0.0193	0.0055	0.0002	0.0000
	120	0.8724	0.5547	0.3789	0.2214	0.1082	0.0434	0.0141	0.0037	0.0001	0.0000
	∞	0.8677	0.5319	0.3520	0.1967	0.0907	0.0339	0.0101	0.0024	0.0000	0.0000

Table B-4 Continued

df_N	df_E	\multicolumn{10}{c}{ϕ}
		0.5	1.0	1.2	1.4	1.6	1.8	2.0	2.2	2.6	3.0
7	2	0.9363	0.8963	0.8736	0.8476	0.8185	0.7868	0.7527	0.7168	0.6410	0.5627
	4	0.9245	0.8368	0.7811	0.7144	0.6387	0.5571	0.4735	0.3916	0.2460	0.1376
	6	0.9157	0.7878	0.7042	0.6054	0.4978	0.3897	0.2895	0.2035	0.0846	0.0278
	8	0.9090	0.7492	0.6449	0.5247	0.4002	0.2841	0.1868	0.1133	0.0323	0.0065
	10	0.9038	0.7189	0.5992	0.4652	0.3328	0.2174	0.1288	0.0689	0.0143	0.0019
	12	0.8996	0.6947	0.5636	0.4207	0.2852	0.1738	0.0944	0.0454	0.0072	0.0007
	14	0.8961	0.6750	0.5353	0.3866	0.2505	0.1439	0.0726	0.0320	0.0041	0.0003
	16	0.8933	0.6588	0.5125	0.3598	0.2243	0.1226	0.0582	0.0238	0.0025	0.0001
	18	0.8908	0.6452	0.4936	0.3383	0.2041	0.1070	0.0482	0.0185	0.0017	0.0001
	20	0.8888	0.6336	0.4779	0.3208	0.1882	0.0951	0.0409	0.0149	0.0012	0.0000
	22	0.8870	0.6238	0.4646	0.3062	0.1753	0.0858	0.0355	0.0123	0.0009	0.0000
	24	0.8854	0.6152	0.4532	0.2940	0.1647	0.0785	0.0314	0.0105	0.0007	0.0000
	26	0.8840	0.6077	0.4433	0.2836	0.1559	0.0725	0.0282	0.0091	0.0005	0.0000
	28	0.8828	0.6011	0.4347	0.2747	0.1485	0.0676	0.0256	0.0080	0.0004	0.0000
	30	0.8817	0.5952	0.4272	0.2669	0.1421	0.0634	0.0234	0.0071	0.0003	0.0000
	40	0.8776	0.5737	0.3998	0.2396	0.1206	0.0501	0.0170	0.0046	0.0002	0.0000
	60	0.8730	0.5504	0.3713	0.2124	0.1005	0.0387	0.0119	0.0029	0.0001	0.0000
	120	0.8679	0.5253	0.3417	0.1857	0.0821	0.0290	0.0080	0.0017	0.0000	0.0000
	∞	0.8622	0.4983	0.3112	0.1597	0.0656	0.0211	0.0052	0.0010	0.0000	0.0000
8	2	0.9365	0.8971	0.8747	0.8490	0.8203	0.7889	0.7553	0.7198	0.6448	0.5671
	4	0.9274	0.8374	0.7817	0.7149	0.6391	0.5574	0.4735	0.3914	0.2456	0.1371
	6	0.9158	0.7869	0.7024	0.6023	0.4935	0.3845	0.2839	0.1981	0.0809	0.0259
	8	0.9088	0.7464	0.6398	0.5173	0.3910	0.2744	0.1777	0.1059	0.0289	0.0055
	10	0.9033	0.7140	0.5910	0.4540	0.3200	0.2049	0.1184	0.0615	0.0118	0.0014
	12	0.8989	0.6878	0.5526	0.4063	0.2697	0.1598	0.0838	0.0387	0.0055	0.0005
	14	0.8951	0.6663	0.5218	0.3696	0.2330	0.1292	0.0624	0.0260	0.0029	0.0002
	16	0.8920	0.6484	0.4968	0.3407	0.2056	0.1077	0.0485	0.0186	0.0017	0.0001
	18	0.8894	0.6334	0.4761	0.3176	0.1846	0.0921	0.0390	0.0139	0.0010	0.0000
	20	0.8871	0.6205	0.4588	0.2988	0.1680	0.0804	0.0323	0.0108	0.0007	0.0000
	22	0.8851	0.6095	0.4441	0.2832	0.1548	0.0713	0.0274	0.0087	0.0005	0.0000
	24	0.8834	0.5999	0.4315	0.2700	0.1439	0.0642	0.0237	0.0072	0.0003	0.0000
	26	0.8819	0.5915	0.4206	0.2589	0.1349	0.0585	0.0208	0.0060	0.0003	0.0000
	28	0.8805	0.5840	0.4111	0.2493	0.1274	0.0538	0.0186	0.0052	0.0002	0.0000
	30	0.8793	0.5774	0.4027	0.2410	0.1209	0.0499	0.0168	0.0045	0.0002	0.0000
	40	0.8746	0.5530	0.3725	0.2120	0.0995	0.0377	0.0114	0.0027	0.0001	0.0000
	60	0.8694	0.5264	0.3408	0.1834	0.0798	0.0275	0.0074	0.0015	0.0000	0.0000
	120	0.8635	0.4975	0.3081	0.1556	0.0623	0.0193	0.0046	0.0008	0.0000	0.0000
	∞	0.8568	0.4663	0.2745	0.1292	0.0472	0.0130	0.0027	0.0004	0.0000	0.0000
9	2	0.9366	0.8977	0.8756	0.8501	0.8217	0.7906	0.7573	0.7221	0.6477	0.5705
	4	0.9249	0.8378	0.7821	0.7153	0.6394	0.5575	0.4735	0.3912	0.2452	0.1366
	6	0.9158	0.7861	0.7007	0.5996	0.4898	0.3800	0.2792	0.1936	0.0778	0.0245
	8	0.9087	0.7439	0.6354	0.5109	0.3832	0.2661	0.1702	0.0998	0.0262	0.0048
	10	0.9029	0.7096	0.5838	0.4442	0.3089	0.1944	0.1099	0.0555	0.0100	0.0011
	12	0.8982	0.6816	0.5428	0.3937	0.2564	0.1481	0.0753	0.0334	0.0043	0.0003
	14	0.8943	0.6584	0.5097	0.3547	0.2182	0.1171	0.0543	0.0216	0.0021	0.0001
	16	0.8909	0.6390	0.4827	0.3241	0.1898	0.0956	0.0409	0.0148	0.0011	0.0000
	18	0.8881	0.6226	0.4604	0.2996	0.1681	0.0801	0.0320	0.0107	0.0007	0.0000
	20	0.8856	0.6086	0.4416	0.2796	0.1511	0.0686	0.0259	0.0080	0.0004	0.0000
	22	0.8835	0.5964	0.4257	0.2630	0.1376	0.0599	0.0214	0.0062	0.0003	0.0000
	24	0.8816	0.5858	0.4120	0.2492	0.1266	0.0531	0.0181	0.0050	0.0002	0.0000
	26	0.8799	0.5765	0.4002	0.2374	0.1176	0.0477	0.0156	0.0041	0.0001	0.0000
	28	0.8784	0.5683	0.3898	0.2274	0.1110	0.0433	0.0137	0.0034	0.0001	0.0000
	30	0.8770	0.5609	0.3807	0.2186	0.1036	0.0397	0.0121	0.0029	0.0001	0.0000
	40	0.8718	0.5337	0.3477	0.1883	0.0825	0.0286	0.0077	0.0016	0.0000	0.0000
	60	0.8660	0.5038	0.3133	0.1587	0.0636	0.0197	0.0046	0.0008	0.0000	0.0000
	120	0.8592	0.4713	0.2778	0.1304	0.0473	0.0129	0.0026	0.0004	0.0000	0.0000
	∞	0.8514	0.4361	0.2417	0.1041	0.0337	0.0080	0.0014	0.0002	0.0000	0.0000

Table B-4 Continued

df$_N$	df$_E$	\multicolumn{10}{c}{ϕ}
		0.5	1.0	1.2	1.4	1.6	1.8	2.0	2.2	2.6	3.0
10	2	0.9368	0.8981	0.8762	0.8510	0.8228	0.7920	0.7589	0.7240	0.6500	0.5732
	4	0.9250	0.8381	0.7825	0.7156	0.6395	0.5575	0.4734	0.3910	0.2448	0.1362
	6	0.9158	0.7854	0.6992	0.5972	0.4865	0.3762	0.2751	0.1898	0.0752	0.0233
	8	0.9085	0.7417	0.6315	0.5053	0.3764	0.2591	0.1638	0.0948	0.0241	0.0042
	10	0.9026	0.7057	0.5774	0.4357	0.2993	0.1854	0.1028	0.0508	0.0086	0.0009
	12	0.8976	0.6761	0.5340	0.3826	0.2448	0.1383	0.0683	0.0293	0.0035	0.0002
	14	0.8935	0.6514	0.4990	0.3417	0.2055	0.1070	0.0478	0.0182	0.0016	0.0001
	16	0.8899	0.6305	0.4702	0.3094	0.1763	0.0856	0.0350	0.0120	0.0008	0.0000
	18	0.8869	0.6128	0.4463	0.2836	0.1541	0.0704	0.0267	0.0083	0.0004	0.0000
	20	0.8843	0.5976	0.4262	0.2627	0.1368	0.0592	0.0210	0.0061	0.0003	0.0000
	22	0.8819	0.5844	0.4091	0.2454	0.1232	0.0508	0.0170	0.0046	0.0002	0.0000
	24	0.8799	0.5729	0.3944	0.2309	0.1122	0.0443	0.0141	0.0035	0.0001	0.0000
	26	0.8780	0.5627	0.3817	0.2186	0.1031	0.0393	0.0119	0.0028	0.0001	0.0000
	28	0.8764	0.5537	0.3705	0.2082	0.0956	0.0352	0.0102	0.0023	0.0001	0.0000
	30	0.8749	0.5456	0.3607	0.1991	0.0893	0.0319	0.0089	0.0019	0.0000	0.0000
	40	0.8692	0.5157	0.3253	0.1678	0.0687	0.0218	0.0053	0.0010	0.0000	0.0000
	60	0.8627	0.4827	0.2884	0.1377	0.0508	0.0142	0.0029	0.0004	0.0000	0.0000
	120	0.8551	0.4467	0.2506	0.1094	0.0359	0.0086	0.0015	0.0002	0.0000	0.0000
	∞	0.8462	0.4047	0.2124	0.0836	0.0240	0.0049	0.0007	0.0000	0.0000	0.0000
12	2	0.9369	0.8989	0.8772	0.8254	0.8245	0.7941	0.7614	0.7268	0.6536	0.5774
	4	0.9252	0.8385	0.7829	0.7159	0.6397	0.5575	0.4731	0.3905	0.2441	0.1355
	6	0.9159	0.7842	0.6968	0.5934	0.4813	0.3700	0.2686	0.1837	0.0713	0.0214
	8	0.9082	0.7379	0.6250	0.4960	0.3653	0.2476	0.1536	0.0869	0.0208	0.0034
	10	0.9019	0.6991	0.5666	0.4213	0.2836	0.1711	0.0917	0.0435	0.0067	0.0006
	12	0.8966	0.6666	0.5192	0.3641	0.2260	0.1227	0.0577	0.0234	0.0024	0.0001
	14	0.8921	0.6391	0.4805	0.3197	0.1847	0.0913	0.0382	0.0135	0.0010	0.0000
	16	0.8882	0.6157	0.4485	0.2849	0.1544	0.0703	0.0265	0.0083	0.0004	0.0000
	18	0.8848	0.5956	0.4219	0.2571	0.1316	0.0557	0.0192	0.0053	0.0002	0.0000
	20	0.8818	0.5783	0.3994	0.2345	0.1142	0.0452	0.0144	0.0036	0.0001	0.0000
	22	0.8792	0.5631	0.3803	0.2160	0.1005	0.0376	0.0111	0.0026	0.0001	0.0000
	24	0.8768	0.5498	0.3638	0.2006	0.0896	0.0318	0.0088	0.0019	0.0000	0.0000
	26	0.8747	0.5381	0.3496	0.1876	0.0808	0.0274	0.0072	0.0014	0.0000	0.0000
	28	0.8728	0.5276	0.3371	0.1766	0.0736	0.0239	0.0059	0.0011	0.0000	0.0000
	30	0.8710	0.5182	0.3261	0.1671	0.0676	0.0211	0.0050	0.0009	0.0000	0.0000
	40	0.8643	0.4831	0.2865	0.1347	0.0485	0.0131	0.0026	0.0004	0.0000	0.0000
	60	0.8565	0.4443	0.2456	0.1044	0.0329	0.0075	0.0012	0.0001	0.0000	0.0000
	120	0.8472	0.4016	0.2042	0.0770	0.0207	0.0039	0.0005	0.0000	0.0000	0.0000
	∞	0.8359	0.3548	0.1632	0.0535	0.0120	0.0018	0.0002	0.0000	0.0000	0.0000

Table B-4 Continued

(b) $p_I = 0.01$

df_N	df_E	\multicolumn{10}{c}{ϕ}
		0.5	1.0	1.2	1.4	1.6	1.8	2.0	2.2	2.6	3.0
1	2	0.9851	0.9705	0.9620	0.9521	0.9408	0.9282	0.9143	0.8991	0.8654	0.8277
	4	0.9809	0.9492	0.9280	0.9012	0.8682	0.8292	0.7843	0.7341	0.6216	0.5014
	6	0.9782	0.9340	0.9030	0.8629	0.8131	0.7541	0.6870	0.6136	0.4589	0.3125
	8	0.9764	0.9236	0.8859	0.8367	0.7759	0.7043	0.6242	0.5387	0.3678	0.2211
	10	0.9752	0.9163	0.8738	0.8184	0.7501	0.6704	0.5824	0.4904	0.3136	0.1725
	12	0.9743	0.9109	0.8650	0.8050	0.7314	0.6462	0.5532	0.4574	0.2787	0.1437
	14	0.9736	0.9068	0.8582	0.7949	0.7174	0.6283	0.5318	0.4336	0.2547	0.1250
	16	0.9730	0.9036	0.8529	0.7870	0.7066	0.6145	0.5156	0.4158	0.2374	0.1121
	18	0.9726	0.9010	0.8487	0.7807	0.6979	0.6036	0.5028	0.4020	0.2243	0.1027
	20	0.9723	0.8989	0.8452	0.7755	0.6908	0.5947	0.4925	0.3910	0.2141	0.0957
	22	0.9720	0.8971	0.8423	0.7712	0.6850	0.5874	0.4841	0.3820	0.2060	0.0902
	24	0.9717	0.8956	0.8398	0.7675	0.6801	0.5813	0.4771	0.3746	0.1994	0.0858
	26	0.9715	0.8943	0.8377	0.7644	0.6758	0.5760	0.4712	0.3683	0.1938	0.0822
	28	0.9713	0.8931	0.8359	0.7617	0.6722	0.5716	0.4661	0.3630	0.1892	0.0792
	30	0.9711	0.8922	0.8343	0.7593	0.6690	0.5677	0.4617	0.3584	0.1852	0.0767
	40	0.9705	0.8886	0.8285	0.7509	0.6578	0.5539	0.4462	0.3424	0.1718	0.0683
	60	0.9699	0.8850	0.8226	0.7423	0.6463	0.5401	0.4308	0.3267	0.1590	0.0608
	120	0.9693	0.8812	0.8165	0.7335	0.6347	0.5261	0.4155	0.3113	0.1468	0.0539
	∞	0.9687	0.8773	0.8102	0.7244	0.6229	0.5120	0.4003	0.2962	0.1354	0.0478
2	2	0.9863	0.9753	0.9688	0.9613	0.9527	0.9430	0.9323	0.9207	0.8945	0.8650
	4	0.9828	0.9567	0.9386	0.9153	0.8862	0.8511	0.8100	0.7635	0.6571	0.5401
	6	0.9803	0.9409	0.9118	0.8730	0.8237	0.7640	0.6951	0.6191	0.4576	0.3052
	8	0.9784	0.9288	0.8910	0.8401	0.7754	0.6982	0.6110	0.5182	0.3358	0.1869
	10	0.9770	0.9196	0.8751	0.8150	0.7393	0.6500	0.5515	0.4498	0.2626	0.1268
	12	0.9760	0.9124	0.8627	0.7957	0.7118	0.6142	0.5085	0.4022	0.2163	0.0934
	14	0.9752	0.9067	0.8529	0.7806	0.6905	0.5869	0.4765	0.3678	0.1854	0.0733
	16	0.9745	0.9021	0.8450	0.7684	0.6736	0.5655	0.4519	0.3420	0.1636	0.0603
	18	0.9740	0.8983	0.8386	0.7585	0.6600	0.5485	0.4326	0.3221	0.1476	0.0513
	20	0.9735	0.8951	0.8331	0.7502	0.6486	0.5345	0.4170	0.3063	0.1354	0.0449
	22	0.9731	0.8924	0.8285	0.7433	0.6392	0.5229	0.4042	0.2936	0.1260	0.0401
	24	0.9728	0.8901	0.8246	0.7373	0.6312	0.5132	0.3936	0.2830	0.1184	0.0364
	26	0.9725	0.8881	0.8212	0.7322	0.6243	0.5048	0.3845	0.2742	0.1122	0.0335
	28	0.9723	0.8863	0.8182	0.7277	0.6182	0.4976	0.3768	0.2667	0.1070	0.0312
	30	0.9721	0.8848	0.8156	0.7238	0.6130	0.4914	0.3701	0.2603	0.1027	0.0293
	40	0.9713	0.8791	0.8060	0.7096	0.5943	0.4693	0.3468	0.2382	0.0885	0.0233
	60	0.9704	0.8731	0.7960	0.6948	0.5749	0.4469	0.3237	0.2170	0.0757	0.0183
	120	0.9695	0.8668	0.7854	0.6794	0.5551	0.4244	0.3011	0.1968	0.0643	0.0143
	∞	0.9686	0.8600	0.7743	0.6634	0.5349	0.4019	0.2789	0.1776	0.0543	0.0111
3	2	0.9867	0.9769	0.9711	0.9644	0.9567	0.9481	0.9385	0.9280	0.9045	0.8779
	4	0.9835	0.9592	0.9421	0.9199	0.8919	0.8580	0.8181	0.7726	0.6678	0.5517
	6	0.9809	0.9427	0.9136	0.8742	0.8237	0.7620	0.6906	0.6117	0.4448	0.2899
	8	0.9790	0.9291	0.8896	0.8357	0.7665	0.6835	0.5902	0.4917	0.3032	0.1576
	10	0.9775	0.9181	0.8703	0.8047	0.7214	0.6234	0.5166	0.4085	0.2191	0.0941
	12	0.9763	0.9093	0.8547	0.7800	0.6861	0.5776	0.4625	0.3504	0.1675	0.0615
	14	0.9753	0.9021	0.8419	0.7600	0.6580	0.5421	0.4220	0.3086	0.1343	0.0434
	16	0.9746	0.8961	0.8314	0.7437	0.6354	0.5142	0.3910	0.2776	0.1118	0.0325
	18	0.9739	0.8910	0.8227	0.7302	0.6169	0.4917	0.3666	0.2540	0.0958	0.0256
	20	0.9734	0.8868	0.8152	0.7188	0.6016	0.4733	0.3471	0.2355	0.0841	0.0209
	22	0.9729	0.8831	0.8089	0.7092	0.5886	0.4580	0.3311	0.2207	0.0752	0.0175
	24	0.9725	0.8799	0.8034	0.7008	0.5776	0.4451	0.3178	0.2087	0.0683	0.0151
	26	0.9721	0.8772	0.7986	0.6936	0.5681	0.4341	0.3066	0.1987	0.0628	0.0132
	28	0.9718	0.8747	0.7944	0.6873	0.5599	0.4247	0.2971	0.1903	0.0584	0.0118
	30	0.9716	0.8725	0.7906	0.6817	0.5526	0.4164	0.2889	0.1831	0.0547	0.0107
	40	0.9705	0.8645	0.7769	0.6614	0.5266	0.3873	0.2606	0.1590	0.0430	0.0074
	60	0.9694	0.8558	0.7622	0.6400	0.4997	0.3582	0.2332	0.1367	0.0334	0.0050
	120	0.9682	0.8464	0.7464	0.6175	0.4721	0.3292	0.2070	0.1163	0.0255	0.0033
	∞	0.9669	0.8361	0.7295	0.5938	0.4439	0.3005	0.1821	0.0978	0.0192	0.0022

Table B-4 Continued

df_N	df_E	\multicolumn{10}{c}{ϕ}
		0.5	1.0	1.2	1.4	1.6	1.8	2.0	2.2	2.6	3.0
4	2	0.9869	0.9777	0.9723	0.9660	0.9587	0.9506	0.9416	0.9317	0.9096	0.8844
	4	0.9838	0.9604	0.9438	0.9221	0.8946	0.8612	0.8217	0.7767	0.6725	0.5566
	6	0.9812	0.9433	0.9139	0.8738	0.8219	0.7585	0.6848	0.6036	0.4330	0.2767
	8	0.9792	0.9284	0.8873	0.8306	0.7575	0.6697	0.5716	0.4691	0.2776	0.1363
	10	0.9776	0.9160	0.8650	0.7944	0.7047	0.5996	0.4865	0.3745	0.1867	0.0726
	12	0.9763	0.9056	0.8464	0.7647	0.6622	0.5452	0.4236	0.3087	0.1330	0.0424
	14	0.9752	0.8969	0.8309	0.7403	0.6281	0.5027	0.3765	0.2620	0.0998	0.0270
	16	0.9743	0.8896	0.8178	0.7200	0.6003	0.4691	0.3405	0.2279	0.0783	0.0184
	18	0.9736	0.8834	0.8068	0.7030	0.5774	0.4420	0.3124	0.2023	0.0636	0.0133
	20	0.9730	0.8780	0.7974	0.6886	0.5583	0.4199	0.2901	0.1825	0.0533	0.0101
	22	0.9724	0.8734	0.7892	0.6763	0.5421	0.4015	0.2719	0.1670	0.0457	0.0079
	24	0.9719	0.8693	0.7821	0.6656	0.5283	0.3861	0.2570	0.1545	0.0400	0.0064
	26	0.9715	0.8657	0.7759	0.6563	0.5164	0.3730	0.2445	0.1442	0.0355	0.0054
	28	0.9711	0.8625	0.7704	0.6482	0.5060	0.3617	0.2340	0.1357	0.0320	0.0046
	30	0.9708	0.8597	0.7655	0.6409	0.4969	0.3519	0.2249	0.1286	0.0292	0.0040
	40	0.9695	0.8491	0.7473	0.6145	0.4643	0.3176	0.1942	0.1051	0.0207	0.0023
	60	0.9682	0.8374	0.7275	0.5864	0.4306	0.2836	0.1653	0.0844	0.0143	0.0013
	120	0.9666	0.8245	0.7060	0.5566	0.3962	0.2504	0.1386	0.0665	0.0096	0.0007
	∞	0.9649	0.8103	0.6828	0.5253	0.3614	0.2185	0.1144	0.0513	0.0063	0.0004
5	2	0.9870	0.9782	0.9730	0.9669	0.9600	0.9521	0.9435	0.9340	0.9126	0.8884
	4	0.9840	0.9611	0.9448	0.9233	0.8961	0.8629	0.8237	0.7789	0.6749	0.5591
	6	0.9814	0.9435	0.9138	0.8729	0.8199	0.7550	0.6795	0.5965	0.4231	0.2663
	8	0.9793	0.9276	0.8850	0.8258	0.7494	0.6578	0.5559	0.4504	0.2575	0.1207
	10	0.9776	0.9138	0.8600	0.7852	0.6899	0.5792	0.4615	0.3471	0.1625	0.0581
	12	0.9762	0.9021	0.8387	0.7510	0.6413	0.5174	0.3914	0.2757	0.1084	0.0306
	14	0.9750	0.8920	0.8206	0.7224	0.6017	0.4690	0.3391	0.2257	0.0763	0.0176
	16	0.9740	0.8835	0.8052	0.6984	0.5692	0.4306	0.2994	0.1898	0.0564	0.0109
	18	0.9732	0.8761	0.7920	0.6782	0.5423	0.3998	0.2688	0.1633	0.0435	0.0073
	20	0.9725	0.8696	0.7806	0.6609	0.5198	0.3746	0.2446	0.1433	0.0347	0.0051
	22	0.9718	0.8640	0.7706	0.6460	0.5007	0.3538	0.2252	0.1278	0.0284	0.0037
	24	0.9713	0.8590	0.7619	0.6330	0.4844	0.3363	0.2093	0.1156	0.0239	0.0029
	26	0.9708	0.8546	0.7543	0.6217	0.4704	0.3216	0.1962	0.1057	0.0205	0.0023
	28	0.9704	0.8507	0.7474	0.6118	0.4581	0.3089	0.1851	0.0976	0.0179	0.0018
	30	0.9700	0.8472	0.7413	0.6029	0.4474	0.2980	0.1758	0.0909	0.0158	0.0015
	40	0.9685	0.8339	0.7186	0.5705	0.4090	0.2601	0.1446	0.0695	0.0100	0.0007
	60	0.9668	0.8189	0.6935	0.5359	0.3696	0.2232	0.1163	0.0516	0.0061	0.0003
	120	0.9650	0.8023	0.6660	0.4992	0.3298	0.1882	0.0913	0.0372	0.0035	0.0002
	∞	0.9628	0.7835	0.6360	0.4606	0.2901	0.1556	0.0699	0.0259	0.0020	0.0000
6	2	0.9871	0.9785	0.9735	0.9675	0.9608	0.9532	0.9447	0.9355	0.9147	0.8910
	4	0.9841	0.9616	0.9454	0.9241	0.8971	0.8640	0.8250	0.7802	0.6764	0.5605
	6	0.9815	0.9435	0.9135	0.8720	0.8180	0.7518	0.6749	0.5905	0.4149	0.2578
	8	0.9794	0.9267	0.8829	0.8216	0.7424	0.6477	0.5428	0.4351	0.2417	0.1090
	10	0.9776	0.9118	0.8556	0.7770	0.6772	0.5618	0.4406	0.3248	0.1442	0.0480
	12	0.9761	0.8988	0.8318	0.7388	0.6230	0.4938	0.3647	0.2492	0.0905	0.0230
	14	0.9748	0.8876	0.8113	0.7064	0.5785	0.4402	0.3083	0.1971	0.0600	0.0120
	16	0.9737	0.8778	0.7936	0.6790	0.5418	0.3978	0.2659	0.1604	0.0419	0.0068
	18	0.9728	0.8692	0.7783	0.6556	0.5113	0.3639	0.2335	0.1339	0.0306	0.0042
	20	0.9720	0.8617	0.7650	0.6356	0.4857	0.3363	0.2082	0.1142	0.0232	0.0027
	22	0.9713	0.8551	0.7533	0.6183	0.4641	0.3136	0.1881	0.0992	0.0182	0.0019
	24	0.9707	0.8493	0.7430	0.6032	0.4456	0.2946	0.1719	0.0876	0.0147	0.0013
	26	0.9701	0.8441	0.7339	0.5900	0.4297	0.2787	0.1586	0.0784	0.0121	0.0010
	28	0.9696	0.8394	0.7258	0.5783	0.4158	0.2651	0.1476	0.0710	0.0102	0.0008
	30	0.9692	0.8351	0.7185	0.5679	0.4037	0.2533	0.1383	0.0649	0.0088	0.0006
	40	0.9675	0.8191	0.6911	0.5299	0.3605	0.2133	0.1080	0.0462	0.0049	0.0002
	60	0.9655	0.8008	0.6607	0.4891	0.3166	0.1753	0.0816	0.0315	0.0026	0.0001
	120	0.9633	0.7800	0.6271	0.4459	0.2728	0.1402	0.0595	0.0205	0.0013	0.0000
	∞	0.9607	0.7563	0.5901	0.4009	0.2301	0.1089	0.0417	0.0128	0.0006	0.0000

Table B-4 Continued

df_N	df_E	\multicolumn{10}{c}{ϕ}
		0.5	1.0	1.2	1.4	1.6	1.8	2.0	2.2	2.6	3.0
7	2	0.9872	0.9787	0.9738	0.9680	0.9614	0.9539	0.9456	0.9365	0.9161	0.8929
	4	0.9842	0.9619	0.9459	0.9247	0.8977	0.8648	0.8258	0.7811	0.6773	0.5613
	6	0.9816	0.9435	0.9132	0.8711	0.8163	0.7490	0.6710	0.5854	0.4082	0.2510
	8	0.9794	0.9260	0.8810	0.8179	0.7363	0.6390	0.5317	0.4224	0.2290	0.1000
	10	0.9775	0.9100	0.8516	0.7699	0.6661	0.5469	0.4231	0.3065	0.1299	0.0407
	12	0.9760	0.8959	0.8256	0.7280	0.6070	0.4735	0.3423	0.2278	0.0770	0.0178
	14	0.9746	0.8835	0.8029	0.6922	0.5581	0.4156	0.2828	0.1744	0.0482	0.0085
	16	0.9735	0.8726	0.7831	0.6615	0.5176	0.3698	0.2385	0.1375	0.0319	0.0044
	18	0.9724	0.8629	0.7658	0.6353	0.4840	0.3333	0.2049	0.1113	0.0221	0.0025
	20	0.9716	0.8544	0.7506	0.6127	0.4558	0.3038	0.1791	0.0923	0.0160	0.0015
	22	0.9708	0.8469	0.7373	0.5931	0.4319	0.2796	0.1587	0.0781	0.0120	0.0010
	24	0.9701	0.8401	0.7254	0.5760	0.4115	0.2596	0.1425	0.0673	0.0093	0.0006
	26	0.9695	0.8341	0.7149	0.5610	0.3940	0.2429	0.1294	0.0589	0.0074	0.0005
	28	0.9689	0.8287	0.7055	0.5477	0.3787	0.2286	0.1186	0.0522	0.0060	0.0003
	30	0.9684	0.8237	0.6971	0.5359	0.3654	0.2165	0.1096	0.0469	0.0050	0.0002
	40	0.9665	0.8048	0.6651	0.4926	0.3182	0.1754	0.0810	0.0309	0.0025	0.0001
	60	0.9642	0.7830	0.6294	0.4462	0.2709	0.1375	0.0572	0.0193	0.0011	0.0000
	120	0.9616	0.7580	0.5896	0.3973	0.2246	0.1038	0.0384	0.0112	0.0005	0.0000
	∞	0.9585	0.7290	0.5456	0.3467	0.1807	0.0751	0.0244	0.0062	0.0002	0.0000
8	2	0.9872	0.9789	0.9740	0.9683	0.9618	0.9544	0.9463	0.9373	0.9172	0.8943
	4	0.9843	0.9621	0.9462	0.9251	0.8982	0.8653	0.8264	0.7817	0.6779	0.5619
	6	0.9817	0.9435	0.9128	0.8703	0.8148	0.7467	0.6676	0.5811	0.4026	0.2454
	8	0.9794	0.9252	0.8793	0.8147	0.7311	0.6315	0.5223	0.4117	0.2186	0.0928
	10	0.9775	0.9084	0.8481	0.7635	0.6564	0.5341	0.4082	0.2912	0.1185	0.0352
	12	0.9758	0.8933	0.8201	0.7184	0.5930	0.4559	0.3234	0.2101	0.0668	0.0142
	14	0.9744	0.8798	0.7953	0.6794	0.5401	0.3943	0.2614	0.1560	0.0396	0.0063
	16	0.9732	0.8678	0.7735	0.6458	0.4963	0.3458	0.2157	0.1193	0.0248	0.0030
	18	0.9721	0.8571	0.7543	0.6169	0.4598	0.3072	0.1815	0.0938	0.0163	0.0016
	20	0.9711	0.8477	0.7374	0.5919	0.4292	0.2762	0.1554	0.0756	0.0113	0.0009
	22	0.9703	0.8392	0.7224	0.5702	0.4034	0.2510	0.1352	0.0624	0.0081	0.0005
	24	0.9695	0.8316	0.7091	0.5512	0.3814	0.2302	0.1193	0.0524	0.0060	0.0003
	26	0.9689	0.8247	0.6972	0.5345	0.3625	0.2129	0.1065	0.0449	0.0046	0.0002
	28	0.9682	0.8185	0.6866	0.5198	0.3461	0.1983	0.0962	0.0389	0.0036	0.0001
	30	0.9677	0.8129	0.6770	0.5067	0.3318	0.1859	0.0876	0.0343	0.0029	0.0001
	40	0.9655	0.7911	0.6406	0.4584	0.2815	0.1447	0.0611	0.0209	0.0012	0.0000
	60	0.9630	0.7658	0.5995	0.4070	0.2318	0.1079	0.0402	0.0118	0.0005	0.0000
	120	0.9600	0.7362	0.5536	0.3531	0.1843	0.0765	0.0247	0.0061	0.0002	0.0000
	∞	0.9563	0.7016	0.5028	0.2981	0.1406	0.0512	0.0141	0.0029	0.0000	0.0000
9	2	0.9872	0.9790	0.9742	0.9686	0.9621	0.9549	0.9468	0.9380	0.9181	0.8954
	4	0.9843	0.9623	0.9464	0.9254	0.8986	0.8657	0.8268	0.7821	0.6783	0.5623
	6	0.9817	0.9434	0.9125	0.8696	0.8135	0.7446	0.6647	0.5774	0.3978	0.2407
	8	0.9794	0.9246	0.8778	0.8119	0.7265	0.6251	0.5142	0.4025	0.2099	0.0871
	10	0.9774	0.9070	0.8450	0.7579	0.6479	0.5229	0.3953	0.2782	0.1093	0.0310
	12	0.9757	0.8909	0.8151	0.7098	0.5806	0.4407	0.3073	0.1955	0.0587	0.0116
	14	0.9742	0.8764	0.7884	0.6679	0.5242	0.3759	0.2433	0.1410	0.0331	0.0047
	16	0.9729	0.8634	0.7647	0.6316	0.4774	0.3249	0.1966	0.1047	0.0197	0.0021
	18	0.9718	0.8518	0.7438	0.6002	0.4384	0.2847	0.1621	0.0800	0.0124	0.0010
	20	0.9708	0.8414	0.7252	0.5730	0.4057	0.2525	0.1361	0.0628	0.0081	0.0005
	22	0.9698	0.8320	0.7086	0.5493	0.3782	0.2265	0.1162	0.0504	0.0056	0.0003
	24	0.9690	0.8235	0.6939	0.5286	0.3548	0.2053	0.1007	0.0414	0.0040	0.0002
	26	0.9683	0.8159	0.6807	0.5104	0.3347	0.1877	0.0885	0.0346	0.0029	0.0001
	28	0.9676	0.8090	0.6689	0.4943	0.3174	0.1730	0.0786	0.0294	0.0022	0.0001
	30	0.9670	0.8026	0.6581	0.4799	0.3023	0.1606	0.0706	0.0254	0.0017	0.0000
	40	0.9646	0.7780	0.6174	0.4273	0.2497	0.1199	0.0464	0.0143	0.0006	0.0000
	60	0.9618	0.7490	0.5712	0.3714	0.1986	0.0848	0.0283	0.0073	0.0002	0.0000
	120	0.9583	0.7148	0.5194	0.3133	0.1508	0.0562	0.0158	0.0033	0.0001	0.0000
	∞	0.9542	0.6745	0.4620	0.2549	0.1085	0.0345	0.0080	0.0014	0.0000	0.0000

Table B-4 Continued

df_N	df_E	\multicolumn{10}{c}{ϕ}
		0.5	1.0	1.2	1.4	1.6	1.8	2.0	2.2	2.6	3.0
10	2	0.9873	0.9791	0.9744	0.9688	0.9624	0.9552	0.9472	0.9385	0.9188	0.8963
	4	0.9844	0.9625	0.9466	0.9256	0.8989	0.8660	0.8271	0.7825	0.6786	0.5625
	6	0.9817	0.9433	0.9123	0.8690	0.8124	0.7428	0.6622	0.5742	0.3938	0.2367
	8	0.9794	0.9240	0.8765	0.8094	0.7225	0.6195	0.5072	0.3947	0.2026	0.0823
	10	0.9774	0.9057	0.8422	0.7529	0.6404	0.5131	0.3842	0.2672	0.1017	0.0277
	12	0.9756	0.8888	0.8106	0.7022	0.5696	0.4273	0.2935	0.1831	0.0523	0.0097
	14	0.9741	0.8734	0.7822	0.6575	0.5101	0.3597	0.2279	0.1285	0.0282	0.0037
	16	0.9727	0.8594	0.7567	0.6187	0.4605	0.3068	0.1805	0.0928	0.0160	0.0015
	18	0.9715	0.8469	0.7341	0.5850	0.4193	0.2652	0.1459	0.0690	0.0096	0.0007
	20	0.9704	0.8355	0.7139	0.5558	0.3848	0.2322	0.1201	0.0527	0.0060	0.0003
	22	0.9694	0.8253	0.6959	0.5303	0.3558	0.2057	0.1007	0.0413	0.0039	0.0002
	24	0.9685	0.8160	0.6798	0.5080	0.3312	0.1841	0.0858	0.0331	0.0027	0.0001
	26	0.9677	0.8076	0.6653	0.4883	0.3102	0.1665	0.0741	0.0270	0.0019	0.0001
	28	0.9670	0.7999	0.6523	0.4709	0.2921	0.1518	0.0649	0.0225	0.0014	0.0000
	30	0.9664	0.7929	0.6405	0.4555	0.2764	0.1395	0.0574	0.0190	0.0010	0.0000
	40	0.9638	0.7655	0.5955	0.3989	0.2220	0.0998	0.0355	0.0098	0.0003	0.0000
	60	0.9606	0.7328	0.5443	0.3390	0.1702	0.0668	0.0200	0.0045	0.0001	0.0000
	120	0.9568	0.6939	0.4869	0.2776	0.1232	0.0411	0.0101	0.0018	0.0000	0.0000
	∞	0.9520	0.6475	0.4234	0.2170	0.0832	0.0230	0.0045	0.0007	0.0000	0.0000
12	2	0.9873	0.9793	0.9746	0.9691	0.9628	0.9557	0.9478	0.9392	0.9198	0.8977
	4	0.9844	0.9627	0.9469	0.9260	0.8993	0.8665	0.8276	0.7829	0.6790	0.5628
	6	0.9818	0.9432	0.9118	0.8679	0.8104	0.7398	0.6581	0.5689	0.3872	0.2304
	8	0.9794	0.9231	0.8743	0.8052	0.7158	0.6101	0.4956	0.3819	0.1910	0.0750
	10	0.9773	0.9035	0.8375	0.7445	0.6277	0.4968	0.3661	0.2494	0.0900	0.0228
	12	0.9754	0.8850	0.8029	0.6890	0.5509	0.4050	0.2708	0.1635	0.0429	0.0071
	14	0.9738	0.8680	0.7713	0.6396	0.4860	0.3329	0.2030	0.1092	0.0212	0.0024
	16	0.9723	0.8523	0.7426	0.5963	0.4318	0.2768	0.1549	0.0749	0.0110	0.0009
	18	0.9710	0.8380	0.7169	0.5585	0.3868	0.2333	0.1206	0.0529	0.0060	0.0003
	20	0.9698	0.8250	0.6938	0.5256	0.3493	0.1991	0.0958	0.0384	0.0035	0.0001
	22	0.9687	0.8131	0.6730	0.4969	0.3179	0.1721	0.0775	0.0286	0.0021	0.0001
	24	0.9677	0.8023	0.6543	0.4717	0.2914	0.1505	0.0638	0.0219	0.0013	0.0000
	26	0.9668	0.7924	0.6376	0.4496	0.2690	0.1330	0.0533	0.0171	0.0009	0.0000
	28	0.9659	0.7833	0.6223	0.4300	0.2498	0.1187	0.0452	0.0136	0.0006	0.0000
	30	0.9652	0.7750	0.6086	0.4127	0.2333	0.1069	0.0389	0.0110	0.0004	0.0000
	40	0.9622	0.7419	0.5556	0.3492	0.1770	0.0701	0.0212	0.0048	0.0001	0.0000
	60	0.9584	0.7019	0.4951	0.2833	0.1256	0.0417	0.0101	0.0018	0.0000	0.0000
	120	0.9537	0.6534	0.4271	0.2173	0.0819	0.0220	0.0041	0.0005	0.0000	0.0000
	∞	0.9476	0.5948	0.3530	0.1552	0.0479	0.0100	0.0015	0.0001	0.0000	0.0000

Table B-5 F_{max} Distribution

(a) $p_1 = 0.05$

df_E	\multicolumn{11}{c}{k, number of variances}
	2	3	4	5	6	7	8	9	10	11	12
2	39.0	87.5	142	202	266	333	403	475	550	626	704
3	15.4	27.8	39.2	50.7	62.0	72.9	83.5	93.9	104	114	124
4	9.60	15.5	20.6	25.2	29.5	33.6	37.5	41.1	44.6	48.0	51.4
5	7.15	10.8	13.7	16.3	18.7	20.8	22.9	24.7	26.5	28.2	29.9
6	5.82	8.38	10.4	12.1	13.7	15.0	16.3	17.5	18.6	19.7	20.7
7	4.99	6.94	8.44	9.70	10.8	11.8	12.7	13.5	14.3	15.1	15.8
8	4.43	6.00	7.18	8.12	9.03	9.78	10.5	11.1	11.7	12.2	12.7
9	4.03	5.34	6.31	7.11	7.80	8.41	8.95	9.45	9.91	10.3	10.7
10	3.72	4.85	5.67	6.34	6.92	7.42	7.87	8.28	8.66	9.01	9.34
12	3.28	4.16	4.79	5.30	5.72	6.09	6.42	6.72	7.00	7.25	7.48
15	2.86	3.54	4.01	4.37	4.68	4.95	5.19	5.40	5.59	5.77	5.93
20	2.46	2.95	3.29	3.54	3.76	3.94	4.10	4.24	4.37	4.49	4.59
30	2.07	2.40	2.61	2.78	2.91	3.02	3.12	3.21	3.29	3.36	3.39
60	1.67	1.85	1.96	2.04	2.11	2.17	2.22	2.26	2.30	2.33	2.36
∞	1.00	1.00	1.00	1.00	1.00	1.00	1.00	1.00	1.00	1.00	1.00

(b) $p_1 = 0.01$

df_E	\multicolumn{11}{c}{k, number of variances}
	2	3	4	5	6	7	8	9	10	11	12
2	199	448	729	1036	1362	1705	2063	2432	2813	3204	3605
3	47.5	85	120	151	184	21(6)	24(9)	28(1)	31(0)	33(7)	36(1)
4	23.2	37	49	59	69	79	89	97	106	113	120
5	14.9	22	28	33	38	42	46	50	54	57	60
6	11.1	15.5	19.1	22	25	27	30	32	34	36	37
7	8.89	12.1	14.5	16.5	18.4	20	22	23	24	26	27
8	7.50	9.9	11.7	13.2	14.5	15.8	16.9	17.9	18.9	19.8	21
9	6.54	8.5	9.9	11.1	12.1	13.1	13.9	14.7	15.3	16.0	16.6
10	5.85	7.4	8.6	9.6	10.4	11.1	11.8	12.4	12.9	13.4	13.9
12	4.91	6.1	6.9	7.6	8.2	8.7	9.1	9.5	9.9	10.2	10.6
15	4.07	4.9	5.5	6.0	6.4	6.7	7.1	7.3	7.5	7.8	8.0
20	3.32	3.8	4.3	4.6	4.9	5.1	5.3	5.5	5.6	5.8	5.9
30	2.63	3.0	3.3	3.4	3.6	3.7	3.8	3.9	4.0	4.1	4.2
60	1.96	2.2	2.3	2.4	2.4	2.5	2.5	2.6	2.6	2.7	2.7
∞	1.00	1.0	1.0	1.0	1.0	1.0	1.0	1.0	1.0	1.0	1.0

Values in the column $k = 2$ and in the rows $df_E = 2$ and ∞ are exact. Elsewhere the third digit may be in error by a few units for the 5 percent points and several units for the 1 percent points. The third digit figures in brackets for $df_E = 3$ are the most uncertain.

This table is taken from Table 31 in Pearson and Hartley (1966). Reproduced with the kind permission of the trustees of *Biometrika*.

Table B-6 Curves of constant power for tests on main effects

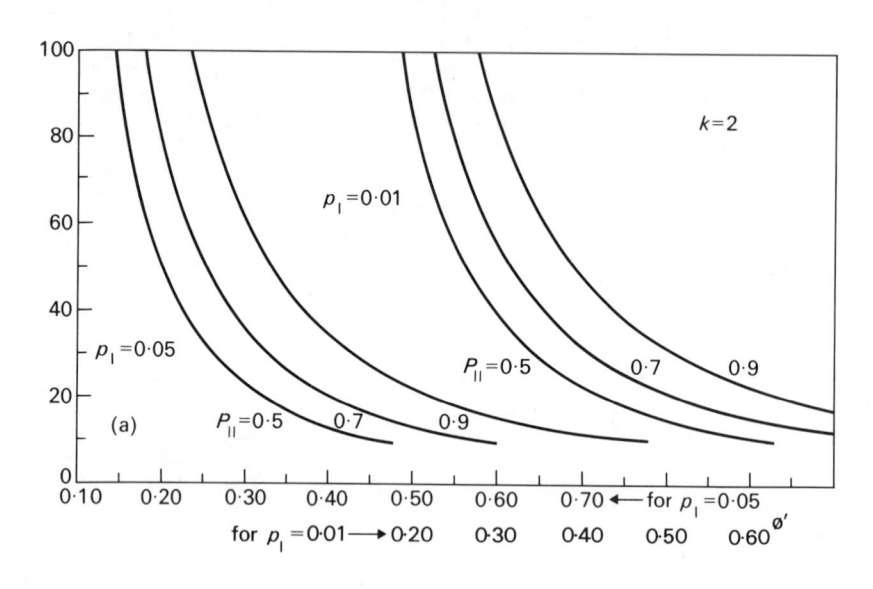

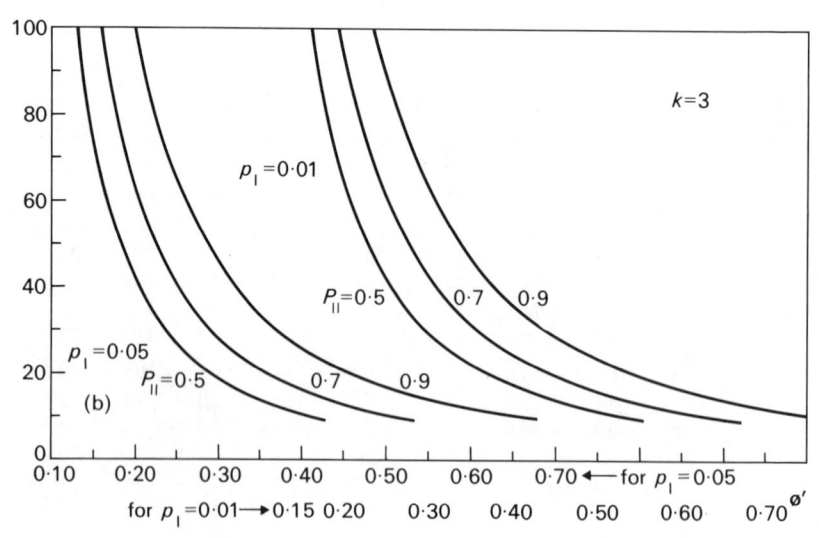

Table B-6 Continued

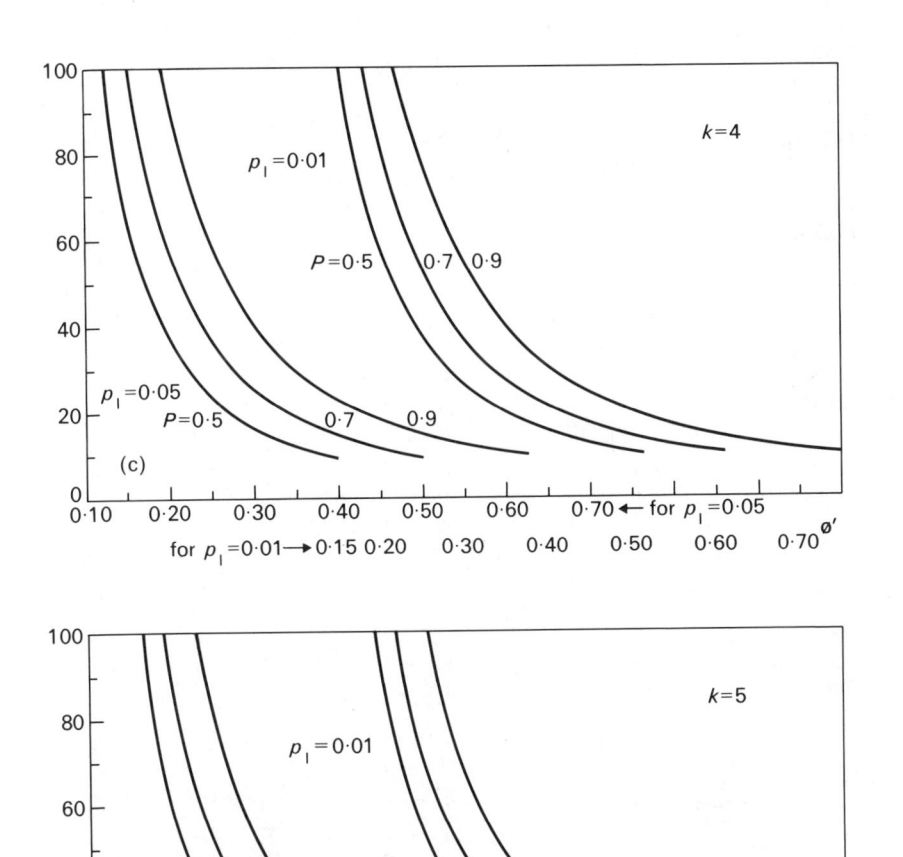

Note: k = number of levels of factor.
Reproduced from Feldt and Mahmoud (1958) with the kind permission of the authors and the editors of *Psychometrika*.

Table B-7 Orthogonal polynomial coefficients

k	Polynomial	1	2	3	4	5	6	7	8	9	10	ΣC_i^2	λ
3	Linear	−1	0	1								2	1
	Quadratic	1	−2	1								6	3
4	Linear	−3	−1	1	3							20	2
	Quadratic	1	−1	−1	1							4	1
	Cubic	−1	3	−3	1							20	10/3
5	Linear	−2	−1	0	1	2						10	1
	Quadratic	2	−1	−2	−1	2						14	1
	Cubic	−1	2	0	−2	1						10	5/6
	Quartic	1	−4	6	−4	1						70	35/12
6	Linear	−5	−3	−1	1	3	5					70	2
	Quadratic	5	−1	−4	−4	−1	5					84	3/2
	Cubic	−5	7	4	−4	−7	5					180	5/3
	Quartic	1	−3	2	2	−3	1					28	7/12
	Quintic	−1	5	−10	10	−5	1					252	21/10
7	Linear	−3	−2	−1	0	1	2	3				28	1
	Quadratic	5	0	−3	−4	−3	0	5				84	1
	Cubic	−1	1	1	0	−1	−1	1				6	1/6
	Quartic	3	−7	1	6	1	−7	3				154	7/12
	Quintic	−1	4	−5	0	5	−4	1				84	7/20
	Sextic	1	−6	15	−20	15	−6	1				924	77/60
8	Linear	−7	−5	−3	−1	1	3	5	7			168	2
	Quadratic	7	1	−3	−5	−5	−3	1	7			168	1
	Cubic	−7	5	7	3	−3	−7	−5	7			264	2/3
	Quartic	7	−13	−3	9	9	−3	−13	7			616	7/12
	Quintic	−7	23	−17	−15	15	17	−23	7			2184	7/10
	Sextic	1	−5	9	−5	−5	9	−5	1			264	11/60
9	Linear	−4	−3	−2	−1	0	1	2	3	4		60	1
	Quadratic	28	7	−8	−17	−20	−17	−8	7	28		2772	3
	Cubic	−14	7	13	9	0	−9	−13	−7	14		990	5/6
	Quartic	14	−21	−11	9	18	9	−11	−21	14		2002	7/12
	Quintic	−4	11	−4	−9	0	9	4	−11	4		468	3/20
	Sextic	4	−17	22	1	−20	1	22	−17	4		1980	11/60
10	Linear	−9	−7	−5	−3	−1	1	3	5	7	9	330	2
	Quadratic	6	2	−1	−3	−4	−4	−3	−1	2	6	132	1/2
	Cubic	−42	14	35	31	12	−12	−31	−35	−14	42	8580	5/3
	Quartic	18	−22	−17	3	18	18	3	−17	−22	18	2860	5/12
	Quintic	−6	14	−1	−11	−6	6	11	1	−14	6	780	1/10
	Sextic	3	−11	10	6	−8	−8	6	10	−11	3	660	11/240

Note: The coefficients under the last column, labeled λ, may be used to estimate the regression coefficient corresponding to that trend. For details on this procedure see Winer (1971, p. 183).

This table is abridged from Table 47 in Pearson and Hartley (1966). Reproduced with the kind permission of the trustees of *Biometrika*.

REFERENCES

Anderson, Richard Loree, and Bancroft, Theodore Alfonso (1952). *Statistical Theory in Research.* New York: McGraw-Hill.
Anscombe, F. J., and Tukey, John W. (1963). "The Examination and Analysis of Residuals," *Technometrics,* **5,** 141–160.
Aronson, Elliot, and Carlsmith, J. Merrill (1968). "Experimentation in Social Psychology," in *Handbook of Social Psychology,* Vol. II, 2nd ed., Lindzey, Gardner and Aronson, Elliot (eds.). Reading, Mass.: Addison-Wesley.
Banks, Seymour (1965). *Experimentation in Marketing.* New York: McGraw-Hill.
Bartlett, M. S. (1937). "Properties of Sufficiency and Statistical Tests," *Proceedings of the Royal Society of London,* **A160,** 238.
Blalock, H. M. Jr. (1961). *Causal Inferences in Nonexperimental Research.* Chapel Hill, N.C.: University of North Carolina Press.
Box, G. E. P. (1953). "Non-Normality and Tests on Variances," *Biometrika,* **40,** 318–335.
Box, G. E. P. (1954). "Some Theorems on Quadratic Forms Applied in the Study of Analysis of Variance Problems: I. Effect of Inequality of Variances in the One-Way Classification," *Annals of Mathematical Statistics,* **25,** 290–302.
Brown, Rex V. (1969). *Research and the Credibility of Estimates.* Cambridge, Mass.: Division of Research, Graduate School of Business Administration, Harvard University.
Campbell, Donald T. and Stanley, Julian C. (1966). *Experimental and Quasi-Experimental Designs for Research.* Chicago: Rand McNally.
Cochran, William G. (1957). "The Analysis of Covariance: Its Nature and Uses," *Biometrics,* **13,** 261–281.
Cochran, W. G. (1968). "Errors of Measurement in Statistics," *Technometrics,* **10,** 637–666.
Cochran, William G., and Cox, Gertrude M. (1957). *Experimental Designs,* 2nd ed. New York: John Wiley.
Cohen, Jacob, and Cohen, Patricia (1975). *Applied Multiple Regression/Correlation Analysis for the Behavioral Sciences.* New York: John Wiley.
Colcord, C., and Deming, L. S. (1936). "The One-Tenth Percent Level of 'Z'," *Sankhyā,* **2,** 423–424.
Coleman, Richard P. (1961). "The Significance of Social Stratification in Selling," in *Marketing: A Maturing Discipline,* Martin L. Bell (ed.). Chicago: American Marketing Association, pp. 171–184.
Conger, Anthony J, (1974). "A Revised Definition for Suppressor Variables: A Guide to Their Identification and Interpretation," *Educational and Psychological Measurement,* **34,** 35–46.
Cooley, William W., and Lohnes, Paul R. (1971). *Multivariate Data Analysis.* New York: John Wiley.
Coons, Irma (1957). "The Analysis of Covariance as a Missing Plot Technique," *Biometrics,* **13,** 387–405.
Cox, D. R. (1958). *The Planning of Experiments.* New York: John Wiley.

Cramer, Elliot M. (1972). "Significance Tests and Tests of Models in Multiple Regression," *The American Statistician*, **26**(4), 26–30.

Dixon, W. J., and Massey, F. J. Jr. (1969). *Introduction to Statistical Analysis*, 3rd ed. New York: McGraw-Hill.

Donaldson, Theodore S. (1968). "Robustness of the *F*-Test to Errors of Both Kinds and the Correlation Between the Numerator and Denominator of the *F*-Ratio," *Journal of the American Statistical Association*, **63**, 660–676.

Draper, N. R., and Smith, H. (1966). *Applied Regression Analysis*. New York: John Wiley.

Farrar, Donald E., and Glauber, Robert R. (1967). "Multicollinearity in Regression Analysis: The Problem Revisited," *Review of Economics and Statistics*, **49**, 92–107.

Feldt, Leonard S. (1958). "A Comparison of the Precision of Three Experimental Designs Employing a Concomitant Variable," *Psychometrika*, **23**, 335–353.

Feldt, Leonard S., and Mahmoud, M. W. (1958). "Power Function Charts for Specification of Sample Size in Analysis of Variance," *Psychometrika*, **23**, 201–210.

Ferguson, George A. (1959). *Statistical Analysis in Psychology and Education*. New York: McGraw-Hill.

Fisher, Sir Ronald Aylmer (1925). *Statistical Methods for Research Workers*. Edinburgh: Oliver and Boyd.

Fisher, Sir Ronald Aylmer, and Yates, Frank (1953). *Statistical Tables for Biological, Agricultural, and Medical Research*, 4th ed. Edinburgh: Oliver and Boyd.

Fisher, Sir Ronald Aylmer, and Yates, Frank (1974). *Statistical Tables for Biological, Agricultural, and Medical Research*. Harlow: Longman, pp. 80–82.

Fleiss, Joseph L. (1969). "Estimating the Magnitude of Experimental Effects," *Psychological Bulletin*, **72**, 273–276.

Frank, Ronald E., and Green, Paul E. (1968). "Numerical Taxonomy in Marketing Analysis: A Review Article," *Journal of Marketing Research*, **5**, 83–94.

Games, Paul A., and Lucas, Patrick A. (1966). "Power of the Analysis of Variance of Independent Groups on Non-Normal and Normally Transformed Data," *Educational and Psychological Measurement*, **26**, 311–327.

Geary, R. C., and Leser, C. E. V. (1968). "Significance Tests in Multiple Regression," *The American Statistician*, **22**(1), 20–21.

Geisser, S., and Greenhouse, S. W. (1958). "An Extension of Box's Results on the Use of the *F* Distribution in Multivariate Analysis," *The Annals of Mathematical Statistics*, **29**, 885–891.

Ghiselli, Edwin E. (1964). *Theory of Psychological Measurement*. New York: McGraw-Hill.

Glass, Gene V., Peckham, Percy D., and Sanders, James R. (1972). "Consequences of Failure to Meet Assumptions Underlying the Fixed Effects Analysis of Variance and Covariance," *Review of Educational Research*, **42**, 237–288.

Gorsuch, Richard L. (1973). "Data Analysis of Correlated Independent Variables," *Multivariate Behavioral Research*, **8**, 89–107.

Greenhouse, Samuel W., and Geisser, Seymour (1959). "On Methods in the Analysis of Profile Data," *Psychometrika*, **24**, 95–112.

Greenwald, Anthony G. (1976). "Within-Subject Designs: To Use or Not to Use," *Psychological Bulletin*, **83**(2), 314–320.

Hald, A. (1952). *Statistical Tables and Formulas*. New York: John Wiley.

Hartley, H. O. (1950). "The Maximum *F*-Ratio as a Short-cut Test for Heterogeneity of Variance," *Biometrika*, **37**, 308–312.

Hays, William L. (1963). *Statistics for Psychologists*. New York: Holt, Rinehart and Winston.

Hays, William L., and Winkler, Robert L. (1971). *Statistics: Probability, Inference, and Decision*. New York: Holt, Rinehart and Winston.

Horsnell, G. (1953). "The Effect of Unequal-Group Variances on the *F*-Test for the Homogeneity of Group Means," *Biometrika*, **40**, 128–136.

Huynh, Huynh, and Feldt, Leonard S. (1970). "Conditions Under Which Mean Square Ratios in Repeated Measurements Designs Have Exact *F*-Distributions," *Journal of the American Statistical Association*, **65**, 1582–1589.

Johnston, J. (1972). *Econometric Methods*, 2nd ed. New York: McGraw-Hill.
Kaplan, Abraham (1964). *The Conduct of Inquiry*. San Francisco: Chandler.
Kendall, M. G., and Stuart, A. (1963). *The Advanced Theory of Statistics*, Vol. 1. London: Griffin & Co.
Kish, Leslie (1967). *Survey Sampling*. New York: John Wiley.
Lindquist, E. F. (1953). *Design and Analysis of Experiments in Psychology and Education*. Boston: Houghton Mifflin.
Maxwell, Scott, and Cramer, Elliot M. (1975). "A Note on Analysis of Covariance," *Psychological Bulletin*, **82**, 187–190.
Mayer, Charles (1970). "Assessing the Accuracy of Marketing Research," *Journal of Marketing Research*, **8**, 285–291.
McCall, Robert B., and Appelbaum, Mark I. (1973). "Bias in the Analysis of Repeated Measures Designs: Some Alternative Approaches," *Child Development*, **44**, 401–415.
Merrington, Maxine, and Thompson, Catherine M. (1943). "Tables of Percentage Points of the Inverted Beta (F) Distribution," *Biometrika*, **33**, 73–88.
Milliken, George A., and Graybill, Franklin A. (1972). "Interaction Models for the Latin Square," *Australian Journal of Statistics*, **14**, 129–138.
Neter, John (1970). "Measurement Errors in Reports of Consumer Expenditures," *Journal of Marketing Research*, **7**, 11–25.
Neyman, J., and Pearson, E. S. (1928). "On the Use and Interpretation of Certain Test Criteria for Purposes of Statistical Inference," *Biometrika*, **20A**, 175–240.
Nie, Norman H., Hull, C. Hadlai, Jenkins, Jean G., Steinbrenner, Karen, and Bent, Dale H. (1975). *Statistical Package for the Social Sciences*, 2nd ed. New York: McGraw-Hill.
Patnaik, P. B. (1949). "The Noncentral χ^2- and F-Distributions and Their Approximations," *Biometrika*, **36**, 202–232.
Pearson, E. S., and Hartley, H. O. (1966). *Biometrika Tables for Statisticians*, Vol. 1, 3rd ed. New York: Cambridge.
Pope, P. T., and Webster, J. T. (1972). "The Use of an F-Statistic in Stepwise Regression Analysis," *Technometrics*, **14**(2), 327–340.
Robson, D. S. (1959). "A Simple Method for Construction of Orthogonal Polynomials when the Independent Variable is Unequally Spaced," *Biometrics*, **15**, 187–191.
Rosenthal, Robert (1966). *Experimenter Effects in Behavioral Research*. New York: Appleton-Century-Crofts.
Rulon, P. J., and Brooks, W. D. (1968). "On Statistical Tests of Group Differences," in *Handbook of Measurement and Assessment in Behavioral Sciences*, Dean K. Whittla (ed.). Reading, Mass.: Addison-Wesley.
Scheffé, Henry (1959). *The Analysis of Variance*. New York: John Wiley.
Searle, S. R. (1971). *Linear Models*. New York: John Wiley.
Seigel, S. (1956). *Nonparametric Statistics*. New York: McGraw-Hill.
Smith, H. Fairfield (1957). "Interpretation of Adjusted Treatment Means and Regressions in Analysis of Covariance," *Biometrics*, **13**, 282–308.
Sokal, Robert R., and Sneath, Peter H. A. (1963). *Principles of Numerical Taxonomy*. San Francisco: W. H. Freeman.
Srivastava, A. B. L. (1959). "Effect of Non-Normality on the Power of the Analysis of Variance Test," *Biometrika*, **46**, 114–122.
Tiku, M. L. (1967). "Tables of the Power of the F Test," *Journal of the American Statistical Association*, **62**, 525–539.
Van de Geer, John P. (1971). *Introduction to Multivariate Analysis for the Social Sciences*. San Francisco: W. H. Freeman.
Wilk, M. B., and Kempthorne, Oscar (1957). "Non-Additivities in a Latin Square Design," *Journal of the American Statistical Association*, **52**, 218–231.
Winer, B. J. (1971). *Statistical Principles in Experimental Design*, 2nd ed. New York: McGraw-Hill.

AUTHOR INDEX

Anderson, R. L., 86
Anscombe, F. J., 48, 81
Appelbaum, M. I., 150, 151
Aronson, E., 67

Bancroft, T. A., 86
Banks, S., 118
Bartlett, M. S., 42, 174
Bent, D. H., 207
Blalock, H. M., 113, 207
Box, G. E. P., 43, 45, 148, 150, 158
Brooks, W. D., 36
Brown, R. V., 67

Campbell, D. T., 113
Carlsmith, J. M., 67
Cochran, W. G., 117, 118, 134, 171, 174, 197
Cohen, J., 231
Cohen, P., 231
Colcord, C., 253
Coleman, R. P., 62
Conger, A. J., 218, 219
Cooley, W. W., 151, 223, 224, 231
Coons, I., 174
Cox, D. R., 63, 113, 118, 134
Cox, G. M., 117, 118, 134
Cramer, E. M., 175, 227

Deming, L. S., 253
Dixon, W. J., 253
Donaldson, T. S., 53, 54
Draper, N. R., 48, 230

Farrar, D. E., 228, 230
Feldt, L. S., 35, 145, 198, 199, 265

Ferguson, G. A., 26, 48
Fisher, R. A., 26, 120, 239
Fleiss, J. L., 36
Frank, R. E., 62

Games, P. A., 51
Geary, R. C., 227
Geisser, S., 150
Ghiselli, E. E., 197
Glass, G. V., 43, 47, 49, 55–57, 187, 194
Glauber, R. R., 228, 230
Gorsuch, R. L., 224
Graybill, F. A., 130
Green, P. E., 62
Greenhouse, S. W., 150
Greenwald, A. G., 141

Hald, A., 253
Hartley, H. O., 42, 239, 254, 263, 266
Hays, W. L., 3, 26, 29, 36
Horsnell, G., 46, 47
Hull, C. H., 207
Huynh, H., 145

Jenkins, J. G., 207
Johnston, J., 40, 197, 198, 210

Kaplan, A., 207
Kempthorne, O., 130
Kendell, M. G., 49
Kish, L., 67

Leser, C. E. V., 227
Lindquist, E. F., 44

Lohnes, P. R., 151, 223, 224, 231
Luens, P. A., 51

McCall, R. B., 150, 151
Mahmoud, M. W., 35, 265
Massey, F. J., 253
Mayer, C., 67
Maxwell, S., 175
Merrington, M., 253
Milliken, G. A., 130

Neter, J., 67
Neyman, J., 27
Nie, N. H., 207
Norton, D. W., 44

Patnaik, P. B., 33
Pearson, E. S., 27, 49, 239, 254, 263, 266
Peckham, P. D., 43, 47, 49, 55–57, 187, 194
Pope, P. T., 231

Robson, D. S., 85
Rosenthal, R., 67
Rulon, P. J., 36

Sanders, J. R., 43, 47, 49, 55–57, 187, 194
Scheffé, H., 41, 43, 45, 53, 69, 113, 163
Searle, S. R., 165, 167
Seigel, S., 18
Smith, H., 48, 230
Smith, H. F., 171, 173
Sneath, P. H. A., 62
Sokal, R. R., 62
Srivastava, A. B. L., 50
Stanley, J. C., 113
Steinbrenner, K., 207
Stuart, A., 49

Thompson, C. M., 253
Tiku, M. L., 255
Tukey, J. W., 48, 81

Van de Geer, J. P., 223
van der Vaart, H. R., 43

Webster, J. T., 231
Wilk, M. B., 130
Winer, B. J., 3, 26, 36, 69, 90, 118, 134, 161, 167, 266
Winkler, R. L., 26, 29, 36

Yales, F., 120, 239

SUBJECT INDEX

Additivity, 6, 65–67, 80–82

BioMedical computer programs, 95–98, 100–110, 131–133, 142–143

Compound symmetry:
 defined, 144–145
 significance test, 148–150
Computer data analysis, 90–110
 (*see also* BioMedical computer programs; Statistical Package for the Social Sciences computer programs)
Contrasts, general linear:
 computer analysis, 104–110
 defined, 82
 degrees of freedom, 84
 independent questions, 84
 orthogonal, 84–85
 significance, 83–84
 (*see also* Orthogonal polynomials)
Correlated independent variables (*see* Multicollinearity)
Correlation:
 among independent variables, 16
 simple, zero-order, 14–15, 218
 (*see also* Multicollinearity)
Covariance, analysis of:
 adjusted treatment means, 181–182, 185–186
 assumptions, 175–176, 186–198
 comparisons with randomized blocks, 198–199
 factorial designs, 199–203
 graphical interpretation, 182–183, 192–193
 multiple covariates, 203
 orthogonal polynomials, 185
 partitioning sums of squares, 176–181
 power, 185
 research uses, 171–174
 significance tests, 185–186
 structural models, 174–175
Crossed designs, 61

Degrees of freedom, 17, 84
Design matrix:
 construction, 22–23
 covariance analysis, 183, 189
 defined, 4, 9, 22
 factorial designs, 69–71
 orthogonal polynomials, 86–88

Error, statistical versus direct control, 169–170, 198–199
Expected mean squares, rules for constructing, 161–162
Expected value:
 defined, 29
 mean squares, 29–30

F distribution:
 central F, 32
 non-central F, 32–33
 relationship to other distributions, 36–37
F test:
 approximate non-central F, 33
 defined, 30
 grand mean, 76–77
 interaction effects, 76
 main effects, 76
 planned sample size, 34–35
 power 31–35, 78
 significance, 31–32, 34–35

SUBJECT INDEX

single parameter, 77–78
  (*see also* specific error assumptions:
     Homogeneity, Independence, Normality;
     and Statistical distribution characteristics)
Factorial designs:
  assumptions, 65–69
  covariance analysis, 199–203
  orthogonal polynomials, 85–89
  parameter estimates, 71–74
  partitioning sum of squares, 74–76
  power, 78
  research uses, 61–63
  significance tests, 76–78
  structural model, 64–65
Fixed effects model, 68–69

General Linear Model:
  defined, 6
  geometric representation, 12–16
  least squares parameter estimate, 10–11
  matrix form, 8–9
  minimal assumptions, 7–8
  permissible measurement scales, 11, 17–19, 22
  simple examples, 5–6
  terminology and notation, 4–5

Homogeneity:
  covariance, 148–150
  covariance matrices, 155–158
  regression, 188–194
  variance, 42–48, 57
Hypotheses:
  alternate, 27
  construction of significance test, 27–31
  null, 26–27
  statistical, 26–27

Independence, 40–41, 144–145, 148–150
Interactions:
  defined, 64
  graphical interpretation, 79–80
  importance, 61–63
  measurement scale effects, 80–82
  need to test, 90

Latin square designs:
  assumptions, 116–117, 122–134
  efficiency, 117
  expected mean squares, 130–131
  orthogonal polynomials, 121
  orthogonal squares, 121
  power, 123
  relationship to factorial designs, 120
  repeated measures, 159–161
  research uses, 117–118
  standard form, 120–121
  structural model, 119
Least-squared-error criterion, 10
Linearity:
  covariance analysis, 194–196

defined, 6
effects of violation, 7–8

Magnitude of effects, 16, 35–36, 214–215
Main effects:
  defined, 64
  graphical interpretation, 79–80
Measurement scales, types, 17–19
Mixed designs, 162
Models, causal and associative, 79–80
Multicollinearity:
  corrective procedures, 229–230
  defined, 206–207
  effects on parameter estimates, 226–227
  effects on statistical tests, 226–228
  interpretation of regression equation, 211
  model specification, 228
  test for, 228–229

Nesting, 154–155
Normal equation, 8, 10–17
Normality, 48–57

Orthogonal polynomials:
  computer analysis, 100–110
  factorial designs, 85–89
  Latin squares, 123
  repeated measures, 146–148, 153–154
Orthogonalization of independent variables, 223–224

Parameter estimates:
  covariance of, 12
  least squares estimate, 10–11
  unbiasedness, 11–12
Polynomial approximations, 65–66
Post hoc tests, 89–90
Power, 31–35

Random effects model, 68–69, 162–167
Randomized blocks, 112–113, 198–199
Regression analysis:
  adjusted R^2, 215
  assumptions, 210
  beta weights, 209–210, 214
  interpretation, 211–224
  multiple correlation coefficient, 214
  partial correlation, 216–218
  R^2 and beta weights, 215–216
  research uses, 207–208
  semipartial correlation, 216–218
  structural model, 209–210
  structure coefficients, 222–223
  suppressor variables, 218–222
  (*see also* Multicollinearity; Orthogonalization of independent variables; Stepwise regression)
Repeated measures designs:
  adjusted degrees of freedom, 150, 153
  all within designs, 151–154

Repeated measures designs (*continued*):
  assumptions, 144–146, 148–151
  conservative *F* test, 150, 152–153, 155, 159–161
  efficiency, 140–141
  expected mean squares, 145–146, 152–153, 155, 159
  homogeneity of covariance matrices, 155–158
  inflation of significance, 148
  multivariate alternatives, 151
  nested designs, 154–159
  orthogonal polynomials, 146–148, 153–154
  power, 159
  research uses, 140–142
  structural models, 142–144, 151–152, 155, 159

Simple effects, 80
Statistical distribution characteristics:
  actual versus nominal, 38
  kurtosis, 39–40
  moments, 38–39
  skewness, 39–40
Statistical Package for the Social Sciences computer programs, 92–95, 98–99, 122–125, 128, 130, 147, 180–181, 190–191, 196, 212–214
Statistical tests (*see* Contrasts; *F* test)
Stepwise regression, 230–231
Sum of squares, partitioning, 16–17

t test (*see F* test)
Test problems, 24, 58, 84, 111, 123, 134–138, 148, 151–154, 154–161, 162, 199–203, 217–222, 225
Trend analysis (*see* Orthogonal polynomials)

Validity, internal and external, 68
Variance components model, 162–167